SENSORY EXPERIMENTS

Sensory Experiments

PSYCHOPHYSICS, RACE, AND THE AESTHETICS OF FEELING

Erica Fretwell

DUKE UNIVERSITY PRESS   DURHAM AND LONDON   2020

© 2020 DUKE UNIVERSITY PRESS
All rights reserved
Designed by Amy Ruth Buchanan
Typeset in Arno and Avenir by Westchester Publishing Services

Library of Congress Cataloging-in-Publication Data

Names: Fretwell, Erica, [date] author.
Title: Sensory experiments : psychophysics, race, and the aesthetics of feeling / Erica Fretwell.
Description: Durham : Duke University Press, 2020. | Includes bibliographical references and index.
Identifiers: LCCN 2019054741 (print) | LCCN 2019054742 (ebook) | ISBN 9781478009863 (hardcover) |
ISBN 9781478010937 (paperback) | ISBN 9781478012450 (ebook)
Subjects: LCSH: Psychophysics. | Senses and sensation—Social aspects. | Racism—United States—Psychological aspects. | Racism—United States—History—19th century. | Science—Social aspects—United States—History—19th century.
Classification: LCC BF237 .F74 2020 (print) | LCC BF237 (ebook) | DDC 152.10973/09034—dc23
LC record available at https://lccn.loc.gov/2019054741
LC ebook record available at https://lccn.loc.gov/2019054742

DUKE UNIVERSITY PRESS GRATEFULLY ACKNOWL-
EDGES THE UNIVERSITY AT ALBANY, SUNY, WHICH
PROVIDED FUNDS TOWARD THE PUBLICATION OF THIS
BOOK.

IN MEMORY OF STEVEN FRETWELL

CONTENTS

        Acknowledgments IX

        Introduction: NEW SENSATION 1

{ 1 }   *Sight* UNRECONSTRUCTED BODY IMAGES 35

        INTERVAL 1 *Colorful Sounds* 79

{ 2 }   *Sound* THE ACOUSTICS OF SOCIAL HARMONY 87

        INTERVAL 2 *Notes on Scent* 124

{ 3 }   *Smell* PERFUME, WOMEN, AND OTHER VOLATILE SPIRITS 131

        INTERVAL 3 *Olfactory Gusto* 167

{ 4 }   *Taste* SCRIPTS FOR SWEETNESS, MEASURES OF PLEASURE 174

        INTERVAL 4 *Mouthfeel* 213

{ 5 }   *Touch* LIFE WRITING BETWEEN SKIN AND FLESH 221

        Coda AFTERLIVES AND ANTELIVES OF FEELING 257

        Notes 265

        Bibliography 289

        Index 313

ACKNOWLEDGMENTS

This book proceeds from the position that literature gives tangible shape to the amorphous fantasies, feelings, and histories that hover just below legibility. In the spirit of beginning this new relationship with you, dear reader, as though it were an old friendship, here are a few fantasies of how this book became legible to me:

Brian Price and Robert Gunn modeled intellectual curiosity, analytical precision, and deep generosity in ways that opened me up to the kind of person I could become and the kind of company I wanted to keep. It is difficult to overstate the impact that Rob in particular had on my scholarly trajectory. His intellectual companionship and emotional support (I was learning the self-doubt that academic writing produces) made all the difference. Simultaneously, a workshop led by Kyung-Sook Boo catalyzed fruitful kinship with fellow travelers Alicia Christoff and Lindsay Reckson. For more than fifteen years, Lindsay and I have been thinking, feeling, and thinking feeling together. Dear Lindsay: friendship as citational feedback loop.

Other fantasies of origination include reading Michael Taussig's work on colonialism and mimesis in an undergraduate anthropology course. Or a decade later, when I taught a course on Emily Dickinson's poems, and in recognizing the extravagance of her introversion came to recognize myself. Still another: high school English teacher Beverly Wheeler (née Porrazzo) taught me formal analysis, which thickened the immediate pleasure of reading with titillating intellectual drama.

Tina Campt, Cathy Davidson, Thavolia Glymph, Karla FC Holloway, and Rebecca Stein all pushed me to think more rigorously and more capaciously about everything. Tom Ferraro encouraged me to pursue the intuitions that originate in the solar plexus, no matter how kooky they might appear. Fred Moten's intellectual generosity is a kind of grace (I may be Jewish but we are all Protestants anyway, h/t Tracy Fessenden). Priscilla Wald's intellectual kinship, steadfast support, and profound compassion have been foundational to all iterations of this book. In the seminar room, on the East Campus street hockey court, and in bars long since gone (RIP Joe & Jo's), I was lucky enough to move among people of unsurpassed passions: Lindsey Andrews practices thinking as radical sociality; Ashon Crawley models criticism as a creative practice; Nihad Farooq doles out care and brilliance in equal measure; Britt Rusert was a mentor to me, although she may not have known it; Casey Wasserman schooled me in the gospel of James Brown. The Franklin Humanities Institute provided a fantastic year of dissertation writing and reading, and it brought me into contact with some of my favorite people: Ignacio Adriasola, Natalie Carnes, and Brian Goldstone. Hey, guys, I'm glad we found one another. Layla Aldousany, Leah Allen, Sarah Almond, Anne-Marie Angelo, Fiona Barnett, Kaila Brown (Joy Division helps me keep your memory), Christopher Catanese, Meredith Farmer, Anne Gulick, Alexis Gumbs, Nathan Hensley, Patrick Jagoda, Keith Jones, Lisa Klarr, Kevin Modestino, Tim Wientzen, Jenny Woodruff, and Timothy Wright helped me figure things out. So too did the companions many of us found along the way, most of whom have moved on to happier trails: Rufus, Max, Liza, Clark, Astro, Fido and Jada, Jack, and Casey. Special thanks to my doghter and kindred spirit Clementine, who buoyed me through grad school loneliness and those bad relationships you have in your twenties. Miss you, darling.

However this book got its start, many people have contributed to its incubation, recognizing my project in ways I had not (yet). Some have heard, read, or responded to portions of this book, while others have offered personal encouragement and professional advice along the way. For all these kindnesses and more, thank you, Sari Altschuler, John Levi Barnard, Dorri Beam, Nancy Bentley, Sarah Blackwood, Pat E. Chu, Matt Cohen, Michael Collins, Peter Coviello, Brad Evans, Erin Forbes, Brian Hochman, Monica Huerta, Toni Wall Jaudon, Catherine Keyser, Lauren Klein, Sarah Lincoln, Dana Luciano, Cody Marrs, Molly McGarry, Rachael Nichols, Carrie Noland, Eden Osucha,

Samuel Otter, Jamie Pietruska, Samantha Pinto, Sophia Roosth, Kelly Ross, Kyla Schuller, Susan Schweik, Gillian Silverman, Gus Stadler, Ed Sugden, Kyla Wazana Tompkins, and Marta Werner. Merci, Christen Mucher, Tessa Paneth-Pollak, and Jordan Stein for your casual expertise in French. J. Michelle Coghlan, Nicholas Gaskill, Justine Murison, and Emily Ogden are my ideal readers and, praise the gods, they have been my real readers, too.

Many thanks to the audiences at the Université Paris-Diderot, Katholische Universität Eichstätt-Ingolstadt, and the Center for Cultural Analysis at Rutgers University. Cécile Roudeau and Julia Faisst are unmatched in their hospitality. Thanks to the fellows at the Freiburg Institute for Advanced Studies, especially Barbara Mennel, as well as to Laura Bieger, Dustin Breitenwischer, and Winfried Fluck. The 2016 C19 seminar led by Laura Wexler and Shawn Michelle Smith was especially fruitful; I am thankful to them and to the seminar participants for their crucial insights. Gratitude is equally due to Eric Lott, whose seminar at the 2010 Futures of American Studies Institute involved lively conversations with Ashley Carson Barnes, Alex Black, John Charles, Alex Corey, Michele Fazio, Brigitte Fielder, Jack Hamilton, Elissa Underwood Marek, Ann Mattis, Philip Nel, Jonathan Senchyne, and, providentially, Todd Carmody.

This book has received support from the American Philosophical Society and from the vw-Mellon Foundation. I was able to spend my first semester back from maternity leave doing only research (teaching- and service-free) thanks to the Dr. Nuala McGann Drescher Leave Award, sponsored by New York State United University Professions, ever fighting the good fight. Support unions! The University at Albany Faculty Research Awards Program covered important research-related expenses.

I am lucky to work in a department that actively protects the research time of junior faculty, especially under conditions of calculated scarcity. My colleagues at the University at Albany (SUNY) have taken on additional labor, and I am eager to pay it forward. Thanks to comrades Richard Barney, Bret Benjamin, Jeff Berman, Helen Elam, Glyne Griffith, Mike Hill, Aashish Kaul, Eric Keenaghan, Kir Kuiken, Michael Leong, James Lilley, Ineke Murakami, Wendy Raphael Roberts, Helene Scheck, Ed Schwarzchild, Charles Shepherdson, Paul Stasi, Laura Tetreault, Lynne Tillman, and Laura Wilder. And I do not want to think where I would be without the profound patience and the institutional knowledge of Lynn Bearup, Kathleen Cummings, Liz Lauenstein (much missed), and Karen Williams. Bianca Englese has been immensely helpful in the short time since she arrived.

Gordon Hutner supported this book early on and provided important professional guidance. It was a sheer pleasure to work with Eric Zinner and Dolma Ombadykow at NYU Press; many thanks to series editors David Kazanjian, Elizabeth McHenry, and Priscilla Wald for their advocacy. I am happily and endlessly indebted to the two readers for NYU Press as well as to Hsuan Hsu and the second reader for Duke University Press. Thank you for your rigor, for your profound care, for seeing my book for what it was while guiding me toward what it could become. Elizabeth Ault at Duke University Press has been with me every step of the way; I couldn't ask for a steadier, more supportive editorial hand. Thank you to Kate Herman, Ellen Goldlust, and all those at Duke University Press who have worked behind the scenes (or rather, between the covers) to make this book happen.

Stephanie Foote generously invited me to edit a special issue of *Resilience: A Journal of the Environmental Humanities* on sensory studies. Thanks to the journal's editors and to the issue's contributors, whose brilliant essays helped shape the book. Portions of an earlier version of chapter 4 appeared as "Emily Dickinson in Domingo," *J19: The Journal of Nineteenth-Century Americanists* 1, no. 1 (2013), and portions of an earlier version of chapter 5 appeared as "Stillness Is a Move: Helen Keller and the Kinaesthetics of Autobiography," *American Literary History* 25, no. 3 (2013).

For all the forms that their companionship has taken, thank you to Sarita Cannon, Lina Assad Cates, Sam Contis, Andrea Haslanger, Kaitlin Hedberg, Katherine Hunt, Drew Kane, Vesna Kuiken, Anna Lyman, Wendy and Jesse Roberts, Tanaz Moghadam, and Kendra Sena. I'm so lucky to be in your orbit. And everlasting thanks to the family: Esther, Fay and Gordon, Roslyn (much missed), Jeff, Jenny, Stu, Amanda and John, Andrew and Jamie, Jan and Charlene, and the whole Carmody crew. Wendy and Padraic clocked in months of childcare so that I could get this book done. I continue to reap the benefits from the impassioned curiosity and unconditional love that Robin and Steve practiced. Thanks for all that you do, Mom. Miss you, Dad, every single day.

Noam brings the sunshine. Ruby brings the silly. Todd brings it. Whether focused on big questions, finer points, or schematic issues, his sharp eye has made this book what it is. He has read multiple (nay, multitudinous) drafts of every single page you are about to read—all in addition to his own work researching, writing, and teaching under precarious conditions, and all in addition to the lifelong work of forging a shared life together as partners and parents. This abundance of love is humbling, and it tests the limits of language.

Introduction

NEW SENSATION

> All men are not created equal in the pursuit of sights, sounds, olfactory and other sense perceptions....
> There are more states of consciousness than there are States of the Union.
> —"A Case for Sympathy," *Harper's Weekly*
>
> $g = k (\log b/b)$
> —Gustav Fechner, *Elements of Psychophysics*

As the nineteenth century came to a close, African American thinker, writer, and activist W. E. B. Du Bois responded to a long-standing query "between me and the other world." How does it feel to be a problem? "It is a peculiar sensation, this double consciousness, the sense of always looking at one's self through the eyes of others, of measuring one's soul by the tape of a world that looks on in an amused contempt and pity. One feels his twoness—an American, a Negro; two souls, two thoughts, two unreconciled strivings."[1] Reflecting on the internal turbulences of the so-called Negro Problem—the pathologizing discourse of black immorality and indolence that took hold after Reconstruction—Du Bois famously describes double consciousness, the concept of a sense of self shaped by the outside world, by other people's perceptions. Du Bois considered double consciousness the defining feature of black life, more elemental even than social structures of racial subordination such as sharecropping. Today *How does it feel to be a problem?* tells a familiar story about the lived experience of the color line under Jim Crow segregation—so familiar, in fact, that we risk losing sight of how counterintuitive this question would have been to Du Bois's first readers. What do everyday feelings have to do with entrenched racial hierarchies? What makes consciousness germane to notions of human difference, the purview first of natural history and then of natural science? Why might qualitative sensations be a useful tool for social analysis? Du Bois's enduring account of double consciousness boldly claims what we likely take for granted: that feeling is part of what it means to "be a problem," that the meaning ascribed to blackness (rather than blackness as such) is the problem. For Du Bois to limn the perceptual reality of racial difference, a new conceptual framework for consciousness had to be built. Psychophysics, the science of sense experience, supplied this framework—along with new experimental methods, new regulatory techniques, and a new aesthetics. To uncover how being a problem became a matter of consciousness, then, is to encounter the creative uses to which psychophysics was put under a social order that constructed human difference as a problem.

Developed and practiced by E. H. Weber, Gustav Fechner, and Hermann von Helmholtz between 1840 and 1880, psychophysics was an experimental science that tested people's subjective responses to auditory, gustatory, olfactory, tactile, and visual stimulation. It was the immediate precursor to experimental psychology but today is largely hidden from view. Psychophysics appears sparingly in histories of pragmatism (C. S. Peirce corresponded with Helmholtz) and of psychoanalysis (Sigmund Freud attended some of Fechner's lectures). The most rigorous accounts of it are to be found in media history; scholars from Friedrich Kittler to Jonathan Crary have argued that psychophysics, as the first science to isolate, measure, and map out human perceptual functions, paved the way for new technologies like the phonograph and, more nefariously, ushered in new techniques of bodily discipline that ensured a more "productive, manageable, and predictable" subject.[2] Today's critical landscape therefore offers a bifurcated view of psychophysics: as either a footnote in the history of ideas or a hegemonic science in the service of liberal biopower. One consequence of this bifurcation is that we have forgotten what psychophysics also made possible: a new theory of sense experience as a fundamentally creative endeavor that orients body-subjects to each other in ways that may reflect but might also refract dominant social formations.

Psychophysics was a science. But more precisely, and by way of metaphor, it was a triptych, a multifaceted field of knowledge that treated sense experience as the hinge attaching empiricism, aesthetics, and metaphysics; it advanced sense experience as a vector of lived know-how, as the embodied habitus of emotional reflection, and as a relational sign that correlates mind and matter. These concepts were far from esoteric and in fact found a wide audience via general periodicals, the most influential means in the nineteenth century of spreading scientific views to the public.[3] But whereas other sciences reached U.S. audiences in books and lecture halls as well, for psychophysics, Americans relied almost exclusively on secondhand reports because the texts were rarely translated into English.[4] The public learned about psychophysics through essays such as botanist C. J. Sprague's "What We Feel" (1867), which informed readers of the *Atlantic Monthly*, "It would seem folly for anyone to maintain that grass is not green, that sugar is not sweet, that the rose has no odor and the trumpet no tone, [yet] the greenness, the sweetness, the fragrance, the music, are not inherent qualities of the objects themselves, but are cerebral sensations."[5] In this fashion, a host of cultural critics and science writers repackaged psychophysics to nonexpert readers. That their essays ran alongside editorials, poems, and advertisements meant that psychophysics was tightly woven into the fabric of U.S. politics, art, and commerce. The century's dynamic textual milieu thus secured the new relevance of "what we feel" to the cultural conditions shaping what feeling can mean.

While psychophysics circulated widely in the United States, it found a foothold there because it suggested a model of interiority that partook of yet simultaneously moved past the biological materials (nerves, blood, etc.) now coming to define human difference. Between 1860 and 1910—an epoch bookended by Fechner's naming of the science and the death of his U.S. philosophical heir William James—the pronounced attention to the senses marked a response to concerns about a social order increasingly sponsored by biology. In its own moment, psychophysics moved along a trajectory asymptotic to that of evolutionary racial science: individual variations in sense experience approached but did not quite align with the new biological theories of human variation powered by the concept of heredity. Notably, evolutionary science considered race a plastic substance and, more specifically, the neurophysiological capacity to feel—the responsiveness of the nerves to external stimulation—a means of accelerating racial and species development.[6] Psychophysics did not directly address human biology, but it did claim that feeling was both embodied *and* irreducible to bodily processes: a material phenomenon that nonetheless exceeds the nervous and viscous matter of race. By studying feeling on the incipient phenomenological terrain of lived experience, rather than on the older epistemological grounds of sentiment, psychophysics equipped Americans with the means to pressure dominant classifications of the human while articulating the inner reality of biologized social taxonomies.

This book recovers the U.S. cultural life of psychophysics to tell the story of how human difference became a sensory (auditory, gustatory, olfactory, tactile, and visual) experience. It argues that postbellum writers and thinkers drew on this forgotten science to conduct their own sensory experiments into the emotional microdynamics of being and belonging. Their creative work both explored and exploited bodily sensations, pressed in on by historical events (the Civil War), social reform (racial uplift), restrictive stereotypes (the super crip), cultural institutions (domesticity), and biopower (eugenics)—all while sketching out possibilities for intimacies and attachments that might evade their disciplinary effects. Psychophysics motivated writers, artists, and cultural producers in different ways and to different ends. Spanning medical case studies, memoirs, photographs, perfumes, poems, novels, and recipes, these projects signaled a shared effort to elucidate the utterly ineluctable but always incomplete project of subjectification from within and below. Attuned to this dynamic archive, *Sensory Experiments* tells an alternate story of modern social formation: of how the scientific fracturing of feeling into an assemblage of fine-grained perceptions engendered small-scale techniques of differentiation (i.e., racialization and gendered sexualization) as well as new genres for calibrating the collective yet contingent meanings of human difference. This story reveals that in the postbellum period, the generic "formalism" of the five senses became a vehicle for a critique of sensorial discipline and an affirmation of sensory world making.

The creative project that constellated around psychophysics aimed to make bodily difference fundamental to the fact of consciousness. I call this project *psychophysical aesthesis*. Aesthesis is the etymological root of *aesthetics*, denoting the "perception of the world by the senses," and it nicely encapsulates the psychophysical revaluation of sensation as lived experience.[7] The texts gathered under psychophysical aesthesis are all animated by the tension between biological configurations of human difference and more "occult" modes of consciousness, feelings that are profoundly embodied and embedded in the world yet escape complete empirical capture. Neither inherently disciplinary nor inherently liberatory, psychophysical aesthesis enforced the vulnerability of some groups while certifying the experiential reality of that vulnerability. What emerged, then, was a seemingly redundant "aestheticization" of the senses: sight, sound, smell, taste, and touch became embodied conventions, or what I call *genres of feeling*, that mediate the fluctuating relation between self and social world. Contra the collective consciousness or identity formations that typically predominate in accounts of the nineteenth century, these sensory feelings constitute decidedly *in*formal or even microhistorical modes of relation that do not consistently serve definable social forms—they move among subjects who strive to, refuse to, or simply do not see themselves as part of a particular group or community. In this book, a specular image, the lilt of a voice, a whiff of perfume, a sweet aftertaste, and a caress are all sites of ever-shifting social meanings and shared possibilities.

Advancing psychophysical concepts and methods, the U.S. project of psychophysical aesthesis reframed the sensory body as a problem not simply of politics or epistemology but of ontology. Indeed, psychophysics itself is something of the secret ingredient baked into our most robust accounts of feeling, especially the phenomenological and the posthumanist strains of affect theory. By centering the body in individual sense experience, psychophysics laid the grounds for landmark feminist and queer phenomenologies, which study the uneven impact of power on everyday embodiment and emotions.[8] At the same time, the psychophysical theory of feeling as intersubjective, as a process of relation between mind and matter, inflects critical orientations like the new materialisms. This tradition in particular, influenced by the philosophy of relational ontology advanced by thinkers from Baruch Spinoza to Gilles Deleuze and Brian Massumi, is largely organized around the axiom that to affect is to be affected.[9] Accordingly, affect appears as a preconscious intensity that moves through porous bodies, operates through flux rather than fixity, and installs immanent relationality in place of individual agency. As a central yet neglected node in the critical genealogy of affect, then, psychophysics today is likely to feel more familiar than foreign, a rather uncanny return borne out in the language of thresholds, intensities, and wavelengths, as well as in the just-noticeable, nonlocalizable affects we have taken to calling "ambient." *Sensory Experiments* moves backward into psychophysics to extend our theories of affect further—toward a more thoroughgoing account of how bodies differentially amass ontological weight, of how gendered, raced, and disabled being (rather than gender, race, and disability as such) becomes "a problem." This psychophysical history of affect helps us recover the barely perceptible yet full-bodied feelings that structure the existential drama of everyday living, from an amputee whose phantom limbs call life itself into question to a cook whose sweet tooth turns domesticity into a feral state of being.

At the interface of science studies and affect theory, where a lost science gives way to a materialist account of ordinary feeling, *Sensory Experiments* illuminates the new psychophysical methods for determining and new languages for describing what human difference feels like. Having catalyzed a notable turn away from the regulation of raw sensation and a turn toward the psychical remainder thereof, psychophysics constitutes an important if ignored entry point into the storied entanglement of affect and power. Viewing the sensory body as at once a corporeal and creative phenomenon—as biological yet stretching into the domain of the symbolic, where worlds signify in the process of their own becoming, where vertical social arrangements might not be sustained—psychophysics furnishes us with an account of feeling that is disciplinary but not strictly so. It is therefore poised to intervene in the characterization of sentimentality as the definitive means of managing affect in the nineteenth century. In short, psychophysics is the vehicle by which we arrive at the meanings of human difference installed and imagined by sensory experiences. This new genealogy brings into view psychophysical aesthesis, which transformed the senses into genres of feeling, the intimate modes of relation (to the dead, to family, to the air, to dessert, to oneself) mediating the ontological differentiation of people and things. Taken together, these genres of feeling offer an important account of the psychical depths of "external" power structures: spirit photographs activate an existential crisis that is also a racial one; acoustic resonance models social harmony; synthetic perfumes denature queer and cross-racial desires; sweetness occasions aesthetic lawlessness; and touch tells a story of self deformation. In what follows, I establish psychophysics as a "speculative science" that enjoins physiology to metaphysics, then elucidate the two main concepts animating psychophysical aesthesis: *perceptual sensitivity*, a mode of sense discrimination that crosscuts aesthetics and eugenics, and the *sign theory of perception*, which holds that sense experience is both a material and semiotic relation between self and world. This framework shows that the five senses became bodily techniques for navigating the emotional vicissitudes of the postbellum era's vertiginous social landscape while serving the book's broader insistence that being a problem is a sensory configuration.

A SPECULATIVE SCIENCE

What attracted U.S. thinkers and writers to psychophysics was its conceptual flexibility. Taking shape as the modern research university took hold, in a moment when academic disciplines were coagulating but had yet to calcify into distinct research programs, psychophysics straddled empiricism and metaphysics; it wagered that science could still be a philosophy. Offering up measurements that doubled as meditations, psychophysics bridged the widening gap between the epistemic communities of natural science and the humanities, or "human sciences." It was uniquely poised to do so because it was not a formal discipline; E. H. Weber was a professor of anatomy, Hermann von Helmholtz was a professor of physiology and then of physics, and Gustav Fechner was a professor of physics who lectured on philosophy. Within this disciplinary context, psychophysics was less a discrete field and more of an orientation, defined by science historian Lynn Nyhart as "a cohesive group [of people], usually with an identifiable philosophical approach to their investigations."[10] I track that philosophical approach through Fechner, who believed that "speculative philosophy could supply a theoretical framework for the hard facts and formulas later discovered by science."[11] Fusing experimentation and speculation, Fechner practiced psychophysics as what I call a *speculative science*, which made it possible to theorize feeling as a relation between material and mental phenomena.

To call a science "speculative" might seem an oxymoron. After all, speculation typically plays the foil to the practical applications of reason codified by Francis Bacon's scientific method. I describe psychophysics as a speculative science because it operated at the nexus of two meanings of *speculative*: the abstract and the aspirational. Psychophysical researchers like Fechner saw themselves as redressing the abstract philosophy of mind by using experimental methods to prove the soul's autonomy and a priori organic unity. As Louis Menand remarks in his cultural history of pragmatism, the "true ambition" of psychophysics was not to "reduce mental phenomena to physical laws, but to solve traditional philosophical problems using laboratory methods."[12] Here, psychophysics resonates with the "fugitive science" practiced by the many antebellum African Americans who produced alternative knowledges in "the quest for and name of freedom."[13] Psychophysics was neither institutionally nor politically fugitive, but like fugitive science it used empiricism to ground philosophies of existence in the lived world. And in the process of "physiologizing" speculative traditions—that is, studying the soul through the materiality of the mind—psychophysics landed on another kind of speculation: the idea that sense experience is a contemplative and conjectural activity, or in David Kazanjian's eloquent language, a "comprehension of the ongoing, dynamic relationship" between self and world unfolding in a subjunctive temporality.[14] Under psychophysics, sense experience is not a stable reflection of the object world but a bodily cognition that anticipates a particular perception (e.g., the color green) as it is being physically processed. Like other speculative enterprises that used everyday practices to launch more existential reflections—including didactic writing and black settler correspondences—psychophysics offered a theory of feeling as material but not mechanistic, as mundane yet cosmically meaningful.[15] It was a speculative science in both senses of the term, for it fused inductive and deductive logic—answering philosophical questions in the laboratory—while reframing sense experience as a dynamic process of becoming.

A speculative science is a difficult balancing act. Nineteenth-century thinkers tended to view psychophysics either as too speculative or not speculative enough. In *Principles of Psychology* (1890), William James derided psychophysics as the science of "representing sensations by numbers" and lamented the "microscopic psychology that has arisen in Germany," so intent on defining "the *elements* of mental life" that its "method taxes the patience to the utmost, and could hardly have arisen in a country whose natives could be *bored*. . . . There is little of the grand style of these new prism, pendulum, and chronograph-philosophers. They mean business, not chivalry."[16] In James's view, to measure the minutiae of mental life is to sap introspection of its romance, thereby reducing consciousness to something decidedly less than the sum of its vibrant parts. Yet in a later passage rich with dramatic irony, James dismisses Fechner as a "mystic and an experimentalist, . . . as loyal to his facts as to his theories. But it would be terrible if even such a dear old man as this could saddle our Science forever with his patient whimsies."[17] This criticism is James at his least Jamesian; here he sounds more like one of the New Psychologists trained by Fechner's colleague Wilhelm Wundt in the 1880s, many of whom (including G. Stanley Hall, E. B. Titchener, and Hugo Münsterberg) inched psychology further away from ontological whimsy and ever closer to positivism. While running James's psychology laboratory at Harvard, for instance, Münsterberg took to the *Atlantic Monthly* to declare psychophysics a "blunder."[18] By the turn of the twentieth century, James's own whimsies began to appear outdated. Perhaps recognizing himself in the mystic-experimentalist, James ended his career revaluing Fechner as a "philosopher in the 'great' sense of the term" and heaped praise on his "panpsychic worldview."[19] Although psychophysics had been discarded as a failed science, James spent his final years insisting on the fruitfulness of its underlying speculations.

When it came to psychophysics, in other words, James had wanted to separate the philosophical wheat from the scientific chaff. But the numbers that James disdained were entirely fundamental to the worldview that he lauded.

These numbers, in fact, were born of an age-old philosophical impasse: the mind-body problem, whether there is a distinction between mind and matter (dualism) or a unifying reality holding them together (monism). Scientific materialism, grounded in the empiricist philosophy that claims must derive from observable phenomena, posited that nature fully explains the world. Conversely, idealism insisted on a transcendent principle (e.g., God, vital force) for explanation. As a medical student in the 1820s, Fechner predictably subscribed to materialism. But then a friend loaned him naturalist Lorenz Oken's *Elements of Physiophilosophy* (1802), which argues that a higher consciousness animates and unifies the world—hence matter and mind are two sides of the same ontological coin. Fechner quickly embraced Oken's monism, which put him at odds with the scientific community. The following decade, while teaching physics at the University of Leipzig, he used the pseudonym Dr. Mises to pen philosophical tracts and satirical rants that lambasted the arrogance of medicine and science. But in these texts Fechner also sketched out what he called the "day view." Contra the "night view" of a mechanistic world, the day view holds that to study only the material features or only the immaterial features of nature is to overlook the connection of all things. Where the physicist sees life as matter demonstrating certain properties under certain conditions, the philosopher sees it as a complex of emotions and ideas. The day view joins the two perspectives: it affirms that the mind (via the nerves) is explicable by the laws of nature but argues that consciousness is not, while affirming the soul's agency but arguing that this agency arrives immanently in the world. What emerges here is a transcendental materialism. In *Nanna; or, On the Soul Life of Plants* (1848) and *Zend-Avesta* (1851), Fechner used the day view to claim that all organic matter, from rocks and stars to insects and human beings, has a soul and that the universe is a manifold living organism made up of these interlocking soul systems. This notion of interconnected consciousness resonates with transcendentalism—especially Ralph Waldo Emerson's claim of "an occult relation between man and vegetable"—although the New England philosophy subordinates the material to the ideal, whereas the day view sees the two as inherently linked.[20] A way to uphold materialism without abandoning idealism, the day view replaced God and nature with consciousness as a universal ordering principle.

In the decades during which Fechner developed the day view, which is the conceptual foundation of psychophysics, experimental physiologist E. H. Weber (Fechner's adviser and then colleague at the University of Leipzig) laid out the methodological foundation of psychophysics. Credited by Fechner as the "father of psychophysics," Weber was the first scientist to examine sensation as a subjective experience and, further, to quantify it by using experimental methods. This research marked a major shift in the science of mind. Weber's object of analysis was not the sense impression, a unit of feeling routed through the nerves, but rather sense experience, the lived awareness of feeling. To investigate sense experience, he tested out the relation between sensory input and perceptual intensity. In laboratory settings, Weber exposed test subjects (white men) to a physical stimulus (e.g., light), then increased the magnitude in small increments (e.g., watts), and then numerically recorded subjects' perception (e.g., brightness) of those increases. In one experiment, blindfolded subjects held equally weighted objects in each hand while Weber slowly increased the weight of one object until they perceived a difference between the two. These tests led Weber to postulate a perceptual *threshold*: a quantifiable point that a physical stimulus must cross before the perceiver can detect a change in sensation. The minimum amount of stimulus increase needed to cross the threshold was a unit of measurement that he called the *just-noticeable difference* (JND). The threshold and the JND established an empirical correspondence between mind and matter, inner life and the external world. By experimenting with people's qualitative experience of physical changes in the environment, Weber reframed consciousness as "the accumulation of minute mental registrations of difference, or small acts of discrimination."[21] Quantitative analysis of the experiential dimension of sensation—that is, of feeling's qualities—set the science of psychophysics in motion: the experimental study of feeling from an immanent point of view.

Fechner directly adopted Weber's experimental design. In 1850, he began pursuing the cosmic goal of resolving the mind-body problem on an impossibly small scale: by quantitatively correlating gradations of physical stimulation to the slight differences in sensation that a person felt. What emerged was the day view science of psychophysics, which Fechner defined in *Elements of Psychophysics* as "an exact theory of the functionally dependent relation of body and soul, or more generally, of the material and the mental."[22] By paying attention to the individual peculiarities of our perceptions, by discovering personal variations in sense experience, we can approximate the common reality or principle holding body and soul together. Fechner spent the rest of his career assaying the body-soul relation by studying the subjective recognition of the change produced by a stimulus. To do so he established the *sensitive threshold* as the point where a "stimulus or change in stimulus becomes noticeable or disappears."[23] These tests led Fechner to conclude that the relation between matter and mind—stimulus and sensation—is not proportional, as Weber had claimed, but logarithmic: "The magnitude of the sensation (g) is not proportional to the absolute value of the stimulus (b), but rather to the logarithm of the magnitude of the stimulus, when this last is expressed in terms of its threshold value (b)."[24] This logarithmic formula means that as a stimulus increases in magnitude, the corresponding sensation intensifies to a lesser degree. For example, as light increases, it becomes more difficult to perceive the change in brightness; we are more conscious of the subjective difference in brightness between a dark room and one lit with a 25-watt bulb than between a room lit with a 100-watt bulb and one with a 125-watt bulb, although the objective difference in light (25 watts) is the same. Known as the *law of psychophysical parallelism*, the equation $g = k (\log b/b)$ is the cornerstone of psychophysics. It is an empirical expression of the day view: material life and mental life correlate, are "functionally dependent," but do not directly affect each other. Whereas the night view states that matter determines mental processes, psychophysical parallelism upholds the monistic day view that mind and matter, soul and body, are interrelated but not causally related phenomena.

Using mathematics to answer metaphysical questions might appear an overzealous empiricism. In fact, the refusal to establish a direct link between body and mind pushed Fechner in the opposite direction—toward bold extrapolation. To justify his methods, he allowed that there are "difficulties of measurement in our psychophysical domain, difficulties which do not exist in purely physical or astronomical areas," but insisted that these "difference[s] only mean that the sphere of inquiry must be widened, and considerations introduced which do not exist in other areas."[25] Our limited access to consciousness is not a limitation but an invitation to expand what counts as phenomena. We can see why James came around to Fechner—and why Fechner's biographer Michael Heidelberger describes his subject as "a radical empiricist with a phenomenalist outlook."[26] In the last decade of his career, while he was praising Fechner's philosophy, James developed the philosophy of radical empiricism. Whereas the "ordinary empiricism" of Enlightenment thinkers like John Locke and David Hume isolates distinct particles at the expense of seeing larger connections in the world, with radical empiricism experience includes both the particulars and the relations between those particulates: "For such a philosophy, *the relations that connect experiences must themselves be experienced relations, and any kind of relation experienced must be accounted as 'real' as anything else in the system.*"[27] The day view can be understood as an iteration of radical empiricism, a philosophy of science that thickens Fechner's earlier claim that calculating minute variations in sensation does not reduce the world to numbers but rather produces more connections in the world, more interlocking souls. Epitomized by the law of psychophysical parallelism, psychophysics sought to interweave the hard facts of material life with, following James, "the *wild* facts" of mental life.[28] Yoking physiology and philosophy, psychophysics undid ordinary empiricism in the process of practicing it.

Moving from natural philosophy to experimental procedures and an incipient radical empiricism, psychophysics was a speculative science that "combined elements of the vitalism that had been popular in Romantic scientific thought with a commitment to a severely nomothetic approach to science that would appeal to the extreme positivist," writes historian Woodruff D. Smith.[29] This Romantic scientific thought was shed by century's end. When Wundt's New Psychology replaced psychophysics, it relegated the body-soul problem to philosophy and kept the experimental study of introspection for itself. In an 1893 essay in *McClure's* on James's psychology laboratory, Herbert Nichols declared the "study of the mind an established natural science, here, at sober universities, and free of spooks and mediums."[30] So rang the death knell of psychophysics. Yet general readers in North America continued to discuss the law of psychophysical parallelism, described in the *New Englander and Yale Review* as "a *metaphysical* theory [that] what we call matter and what we call soul are but sides [of] one and the same reality."[31] Although on the wane in scientific circles, psychophysics remained an appealing framework for meditating on the grand implications of the measured mind. A science that sought to explain the world without explaining it away, it traded the *what* of sensation (impressions) for the *how* of sensation (experience), split feeling into a set of sense-specific experiences, and used quantitative analysis to prove metaphysical hypotheses. As a speculative science, psychophysics studied the interrelation of organic life and soul life to arrive at definitive proof that human consciousness is material yet elastic enough to accommodate the will.

SENSITIVE SUBJECTS

The psychophysical account of consciousness as equally embodied and ensouled had significant social value. The experimental study of sense experience (taste, touch, sight, sound, and smell) led Fechner to develop the concept of perceptual sensitivity: the psychophysical process of discerning fine gradations of sensation, such as varying levels of brightness. Once perceptual sensitivity migrated into cultural arenas, it became an affective capacity that moved aslant the dominant discourses of sensibility and sentimentality. These familiar discourses turn on the concept of sentiment, defined as the emotional reflection arising from sense impressions. In the eighteenth century, empiricism joined with social philosophy to form sentimentalism, a moral epistemology that considers sentiment the guide to truth. Sentimentalism underwrote the bourgeois project of sensibility, which made the subject's cultivation of sympathy, or "fellow feeling," necessary for social membership. In the United States, sentimentalism underwrote sentimental literature, a popular if maligned women's genre that features scenes of heightened emotion, but it was more of an ideology—one that put women's "natural" capacity for sentiment in the service of social reform, such as abolitionism. Sentiment has proved an important framework for showing how feeling operates as a regulatory apparatus; scholars such as Lauren Berlant, Kyla Schuller, and Laura Wexler have powerfully revealed sentimentality's collaborations with consumer culture, life science, and imperialism in propping up taxonomies of race, gender, and class.[32] But like any frame, sentiment restricts as much as it focuses our view. What happens to feeling when sensation shears away from sentiment? Psychophysics, spinning sentiment on its axis with metaphysical rather than moral concerns, suggests one possibility: it becomes the embodied locus of affective judgment, lodging the racial body at the core of the "science of sensitive knowing" called aesthetics.[33]

The era's new discourse of perceptual sensitivity was born of the entanglement of psychophysics and evolutionary racial science. At first glance, the two sciences have little in common: psychophysics investigates psychological variations in individual sense experience while evolutionary racial science investigates biological variations in species over time. They were, in fact, complementary. Fechner and Helmholtz considered psychophysics "consistent with Darwin's theory of evolution and a supplement to it," and conversely Darwin cited their psychophysical research in his study of sexual selection, *The Descent of Man* (1871).[34] Over the course of the century, thinkers moved away from viewing the body "as an entity determined by God and toward viewing it as raw material malleable under man's direction," Carolyn Thomas de la Peña points out.[35] In particular, dominant paradigms of evolution held that species change depends on this malleability and self-directed improvement. What determines success, Darwin argued, is an organism's ability to adapt to its environment, its capacity to acquire and transmit slight biological variations to offspring. The scientific effort to embed human beings in nature heightened the need to determine the mind's place in nature as well. Influenced by Darwin's studies and the earlier work of Jean-Baptiste Lamarck, evolutionary thinkers deemed perceptual sensitivity a mechanism of adaptation. Further, they turned it into an aesthetic project of racial perfection that I call *sensitivity training*.

Before mapping out this regime of perceptual sensitivity, it is worth establishing that the senses have always been a metric of species, and by extension racial, difference. In *De Anima (On the Soul)*, Aristotle divided the perceptual faculty into five senses—meant to correspond to the elements of water, ether, earth, air, and fire—and arranged them based on their proximity to reason. In the following order, the senses of sight, sound, and smell were specific to human consciousness, and the senses of taste and touch to animal consciousness. In the eighteenth century, following naturalist Carl Linnaeus's taxonomic classifications, the Aristotelian sensory hierarchy became an attractive tool for advancing racial taxonomies. It certainly appealed to Lorenz Oken, whose speculative theory of an integrated totality of consciousness had inspired Fechner's day view. Notably, the subtitle of Oken's *Elements of Physiophilosophy* is *The Theory of the Senses, with the Classification of the Animals Based on It*. Oken divided animal life into five classes, then he invented Latin names for each class based on the sense that ostensibly dominated their mental faculty, and finally he ranked these classes accordingly: *Dermatazoa* (invertebrates), ruled by touch; *Glossozoa* (fish), ruled by taste; *Rhinozoa* (reptiles), ruled by smell; *Otozoa* (birds), ruled by sound; and the highest form, *Ophthalmozoa* (mammals), ruled by sight.[36] Oken then applied this schema to human "classes":

1. The Skin-Man is the *Black*, African.
2. The Tongue-Man is the *Brown*, Australian-Malayan.
3. The Nose-Man is the *Red*, American.
4. The Ear-Man is the *Yellow*, Asiatic-Mongolian.
5. The Eye-Man is the *White*, European.[37]

This sensory taxonomy of racial groups combines classical psychology with natural history, the study of organic life through observation. In an era when natural history sponsored the white supremacist projects of settler colonialism and transatlantic slavery, Oken evolutionizes the Aristotelian sensory hierarchy, narrating species progress as sensory progress. The path from savage to civilized, from black to white, leads from touch to sight. Far from pure abstraction or idealism, his philosophy of a monistic world animated and unified by God was steeped in the natural world, powered by the progressive sensory arrangement of animal and racial classes.

When it came to explaining organic life, the transition from natural history (i.e., ethnology, phrenology, etc.) to natural science (astronomy, chemistry, physics, biology, and geology) in the nineteenth century helped push theories of human difference inward. Accordingly, perceptual sensitivity replaced the sense organs as markers of evolutionary development. To be sure, perceptual sensitivity began as a strictly psychophysical concept. Fechner explained in his *Elements of Psychophysics*, "In general, the term *sensitivity* means no more than what is otherwise referred to by the terms *irritability*, *excitability*, or *sensibility*. . . . However, insofar as all sensations depend on inner processes, one could well relate the term sensitivity to its underlying psychophysical process instead of to sensation."[38] Fechner draws an important distinction between nervous sensitivity and perceptual sensitivity. Nervous sensitivity is a neurophysiological condition, an unregulated state of feeling that arises when a person's nerves are so receptive to external stimulation that they are overly affected by and susceptible to environmental influence. By contrast, perceptual sensitivity is a psychophysical process: the higher mental function of discerning a change in one's sensory state as a result of changes in the physical world, that is, of just noticing the differentia of sensory stimulation. What matters here is not how much one feels but the ability to parse whatever it is that one feels. To catch a whiff of perfume is to be affected by and to *analyze* one's environment. Perceptual sensitivity therefore names the agential capacity to respond to the world by differentiating slight gradations of sensation. These microfeelings, in turn, form the basis of the finer feelings and judgments needed to manage one's place in the world.

Perceptual sensitivity was formulated as an "immediate psychophysical affect, a shock to the brain," that operated as a kind of preconscious substrate of aesthetic feeling.[39] Fechner's later work clarifies this aesthetic function. After establishing a speculative science that "ensouled" empiricism's night view of reality, Fechner took to enfleshing the speculative abstractions of aesthetics. From 1865 to 1875, he used his law of psychophysical parallelism to examine how art objects affect the mind. By simply renaming the sensitive threshold the aesthetic threshold, Fechner was able to determine the intensity that an artwork (stimulus) must have to produce pleasure or displeasure (mental activity). Establishing the kind of quantitative analysis that would become the cornerstone of social science, he surveyed visitors at art exhibitions about their sensory responses to color, form, and line and then used the statistical average of these questionnaires to arrive at a bottom-up definition of beauty and pleasure. In his 1876 study *Vorschule der Aesthetik* (*Introduction to Aesthetics*), Fechner called these empirically derived definitions "aesthetics from below," over and against the Kantian "aesthetics from above" that uses moral ideals to define truth and beauty. In this explicitly artistic context, Fechner framed perceptual sensitivity as a preconscious judgment—or perhaps more precisely as the immanent habitus of reflection—forming the basis of aesthetics.

Fechner's aesthetics from below laid the groundwork for the transformation of the Aristotelian sensory hierarchy into a sensitivity hierarchy. That transformation involved the co-option of psychophysics by evolutionary thinkers. For them, perceptual sensitivity was a psychologized renovation of sensibility, the eighteenth-century discourse that emphasized a person's "capacity to bring intellect to bear on sensory data, to distinguish fine gradations of feeling, and to modulate one's actions accordingly."[40] With perceptual sensitivity, fine-grained feelings are cultivated for the purpose of species progress, not of sensus communis. This refashioning of perceptual sensitivity largely began with Canadian science writer Grant Allen's *Physiological Aesthetics* (1877). In it, Allen used physiological research to rank each of the senses according to their evolutionary development and corresponding delicacy of feeling (sight and sound were at the top, predictably). Advancing the view of evolution as a progression from simple to complex structures, he argued that aesthetics is the "progressive product of progressing fineness and discrimination in the nerves, education, attention, high and noble emotional constitution, and increasing intellectual faculties."[41] Complex sensory structures are "for the advantage of the organism" because they "perfectly align its internal processes with the external environment."[42] The more differentiated the nerve, the finer the feeling, and the finer the feeling, the more adaptable the perceiving body to the changing environment. Hence, perceptual sensitivity facilitates human development by bringing inner life and outer world into a more perfect correspondence. It was now an aesthetic project of cultivation, at the level of each sense, with an evolutionary purpose.

Perceptual sensitivity became a "valued characteristic of civilized cultivation" because it underwrote aesthetic feeling and, by extension, registered the (human) organism's autonomy.[43] The "feeling of difference between consecutive, or co-existing impressions," Scottish thinker Alexander Bain wrote in 1865, is evidence that "we are alive, awake, mentally alert, under the discriminative exercise, and accordingly may be said to be conscious."[44] Awake, alive, alert: perceptual sensitivity allows a person to act with the world rather than react to it. Instead of leading to exhaustion or irritation, it stimulates intellection. On this basis, perceptual sensitivity converged with the Lamarckian theory of impressibility: that an organism's capacity to be affected over time, to glean sense impressions and transmit acquired sentiments to future generations, drives species change. Kyla Schuller persuasively argues that in this era, sentimental biopower turned impressibility into a vector of racialization; a host of institutions disciplined black and indigenous men, women, and children on the basis that they allegedly had unresponsive nervous systems—were impervious to feeling—and therefore were incapable of self-directed improvement.[45] Like impressibility, perceptual sensitivity was thought to drive human development; aesthetic microjudgments fine-tune an organism's relation to its world. Perceptual sensitivity and impressibility thus represent the psychophysical and neurophysiological aspects of evolution. Impressibility holds that quantity of feeling (repeated sense impressions) stimulates biological development, and perceptual sensitivity that quality of feeling (varieties of sense experience) stimulates it. In short, what accelerates species adaptation is the capacity to experience not simply more feelings but more *kinds* of feelings. Perceptual sensitivity allows the embodied mind to respond to and parse the physical world at an exceptionally granular level. In this way, evolutionary racial science remade perceptual sensitivity into an affective capacity that blends sensibility's aesthetic judgments with impressibility's civilizational prerogatives. Whereas impressibility served the broader sentimental imperative of cultivating the capacity for sympathy, perceptual sensitivity channeled affective microjudgments toward the cultivation of aesthetic experiences. Both these scientific theories of feeling were deployed to racialize subjects and manage "life itself" accordingly.

The incorporation of perceptual sensitivity into evolutionary discourse produced a sensitivity hierarchy of humankind: the ordering of racial groups not by their dominant sense but by their capacity to differentiate sensory states. Darwin's cousin Francis Galton first proposed the sensitivity hierarchy. After reading *Elements of Psychophysics*, he adopted Fechner's experimental method to test the perceptual sensitivity of the English population, going so far as to invent a special whistle (a dog whistle) to determine people's varying aural sensitivity.[46] Galton presented his research in *Inquiries into Human Faculty and Its Development* (1883), a book best known for launching eugenics, the program of biologically improving national subjects by enhancing the reproductive success of those considered physically and mentally "fit" for civilization. Galton considered perceptual sensitivity germane to "the cultivation of race, or as we might call it, [the] 'eugenics' question" because it was evidence of a fully developed, differentiated mind.[47] His sensory experiments revealed that "two persons may be equally able just to hear the same faint sound, and they may equally begin to be pained by the same loud sound, and yet they may differ as to the number of intermediate gradations of sensation. The grades will be less numerous as the organization is of a lower order, and the keenest sensation possible to it will in consequence be less intense."[48] Linked to biological "order" and "organization," perceptual sensitivity became a metric of racial difference. After all, one of Galton's major conclusions was that nervous sensitivity is highest among "women of delicate nerves" while perceptual sensitivity "is highest among the intellectually ablest" and lowest among the "wild races," because "a delicate power of sense discrimination is an attribute of a high race."[49] Perceptual sensitivity, or "sense discrimination," now supported racial taxonomies by extending the eugenic project of perfecting the human into the domain of consciousness.

To the extent that the end goal of evolution was a perfect correspondence between organism and world, "sense discrimination" constituted an innate though educable trait powering human development. One can "*educe* the existing [sensory] faculties," Allen had explained in *Physiological Aesthetics*, but "not *produce* new ones. In every department the aim of Education should be so to train each individual that he may use to the best advantage of the organism which heredity and circumstances have given to him."[50] So began a cultural program of training perceptual sensitivity, from the color sense (which Nicholas Gaskill has meticulously documented) to the haptic sense.[51] Italian physician and educator Maria Montessori, for instance, placed tactile sensitivity at the core of her pedagogical program in the hopes of "lay[ing] the groundwork for the subject's perceptual development throughout life, training that would prove essential for their [children's] insertion into the emerging industrial workplace."[52] In 1899, novelist and journalist Theodore Dreiser reported on a similar program for adults. Philadelphia psychologist Elmer Gates had found a way to "separately and rapidly train [the senses] to an acuteness and power of discrimination hitherto unknown," in the interest of guarding against "false or weak registrations of sensations."[53] First, a person establishes his threshold for each sense, and "when the least he can distinguish in these separate fields has been accurately measured the real training begins"; this involves "detecting, perceiving, and discriminating this 'least noticeable difference,' forty or fifty times an hour, for an hour daily during two or three days."[54] It was therefore important to cultivate the sensitivity—the internal, or immanent, faculty of judgment—of each sense, "since the whole intellectual progress of the race depends primarily on this perfect sensory development," Dreiser added.[55] Sensitivity training drove racial progress while guarding against the "feeblemindedness" (in the vocabulary of the era) that threatened racial futurity. Indeed, Italian criminologist Cesare Lombroso's "Sensitivity Test" elucidates the stakes of this training regimen. To ascertain the differential responsiveness of "unfit" individuals, Lombroso sent electric impulses to people's various body parts (genitals, gums, nipples); the less responsive the person, the less intelligent and more inclined to crime and cruelty. Sensitivity to affective stimuli helped classify whole groups of people—mentally ill people, women, people of color, the newly typed homosexual—as pathologically criminal. Adjunct to eugenics and the carceral state, sensitivity training established a set of affective norms that turned "aesthetics from below" into an apparatus of racial science "from above."

Psychophysics split feeling into a set of perceptual sensitivities, which in turn tethered aesthetics to evolutionary discourses. Over the course of the century, perceptual sensitivity transformed from a precognitive process of discerning sensory states into the affective capacity to make aesthetic microjudgments—an immediate calculation about, not a disinterested reflection on, the world. Naming the experiential attunement to different qualities of sensation, it joined impressibility in propelling human development and indexing human difference. But unlike impressibility, perceptual sensitivity did not operate exclusively as an arm of biopower. It also functioned as a kind of "sense method," defined by Elizabeth Freeman as a bodily cognition that opens up those intimacies that "do not always refer to or result in a stable social form but instead *move*, with and against, dominant timings and time."[56] Perceptual sensitivity was a small-scale judgment that remade feeling into an embodied yet elementally speculative—open-ended, subjunctive—structure of experience, and therefore capable of reshuffling the biologized social field.

REMAKING SENSE

In the mid- to late nineteenth century, the experimental study of sense experience gave way to a theory of feeling as a (logarithmic) relation between self and world. As the law of psychophysical parallelism filtered into evolutionary racial science, thinkers such as Allen, Galton, and Dreiser turned their attention to the affective discriminations calibrating that relation; they considered perceptual sensitivity an unevenly developed affective capacity that places people along a scale of development from savagery to civilization. Situating psychophysics in the wider biopolitical field confirms what we would expect to find in the nineteenth century: that the senses had a disciplinary function. But the senses also had unexpected effects. Hermann von Helmholtz's sign theory of perception expanded these sense-specific feelings into embodied conventions—and as a result, the senses served not only as metrics of human difference but also as modes of affective encounter, felt on and through bodies that are always more and other than their biological faculties. Psychophysical feeling proceeds first with perceptual sensitivity, an ongoing process of making microjudgments about the world, and then with the mind's synthesis of those microjudgments into a sign for navigating that world. By tethering the sensory to the symbolic, Helmholtz's sign theory of perception reframed the five senses as organic "forms" that organize material life. What emerged from the tension between perceptual sensitivity and the sign theory of perception was *psychophysical aesthesis*: an aesthetic project positing the five senses as "genres of feeling" that stage the internal dramas of structural oppression. Ultimately, this book proposes, racial difference took shape through the sensory genres—touch, taste, sight, sound, and smell—that allow for aesthetic recalibrations of bodies and subjects to each other and within an unsettled (though at times all-too-rigid) social environment.

Weber and Fechner assayed the role of the psyche in assessing slight changes in the world; Helmholtz assayed the role of the psyche in aggregating those slight changes so that perceiving subjects could act in and on the world. Like Fechner, Helmholtz used experimental methods to study sense experience, but unlike Fechner, he directed his research toward epistemological rather than ontological concerns. Helmholtz's sensory experiments aimed to reconcile competing theories of cognition: conceptual or scientific knowledge (*Wissen*) on the one hand and the lived, practical know-how of "sensible intelligibility" (*Kennen*) on the other. Art historian Zeynep Çelik Alexander explains that in the mid-nineteenth century, amid heated scientific debates about whether judgments are based in thought or in sensation, Helmholtz proposed an "alternative epistemic principle based on the body rather than the mind" called *aesthetic induction*.[57] Complementing Fechner's *aesthetics from below*, aesthetic induction names the intellectual content of sensation; it claims that in the act of sensing, knowing is already taking place. Whereas perceptual sensitivity was a discriminative activity that became a disciplinary apparatus, the sign theory was a mode of aesthetic induction that became a creative act: feeling a relation between self and world that is equal parts calculation and imagination. By framing sense experience as a sign, Helmholtz made it possible for U.S. writers to reconfigure feeling as a sense-specific genre that stabilizes without cementing one's place in the world.

Aesthetic induction added another layer to Fechner's psychophysical law: the relation between mind and matter is not simply logarithmic but semiotic—a sign. Showing how the sign theory of perception gave way to "genres of feeling," however, first requires establishing how Helmholtz remade sense altogether. After all, since classical antiquity, sense experience had been considered a mirror or carbon copy of the object world. In Aristotle's famous example, a gold signet ring pressed into a block of sealing wax leaves behind the design (form) but not the gold (matter), and so too objects impress sensations on the mind—hence "sense impression." Drawing on Aristotle, Enlightenment thinkers like Locke developed the "impression theory of sensation," which posits that the mind is a blank slate and that sense impressions, stamps of reality endowed with preformed meaning, are its only source of knowledge.[58] But as experimentation began replacing observation in the study of mind, where the philosopher had once seen a tabula rasa, the physiologist now saw an active organ powered by nerves. In the 1820s, physiologist Johannes Müller (Helmholtz's adviser) discredited the impression theory. He proposed the "law of specific nerve energies," the theory that through the nerves, the mind receives "knowledge of certain qualities or conditions, not of external bodies, but of the nerves of sense themselves; and these qualities of the nerves of sense are all different, the nerve of each sense having its own peculiar quality."[59] The law's first implication is that the nerves are not hollow vessels or neutral conduits but "thick" structures that leave their own mark on the messages they convey. In fact, Müller believed that he had found the physiological equivalent of Kant's innate categories of thought, the a priori mental concepts that act as intermediates between self and world. Because Müller's law attributed sense experiences to the innate configuration of the nerves, its main provocation was that "our knowledge of the world reflects the structure of our nervous system" rather than the object world.[60] The color green, for instance, is not a property of grass but an effect of the optic nerves. In more nihilistic assessments of this law, what we feel is an arbitrary sign with no stable point of reference. There is no "green"; all reality is subjective.

In addition to overturning the impression theory of sensation, the law of specific nerve energies initiated what Jonathan Crary calls the "separation of the senses," the atomization of the feeling body into isolated perceptual functions.[61] For Müller, the senses were organically distinct mediums: five types of nerves, each corresponding to one of the five senses. In claiming the functional autonomy and organic specificity of the senses, Müller posited what might be called a *formalization* of the senses. Reconciling the form/matter distinction set out by Aristotle and advanced by Enlightenment empiricists, Müller's law suggests that the senses are not impressions of the world but, rather, distinct physiological forms that actively shape it. Through the senses, consciousness leaves its imprint on the world—not, as Locke had claimed, the other way around. The sensory nerves determine what kind of sensation a stimulus will become; an optic nerve transposes electricity into retinal "floaters," whereas a tactile nerve turns it into heat. The nerves serve as the internal rules of coherence governing the experiential form a stimulus will take: whether electricity will feel bright or feel hot. The five senses were now organic forms—and the seed of *aesthesis*.

A science "born directly out of Müller's physiology," psychophysics used lived experience to find a middle ground between sensory physiology (feeling is subjective) and the impression theory of sensation (feeling reflects objective reality).[62] Weber, Fechner, and Helmholtz argued that sense experience is material but not strictly so—it is shaped, but not entirely governed, by nerve structure. They agreed with Müller that everyone sees the color green slightly differently due to variations in physiological makeup. Nonetheless, they contended, by studying the individual peculiarities of sense experience—the psychological component of sensation—we can determine the common quality or reality that unifies these subjective variations. In the 1850s and 1860s, while Fechner pursued this problem by testing people's perceptual sensitivity, Helmholtz put forth studies of sense experience that shifted the study of feeling away from Müller's physiological determinism and closer to radical empiricism. In his *Treatise on Physiological Optics* (1867), Helmholtz revealed that the retina is physiologically prone to distortions and gaps in the field of vision but that the mind fills in these lacunae through "unconscious inferences." A term that covers habit and learned associations, *unconscious inference* is the psychical mechanism that holds inner and outer worlds together. It synthesizes inner know-how with data received from the nerves to construct a coherent picture of the world. Sense experience is neither the projection of an object onto the mind (Locke's theory) nor a mix of concepts and intuitions (Kant's theory, which Müller "physiologized") but an unconscious activity that makes physical stimulation intelligible to the mind. Helmholtz duly viewed feeling as a product of both nerve structure (matter) and experience (mind)—a physiologically scripted yet psychologically supple configuration.

Helmholtz's notion of unconscious inference remade sense experience into a kind of aesthetic experiment: "The correspondence between the external world and the Perceptions of Sight rests . . . upon the same foundation as all our knowledge of the actual world—on *experience,* and on constant *verification* of its accuracy by experiments which we perform with every movement of our body."[63] Sense experience is not a reflection stripped of embodiment but a learning activity, an "experimental loop of perception, action, [and] consequence"—a central tenet of pragmatism.[64] And what makes it an aesthetic experiment is that, although undertaken for the practical purpose of facilitating the body's successful habitation of the world, its "verifications" are shot through with speculations, with subjunctive formulations about what a particular sensation will become. Echoing Helmholtz in his own way, William Connolly has recently described sense experience as "an anticipatory structure" that organizes the "rapidly changing contexts of everyday life."[65] To perceive green is to anticipate and respond to that color in the process of its own becoming. Feeling falls within the bounds of the physiological parameters of the nerves while remaining psychically provisional at an individual level. Within this conceptual framework, sense experience is a quotidian experiment, an everyday activity, that follows a general pattern or formula (psychophysical parallelism) while remaining open ended and ongoing.

Together, the notion of unconscious inference and experience-as-experiment made it possible to remake sense into a sign. Sense experience is "a *practical* truth," Helmholtz argued. "Our representation of things *cannot* be anything other than symbols, naturally given signs from things, which we have learned to use in order to control our motions and actions. When we have learned to read those signs in the proper manner, we are in a condition to use them to orient our actions such that they achieved their intended effect."[66] Green is a color that everyone sees slightly differently, yet the more we experience green, the more it acquires predictability and stability, which is why most of us agree on its general bounds—that, for instance, green is not orange. Locke would say that green is a mimetic copy of grass imprinted on the mind (i.e., objective reality); Müller would say that it is an effect of the optic nerves (wholly subjective); Helmholtz reconciled the two by saying that although green has no inherent connection to grass, it becomes objectively real the more it is subjectively experienced. Here the sign theory joins the law of psychophysical parallelism in offering a theory of sensation as relational, insofar as the "distinction between physical and mental, inner and outer—a distinction that is always fallible and revisable—can only be made by interacting with other people. What is inside or outside is *defined socially*."[67] If relations are real and feeling is relational, goes the day view syllogism, then feelings are real things in the world. Once remade into a sign, sense experience becomes an ongoing act of interpretation—not a "hard" fact but a situational fact that orchestrates without overdetermining new connections between self and world.

Helmholtz's innovation was to claim that sense experience is real not despite but because of its mediating function; now that signs are a "practical truth," the symbolic is woven into the very fabric of lived experience. Crucially, then, the conceptual arc that leads from Müller's separation of the senses to Helmholtz's sign theory of perception—from the five senses as organic forms to the five senses as psychophysical signs—sets psychophysics along a critical trajectory that moves from Raymond Williams's "structures of feeling" to Lauren Berlant's redefinition of genre as a social convention. At base, "structure of feeling" refers to the "affective elements of consciousness and relationships" viewed as social phenomena—the emotions that shape individual, collective, and political life in a specific time and place.[68] Berlant's illuminating work on the "historical sensorium" (the affects, moods, and atmospheres that negotiate the present in any historical moment) expands these structures of feeling into genres. More than a mode of recognition between reader and literary text, genre names "a sign for shared worldmaking."[69] As Berlant describes it,

> A genre is an aesthetic structure of affective expectation, an institution or formation that absorbs all kinds of small variations or modifications while promising that the person transacting with it will experience the pleasure of encountering what they expected. . . . It mediates what is singular, in the details, and general about the subject. It is a form of aesthetic expectation with porous boundaries allowing complex audience identifications. . . . To call an identity like a sexual identity a genre is to think about it as something repeated, detailed, and stretched while retaining its intelligibility, its capacity to remain readable or audible across the field of all its variations.[70]

With its insistence on small variations and porous boundaries, Berlant's description of genre is indebted to a psychophysical logic. Yet she pushes that logic further into the social domain of the "conventionalized symbolic."[71] Genre is a form of recognition, a set of attachments and identifications processed in the prerational domain of experience that makes historical moments legible to us. Once genre dilates to include not only literary norms but also social norms, it becomes a "bundle of promises" that bridges the "cultural feelings [that] find their place in how you find yourself."[72] To say that we live genre is to challenge facile distinctions between representation and reality, and to recognize the structural proximities that make us intelligible (or not) to one another.

Helmholtz's sign theory of perception is the hinge upon which empiricist theories of sensation (from mimetic imprint to material form to psychophysical sign) and critical theories of feeling (from sign to structure to genre) pivot. It therefore clarifies how the senses came to mediate—not simply mirror—raced, gendered, and disabled embodiment in the postbellum period. In effect, psychophysics turned sense experience into *aesthesis*: the affective locus where embodied immediacy and aesthetic imagining commingle. Within the logic of Fechner's "aesthetics from below" and Helmholtz's "aesthetic induction," the embodied is inherently aesthetic, the lived inherently literary. Accordingly, the perceptual sensitivities that buttressed human difference were also *genres of feeling* structuring the felt experience of that differentiation. The "historical sensorium" of the postbellum period comprised sensory genres for adjusting, at the finest gradation of feeling, relations among body-subjects. The five senses proffered narrative possibilities that organized emotional expectations and social interactions but more specifically, in Amber Musser's locution, made "the embodiment of difference" central to the "structural aspect of sensation."[73] By excavating the scientific contexts in which feeling became a "structure," we can better recognize the conceptual work of the senses and their stakes—organizing the body's fitful relation to the social world while remaining open to spheres of multiplicity that biopolitical governance cannot fully control.

PSYCHOPHYSICAL AESTHESIS

The psychophysics of feeling—involving a set of sense-specific experiences that bridge mind and matter, the affective substrate of aesthetic judgment, and perceptual signs holding self and world together—elucidates the process by which sense experience acquired ontological value in the late nineteenth century. As a speculative science, psychophysics made possible a new understanding of consciousness as embodied but not strictly biological. Psychophysical aesthesis constellated around this new development and experimented further with the existential, aesthetic, and social possibilities thereof.

This project attunes us, I contend, to the status of the five senses as genres of feeling that structure the ontological possibilities and pitfalls of becoming a particular historical body-subject—and that occasion further meditations on the perceptual habits and sensory ways of being that might be cultivated to instantiate alternative selves or social collectivities.

Indeed, this dramatic transformation in the conception of feeling directs us toward the new apprehension in the late nineteenth century of race as a "matter" of consciousness. As periodicals like *Littell's Living Age* reported that "a number of physiologists, chiefly German, have occupied themselves with measuring the sensibilities of our organism," these psychophysical measurements and metaphysical theories equipped creative and critical thinkers with the means to unloose the tightening hold of biology on human difference and, by extension, the dominant social order.[74] Thus was born psychophysical aesthesis: the project that extended "aesthetics from below" and "aesthetic induction" into a formally aesthetic domain (e.g., literature, perfumery, photography) to explore the genres of feeling that mediate biologized social arrangements. From 1860 to 1910, a range of U.S. writers explored human difference as a (logarithmic) relation between body and soul, as a mode of feeling that moves through the biological materials of blood and nerves yet is irreducible to them. They exploited rather than shied away from the irresolvable tension inhering in psychophysics, between sensitivity discourse and sensory genres. Even as perceptual sensitivity entered into biological paradigms of the human, psychophysical aesthesis sought to remake race, gender, and disability as processes or activities of embodied consciousness—as a "functionally dependent" though not deterministic "relation of body and soul," as Fechner would say. Organized around the psychical or experiential remainder of bodily difference, psychophysical aesthesis advanced the proposition that being a problem can be a feeling.

In its exploration of what feeling makes in the world, psychophysical aesthesis did not simply draw on psychophysics but actively advanced and even amended it. *Sensory Experiments* joins recent scholarship that explores the flexibility of literature as a mode of scientific inquiry, from Amanda Jo Goldstein's delineation of Romantic poetry as a "sweet science" for investigating organic life and Natalia Cecire's account of the epistemic virtues performed by twentieth-century experimental poetry to Britt Rusert's and Kyla Schuller's important recoveries of minoritized science practitioners in the nineteenth-century United States.[75] In keeping with the important work of these and other scholars, this book illuminates the professional science of Weber, Fechner, and

Helmholtz but gives equal if not more weight to the little-known public thinkers who disseminated psychophysical concepts and methods in magazines like *Harper's Monthly, Popular Science Monthly*, and *Lippincott's*: critics Henry T. Finck and Grant Allen, German émigrés and physicians Julius Bernstein and Ernst Gryzanowski (a friend of William James and historian Henry Adams), and early psychologists Joseph Jastrow and Havelock Ellis (best known for his work in sexology). Reading psychophysics at once through and beyond its main practitioners illuminates unfamiliar stories about familiar figures: nerve specialist S. Weir Mitchell features not as the inventor of the notorious "rest cure" for bourgeois women but as a beleaguered surgeon who had to use fiction to establish the phantom limb as a fact, while novelist Pauline Hopkins is more of an acoustician testing out the relevance of consciousness to kinship. At the same time, this book recognizes the alternate spaces in which many Americans investigated the experiential bounds of social discipline: the lady's toilette and the kitchen, not simply the university laboratory, are sites of sensory experimentation. In charting the cultural circuits through which psychophysics moved in the late nineteenth and early twentieth centuries, *Sensory Experiments* uncovers the psychophysical experiments—both scientific and literary—that moved sense experience into aesthesis.

Psychophysical aesthesis extended rather than served as a mere venue for scientific concepts. Precisely because psychophysics remade the senses into both a lived experience and a symbolic event—a learning activity shot through with imaginative signification—literature became an important medium for elaborating the aesthetic processes inhering in sensory embodiment. The texts advancing psychophysical aesthesis traverse the literary genres that emerged, were consolidated, or were recalibrated in the postbellum period. What distinguishes psychophysical aesthesis from other literary projects in this era is the purposeful deployment of psychophysics—in the language of parallelism, just-noticeable differences, and thresholds—to stage the internal drama of racialized difference, to reroute social arrangements through the diffuse entanglements of inner and outer worlds. Favoring barely conscious transactions over clearly defined events, psychophysical aesthesis attends to the slight sensory changes that acquire significant social meanings, the fleeting sensations that become scenes of negotiation among those seeking to stabilize their place in an unsettling world. This preoccupation with the small affects mediating the biopolitical management of life takes a particular thematic shape: impossible forms of embodiment, either bodies on the verge of becoming spirits or spirits (consciousness) excessive in their corporeality.

Sensory Experiments features body images that are more real than bodies; utopian sounds that imbue "pure being" with racial purity; decadent perfumes that turn women's biological essence into a chemical essence; dessert recipes that enflesh the domestic angel; and fingers that tell a queerly doubled life story. Psychophysical aesthesis put the logarithmic push and pull of the body-soul relation in direct contact with the emotional ups and downs of the everyday. As a result, the feeling body became a physiologically formal yet psychically flexible assemblage. And by expanding on the literariness of sensation itself—aesthesis, genres of feeling—psychophysical aesthesis remade literature as such into a flexible kind of body, capable of using its own capacious materiality to amend the narratives of social life that it invokes.

Taking a cue from its object of study, *Sensory Experiments* examines literature and sensation in the same way that psychophysics studied mind and matter: as correlated but not causally related. My method is to track scenes in which human difference becomes a problem of consciousness across texts that stage the interrelation of literary genre and lived genre—neither reducible to the other but each transducing the energy of the other. This approach is indebted to the theoretical traditions that attend to the entanglement of experience and language, troubling the entrenched binary of immediacy and mediation. Bruno Latour's sociological study of olfactory sensitivity in the French perfume industry elucidates this book's methodology. In "How to Talk about the Body?" Latour analyzes the "olfactory training" that perfume apprentices must undergo, which involves using an odor kit—a sample of fragrances—that "is not part of the body as traditionally defined, [but] it certainly is part of the body understood as 'training to be affected.'"[76] The odor kit sensitizes the perceiver by equipping her with language, for at the end of the training session, "the word 'violet' carries at last the fragrance of the violet and all of its chemical undertones. Through the materiality of the language tools, words finally carry worlds. What we say, feel and act is geared on differences registered in the world."[77] *Violet* is a descriptor and a performative, realizing an experience that had not consciously existed before. As Nicholas Gaskill, thinking with Latour, writes, "language has the power to augment the sensory encounter with the world."[78] Psychophysics offers an early iteration of this theoretical position. It bypassed the facile opposition of concrete sensations and abstract signs, instead reconciling empiricist and speculative, scientific and aesthetic ways of knowing. Psychophysical aesthesis extends this proposition by demonstrating that literature is a sensitizing mechanism, not merely a representation but an amplification of experience. Thus, to explore the proximities of lived and literary genres is to posit literature as a technology or "kit" that has the potential to reproduce—not copy but produce *more*—feeling and, in the key of radical empiricism, to create more connections to the world by registering more differences in it.

Collating various writers and artists who refused the bifurcation of language and life (including Kate Chopin, Emily Dickinson, Sadakichi Hartmann, and Pauline Hopkins as well as William Dean Howells, who appears throughout in small increments), psychophysical aesthesis marks a decisive effort to return aesthetics to its origins in bodily sensation, to aesthesis. It is a project that reaches back to classical antiquity, which according to Daniel Heller-Roazen recognized that "each individual sense (vision, smell, etc.) is its own *aesthesis*."[79] For the writers under discussion, sensation is not the corporeal springboard for reaching the heights of transcendent feeling; instead those finer feelings dwell within the body. In many ways, the "aesthetic turn" of the past twenty years is in fact a return to aesthesis, a return to the sensory body, and a recognition of aesthetics "as a form of cognition, achieved through taste, touch, hearing, smell—the whole corporeal sensorium," in the words of Susan Buck-Morss.[80] *Sensory Experiments* is indebted to the New World contexts of aesthetics that Elizabeth Maddock Dillon has excavated, particularly eighteenth-century "Atlantic aesthesis": the material circuits that linked Native and European populations and that constituted a "commoning" rooted in sense experience, contra the Kantian sensus communis delivered from above.[81] Conceptually dovetailing with "Atlantic aesthesis," psychophysical aesthesis continues the important work of recovering the flesh at the center of aesthetics—and more broadly, the interanimation of aesthetics and biopower. But its aim is less to recover a "commons" of taste than to chronicle the translation of sense experience into a set of conventions that holds a world in common. This book duly views psychophysical aesthesis as a world-making activity, a historically specific project that encompassed the lived realities and lofty reveries drawing disparate individuals into relation.

Partaking of the current recrudescence of aesthetics and of posthumanist perspectives on affect, *Sensory Experiments* builds on important accounts of the sensory body in the long nineteenth century, from the "politics of anxiety" in the antebellum United States to the "transatlantic feelings" sparked by the Paris Commune and the ecstatic religious performances that realized racial difference.[82] Its aim is to uncover the story of how the senses became at once sites of bodily discipline and aesthetic structures organizing the experience of that discipline. It focuses primarily on white-authored and black-authored texts to elucidate the social problems and contradictions with which psychophysical aesthesis grappled. Of course, "being a problem," to return to Du Bois, was by no means limited to African Americans in the postbellum period; the general public viewed Native Americans, people with physical and cognitive disabilities, Asian and non-Protestant European immigrants, among others, as "problem" populations. And, of course, race is a highly mobile configuration, a complex mode of arranging power that is consistent neither in its operations nor in its effects. Yet what is consistent, as many critics have demonstrated, is that in the United States, blackness functions as the most inferior racial position, and it governs all other distinctions. In Europe and North America, white supremacy uses blackness as the yardstick against which a person's distance from whiteness is measured. Lorenz Oken's sensory hierarchy of racial development—the European "Eye-Man" at the top and the African "Skin-Man" at the bottom—bears out this historical truth. Although psychophysical aesthesis includes the work of those writing from various and variously entangled subject positions, and although there are limitations to focusing on the black/white racial dyad, the goal of this book is to elaborate the genres of feeling that mediated the inner experience of moving along a racial spectrum anchored at opposite ends by blackness and whiteness.

At the same time, *Sensory Experiments* emphasizes that the forms of "complex embodiment" traveling under the sign of disability move in and out of racial hierarchies.[83] As David T. Mitchell and Sharon Snyder have argued, the late nineteenth century witnessed the rise of the "eugenic Atlantic," the deployment of biological inferiority to constitute race and disability as mutual projects of human exclusion. This book is indebted to recent scholarship that investigates disability as an entry point into, and a central modality of, racialized experiences. Jasbir Puar's analysis of neoliberal biopower, for instance, reveals how groups are marked "as those in decay" based on "what capacities they can and cannot regenerate," such that whiteness signifies as "the capacity for capacity."[84] As an affective-aesthetic capacity, perceptual sensitivity differentially binds disability to race, class, and gender. Although the phantom limb, as chapter 1 shows, is a feeling that seems to diminish the amputee soldier's claim to whiteness, it confers his "liveliness" over and against the "injured" population of ex-slaves. Yet it is equally true that disability studies scholarship, with its focus on "the materiality of impairment," clarifies the centrality of complex embodiment to this book.[85] Recognizing the "interbodily potentials, desires, and moments" that structure disabled life, following Melanie Yergeau, means recognizing the aim of psychophysical aesthesis: to understand what bodies can make in and of the world, to speak bodily variation from the inside (no matter how porous "inside" is), and to model life on interdependence rather than independence.[86] Helen Keller's *The Story of My Life* at first appears a conventional narrative of "overcoming" disability, as I discuss in chapter 5, but in fact it exploits tactile sensitivity to transform autobiography into a genre of selves. Keller is therefore a germinal seed in contemporary critical efforts to reconcile the social construction of disability with the lived experience thereof. The cultural collocations of difference in the postbellum United States reveal that experiences of disability not only intersected with racialized experiences but also activated psychophysical aesthesis, which assesses not what feeling is but what it can do.

OVERVIEW: SENSITIVITY AND SYNAESTHETICS

In five chapters, each devoted to a specific sense, *Sensory Experiments* tells the story of how racial difference became a sensory experience. As such, it tracks the material circuits of sensory activity as they structure an impossible desire for social attachments that simultaneously transcend the body and secure its biological particularity. Beginning with the seemingly immaterial sense of sight, chapter 1 uncovers the immediate precursor to and impetus for the concept of the "body image": the phantom limb, which revealed the existence of a psychological body that animates the physical one, and as such provoked a crisis of seeing that inflected the national crisis of the Civil War. Within the context of Fechner's theory of "heavenly vision," S. Weir Mitchell's identification of the phantom limb in amputee soldiers and William Mumler's spirit photographs constituted distinct "body images" that turned sight into a sense of its own loss. This mode of "not-seeing" dilated the real, and realism itself, to include the occult—though in so doing depicted "spirited" white bodies as particularly capable of feeling loss. Chapter 2 also pursues the problem of what happens to bodies that become spirits by pursuing the relation between psychophysical acoustics and post-Reconstruction utopian fiction. Edward Bellamy and Pauline Hopkins both leverage in their novels Helmholtz's resonant theory of hearing as a vehicle of transpersonal consciousness, the ontological basis of alternate worlds of "pure being" that can nonetheless certify racial purity. Uncovering the tension between acoustics and eugenics, the chapter focuses on shared efforts in *Looking Backward, 2000–1887* and *Of One Blood* to fold auditory sensitivity into narratives of evolutionary development while retaining the egalitarian possibilities of social harmony.

The book then moves from the theories that emerged from psychophysics proper to the psychophysical ideas further developed by perfumers, cooks, and activists. Chapter 3 excavates the chemical and racial science behind synthetic perfumery to consider the intoxicating pleasures—of queer intimacy and cross-racial desire—that can easily shade into toxic peril. A compound that mixes organic and inorganic materials, synthetic perfume unsettled social boundaries at the level of the free-floating odors that diffuse rather than contain sexual and racial difference. Yet in the naturalist fictions of Kate Chopin, these perfumes paradoxically mediate the "stuckness" of the New Woman, for whom free-floating embodiment is more perilous than pleasing. Moving from an atmospheric aesthetics to a mode of apparent self-containment, chapter 4 excavates the racial bodies underwriting the new status of taste as the "soul" of food. In the tension between culinary science and gastronomy, sweetness became the most transcendent component of eating—and the most primitive. Women, the main cooks in the house, used their sweet tooth to experiment with this paradox. A comparative analysis of several Afro-Caribbean black cake recipes, followed by analysis of Emily Dickinson's culinary and poetic engagement with Domingo, shows how women cooks rendered gustatory and aesthetic delicacy a carnal mode of consciousness. Where taste reveals the fleshiness at the inner core of finer feeling, touch in chapter 5 poses questions about consciousness rendered only by external contact. An object of psychophysical study and herself a psychophysical practitioner, Helen Keller authored autobiographies that turned touch into a "double sensation" of self-as-other. Analyzing *The Story of My Life* as a story of many selves and then in conjunction with W. E. B. Du Bois's collective autobiography, *The Souls of Black Folk*, elucidates the touches that reorganize selfhood into a third-person narrative.

I offer "thick descriptions" of each sense as it was steeped in specific scientific claims, political discourses, and cultural practices. My method is indebted to the field of sensory studies, especially historian Mark M. Smith's work on the senses and race in the nineteenth century.[87] Most monographs within this important field are organized around a single sense, to offer historical depth. However unwittingly, this strategy implicitly reifies the singularity of a given sense by effacing its connections with other experiential modalities. Furthermore, it risks reproducing the Aristotelian hierarchy—the Western canon of taste, touch, sight, sound, and smell—that has been used to buttress racial and species taxonomies. As the interdisciplinary formation first of visual studies and then of sound studies in the past twenty years suggests, scholars continue to value as worthy objects of study only those senses that sit atop hierarchies of intellection (Aristotle's human/animal distinction), of race (Lorenz Oken's taxonomy from the white eye-man to the black skin-man), and of aesthetics (Grant Allen's taxonomy from sight to taste). The fact that the senses of taste, touch, and smell have yet to be organized into coherent subfields (although taste does at times fly under the banner of food studies) suggests that humanist inquiry has not yet divested itself of the imperialist, anthropocentric frameworks that subordinate the "corporeal" senses to the "noncontact" ones. By allocating equal epistemological and aesthetic value to each of the five senses, *Sensory Experiments* aims to level vertical schemas of sensory feeling and, in turn, draw cultural studies into conversation with the racist logics of its own field formations.

With each chapter devoted to a single sense, this book may level the sensory hierarchy, but it still retains the Western fiction of a "five-sense sensorium," to borrow Marshall McLuhan's term.[88] Psychophysics certified that fiction by studying consciousness as a set of sense-specific capacities. It also offered a fruitful means for undoing these distinctions: synaesthesia. Defined by neuroscientist Richard Cytowic as the "capacity for [the] anomalous binding" of otherwise distinct sensations (e.g., a yellow smell), synaesthesia covers a range of experiences involving the commingling of sensations.[89] History is replete with isolated reports and individual case studies of synaesthesia, but Fechner was the first to systematically study it as part of his "aesthetics from below." Of the hundreds of museumgoers he surveyed, seventy-three associated specific colors with specific figures. Francis Galton—commonly credited with "discovering" synaesthesia, likely because Fechner's *Vorschule der Aesthetik* has yet to be translated into English—later used Fechner's questionnaires to study the same phenomenon. In *Inquiries into Human Faculty and Its Development* he discussed the evolutionary merits of perceptual sensitivity as well as the peculiarities of "color associations" and "visualized numerals." Perceptual sensitivity produced its doppelgänger: the sensory experiences that do not yield emotional distinctions but instead forge likeness and unity.

Fin de siècle symbolists and like-minded artists embraced synaesthesia as a mystical gift and a means of access to occult knowledge, while social critics viewed it as a symptom of degeneracy. Galton pointed out that synaesthesia is an anomaly and a heritable trait but did not consider it an index of biological inferiority. Yet given its place in *Inquiries*, synaesthesia is necessarily bound to eugenics. In the 1880s, it filtered into social Darwinist narratives of white racial decline. If evolution is a process of an organism's physical and psychological differentiation, then synaesthesia is a measure of primitive simplicity, an embodied mind unable to calibrate its relation to the world and adapt accordingly. This was the argument that Austrian physician Max Nordau made in his indictment of European decadence, *Degeneration* (1892). Nordau drew on the work of pharmacologist Raphäel Dubois, whose study of bioluminescence revealed that the paddock (the ancestral mollusk) hears, feels, tastes, and smells all at once. Nordau claimed that synaesthetic experience "relinquishes the advantages of the differentiated perceptions of phenomena, and carelessly confounds the reports conveyed by the particular senses. It is a retrogression to the very beginning of organic development. It is a descent from the height of human perfection to the low level of the mollusk... and the return from the consciousness of man to that of an oyster."[90] Perceptual sensitivity was an affective capacity driving evolution and art. Conversely, synaesthesia was an anomaly that pitched human beings backward in time, past the primates and reptiles to the bivalves. Contra the racial project of perceptual sensitivity, it threatened the progressive arc of aesthetic and social order.

The scientific history of synaesthesia reveals the dialectic of distinction and dissolution that animates the project of psychophysical aesthesis—and this book. Perceptual sensitivity upholds a classificatory logic, whereas synaesthesia runs the risk of aesthetic formlessness. *Sensory Experiments* embraces this risk. It attends to synaesthesia as a "fugitive interval," to borrow from William Connolly, between the "reception of sensory experience" and the cultural "organization of perception."[91] Interrupting perceptual order and this book's organization are four fugitive intervals that excavate the era's synaesthetic experiments: the invention of color music paradoxically doubles as sensitivity training; smell concerts bind acoustics to perfume's Orientalist aesthetics; a fictive "yellow smell" renders bourgeois bodies indistinguishable from primitive ones; and a contemporary Sugar Baby solicits the "mouthfeel" of enslavement by conjuring an antebellum salt lick. Thus, in the process of bridging sense-specific genres of feeling, synaesthesia becomes this book's *dis*organizing principle, an internal disruption of its organizing logic. This arrangement aims not to rehearse the contrapuntal movement of regulation (perceptual sensitivity) and resistance (synaesthesia) but instead to emphasize the interpenetration of these two new varieties of sensory experience in the always-tenuous processes of subjectification. In the structural oscillation between sensitive chapters and synaesthetic intervals, between genres of feeling and the anomalous bindings they generate, *Sensory Experiments* crosses the very thresholds it studies. Only then might we enter into the story of how "being a problem" became a matter of consciousness, of how subjective feeling became an objective fact.

Sight

{ 1 }

UNRECONSTRUCTED
BODY IMAGES

> [Man] is seized with a longing, a foreboding, or a joy, which he is quite unable to account for; he is urged to a force of activity, or a voice warns him away from it, without his being conscious of any special cause. These are the visitations of spirits, which think and act in him from another center than his own.
> —Gustav Fechner, *The Little Book of Life after Death*
>
> Missing me one place search another.
> —Walt Whitman, *Leaves of Grass*

Does everybody have two bodies? While working during the Civil War as a contract surgeon at the U.S. Army Hospital for Injuries and Diseases of the Nervous System, Philadelphia physician S. Weir Mitchell began to suspect this was the case. The amputee soldiers that he treated claimed to have sensations in limbs that, by any empirical standard, no longer existed. In 1871, Mitchell named this perceptual "image or memory of a body part" *phantom limb*.[1] In the same decade that Hermann von Helmholtz redefined sensation as a labile sign mediating body and mind, Mitchell defined the phantom limb as a psychological yet materially felt body part. Although he had no direct link to the German science, Mitchell contributed to psychophysical research by assaying the psychical dimensions of physical embodiment. Indeed, his case studies laid the conceptual groundwork for the body image, identified in 1911 by neurologist Henry Head as the preconscious representation of the body that governs physical movement in time and space—the "mental body" in the material body. Neuroscientists today classify the phantom limb as a "body image disturbance" because it arises when, following amputation, the body image no longer "matches" the body's new physical configuration. This failed correspondence between mind and body, representation and reality, psychical fiction and physical fact, preoccupied Mitchell and the general public. Stories of amputee veterans suffering horrifically from phantom limb pain posed the question: If a fabricated anatomy can be real, then what happens when a *mis*representation governs reality?

This query was sparked by, but reached well beyond, the phantom limb. The historical conditions that made the identification of the phantom limb possible involved the convergence of two large-scale crises: the epistemological crisis of seeing and the national crisis of the U.S. Civil War. Historiographical accounts typically claim that the Civil War heralded the "visual epistemology of modernity itself," in part because it was the first war to be extensively documented through the new medium of photography.[2] But rather than secure the cultural hegemony of the visual, the war intensified reservations about seeing, which by this time had taken something of an epistemological hit. Physicists had proved that forces invisible to the human eye shape the visible world, while ophthalmologists revealed that the eye is physiologically inclined to misperceive the visible world. By midcentury, these twinning revelations had come to underwrite a newly materialist ontology of the soul: that it is a form of invisible energy that materially exists within and among (not transcendentally above) organic life. This ontology was advanced primarily by American spiritualism, a religious and reform movement built on the belief that the living can communicate with the dead. Spiritualism was established in 1848 and by 1871 counted more than two million followers, due to the war's massive scale of death and the fact that most of the dead never made it back home for burial. "Mothers are losing their children by death; fond fathers unwillingly give up the only son of their name to the grave; each day how many die, some of whom are ... bitterly mourned by the survivors," a writer for the *Nation* acknowledged. "It is vain to look for a speedy ending to a belief that offers the living one more opportunity to speak with the beloved dead."[3] Spiritualism was often lambasted as humbuggery, and spirit mediums denigrated as hysterical women. But even those who did not subscribe to spiritualism found comfort in a world where nobody is absent, and everybody is present in one form or another. When it came to the unseen world of spirits, general attitudes held, à la the governess in Henry James's gothic novella *The Turn of the Screw* (1898), that "not seeing is the strongest of proof."[4]

As sight transformed into a sense of its own absence, *not-seeing* (to use James's phrase) came to mediate the feelings of loss that saturated the 1860s. It emerged as a perceptual modality sensitive to the liveness of visibly absent bodies. The phantom limb was one such body that required not-seeing, as did the spirit photograph—to far more controversial ends. In 1862, Boston engraver and amateur photographer William Mumler, with his wife, the spirit medium Hannah Mumler, invented spirit photography: portraits of a subject in the company of a shadowy figure identified as a spirit. The camera seems an unlikely instrument for not-seeing, given that it actually widened the horizon of human sight. Yet Shawn Michelle Smith argues that a certain blindness or nonvisibility has haunted the camera since its invention in 1839, for photography "demonstrated how little is ordinarily visible, giving one the unnerving sense of living in a world only partially perceived."[5] Spirit photography in particular staged not-seeing by depicting figures so barely visible as to reveal more about what cannot be seen than what can. Enjoining spirit communication to the "tempting accuracy of new technologies of reproduction," spirit photographs remained popular no matter how many experts publicly debunked Mumler's work.[6] Set within a culture of loss permeated by spiritualist practices, spirit photographs circulated alongside phantom limbs as fictions of wholeness.

The body image is a useful heuristic for exploring the loss mediated by not-seeing because it illuminates two phantasmatic bodies that existed at the threshold of visibility: the phantom limb and the spirit photograph. To call these fantasies *body images* is to understand them as a problem of consciousness—whether conscious feelings are real and come from within (the mind) or without (matter), and whether consciousness as such is its own body. *Body image* points to a historical moment when body and mind were set into a relation of mutual haunting; consciousness became the spirit possessing the body (phantom limb), and embodiment shadowed consciousness (spirit photography). Further, these psychical or spiritual bodies activated not-seeing, and they vexed distinctions between reality and fiction. Whereas the phantom limb deceives the amputee into feeling a body part he lacks, the spirit photograph deceives the viewer into believing the dead are present. What proved unsettling, however, was not the body image's deceptiveness but the emotional reality it conveyed. The phantom limb reveals more about the amputee's mind than his body, and spirit photographs more about the viewer's inner state than the objective reality of spirits. As two sides of the same psychophysical coin—the body a psychical sensation, the spirit a physical stimulus—the phantom limb and spirit photograph opened up mourners to the material properties of their own grief.

These body images constitute scenes of not-seeing, for only through the manipulation and subversion of the visual can they be either accessed or rendered. A perceptual modality attuned to the animacy rather than the visibility of matter, not-seeing became a way of knowing and thereby claiming the reality of ghostly forms. As redefined by Mel Y. Chen, animacy names the degree to which matter is considered to have potentiality, sentience, and agency.[7] In the mid- to late nineteenth century, not-seeing certified the perceptual reality of a body and did so based not on which side of the life/death binary it fell but according to its relative animacy, the degree to which it has the vital capacity to affect others. The animacy of these body images—the phantom limb physically moves the amputee's stump, and the spirit photograph emotionally moves the viewer—partook of a broader deployment of the grieving body "as the index of a temporality apart from the linear paradigm of 'progress.'"[8] It was also a vector of racialization, buttressing the hierarchical arrangement of variously wounded subjects (white and black soldiers, white mothers) according to the supposed liveliness of their own bodies. Notably, once neurologist William Hammond concluded his tenure as U.S. Army general surgeon, during which he established the U.S. Army Medical Museum to archive physical specimens and medical photographs of injury, he took to the *North American Review* to deride spiritualism, arguing that although "things are never seen ... as they exist," those who "believe in the materiality of spirits" are "savages."[9] Animacy made the phantom limb appear to be a far more "self-possessed" body than the amputee himself, whereas the capacity of Mumler's spirits to affect viewers ended up affirming the viewer's, not the spirit's, vitality. The ghostly body of grief suddenly came to "matter" more than ever, but the materiality of loss kept alive—or kept lively—racialized hierarchies of feeling that endured well beyond the war.

Dissolving fragile distinctions between life and death, fact and fiction, as well as mental and material worlds, phantom limbs and spirit photographs tell a story about unreconstructed subjects, those unable to (or who refused to) adapt to new political conditions. Understood as early iterations of the body image, these phenomena emphasize the psychophysical correspondence between mind and body—one that hews toward a materialist ontology of the soul—by pushing at the limits of visual perception. They therefore underscore the conceptual commonalities between spiritualist discourses and psychophysics, in particular Gustav Fechner's panpsychical theory of consciousness as a "heavenly vision." Even though Fechner held spiritualism in low regard, his recognition of "the discrepancy between sensuous experience and transcendental matter on the one hand" while stipulating "their mutual translatability and interdependency on the other" influenced spiritualists.[10] This point of conceptual contact helps explain how discursive and technological practices that made a claim to the real—Mitchell's medical case studies of psychologically "reconstructed" bodies, Mumler's photographs of physically "reconstructed" families, and literary fictions of Reconstruction like Henry James's *The Bostonians* (1885)—advanced a psychophysical theory of feeling shot through with spiritualist not-seeing. It also fruitfully reframes spiritualist projects of psychophysical aesthesis as a deeply realist effort to fill in the "blind spots" of the main genre for documenting Civil War losses: medical photography. As formalized by psychophysical aesthesis, these body images highlight the raced subjects pushed below what William Connolly calls the "threshold of political visibility inside every domain of life."[11] In so doing, they inculcate the unreconstructed feelings that set not-seeing alongside wider processes of racialization—all while staging the literariness of lived sensation.

SPIRITS ON THE THRESHOLD

In 1885, three years after the formation of the Society for Psychical Research in Great Britain, William James founded the American Society for Psychical Research to scientifically study paranormal phenomena. Up until this point, spiritualism had been the primary though less professionalized arena for such experiments, performed in living rooms rather than laboratories. Spiritualism mixed popular religion and popular science, as spirit mediums—mostly women—used scientific language, media, and methods to "test the unseen boundary between this world and the next," to the condemnation of most "men of science," Molly McGarry writes.[12] Many spiritualists drew on psychophysical research to engage the unseen world, connecting "the intimate physiology of experience" to the "irresistible physics of the universe."[13] Hermann von Helmholtz was an important figure but Fechner most of all; he was listed in an *Atlantic Monthly* article, "Transcendental Physics," as among "the men of considerable scientific repute" whom "the spiritualists had taken to heart."[14] In the journal *The Monist*, theologian Paul Carus explained that Fechner "believed in the spirituality of the soul," but he "was not a spiritualist and exhibited a decided dislike for spiritualist séances."[15] Spiritualists learned of Fechner's theory of the afterlife in his theological tract *The Little Book of Life after Death*, published in 1836 and then revised in 1866; the first English translation appeared in 1882, and the first U.S. edition in 1904, with an introduction by William James. In that introduction, James explained Fechner's "day-light view" as the "view that the entire material universe, instead of being dead, is inwardly alive and consciously animated."[16] However spiritualists found Fechner at midcentury, they shared his day view of a universe that is alive and conscious. Accessing the world's ever-present yet imperceptible life forms required eschewing the ocular-centric empiricist paradigm of "enlightenment," of exposing hidden truths, and instead deploying the bodily cognition called not-seeing.

In the 1866 edition of *Life after Death*, Fechner synthesized new scientific theories of light and energy, and he brought those theories to bear directly on the day view he had sketched out decades earlier. In the nineteenth century, it is well known, vision both contracted and expanded. The modernization of the microscope and the telescope allowed human beings to see what was otherwise invisible, yet the act of seeing became an uncertain endeavor. This uncertainty arose in part from Helmholtz's 1851 invention of the ophthalmoscope, an instrument for examining the inside of the human eye. This research led Helmholtz to discredit, in his words, the "widespread conviction" that the eye is "an optic instrument so perfect that none formed by human hands can ever be compared with it."[17] In his monumental *Treatise on Physiological Optics* (1856–67), Helmholtz argued that the field of vision has physiological defects and gaps—including the blind spot, chromatic irregularities, and spherical aberrations—that distort our picture of reality. That we can arrive at a "correct" image of the world is only because of the constant readjustments of ocular muscles and the learned habits that the mind draws from experience. Helmholtz's physiological optics swiftly moved beyond scientific circles across the Atlantic, and it led editorial writers to declare, "All optics is illusion."[18] Of course, ophthalmologists such as Henry Willard Williams (who in 1864 treated Emily Dickinson for eye problems) insisted that if "there be any faculty of the body of preeminent importance and value, it is the faculty of seeing."[19] But now, even if vision was the most important sense, it was no longer an objective one. "Can We Believe Our Eyes?" asked the trade publication *Manufacturer and Builder*. The answer was no. "'Seeing is believing' are the words of the old proverb. . . . Not only do we doubt it, but directly deny it. 'Seeing is deceiving,' at least in many instances."[20]

Equally important to the cultural ascendance of not-seeing was the replacement of Isaac Newton's corpuscular theory of light—the theory that light is composed of particles emitted by a specific source—with Thomas Young's wave theory. In the early nineteenth century, Young argued that light is composed of waves that travel through the medium called "luminous ether," a form of energy that is "all-pervading, invisible, and inarguably *there*, materially so," Gillian Beer explains.[21] In conjunction with the newly recognized physiological fallibility of the eye, the fact that the "all-permeating ether was not available to direct observation" was a point that spiritualists "used to their advantage: seeing is not a prerequisite for believing."[22] Equally if not more important, Young's identification of light waves in space led to further analysis of their movement in time, which involved counting the vibrations of these waves within a given period—their frequency. Such analysis of the nonmechanical forces of heat and light was Helmholtz's earliest endeavor. He determined that the difference between the two is quantitative: heat waves vibrate more frequently than light waves. In an 1847 lecture at the Berlin Physical Society, Helmholtz first posited the *law of the conservation of energy* (or *force*), best known as the first law of thermodynamics and considered one of the century's most influential theories, alongside natural selection. He defined the law accordingly: "the *quantity of force which can be brought into action in the whole of Nature is unchangeable,* and can neither be increased nor diminished."[23] Energy can neither be created nor destroyed; its quantity remains constant. Helmholtz's physiological optics would later dethrone sight as a the seat of universal truth—thereby throwing epistemological weight behind not-seeing—but his law of the conservation of energy first dethroned the "truth" of the visible world by subordinating it to the system of invisible motion that pervades it.

This law's most significant implication was that the world is a closed circuit, not a stable system with an infinite supply of energy. Within this closed circuit, matter is immortal but, crucially, not immutable. Light does not die out but simply takes on a new form: heat. That energy merely changes form, Helmholtz acknowledged, "directs us to something beyond the narrow confines of our laboratories and manufactories, to the great operations at work in the life of the earth and of the universe."[24] Jessica Riskin points out that although Helmholtz was a critic of Romantic science, he nonetheless believed in the Romantic principle of organic unity, and in particular regarded "all moving forces as interconvertible forms of the same essential 'activity,'" so that the "living agency of organisms was integral to a more general living agency of nature itself."²⁵ Aiming to balance Enlightenment beliefs in free will with natural science's mechanistic worldview (i.e., all life ruled by cause and effect), Helmholtz settled on a middle-ground philosophy that Anson Rabinbach describes as transcendental materialism. This philosophy views life "not as mechanical motion . . . but rather [as] the particular form taken by the universal force of motion that propels all of nature."²⁶ Rather than assume a reductive sameness in nature, Helmholtz's law suggested a dynamic yet unified material ontology, whereby electricity, magnetism, light, and heat are all variations of the same single entity: energy. Invisible as well as indestructible, and moving through inorganic and organic matter alike, energy is the transcendental principle omnipresent in nature, perceptible only through its material effects or manifestations. That all living matter (atoms, animals, stars) are subject to the law of the conservation of energy radically reframed the soul as physical matter, a "form of vibrant energy that radiates out of the body even after death."²⁷

It seemed entirely possible, then, that the afterlife was not a bounded space apart from earth, as Christianity taught, but rather an energetic system radiating through it. Fechner thought so. First published under the pseudonym Dr. Mises to protect his reputation as a physicist, Fechner's *The Little Book of Life after Death* claims that human beings pass through three phases of living: a prenatal life, life on earth, and life hereafter. Its claim was as provocative as its methodology. An early elaboration of the day view, *Life after Death* pushes transcendental materialism into a theological domain. Its core claim is that if material and spiritual phenomena comprise two parts of the same whole, then we can use empirical knowledge of the former to draw conclusions about the latter. The day view scientist takes into account what exceeds observation, Fechner explained, specifically the "wonderfully complicated play of vibrations . . . originating in our brain," whereas the night view "man of science only knows and studies the play of waves of a lower order [physical phenomena], little caring for those of a higher order [psychical phenomena]. He does not perceive them, but knowing the principle, he ought not to neglect the inferences that may be derived from it."²⁸ *Life after Death* accordingly describes the continuity of material and mental worlds along a scale of spiritual energy, thereby treating metaphysical questions—from which his colleagues at the University of Leipzig shied away—as a legitimate object of scientific study. If the eye is a fallible organ, then empirical science, driven by observation, cannot definitively disprove the existence of spiritual energy. Is it not possible to infer that the nonliving *are* ether—omnipresent agents that can neither be weighed nor measured yet are unquestionably there?

These questions took on real meaning in 1840, when Fechner experienced firsthand the limits of empirical observation. To study retinal afterimages, he stared at the sun through colored glass, which resulted in a year of near-total blindness and spurred a mental health crisis involving insomnia and anorexia. Following his recovery around 1850, Fechner went about establishing psychophysics and in the 1860s returned to *Life after Death* to retrofit its speculative day view with the new scientific vocabulary that he and Helmholtz had developed in the intervening decades. In the revised *Life after Death* (1866) Fechner buttressed the panpsychical day view with the mechanics of the perceptual threshold, defined in *Elements of Psychophysics* (1860) as the point where we consciously feel a change in sensation. Drawing on his psychophysical research, Fechner argued in *Life after Death* that the perceptual threshold, not death, separates the living from the nonliving: "The empirical law of the reciprocity of body and mind states that consciousness is extinguished whenever the bodily activity on which it is dependent sinks below a certain degree of power, called the Threshold."[29] In *Elements*, Fechner had used the wave as a figure for the rise and fall of this bodily activity: "In each wave the part that rises above the threshold is . . . connected with a single consciousness. Whatever lies below the threshold, being unconscious, separates the conscious crests, although it is still the means of physical connection."[30] To illustrate this spatiotemporal movement, *Elements* includes an image of a sinusoidal waveform crossing a horizontal line, the threshold (figure 1.1). As the wave rises, it crests into an individual moment of human consciousness, and as it falls below the threshold, it rejoins a collective consciousness. For Fechner, consciousness is present when the bodily energy "underlying the activity of the mind is raised beyond the degree which we call the threshold," so that the "summits of the waves of our psychophysical activity move and change from place to place, though confined in this life to our body."[31] In *Life after Death*, he maps this psychophysical theory onto his panpsychical theology: when an organism is living, its spiritual energy peaks into individual consciousness, and when nonliving, that energy sinks into the "world soul," conceived of as a below-threshold stimulus.

In other words, *Life after Death* extends mind-body parallelism to the universe; the cosmos is an ensouled body, endowed with a consciousness in which all life forms unconsciously participate. The psychophysical language of the threshold, the stimulus, and waves of energy are elemental to Fechner's

zugleich dadurch darstellen können, dass wir alle Wellen in Zusammenhang verzeichnen; aber nicht oberhalb, sondern unterhalb der Schwelle zusammenhängen lassen, nach diesem Schema:

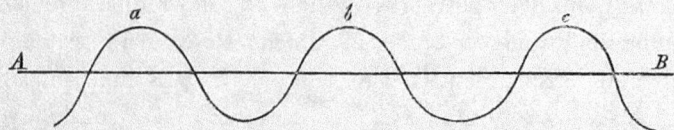

Hier stellen a, b, c drei Organismen oder vielmehr die psychophysischen Hauptwellen dreier Organismen vor, AB die Schwelle. Was von jedem Wellenberge die Schwelle überragt, hängt in sich zusammen und trägt ein einiges Bewusstsein; was unter der

FIG. 1.1 Illustration of waves of consciousness, from Gustav Fechner's *Elements of Psychophysics* (1860).

claim about the immortality of consciousness. Indeed, echoes of Helmholtz ring in his assertion that "conscious energy is in fact never produced afresh, nor can it be absolutely destroyed. Similar to the body with which it is connected, it may change its place, form, and activity, in time and space."[32] Once relocated from the physical to the psychical part of the universe, consciousness leaves behind the sentient body to become a sensory stimulus. Once part of this world soul, consciousness *is* a light wave, a sound wave, and so forth. As elaborated in the appendix "On the Principle of Heavenly Vision," this new manifestation suggests the "heavenly vision" of the nonliving. Souls are forms of energetic matter that "appear to each other immediately and in their full intensity"—contra the "earthly vision" that cannot perceive these bodies directly but can only perceive "their images on the retina."[33] Yet because these souls are physical stimuli, they can affect the "earthly vision" of the living. When we visualize the deceased in a memory or a dream, or see them "out there" (i.e., a mirage), we behold not an illusion but a material reality. Fechner explains:

> Did you take the faint image in which a dead person appears in your memory for a mere inward semblance? If so, you have mistaken it; it is more than that, it is your friend's own self. His former shape is still the garment of his soul ... free from earthly burdens, changing its place in a moment, at the call of every person who thinks of him, or even entering into your mind of his own accord.... You also have heard of ghosts appearing—what the

doctors call illusions or hallucinations. They are indeed hallucinations of the living, but, at the same time, real manifestations of the dead. The faint images in our memory are such manifestations, those vivid apparitions are only the more so.[34]

This is a radical proposition: that representations are real things in the world. Scientists like John Draper took to monthly magazines to inform the public that such "ghosts" are in fact retinal afterimages, visual images retained in the mind's eye long after "the reality has appeared."[35] Fechner, however, insisted that these mental images are material forms, that retinal afterimages are physical manifestations of the nonliving soul. He did so on the basis that spirits are material beings endowed with a consciousness of their own, entering into the minds of the living as internal visions or hallucinations. The "peculiar reversed-out ghosts that dance before [the] eyes" are entirely real because spirits are visual stimuli.[36] What this means, Paul Carus explained, is that afterimages are not "mere abstractions or [a] sham but the true presence of the souls of our beloved ones."[37] To the extent that felt experience is a fact in the world, the optical illusion is wholly objective.

Fechner's ability to bring thermodynamics to bear on theology was important to midcentury conceptions of the nonliving as agential matter—a theory that spiritualists promoted. In his claim that souls are light waves that stimulate internal or psychical images (i.e., memories, dreams), Fechner's psychophysical theory of life after death buoyed other materialist ontologies of soul life. "Both invisible ether and invisible matter form but one grand universe, in which the sum of energy remains constant, though the order of its distribution endlessly varies."[38] The author of this statement could easily be Fechner, though it is in fact U.S. theologian John Fiske. In the *Atlantic Monthly*, he elaborated upon the "hypothesis of an unseen world in which psychical phenomena persist in the absence of material conditions."[39] Although aligned with spiritualism, the day view was adapted by anyone who disagreed with the night view. In a *North American Review* article, "Ghost Seeing," for instance, minister Frederic Hedge echoed Fechner by chiding the "one-sided culture of physical science" for rejecting the "unseen world where science cannot reach, and which enfolds the visible as space encompasses sun and planet."[40] Not only religious but also scientific thinkers challenged night view empiricisms. A writer for the *Scientific American* acknowledged, for instance, that mirages "are not to be attributed wholly to the exercise of the imagination, and no explanation, founded on the law of optics, has, as yet, been made" to disprove their reality.[41] Predicated on Helmholtz's work in thermodynamics and optics as well as on Fechner's theory of spirit life as below-threshold stimuli, not-seeing demonstrated that it was impossible to deny the material endurance of the soul. What emerged from this epistemological flux were two new "transcendental materialist" bodies that breached the psychophysical threshold separating the living from the nonliving: phantom limbs and photographic spirits.

NOT-SEEING THINGS

Physiological optics shifted epistemological value from seeing to not-seeing, while thermodynamics proposed a materialist ontology of energy, a transcendental principle that could unify not simply body and soul but living and nonliving. These developments suggested that invisible matter was as real as any objective phenomenon. Fechner, however, found that the former was actually *more real* than the latter. As Carus noted in his 1906 review of *Life after Death*, one of Fechner's more provocative claims is that the "reality of the soul life" trumps reality itself; not only are psychical images "actual events but they are even more real than material objects."[42] For proof, Fechner need have looked no further than S. Weir Mitchell's identification of the phantom limb, a psychical image that seemed more real than the physical body. Unlike Fechner, Mitchell was a night view "man of science" who insisted that facts be derived from observation. He also was a physician who staked his authority on the *medical gaze*—Foucault's term for the institutionalized way of looking that subjects the patient's body to visual scrutiny and establishes the doctor as a producer of truth. Mitchell found it strange enough that, among the amputees he treated, when "a limb has been cut off the sufferer does not lose the consciousness of its existence," as though limbs can convert from physical to psychical matter.[43] But more startling than the phantom limb, he explained, was that amputees have "a sense of its existence so vivid as to be more definite and intrusive than is that of its truly living fellow member."[44] In Fechnerian terms, the phantom limb was a form of soul life that exceeded external reality. As a body that yielded to not-seeing rather than to observation and that seemed to partake of the unseen world more than the visible one, the phantom limb forced Mitchell onto the psychophysical terrain of mind-body parallelism. It also forced him to entertain the possibility that experiential fictions might be more real than empirical facts.

It makes a certain kind of sense, then, that the first medical case study of the phantom limb took the form of fiction: Mitchell's "The Case of George Dedlow," which appeared in the *Atlantic Monthly* in 1866. The story is presented as a self-reported case study, tracking the titular narrator's transformation from surgeon to Union cavalryman to quadruple amputee. While recovering from his amputations, Dedlow begins experiencing phantom limb pain that medical science cannot remedy. As a result, he is forced to seek healing at a séance, where he is briefly reunited with the spirits of his lost limbs. Dedlow is presented as one duped by the fiction of bodily wholeness spun by his phantom limbs. But "The Case of George Dedlow" itself duped the reading public into mistaking fiction for fact. Assuming the case study true, readers of the *Atlantic* started a collection for Dedlow, and others sought audience with him at the Philadelphia hospital where most of the story is set. In a speech made at the American Medical Association fifty years later, Mitchell recalled, "George Dedlow must have seemed very real. At the close of the story, he—a limbless torso—is carried to a spiritualist meeting, where the spirits call up his lost legs and he capers about for a glorious minute. The spiritualist journals seized on this as new proof of the verity of their belief. Imagine that!"[45] But were the spiritualists deceived? Was not the joke on Mitchell, the physician whose object of study had to be a sensationalist trope to become a scientific truth? Neurologist Oliver Sacks has credited Mitchell with proving that phantom limbs "were 'real'—neurological constructs dependent on the integrity of the brain, the spinal cord, and in the remaining proximal portions of the sensory and motor nerves of the limb."[46] Mitchell proved the reality of phantom limbs but seemed fairly uncertain about what "reality" meant: he classified phantom limbs as sensory "delusions" and "hallucinations." Mitchell's discursive corpus—the fictional "George Dedlow," the essay "Phantom Limbs" (1871), and the medical textbook *Injuries of Nerves and Their Consequences* (1872)—is a mix of case study and gothic sensationalism that uses generic indeterminacy to express the indeterminate ontology of the phantom limb. As such, these texts are constitutive rather than reflective of Mitchell's medical research—a means of further testing out the various fictions that structure reality.

That Mitchell considered fiction the most appropriate venue for presenting his research can be attributed as well to the transitional moment in mid-century science when Romantic paradigms were ceding ground to a more rigid positivism. Like Fechner, who used Dr. Mises to veil his psychophysical theory of life after death, Mitchell hid behind George Dedlow, the ostensible author of the case. The story begins with Dedlow's prefatory explanation for why a general periodical (the *Atlantic*) rather than a professional journal is publishing his case: "The following notes of my own case have been declined ... by every medical journal ... because the psychical deductions to which they have led me are not of medical interest."[47] Dedlow's diegetic peer reviewers refused his case study because they subscribe to night view empiricism, which makes no room for "psychical deductions." This brief remark signals to readers that what follows is a dramatic departure from medicine's epistemological and professional norms. Indeed, Dedlow is not simply the narrator but a physician and a patient as well. As such, he combines the narrative perspective of the disinterested observer with "the empathetic viewpoint of the person experiencing the phantoms."[48] In tracking these phantoms, the case study shifts from the former perspective to the latter. The ghostly body driving Dedlow toward profound abjection also drives the story from seeing to not-seeing, ultimately redefining life in terms of the animacy, not the visibility, of the body.

"The Case of George Dedlow" begins with clinical descriptions of the wounds and infections that Dedlow incurs, which require the successive amputation of both his arms and legs. The increasing survival rate of amputation during the Civil War meant that amputee veterans constituted a highly visible class of disabled citizens. In his essay "Phantom Limbs," Mitchell recounted that "every man's loss was visible, and hundreds of men, less by a leg or an arm ... presented sights at once pitiable and singular."[49] Through parades and portraiture, veterans turned that pity into a positive "empty sleeve discourse" that framed amputation as "visual evidence of courage."[50] Yet as a quadruple amputee, Dedlow possesses a disability that registers not in the key of honorable pity or of patriotic heroism but in the key of the unsightly, the ugly—less a veteran and more a beggar.[51] After all, Dedlow sees himself as a freak, a "useless torso, more like some strange larval creature than anything of human shape."[52] He inhabits the domain of sensationalism, a cultural mode that emphasizes "materiality and corporeality, even or especially to the point of thrilling and horrifying readers."[53] Further, this "larval" body raises the questions of whether Dedlow is human and whether he is alive. An altogether existential crisis unfolds:

> Still more remarkable, however, were the physical [*sic*] changes, which I now began to perceive. I found to my horror that at times I was less conscious of myself, of my own existence, than used to be the case.... At times the conviction of my want of being myself was overwhelming and most painful. It was, as well as I can describe it, a deficiency in the egoistic sentiment of

individuality.... Would such a being, I asked myself, possess the sense of individuality in its usual completeness, even if his organs of sensation remained, and he were capable of consciousness?... I thus reached the conclusion that a man is not his brain, or any one part of it, but all of his economy, and that to lose any part must lessen this sense of his own existence.[54]

When you amputate the body, you amputate the spirit. Dedlow has arrived at Fechner's law of psychophysical parallelism: a change in physical state correlates to a change in psychological state. So inextricably linked are body and mind that even the likely typo "physical changes"—changed to *psychical* in the 1900 reprint of "The Case of George Dedlow"—redoubles the easy slippage between the two.[55] Dedlow concludes that he is "not a happy fraction of a man" and awaits the day when he "shall rejoin the lost members of my corporeal family in another and a happier world!"[56] The physical death of his limbs is bound to other kinds of death—of humanity (now larval), of individuality (not George Dedlow), and of manhood (now a fraction)—which pose the question of whether Dedlow, as his name implies, is not already dead.

The reduction to "bare life" brought on by psychophysical amputation has decidedly racial dimensions. Sari Altschuler astutely points out that Dedlow's phantom limb pain "prompts both medical and philosophical meditations," yet these meditations are also a politically loaded mathematics.[57] The calculation behind Dedlow's manhood is quite specific: he has "lost four fifths of [his] weight" and "at least a third of [his] skin."[58] Translating this existential loss into concrete numbers, the story offers up two fractions that together cite the three-fifths personhood accorded to enslaved black people. Amputation, then, is a loss of white masculinity. Dedlow reproduces what Lauren Berlant calls the "peculiar dialectic between embodiment and abstraction in the post-Enlightenment body politic."[59] According to this dialectic, the public sphere is organized around the figure of the bodiless citizen, the rational subject capable of transcending particularity and implicitly coded as white male. The bodiless citizen thus enshrines white masculinity as the universal standard against which all other body-subjects are differentially marked. At the same time, the public sphere historically has "invested the core of citizenship in the whole, white male body," which U.S. presidents like Theodore Roosevelt performed and pressed into the service of empire.[60] Dedlow synthesizes these two accounts of citizenship in macabre fashion. Little more than torso and head, he is a literalization of the rational subject—all mind, no body. But operating in the key of the unsightly and grotesque, his "embodying" this political ideal diminishes rather than enhances his whiteness and manhood. To be bodiless is not a privilege but a problem, for disability evacuates Dedlow of the "egoistic sentiment of individuality" and therefore any claim to autonomy. As a "fraction of a man," Dedlow lacks the mental capacity needed to transcend and govern his body, and now is more akin to the enslaved black person who is three-fifths a person and legally lacks self-possession.

In this way, the phantom limb functions as a radical troping on liberal self-possession: it becomes a form of spirit possession. As the medical case study shifts its attention from the unsightly body to the unseen body, and its style from grim realism to gothic sensationalism, consciousness itself becomes sensational. What happens, the story asks, when perceptual reality is a ghost story? The phantom limb is a fiction of bodily wholeness spun by a haunted mind—hence the sensationalism encoded in the very term *phantom limb*, as well as the other epithets that Mitchell used for this condition, including *sensory ghost*, *spirit limb*, and *ghostly member*. So haunted is Dedlow by the physical feelings generated by his mind that he becomes susceptible to spiritualism. When another amputee asks him if he believes that all things die, Dedlow responds in the language of thermodynamics: "The soul does not, I am sure; and so as to matter, it merely changes form." This friend, a spiritualist, presses Dedlow: "'But why, then,' said he, 'should not the dead soul talk to the living? In space, no doubt, exist all forms of matter, merely in finer, more ethereal being. You can't suppose a naked soul moving about without a bodily garment; . . . and if its new clothing be of like substance to ours, only of ethereal fineness . . . must it not then possess powers as much more delicate and refined as is the new material in which it is reclad?'"[61] If consciousness is material, and if matter cannot be destroyed, then consciousness must be immortal, simply adorned in the "higher frequency" garb of heat sensations and throbbing pain. According to the logic of Dedlow's friend, phantom limbs constitute rather than contradict the physical body. Reducible neither to body nor mind, and neither to life nor death, phantom limbs are evidence of a divine consciousness that connects physical appearances to subjective consciousness. How else to account for a lost limb that is both imaginary and undeniably material?

Moving from seeing to not-seeing involves the relocation of this internal drama from the army hospital to the spiritualist séance. In a scene suspended between disbelief and comic relief, Dedlow joins an "eclectic doctor," a spirit medium, and an "authoress of two somewhat feeble novels" to communicate with the dead. Sitting around a table, the medium asks him to "think of a spirit," and a "wild idea" comes to mind. Soon after, a "series of irregular knocks" are made on the table, and the authoress decodes these knocks: "'UNITED STATES ARMY MEDICAL MUSEUM, Nos. 3486, 3487.' The medium looked up with a puzzled expression. 'Good gracious!' said I, 'they are *my legs—my legs!*'" Dedlow then recounts:

> Suddenly I felt a strange return of my self-consciousness. I was reindividualized, so to speak. A strange wonder filled me, and, to the amazement of everyone, I arose and walked across the room on limbs invisible to them or me. It was no wonder I staggered, for, as I briefly reflected, my legs had been nine months in the strongest alcohol. At this instant all my new friends crowded around me in astonishment. Presently, however, I felt myself sinking slowly. My legs were going, and in a moment I was resting feebly on my two stumps on the floor. It was too much. All that was left of me fainted and rolled over senseless.[62]

The trope becomes literal; the limbs are indeed phantoms. Once amputated, Dedlow's physical legs were sent to the U.S. Army Medical Museum in Washington, D.C., preserved in vats of alcohol. Once the séance reunites the souls of the "dead" limbs and the living person, Dedlow recovers his self-possession, accentuated by the exclamatory repetition of *my*. Walking on "limbs invisible to them or me," he is reborn a "reindividualized" subject capable of self-directed movement. But this reunion, this self-repossession, is fleeting. The spirits of his legs decide to move on, leaving "all that was left" of Dedlow as allegedly feeble as women's writing (the authoress's novels). Mitchell endorses the reality of phantom limbs only to insist, rather heavy-handedly, that the transcendental materialism advocated by spiritualism has no legs to stand on. Mocking rather than validating the day view of nature, the story's sensational climax establishes the phantom limb as mere hallucination. However much it challenges traditional binaries between the empirical and the speculative, the phantom limb clearly falls in the latter category.

Or does it? Much like the antebellum skeptics who ended up validating the mesmerists they sought to debunk, as Emily Ogden has brilliantly shown, Mitchell is the quintessentially modern subject seeking to manage this occult phenomenon at the moment he conjures it.[63] Indeed, Justine Murison persuasively argues that in attempting to distinguish "good" medicine from "bad" religion, Mitchell ultimately "reinforce[d] the reality of ghosts."[64] Case in point: Dedlow's stagger was not obviously sensational to readers. In 1871,

Sight · 51

Lippincott's printed Mitchell's medical essay "Phantom Limbs," which clarified that "The Case of George Dedlow" was a fiction and that the author never thought it "possible that his humorous sketch, with its absurd conclusion, would for a moment mislead anyone. Many persons, however, accepted it as true"—and so the "present description of what the amputated really feel and suffer may possibly serve to correct such erroneous beliefs as were caused by this *jeu d'esprit*."[65] Mitchell shirks responsibility for the George Dedlow hoax, but an author cannot charge his readers of gullibility when he sought to mislead them. Perhaps more noteworthy is that the scene he considered most absurd was the scene the public viewed as entirely plausible. When it came to the phantom limb, even William James acknowledged, "If there be any distant material object with which a man might be supposed to have clairvoyant or telepathic relations, that object ought to be his own cut-off arm or leg."[66] Further, print culture fostered such "erroneous beliefs." In the middlebrow *Atlantic Monthly*, "The Case of George Dedlow" absorbed credibility from the company it kept, which in that issue included William Cullen Bryant's poem "The Death of Slavery" and journalist Henry Burrage's Civil War essay "Retreat from Lenoir and the Siege of Knoxville." In the pulpier magazine *Lippincott's*, "Phantom Limbs" followed Clara Guernsey's formulaic ghost story "The Cold Hand," about a dead criminal's severed hand and the hapless victims thereof. In that magazine, spatial proximity and thematic similarity forced a likeness between medical cases and gothic stories. The chiastic relation between Mitchell's two accounts—"The Case of George Dedlow" a fiction that seemed real and "Phantom Limbs" a report that seemed fictional—further muddled the already tenuous distinction between the physical and the psychical. Not-seeing converged with print culture to upend the narrative hoax (George Dedlow), itself intended to unveil a psychical hoax (the phantom limb) by verifying its real existence.

"Phantom Limbs" revealed that what amputees "really feel" is not all that different from what Dedlow "falsely" felt. "There is something almost tragical, almost ghastly, in the notion of these thousands of spirit limbs haunting as many good soldiers," Mitchell lamented in *Lippincott's*.[67] In his medical study *Injuries of Nerves and Their Consequences*, he further elaborated the tragedy that the "sense of the existence of the limb" is so strong as to be "even more intense than exists for the remaining member."[68] These "ghostly members" are fictions of bodily presence so convincing as to make the real body seem illusory; they have such a "distinctly material" presence as to "betray" the amputee in the middle of embodied action.[69] In one case, when a "gallant fellow, who had lost an arm at Shiloh," went riding, "he used the lost hand to grasp the reins, while with the other he struck his horse. He paid for his blunder with a fall." In another, a "poor fellow, at every meal for many months, would try to pick up his fork, and failing would be suddenly seized with nausea."[70] These "absurd mishaps" involve valorous men who are victims of a hallucination that only experience can debunk. In *Injuries of Nerves*, Mitchell notes that "with the aid of a faradaic current applied to the nerves of the stump," he was able to "suddenly recall" consciousness of a soldier's amputated limb, and once when he "faradized a case of a disarticulated shoulder . . . [t]he patient suddenly cried aloud, 'Oh, the hand, the hand!' and attempted to seize the missing member. The phantom I had conjured up swiftly disappeared, but no spirit could have more amazed the man, so real did it seem."[71] Perhaps Mitchell's time acting the "quack" who engineers phantom pain is what spurred him to engineer the fake case study "The Case of George Dedlow." In both instances, rather than unmask or debunk the phantom limb as the mind's "betrayal" of the body, these cases instead end up certifying the convertibility of mental and material life.

Through specular language and sensationalist tropes, Mitchell's medical cases link phantom limbs to spiritualism's performances of transcendental communion. Even more so than in "The Case of George Dedlow," consciousness becomes in his medical cases a supernatural event that, given prevailing notions of women's frailty and hyper-receptivity, feminize veteran amputees. These cases, more specifically, figure the amputee as a spirit medium, the "credulous instrument employed by the spirit."[72] It was standard practice for doctors to "pathologize mediumship, naming it as a particularly female disease akin to hysteria," manifested through the same bodily repertoires as spirit possession: uncontrolled thrashing, trembling, and jerking.[73] Mitchell's cases duly limn the disabled male body as involved in a set of mediumistic performances bordering on hysterics. The "sensory ghosts" causing their stumps to "shake" and "quiver" in a "crazed" fervor with "spasmodic motions" are all "called up" from within.[74] Mitchell's feminization of disability accords with the rest cure that he later developed, first to cure soldiers' battle fatigue and then, in the 1880s, to cure the newly fatigued middle-class white people suffering from "nervous exhaustion." In Nancy Cervetti's biography of Mitchell, she observes that the phantom limb—the transformation of physical trauma into a psychological manifestation—paved the way for Mitchell's understanding of neurasthenia as "the transformation of emotional trauma into somatic manifestations."[75] The phantom limb functioned as the masculine obverse of neurasthenia, but it also plagued a feminized population. Anticipating the neurasthenic white woman while drawing on figurations of the spirit medium as a hysteric, the amputee soldier is possessed by an internal ghost that pushes him even further from his "natural" properties of vitality and rationality.

This feminization is simultaneously a racialization. Across these cases, the psychical ghost does things to the disabled male body. In one gruesome case, a thumb "bent in on the palm" before the hand was amputated continues to "torture the palm which it wounded in life," so that any "attempt to will a movement of the lost part results in utmost pain."[76] Mitchell's patients appear far less lively than the phantoms possessing them. Even Dedlow's "dead" limbs are strong enough to move his torso across the floor; they are not brought back to life but rather bring him back to life, "reindividualizing" him. Because they are figured as animate—having will, agency, and autonomy—these spirits are coded as white. This whiteness, however, does not transfer to the survivors. As previously discussed, because disability fractures self-possession, it diminishes any claim to whiteness. Disability racializes the white veteran as well by ascribing animatedness to his body, a concept developed by Sianne Ngai to describe an affective condition associated with the "overly emotional racialized subject, abetting his or her construction as unusually receptive to external control."[77] Animatedness "resembles a kind of mechanization" and here characterizes Mitchell's patients as puppets incapable of independent action.[78] The relation of the amputee to his phantom limbs is one of animatedness to animacy; his body moves only according to the will of the lively phantom limb. This is why Mitchell's patients appear not unlike the black people whose inner life, psychologist G. Stanley Hall argued, was "dominated by spirits," which made "the next world" seem to them more real than the present one.[79] Like women and people of color, who are "responsive only to external motion and incapable of internal response," the amputee veteran is possessed, not self-possessed."[80] But the phantom limb evidences a distinctly "white" variety of animatedness because it is a sensation that arises from excess interiority rather than from excess receptivity. The phantom limb bears out a white man who is governed *too much* by his psyche, too much by the internal signs (the body image) that his rational faculty cannot override. Animatedness results from a body that disability has rendered excessively white.

Within the historical context of its medical identification, the phantom limb was a body image that crisscrossed contingent designations of race, gender, and disability. As described by Mitchell, it situated wounded bodies not on either side of the life/death binary but instead along a spectrum of vitality, from animatedness to animacy. And as adopted and adapted by spiritualists, the psychophysical day view was the very condition of the phantom limb's possibility. Fechner's philosophy underwrote the psychophysical parallelism and day view epistemology of not-seeing and as such stymied Mitchell's attempted explanations. A psychical response to physical trauma still considered one of the "most elusive afflictions in the repertoire of human illness," phantom limbs struck an uncanny resemblance to spiritualist performance.[81] Across his fictional and medical cases, Mitchell sought to establish the reality of unseen pain without abandoning the empiricist protocols that would secure universal truth against the baseless claims of nonprofessional or vernacular scientists. Above all, however, what perhaps unnerved Mitchell the most was that phantom limbs were an undeniably lived and literary experience—a sensationalistic sensation that dilated physical reality by confounding internal and external bodies.

SEEING NOT-SEEING

The phantom limb was the form that mourning took for Civil War amputees while the spirit photograph gave form to civilians' experience of loss. Yet whereas the phantom limb was a kind of spirit communication that physically tortured survivors, spirit photographs offered solace. In William and Hannah Mumler's photographs, the placid spirits positioned beside or behind the living sitters adopted "the same roles or gestures popular in paintings of the time."[82] These photographic spirits were figures of reassurance rather than terrifying ghosts because they adopted familiar poses and postures. And because they actually *were* familiar: Mumler had a vast archive of photographic subjects to refashion as spirits—that is, the soldiers whose portraits had been taken before they headed off to war. Mumler used the technique of double exposure to produce spirit photographs. He put a used plate glass (already imprinted with a person's image) into his camera in front of a clean plate glass and then photographed his client; the resulting image showed that person adjacent to a faint figure that looked like a ghost but in fact was the figure from the used plate glass, degraded in quality from transferal. In this fashion did a particular kind of "body image" take hold during and after the war—one that, like the phantom limb, reopened time by putting the past in the present and in physical space.

Mumler's spirit photographs sparked instant controversy. Were these photographic ghosts real or not? In 1869, shortly after moving his studio from

Boston to New York City, he was charged with fraud. Widely publicized by national magazines like *Harper's Weekly*, the sensational trial was something of a media circus, with professional humbug P. T. Barnum of all people testifying against the photographer; it takes a con to know a con (figure 1.2). But scientific experts could not definitively *dis*prove spirit photography, so Mumler was acquitted. The court of public opinion remained divided. The *Manufacturer and Builder* called spirit photography a hoax because objects "must be visible to the eye" and illuminated "by light possessing chemical rays" to be photographed.[83] In the agnostic language of litotes, English photographer J. Traill Taylor allowed that the "photographing of an invisible image, whether it be a spirit or a lump of matter[,] is not scientifically impossible."[84] Meanwhile, the spiritualist newspaper *Banner of Light* declared, "No fact in philosophy disproves the power of a spirit to reflect chemical rays."[85] By insisting that the camera can "*prove*—empirically and beyond question—the definite existence of spirit life," spiritualists advanced the psychophysical project of applying empirical methods to psychical phenomena.[86] Not only was the camera more perfect than the fallible human eye, the thinking went, but it also had a lower visual threshold. And a lower visual threshold meant that the camera required less physical stimulation—energy of lower frequency—to make these spirits visible to its mechanical eye.

Spirit photographs consoled mourners by allowing them to see their own not-seeing, offering viewers just enough visual information about the dead to confirm presence in the face of absence. Critics recently have begun to reassess the significant but overlooked role that the Mumlers played in the visual experience of the Civil War. Their spirit photographs typically play the foil to the grim battlefield photographs of Mathew Brady, Andrew Gardner, and Timothy O'Sullivan, whose iconic images of the Civil War dead are considered a harbinger of artistic modernity. Conversely, the Mumlers' spectral images of the dead appear as an "absurd, repugnant, embarrassing episode" in the history of photography, as Marina Warner observes.[87] This general attitude has arisen in part because spirit photography was not only allied with spiritualist practices but also part of sentimental mourning culture; the photographs served as tokens of affection, much like mortuary photography of the 1840s and 1850s. It might be safely wagered that it was only against the fraud and femininity represented by spirit photography that battlefield photographs came to acquire the aura of the real and of the modern. The Mumlers joined Brady, Gardner, and O'Sullivan in documenting the war; they simply did so by making spirits barely visible and thereby making the pain of the bereaved

Vol. XIII.—No. 645.]   NEW YORK, SATURDAY, MAY 8, 1869.   [SINGLE COPIES, TEN CENTS.
$4.00 PER YEAR IN ADVANCE.

SPIRITUAL PHOTOGRAPHY.

The case of the people against WILLIAM H. MUMLER, of 630 Broadway, is one so remarkable and without precedent in the annals of criminal jurisprudence that we devote this page to illustrations bearing upon it. The charge against Mr. MUMLER is that, by means of what he terms spiritual photographs, he has swindled many credulous persons, leading them to believe it possible to photograph the immaterial forms of their departed friends.

The case has excited the profoundest interest, and, strange as it may seem, there are thousands of people who believe that its development will justify the claims made by the spiritual photographer. We shall not attempt to give an expression to our own opinions, but simply to follow the developments of the case through the testimony offered during the first few days of the trial.

It is through the instrumentality of Marshal JOSEPH H. TOOKER that the case has been brought before the courts. He deposes that he was ordered by Mayor HALL to investigate the case, which he did by assuming a false name, and by getting his photograph taken by Mr. MUMLER. After the taking of the picture the negative was shown him, with a clear, indistinct outline of a ghostly face staring out of one corner; and he was told that the picture represented the spirit of his father-in-law. He, however, failed to recognize the worthy old gentleman, and emphatically declared that the picture neither represented his father-in-law, nor any of his relations, nor any person whom he had ever seen or known. With this evidence he had over seen of known. With this evidence the prosecution rested.

The counsel for the defense have brought forward a number of witnesses who testify to the genuineness of spiritual photographs taken for them by Mr. MUMLER. WILLIAM P. SYLER, a photographer, of Poughkeepsie, testifies that MUMLER succeeded in producing spiritual photographs at his gallery in Poughkeepsie, and he was unable to discover how it was done. Judge EDMONDS, one of the most distinguished advocates of spiritualism, deposed that he had two photographs taken by MUMLER; the spirit form in one he thought he could recognize, but not the one in the other. He said: "I believe that the camera can take a photograph of a spirit, and I believe also that spirits have materiality

— not that gross materiality that mortals possess, but still they are material enough to be visible to the human eye, for I have seen them only a few days since I was in a court in Brooklyn when a suit against a life insurance company for the amount claimed to be due on a certain policy was being heard. Looking toward that part of the court-room occupied by the jury, I saw the spirit of the man whose death was the basis of the suit. The spirit told me the circumstances connected with the death; said that the suit was groundless, that the claimant was not entitled to recover from the company, and said that he (the man whose spirit was speaking) had committed suicide under certain circumstances. I drew a diagram of the place at which his death occurred, and on showing it to the counsel, was told that it was exact in every particular."

A large number of witnesses deposed that they recognized the forms of departed friends (in some cases of those long dead) in the photographs taken for them by MUMLER. The most striking case was that of a gentleman of Wall Street, whose deceased wife's features both he and his friends distinctly recognized in a photograph taken for him in this way.

If there is a trick in Mr. MUMLER'S process it has certainly not been detected as yet. To all appearances spiritual photography rests just where the rappings and table-turnings have rested for some years. Those who believe in it at all will respect no opposing arguments, and disbelievers will reject every favorable hypothesis or explanation. Mr. MUMLER has certainly been very fortunate. He has been believed in, in the first place, by a large number of people. He has obtained, again, a good price for his photographs; for who could expect spirits to be called "from the vasty deep" for less than ten dollars per head? And, finally, he has been prosecuted, and thus effectually advertised. Beyond this, the trial, like all legal prosecutions of this nature, will amount to nothing.

In addition to our illustrations of specimens of Mr. MUMLER'S spirit photographs, we give also representations of similar photographs taken by Mr. BOCKWOOD of this city. The latter were taken by natural means, but not so as to escape detection to the trick resorted to to secure the result. Mr. MUMLER has certainly the advantage of a longer experience in the business.

W. H. MUMLER.   MRS. W. H. MUMLER.—BY MUMLER.   SPIRIT PHOTOGRAPH BY MUMLER.

SPIRIT PHOTOGRAPH BY MUMLER.   SPIRIT PHOTOGRAPH BY MUMLER.   SPIRIT PHOTOGRAPH BY MUMLER.

SPIRIT PHOTOGRAPH BY MUMLER.   P. V. HICKEY.—BY ROCKWOOD.   C. B. BOYLE.—BY ROCKWOOD.

SPIRITUAL PHOTOGRAPHY.—[SPECIMENS FURNISHED BY MUMLER AND ROCKWOOD.]

FIG. 1.2 Cover page, *Harper's Weekly*, May 8, 1869.

clearly visible. Simply put, whether or not spirit photography was a hoax, it certainly told a real story.

Even a story meant to debunk spirit photographs can end up affirming their "real" purpose: to offer comfort. This healing function is at the center of Metta Victoria Fuller Victor's short story "The Spirit Photograph," printed in *Harper's Monthly* in 1863 under the pseudonym Seely Register. The story centers on a man named Dudley who mourns "the loss of his wife" after the ship she was sailing to Havana crashed and sank.[88] Intrigued by the "last marvel of spiritualism," Dudley's friend convinces him to visit a photographer who can "fix the shadows of souls as well as bodies—so they say! The spirit of the deceased friend wished for appears beside the picture of the sitter, faint and shadowy . . . but still quite palpable."[89] When, after sitting for the photographer, Dudley sees the picture of himself and his deceased wife "robed in some ethereal texture," he cries out, "She *was* here, as really and truly as I am, or as you are! Oh what happiness is this, to feel that our loved ones are separated from us by so slight a barrier."[90] The image, however, is not a spirit photograph; it is a regular portrait. The wife survived the shipwreck and had been physically standing behind Dudley in the studio. With the happy reunion of husband and wife, "The Spirit Photograph" suggests that spirit photographs are impossible documents—but they are not a callous hoax. Rather, spirit photographs are a homeopathic remedy for the bereaved, for up until the "grand reveal," the image had helped Dudley grapple with loss. From this perspective, the spirit photograph is akin to twenty-first-century neuroscientist V. S. Ramachandran's mirror box, a box with two outward facing mirrors that alleviates phantom pain by tricking the perceiver into thinking that the missing appendage, such as a missing hand, is present (really what the subject sees is the reflection of the "real" hand).[91] The mirror box seems to make good on the promise of spirit photography: optical illusion as analgesic. Taking seriously the camera's role in mediating and ameliorating the grief, trauma, and loss pervading this historical moment, Victor's story frames spirit photography as a fiction of reattachment—with the purpose not to make the dead observable but to make visible the unobservability of the survivor's grief.

This therapeutic function brings spirit photographs, portraits of emotionally wounded civilians, in close alignment with the era's medical photographs of wounded soldiers, portraits of physical wounded soldiers. Yet spirit photographs deployed not-seeing to disavow the work of exposure that the medical gaze performed and that medical photography extended, literally so: doctors were the first medical photographers, a fact that crystallizes the "marriage of medicine to technologies of realism" during the Civil War.⁹² Robert Goler reminds us that the war was the "first large-scale conflict in which medically significant numbers of injuries were photographically recorded."⁹³ In 1862, William Hammond established the U.S. Army Medical Museum (AMM) in Washington, DC, to collect pathological specimens and photographs of injuries. By 1866, the AMM had gleaned more than seventeen hundred images, used either for medical study or as proof of disability for pension claims. Considered "one of the pioneer practitioners of the new visual empiricism," ophthalmologist Reed Bontecou contributed so many photographs to the AMM that they became the core of its collection (figure 1.3).⁹⁴ At Harewood Hospital in Washington, DC, Bontecou used the camera in ways that anonymized rather than valorized his patients, their bodies posed and declothed to reveal their wounds. On these cartes de visite, placards offer identifying information for each subject, now doubly objectified by the doctor and the camera. The portraits bespeak the realist insistence on a "compulsory and compulsive visibility" that lodges meaning in bodily surface, conveys physicality instead of personality, and reduces the individual to a type of injury.⁹⁵ Presented serially in medical albums, they contain the shock of visibly mutilated bodies by laying bare the "truth" of wounding.

Or so it would seem. By containing the shock of mutilation, Tanya Sheehan argues, these images "demonstrated that debilitated military bodies, along with the nation they both symbolized and served, could return to a state of health."⁹⁶ Yet if, according to S. Weir Mitchell, "only about five percent of the men who have suffered amputation never have any feeling of the part as being still present," then nearly every photographed amputee was a George Dedlow.⁹⁷ Had Dedlow been under Bontecou's care, the photograph would have shown his physical body but not his phantom body. A complete visual record of Dedlow's war wounds would require the more discerning eye of William Mumler's camera. Spirit photography represents an important counterarchive, not only because it depicts the emotional wounds of war—the injury to the surviving family—but also because it consoles rather than diagnoses, not-sees rather than exposes, wounds. In the spirit photograph, that wound takes the form of a faint outline of the dead, who can be materialized only by enjoining the camera lens to cosmic intent, the behavior of light to magnetic powers. In his memoir, Mumler insisted that his "ability in taking the likeness of those who have passed on" depended on his wife, Hannah, a "natural clairvoyant" whose "magnetic powers [were] directly connected with spirit photography."⁹⁸ Mumler's day view account figures the camera as an overly

FIG. 1.3 Reed B. Bontecou, Harewood Hospital photograph album (c. 1864–1865), page 15. © Stanley B. Burns, MD, and the Burns Archive, New York, New York.

mechanical eye; it requires spiritual energy to truly see. In *The Veil Lifted: Modern Developments of Spirit Photography* (1894), J. Traill Taylor shored up this idea by arguing that "there is some fluorescent compound in the eyes of such persons not present in those whose are normal, and that it is to this they owe their seeing powers."[99] Whether attributed to the body's magnetic powers or light's chemical properties, the clairvoyant's collaboration with the camera turns spirit photography into an extravisual technology.

Perhaps paradoxically, spirit photography undercut the medical logic of exposure through double exposure, a technique that yields visual obscurity instead of visual clarity. Amateur photographer Oliver Wendell Holmes took note of the not-seeing that double exposure proffers. His *Atlantic* essay "Doings of the Sunbeam" (1863) addresses the simultaneous truthfulness and artifice of the photographic image. Holmes made a point of praising Mathew Brady's straightforward images of the dead of Antietam, "views which the truthful sunbeam has delineated in all their dread reality," and then lambasted Mumler. After giving step-by-step instructions on how to use double exposure to produce spirit photographs, Holmes contemplates the popularity of Mumler's images:

> Mrs. Brown, for instance, has lost her infant, and wishes to have its spirit-portrait taken. Whether it belonged to Mrs. Brown or Mrs. Jones or Mrs. Robinson, King Solomon . . . would be puzzled to guess. But it is enough for the poor mother, whose eyes are blinded with tears, that she sees . . . a rounded something, like a foggy dumpling, which will stand for a face: she accepts the spirit portrait as a revelation for the world of shadows.[100]

Blinded by photographic illusion and her own tears, the viewer sees whomever she wants to see. Whereas Brady's photographs of the dead shock the viewer by illuminating the gruesome reality of war, Mumler's images of the dead yield sentimental tears that further occlude the world "as it is." Although Holmes presents this visual indeterminacy as part of the image's fraud, this indeterminacy in fact situates spirit photography as the obverse, not the opposite, of Brady's realist images of nameless corpses. Like the battlefield scenes that devastated U.S. audiences, Mumler's images of faceless ghosts, stripped of individual identity, are figures of absence that act as "a catalyst for social connection."[101] Precisely because of spirit photography's resistance to visibility, any identity might be attached to these faceless figures, and therefore any mourner can find solace in such images (figure 1.4). The image reconstructs

FIG. 1.4 William Mumler, *Mrs. French*, c. 1862–1875. Courtesy of the Getty Museum, Los Angeles, California.

fractured families and brings impersonal mourners into attachment: not Mrs. Brown *or* Mrs. Jones *or* Mrs. Robinson, but Mrs. Brown *and* Mrs. Jones *and* Mrs. Robinson. Representing the dead as spirits rather than as corpses—replacing corporeality with abstraction—the spirit photograph uses double exposure to conventionalize loss. Double exposure is a type of exposure that doubles as concealment, visualizing spirits so unseeable as to be generic.

The phantom limb is an internal representation of bodily presence, and so too the spirit photograph is an external representation "of the felt presence of absent loved ones," which likewise can be accessed only through not-seeing.[102] Many Americans, whether believers in spiritualism or not, found in spirit photography's disembodied yet material intimacy a way to keep the memory of the dead alive and to express their bonds of affection for those they had lost. Mumler's images initiated and instantiated a community of loss by pushing at the limits of human as well as photographic vision. Take, for instance, his 1872 portrait of Mary Todd Lincoln with the spirits of her deceased husband and son—a picture meant to console not simply the widow but the nation (figure 1.5). In it, we see an opaque woman next to two transparent figures, one of which was the most identifiable American of the nineteenth century, Abraham Lincoln, whose "visibility and familiarity was envisaged as both unifying and comforting bereaved families."[103] But despite the iconic force of Lincoln's face, both he and his son Tad appear on the verge of fading away. They emerge from as they recede into the background. The camera's eye exposes the ghosts, while those ghosts register the impossibility of perfect visibility. Although addressing the same subject matter as Bontecou and Brady, Mumler's spirit photographs—unlike the clinical starkness of Bontecou's medical photographs and the stark clarity of Brady's battlefield photographs—approach the act of looking as an uncertain enterprise, a kind of revelation that does not guarantee disclosure. Barely marked by light, the figures of Lincoln and Tad surrender to the possibility of, *as they agitate ideas about*, visibility. These figurations of an absent presence hover just above and below the threshold of visibility, disappearing into their own appearance, and withholding themselves from us at the same moment we behold them. Mumler's camera does not restabilize vision; it dissolves vision.

The spirit photograph's play of visibility and invisibility is, moreover, what Dana Luciano calls a "play of power across the color line."[104] Not-seeing subverts visual epistemologies, but it still tethers the familial function of spirit photography to its racial function. The mourners featured in Mumler's images, after all, are primarily bourgeois white subjects. Market capitalism helps

FIG. 1.5 William Mumler, *Mary Todd Lincoln with the Spirit of Her Husband President Abraham Lincoln and Son Thaddeus*, 1872. Courtesy of the Allen County Public Library, Fort Wayne, Indiana.

explain this fact. Because Mumler charged ten dollars for a dozen spirit photographs, five times the standard rate for studio portraits, lower-class and nonwhite subjects had limited access to this particular manifestation of the spirit world. Equally if not more important, though, is that in these images white people figure as both living subjects and dead spirits, while Native and black people are figured only as dead spirits. The struggle between body and spirit historically has been central to a "wider notion of the white body, of embodiment, [and] of whiteness involving something that is in but not of the body," Richard Dyer has argued.[105] It is by now axiomatic that to be white is to have a transcendent relation to one's body. By reinforcing historical scientific claims that black people are unable to feel pain and "to 'own' their bodily experiences," spirit photographs attached different meanings to different bodies in pain.[106] Mumler's portraits thus entail a relation between corporeality and interiority that privileges the white body as supremely capable of moving between both the physical and the spiritual world.

The filmy souls that Mumler conjures are stripped of flesh but not of race. Using stock racial tropes that figure Native Americans and Africans as "a vital link between this world and the next," his photographs superimpose colonial relations onto the spirit world.[107] In particular, *Master Herrod with the Spirits of Europe, Africa, and America* perpetuates the "cult of the Vanishing American," a colonial discourse that framed the "extinction" of Native peoples as both spontaneous and inevitable by invoking the Romantic trope of the Native American as a spiritual guide for the white man (figure 1.6).[108] Both a central and a displaced figure in this drama of cross-temporal connection, the indigenous figure embraces if not beatifies the white "master," while his visual disappearance into (and as) the backdrop redoubles the alleged hereditary disappearance and pastness of his people. Taken together, the Native, African, and European ghosts that straddle the threshold of visibility form the very precondition of the photographic subject's full-bodied sovereignty. These ghostly figures are, of course, exposed to different ends. The Native American ghost papers over the ongoing wars waged by settler colonists against indigenous tribes in the 1860s and 1870s—especially when we take into account the way that a contemporaneous photograph of a Dedlow-like man named Benjamin Franklin (a quadruple amputee who lost his limbs to frostbite while fighting Native tribes in Minnesota) sacralizes the wounded white body (figure 1.7). More than play the foil to the feelingfull white body, Mumler's Native American ghost heightens the transcendent properties of white embodiment. In Victorian spirit medium William Stainton Moses's spirit photograph

FIG. 1.6 William Mumler, *Master Herrod with the Spirits of Europe, Africa, and America*, c. 1862–1875. Courtesy of the College of Psychic Studies, London.

FIG. 1.7 Carte de visite of quadruple amputee Benjamin Franklin, ca. 1873. Photographer unknown. © Stanley B. Burns, MD, and the Burns Archive, New York, New York.

album, for instance, *Master Herrod* sits next to *Mrs. Mary Todd Lincoln*.[109] In their serialized relation to each other, the "spirits of Africa and America" index an ancestral past that certifies the white "European spirit" of the sovereign nation-state, which Lincoln's ghost—his gossamer body marking not the ineluctable extinction of inferior races but a racially specific capacity to transcend time and space—embodies as paternal icon and national symbol. Dispossessed, the Native American and African ghosts mark a wayward temporality, while the European spirit allied with Lincoln's iconic figure instantiates whiteness's timelessness.

That people of color appear in Mumler's spirit photographs never as living sitters but only as spirits invests them with a "failed embodiment," as though they are unable to access experiences of pain, contra the white mourners who are "active in their suffering."[110] This dynamic extends beyond the visual presentation of the dead to include the visual presentation of wounded soldiers, as depicted in Bontecou's medical photographs (five in total) of the U.S. Colored Troops. Medical photographs of the wounded black body appear as the obverse of spirit photographs of the dead black body: so opaque as to be impenetrable, rather than so transparent as to be impenetrable. Seriality ensures that in Bontecou's photograph album, the picture of wounded black soldier Charles Harris (see figure 1.3) blends in rather than stands out. Yet the picture of Harris is taken at an odd angle, and Bontecou's photograph of Private Lewis Martin does not capture his body entire (figure 1.8). In both cases, the photographic moment feels and looks decidedly makeshift—far less poised, in the bourgeois mode of portraiture, than the images of wounded white soldiers. Perhaps above all, what sets these images apart is the glossy sheen of Harris's face and of Martin's eroticized bare chest. Lighting is an aesthetic technology that, Richard Dyer has argued, doubles as a racial technology. The difference between glow and shine is crucial to how photography constructs and privileges whiteness. Whereas with glow, "light from within or from above appears to suffuse the body," with shine, "light bounces back off the surface of the skin."[111] Glow betokens a porous body that can absorb light and exude the inner radiance of the soul, whereas shine betokens a dense body that can only refract light. It is unsurprising that photographic lighting was developed to make white skin glow and dark skin shine. Here, studio lighting seals off the wounded black body from feeling pain. Like the Native people who perform their own disappearing act in Mumler's spirit photograph, Bontecou's shiny black subjects stage their inability to absorb pain by fail-

FIG. 1.8 Reed B. Bontecou, *Pvt. Lewis Martin*, c. 1865. Textual Records. Record Group 94: Records of the National Adjutant General's Office, 1762–1984. Courtesy of the National Archives, College Park, Maryland.

ing to absorb light. Further, in 1867 the AMM relocated to the abandoned Ford's Theatre, thereby making the "somber treasure house, devoted to the study of disease and injury, mutilation and death," a "noble monument to Lincoln's memory," as its curator J. J. Woodward wrote.[112] Under the banner of heroic sacrifice, patriotism, and the illusive presence of Lincoln, the AMM became a monument to wounded white masculinity that, like the medical photographs it housed, pushed the injured black body below the threshold of political visibility.

Spirit and medical photographs of the wounded simultaneously emphasize and efface black corporeality. In so doing, they partake of a long tradition of "rendering the Black body hypervisible and invisible simultaneously," following Jasmine Nichole Cobb.[113] These two genres represent black people either as gossamer spirits or as opaque bodies but in both cases subordinate the injuries of slavery to those of the Civil War. Both spirit photographs and medical photographs racialize wounded bodies, but that woundedness functions in different ways. Unlike Bontecou's images, Mumler's photographs validate subjective experiences of pain—and do so through artifice. Yoking the laws of optics to a materialist ontology of the soul, they limn loss through a day view notion of sight as a mode of not-seeing, that is, they construct a visual epistemology that subordinates the eye to magnetic or spiritual energies. Spirit photographs thus join phantom limbs in undoing death by enlivening vision, a perception less about the physics of light waves than the volatile bodies that exceed them. *Volatile* might seem a peculiar characterization, given that Mumler's spirits are remarkably static and two-dimensional. Unlike the lively internal spirits haunting veteran amputees, these externalized spirits appear as stilted as the living photographic subjects seeking comfort—and as still as the corpses Brady depicted in his "still life" images. The volatility of these photographic bodies, however, arises not from their visual appearance but instead from what they do out of frame: move the viewer, as Holmes well knew, likely to tears. Whether a psychical force that animates the wounded white body or a racialized spirit incapable of "owning" its own loss, these body images encode diminished sight as a means of capturing the realities that medical science cannot. Instantiating the epistemological conflict arising when "the real is not the same as the visible," spirit photographs and phantom limbs inculcate a disintegrative vision that displaces the claims of empiricism and the nation-state by affirming the authenticity and racially coded animacy of subjective pain.[114] Across medical case studies and spirit photographs, seeing—pitched against the destabilizing conversions of organic matter from one form to another—begins to look a lot like *not-seeing*.

THRESHOLDS OF POLITICAL VISIBILITY

We have been tracking two sets of body images that took shape in response to the physical and familial losses brought on by the Civil War, two fictions that do not simply claim the mantle of the real but actually dismantle empirical reality. Phantom limbs and spirit photographs are, more specifically, unreconstructed body images—*unreconstructed* as a manifestation of a psyche that has not adjusted to its new lived reality, and *unreconstructed* as a refusal to inhabit a new political milieu. That Mitchell, who disliked Lincoln, identified as one of "the old fellows who are still unreconstructed" ties the always-unfinished body image to the still-unfinished project of Reconstruction.[115] From 1863 to 1877, Reconstruction combined the "legal freedom of Emancipation with the political self-rule and social resources that would make freedom secure and powerful" for African Americans.[116] Once the U.S. government abandoned it for the "greater good" of regional reconciliation, white supremacist laws that reenslaved African Americans took hold, initiating the historical period called "black life at the nadir." In the wake of Reconstruction, the phantom limb and spirit photograph did not die so much as change form. They were material signs no longer of white grief for the dead but now of white hauntedness by the living, specifically by the newly born black citizen. Nonlocalizable, entirely diffuse, yet profoundly felt, blackness becomes in fictions of Reconstruction a below-threshold body whose political visibility requires the perceptual modality of not-seeing.

To be sure, the "black body is always problematic in the field of vision," as Nicole Fleetwood argues.[117] In the field of post-Reconstruction vision, the black body proved especially problematic, at once exposed and invisible, as though simultaneously inhabiting the position of the living and the dead in a spirit photograph. The figure of tragic mulatta Rhoda Aldgate in William Dean Howells's novella *An Imperative Duty* (1891) typifies this dynamic of exposure and effacement. Set in Boston in the early 1870s, the story renders racial embodiment as much a psychical as a biological phenomenon. When Rhoda's aunt Mrs. Meredith reveals to Rhoda her "true" black identity, Rhoda refuses "to accept the loss of her former self, like that of the mutilated man who looks where his arm was, and cannot believe it gone. Like him, she had the full sense of what was lost, the unbroken consciousness of what was lopped away."[118] By likening the "unbroken consciousness" of her whiteness to a phantom limb, Rhoda situates her interiority, or sense of self, at the nexus of the circulatory system and the nervous system. The mixed-race woman yokes the one-drop rule to soul life; the materiality of the spirit is a racially specific kind of material. With her entire existence called into question by a white body that is consciously but not physically present, the tragic mulatta takes the place of the "tragical" amputee haunted too by his diminished whiteness. But the body, not the body image, is the fiction—or rather, the body image is a psychical fiction more real than the legal fiction of race. Because Rhoda sees herself as white, she "is" white, which is why her blackness is effaced the very moment it is exposed. Unlike Frances Harper's titular heroine in *Iola Leroy* (1892), a "mulatta" who is not tragic because she embraces her black identity, Rhoda "has never felt it [black]."[119] For Howells, the emotional drama of biological disclosure activates a not-seeing attuned to the gap between the hereditary and the social—being black versus having been socialized as white—and helps explain why Rhoda would commit herself in marriage to a white doctor (hence, pass as white) rather than commit herself to "her" race.

A legally black person whose body image registers her unreconstructed whiteness, Rhoda is a figure that juxtaposes two models of interiority—the psyche and the blood, mind and racial matter. At the core of *An Imperative Duty* is a psychophysics of passing, Rhoda's decision to push her "one drop" below the threshold of perceptual visibility. Henry James's *The Bostonians* (1885) predates *An Imperative Duty*, but by dramatizing how not-seeing occludes rather than illuminates black life, it conceptually picks up where Howells's novella leaves off. First serialized in the *Century*, a purveyor of plantation fiction and "romances of reunion" in the 1880s, *The Bostonians* is an unreconstructed novel of Reconstruction. Set technically in 1871 but temperamentally in 1861, it describes a family feud that doubles as a battle of the sexes and triples as a Civil War battle reenactment: Boston suffragist Olive Chancellor and her patriarchal Mississippi cousin Basil Ransom fight for the heart and soul of trance speaker Verena Tarrant. Critics have read the novel as "James's ultimate ghost story," partly because James wrote it while grieving his father's death and partly because of its depiction of spiritualism (James, unlike his brother William, was skeptical of spirit mediums).[120] *The Bostonians* is a ghost story, but not because spiritualism takes center stage. It is a ghost story because it is haunted by its own historical backdrop or, to invoke Christina Sharpe, its own climate: Reconstruction.[121] This haunting takes shape as an "obscure hurt"—to borrow James's phrase for his causalgia—that the characters feel but cannot see.[122] Indeed, *The Bostonians* is "an especially acute novel of Reconstruction" that manages to avoid any thoroughgoing political analysis, as Peter Coviello notes.[123] The novel can no more bear to behold its historical setting than its wounded warrior, Olive, "unable to meet her own eyes in the mirror," can behold herself.[124] Olive declares that she "want[s] to know everything that lies beneath and out of sight," yet her dedication to spirit life pushes black life out of sight.[125] Within the context of the unreconstructed body images pervading the post-Reconstruction field of vision, *The Bostonians* asks: Who gets overlooked in the act of not-seeing?

The Bostonians features ideological and regional clashes that manage to leave black citizens beneath and out of sight, below the threshold of visibility. The force behind black invisibility is not Basil, the proudly unreconstructed Southerner ever waving the flag for the Lost Cause, but the peripheral character and feminist foremother Miss Birdseye, "one of the most passionate of the old Abolitionists." Olive brings Basil to a spiritualist meeting "just for the pleasure of seeing her," but Basil has a different view of Miss Birdseye. She is an "essentially formless old woman, who had no more outline than a bundle of hay."[126] Focalized through Basil, the narrator elaborates:

> She was a little old lady, with . . . weak, kind, tired-looking eyes. . . . She had a sad, soft, pale face, which looked as if it had been soaked, blurred, and made vague by exposure to some slow dissolvent. The long practice of philanthropy had not given accent to her features; it had rubbed out their transitions, their meanings. The waves of sympathy, of enthusiasm, had wrought upon them in the same way in which the waves of time finally modify the surface of old marble busts, gradually washing away their . . . details. In her large countenance her dim little smile scarcely showed.[127]

Across the many belittling adjectives used (sad, soft, pale, soaked, blurred, vague, rubbed out, washed away, dim, little, scarcely showing—to name a few), Miss Birdseye appears as one of Mumler's photographic spirits, a "foggy dumpling" whose face has been effaced, though due not to double exposure but instead to overexposure. That is, Miss Birdseye's body is more of a "body image." But unlike the ghosts that Mumler conjured for the private purposes of mourning, Miss Birdseye's faded face is wrought not by a wounded domestic sphere—a household diminished by Civil War casualties—but an overactive public life. For Olive, as with Mumler's clients, the pleasure of seeing Miss

Birdseye is not-seeing her. Instead of seeing her person, Olive sees the "waves" of time that her vague face, like the degraded image wrought by a used glass plate, represents.

That Basil regards Miss Birdseye's "weak" eyesight as part of her facelessness suggests that her easily overlooked person is a reflection of her own physiological tendency to overlook others. The narrative's not-seeing of Miss Birdseye, in other words, is tethered to her own not-seeing. Whereas Olive seeks occult knowledge from beneath and below, her forebear gleans it from high above—as *birdseye* suggests. Miss Birdseye's sight is also an "oversight, an act that sees too much and fails to see," John Funchion observes.[128] And this oversight turns the threshold of perceptual visibility into one of political visibility. Miss Birdseye has a passion for compassion, but not for people:

> [She] knew less about her fellow creatures, if possible, after fifty years of humanitary zeal, than on the day she had gone into the field to testify against the iniquity of most arrangements. Basil Ransom knew very little about such a life as hers, but she seemed to him a revelation of a class, and a multitude of socialistic figures, of names and episodes that he had heard of, grouped themselves behind her. She looked as if she had spent her life on platforms, in audiences, in conventions, in phalansteries, in séances; in her faded face there was a kind of reflection of ugly lecture-lamps.... Since the Civil War most of her occupation was gone; for before that her best hours had been spent in fancying that she was helping some Southern slave to escape. It would have been a nice question whether, in her heart of hearts, for the sake of this excitement, she did not sometimes wish the blacks back in bondage.... She was in love ... only with causes, and she languished only for emancipations.[129]

However misogynist this passage is (and it is), because it is focalized through Basil, it usefully underscores an uncanny similarity between these two seemingly oppositional figures. The uneasy transition described from the antebellum to postbellum social order—the "nonevent of Emancipation," to cite Saidiya Hartman—applies not simply to Miss Birdseye, the unreconstructed abolitionist, but to Basil, the unreconstructed Southerner.[130] Miss Birdseye's transcendent vision, or oversight, is the perceptual and political underbelly of not-seeing. Whereas not-seeing is an apparatus of the transcendental materialist day view—the universe is alive and connected—oversight fails to see these connections. An oblique criticism of Emerson's disembodied transparent eyeball, oversight sees so much that it sees nothing at all. Unlike not-seeing, it lacks visual sensitivity; oversight is a way of seeing that is unable to discern the bodies that compose the field of vision. Hence, "the blacks" appear only to be disappeared by "humanitary zeal." As "the novel's chief figure for historical unfolding," then, Miss Birdseye has transferred her political energies from abolitionism to women's suffrage.[131] But *The Bostonians* takes pains to point out that a bird's eye history is necessarily blind to its own unfolding and as such risks acting on behalf of, or at least buttressing, the political institutions it aims to abolish.

Moreover, the blindness of oversight certifies white racial superiority. Taking a cue from Helmholtz's work in physiological optics, many physicians associated ocular dysfunctions and "diseases of the eye with nervousness and its attendant physical and mental phenomena."[132] In physician George Miller Beard's popular medical book *American Nervousness* (1881), he linked neurasthenia—a depletion of nerve energy caused by the perceptual demands of civilization—to poor eyesight. "Our oculists have constant proof of the nervousness of our age.... Among savages everywhere, near-sightedness is very rare," hence "myopia is a measure of civilization."[133] The myopia and near-sightedness from which white people suffer is a condition of civilization—and in *The Bostonians*, one that renders black people invisible. According to the ophthalmology of "bird's eye" vision, black people are ghostly bodies living below the threshold of white people's vision. Spiritualism functions as the arena in which feminists use *not-seeing* to access truths that patriarchal institutions would not recognize, yet Miss Birdseye displays the ease with which not-seeing shades into a form of racial oversight. In fact, her oversight appears not all that different from Basil's erasure of Reconstruction when he recalls "whipping" carpetbaggers "at political meetings in blighted Southern towns, during the horrible period of reconstruction"—as though Reconstruction was a thing of the past when, in the novel's historical world, it is very much *now*.[134] The proleptic slip reveals how even as gender politics overshadow racial politics in *The Bostonians*, Reconstruction is the antiblack weather that saturates its drama of spirit and bodily possession. James cannot help but adopt, even as he takes aim at, oversight.

The Bostonians shows how white suffragists used not-seeing to challenge unequal distributions of power in a way that overlooked black civic life, rendering it invisible. Oversight becomes, then, a failure of political vision that ends up accommodating rather than vanquishing reactionary politics. The novel makes this clear in the final scene, when the narrator likens Basil's kidnapping of Verena at the Boston Music Hall to John Wilkes Booth's assassination of Lincoln at Ford's Theatre. Just before Verena is about to perform a trance lecture, Basil feels like a young man "who, waiting in a public space, had made up his mind, for reasons of his own, to discharge a pistol at the king or the president."[135] As 1871 cannot shake the events of 1865, white feminist politics prove ill-equipped to prevail over Basil's patriarchal agenda. Once he convinces Verena to abandon her political and personal commitment to Olive, she is consigned to a life of concealment as a private woman rather than as a public speaker. The novel famously ends with Verena "in tears. It is to be feared that with the union, so far from brilliant, into which she was about to enter, these were not the last she was destined to shed."[136] Allied with woman's suffrage, spiritualist oversight becomes an apprehending not of previously invisible subjects but the always-racialized and unincorporated excess of political visibility.

....

Phantom limbs and spirit photographs thrived during the Civil War but did not survive far past it. Spirit photography remained a popular if controversial photographic genre well into the twentieth century, but its originator, Mumler, retired his practice around 1873—one year after Mitchell presented his final medical research on phantom limbs in *Injuries of Nerves*. The phantom limb, in fact, was both born and buried by Mitchell. Although William James thought it "strange that no more systematic effort to investigate the phenomenon should have been made" since Mitchell, he decided to "leave [it] in Dr. Weir Mitchell's hands."[137] The phantom limb lay dormant until World War I produced a new population of veteran amputees, which spurred *Scientific American* to ask, "Just how common is the subject of 'phantom limbs' to the public at large? Just how familiar is it to medical men who have not made a special study of nervous phenomena?"[138] On both counts: not very. But however short-lived its study, the phantom limb had long-lasting effects. In keeping with the law of the conservation of energy, the psychophysical body image that Mitchell tentatively formulated and that Mumler conceptually took up was not destroyed but instead took shape as a different body of knowledge: phenomenology.

In the twentieth century, the body image fell under the purview of modern psychology, but it was philosopher Maurice Merleau-Ponty who explored the ontological remainder of this scientific concept. Merleau-Ponty famously understands the body image as a habituated body: the body that one becomes accustomed to by moving around in the world, encountering objects, and anticipating movements and resistances. Focusing on the role that the body plays in memory, which is not "the constituting consciousness of the past, but an effort to reopen time on the basis of the implications of the present," he argues that the body "is the medium of our communication with time as well as with space."[139] As the memory of a body part, then, the phantom limb is an "ambivalent presence" that keeps the habitual body alive through the refusal of "mutilation."[140] Building on this phenomenological tradition, Sara Ahmed has compellingly reframed whiteness itself as a habitual body, a "style of embodiment" that takes up space "as if it were at home."[141] Ahmed's phenomenology of whiteness as a being-at-home complements recent efforts in black studies to understand the phantom limb as a black diasporic sensation, a condition of not being at home, and a painful yet generative feeling of displacement that radiates across time.

When phenomenology is routed through racial capitalism, the phantom limb becomes an act of expressing mutilatedness, not a refusal of mutilation. Likening African cultural memory to a phantom limb because it "is a sentient recollection of connectedness experienced at the site of rupture," Saidiya Hartman writes that this "recognition entails a remembering of the pained body, not by way of a simulated wholeness but precisely through the recognition of the amputated body in its amputatedness."[142] The wounded body is the enslaved body; the body image disturbance is geocultural disturbance; the medical saw is the slave ship. The phantom limb, then, is neither "a return to an originary plenitude" nor a false consolation but a conscious feeling that takes dislocation as the condition of possibility for the endurance of black social life.[143] It is a trope for what Nathaniel Mackey calls the "cultural dislocation" of black life. "The phantom limb is a felt recovery, a felt advance beyond severance and limitation, that contends with and questions conventional reality, that is a feeling for what is not *there* that reaches beyond as it calls into question what is," Mackey writes. "The phantom limb haunts or critiques a condition in which feeling, consciousness itself, would seem to have been cut off."[144] The phantom limb holds itself apart from the conditions of alienation that produced it, refusing the anesthetizing conditions that have left black people "cut off." It indexes an "underworld imagination" that shifts "perspective between real and unreal, an exchange of attributes between the two," and thereby queries Western ontologies.[145] Remade into a culturally and conceptually Black sensation, the phantom limb names the dis- and re-membering of the Middle Passage, a nonlocalizable and therefore fugitive feeling and a refusal of empirical reality. Viewed through a racial phenomenology partly originating in psychophysics, the phantom limb is more than a sensation of unreconstructed whiteness; it is a "creative reconstruction" of black life.[146]

This account of the phantom limb suggests more broadly that the body image is a displacement of the sensory apparatus. It elucidates that our seeing, like our sensing, is always already displaced and delocalized, that it can be neither confined nor attached to a particular body or body part. Raising questions about the metaphysics of loss, yet deeply historical in its scene of identification and its implications, the body image represents that which is felt but remains nebulous, inconstant, and volatile. In manifesting the uncontainability of feeling, it reveals that all perception is a deception, all optics an illusion—an embodied reality that can be neither verified nor measured. The phantom limb is a psychosomatic condition as well as a cultural phenomenon that emerged from what has been described as the first modern war, fought over the transatlantic institution of slavery. It is a body image, a displacement of consciousness, that suggests a radical continuity between the psychical and the physical and the potential and the actual.

{ INTERVAL 1 }

Colorful Sounds

About the time that fascination with the phantom limb peaked, another flummoxing neurosensory phenomenon arrived on the scene: synaesthesia. In the 1870s, Gustav Fechner began surveying museumgoers about their sensory responses to art, and his 1876 study *Vorschule der Aesthetik* revealed that some individuals had reported on the strange experience of visualizing specific alphabetic or numerical characters in particular colors. This research laid the foundation for the systematic study of what later would be called synaesthesia. "Fechner's psychophysics has no substitute: no amount of fiddling with nerve impulses or brain images can substitute for the observer's report. Even the current craze of functioning imaging starts with the subject's state of mind," in the words of neuroscientist Richard Cytowic.[1] Francis Galton felt the same way. Shortly after the publication of *Vorschule der Aesthetik*, he reproduced Fechner's study. Galton's own survey of people's mental images found its way into *Inquiries into Human Faculty and Its Development*, where he defended the method of using questionnaires and subjects' self-reports to analyze sensory experiences:

> These independent statements powerfully corroborate and explain each other. Therefore, although philosophers may have written to show the impossibility of our discovering what goes on in the minds of others, I maintain an opposite opinion. I do not see why the report of a person upon his own mind should not be as intelligible and trustworthy as that of a traveler upon a new country,

whose landscapes and inhabitants are of a different type to any which we ourselves have seen.[2]

In other words, empirical validity lies in the aggregate; truth emerges in the mutual corroboration of individual reports. In 1912, U.S. psychologist June Downey analyzed similar self-reported accounts for the *Journal of Philosophy, Psychology and Scientific Methods*. She determined that "there is very slight evidence" that Percy Shelley, William Blake, and Edgar Allan Poe "experienced *true synesthesia*."[3] If a first-person description is the basis of diagnosis, if analyzing questionnaires is the only way to study synaesthesia, then why not by parsing "Ozymandias" as well? To be sure, neurological synaesthesia is distinct from the "literary synaesthesia" of cross-sensory language. Yet Downey's method—a psychology experiment that more closely resembles hermeneutics—hints at the impossibility of understanding one without the other. Today synaesthesia remains a cross-disciplinary object, a term defined in *Essentials of Cognitive Neuroscience* and in *A Glossary of Literary Terms* (both of which cite Baudelaire).[4] If neurological or "true" synaesthesia is a commingling of two sensory stimuli (e.g., blue and B-flat) that yields a new sensation (color sound), then is it not a metaphor generated by the mind—a literary event?

As Downey's study bears out, the descriptive method that brought synaesthesia to light was part of, not parallel to, its literary life. In 1871, symbolist Arthur Rimbaud's poem "Voyelles" declared, "A black, E white, I red, U green, O blue: vowels / One day I will tell your latent birth."[5] The idea that certain sounds can stimulate color sensations emerged from several sources, including composer Richard Wagner's theory of the "total work of art," medical case studies about subjective visions (e.g., hallucinations and afterimages), and Charles Baudelaire's poem "Correspondences" (1857), which itself advanced theologian Emanuel Swedenborg's mystical notion of the correspondence of the spiritual and the natural world: "Like long echoes which in a distance are mingled / In a dark and profound unison / Vast as night is and light, / Perfumes, colors and sounds answer one another."[6] For many artists, the correspondence of the senses proved that "the world is knit together, that some underlying unity exists" in the universe.[7] Hermann von Helmholtz's research on the visual and auditory senses made possible new color systems based on the "retina's different sensitivities to discrete light frequencies" as well as a new understanding of the music-color relation as "a physiological experience subject to clinical observation." At the same time, Sarah Pourciau writes, psychophysical parallelism countered night view materialism by enfolding "sound *back* into an all-encompassing science of *Geist* [soul]."[8] Psychophysics separated the senses, yet its underlying day view principles established the grounds upon which avant-garde artists in Europe and North America could claim synaesthesia as evidence of the harmony of the universe. Such is the psychophysical genealogy of Rimbaud's sensory experiments.

In combination with Fechner's and Galton's investigations of letter photisms, "Voyelles" secured synaesthesia as both a scientific object and an aesthetic practice. In fin de siècle Europe and North America, color hearing was not a type of synaesthesia but *was* synaesthesia. Between 1870 and 1883, there were three medical case studies of color hearing, but sixteen case studies in 1884 alone, the year after the publication of "Voyelles." Writing on the problem of color audition in *Popular Science Monthly* (1893), French psychologist Alfred Binet explained that although color hearing has been "discussed in daily papers and literary and scientific reviews; it has been the subject of medical theses and of didactic treatises; it has figured in poetry, in romance, and even in theater," little is "yet known of the question and still less is understood," because the physical laws of sound and color, "which are blended in color hearing," cannot fully explain the psychological experience of "what color hearing is."[9] In an 1894 review of Swiss psychologist Theodore Flournoy's book on color hearing, William James offered a theory of what color hearing is: an affective association.

An atmosphere of emotional tendency of some kind or other is *ready* in all of us to envelop almost any sensorial impression and idea; and in chosen individuals on a given occasion, some accidental coincidence in the mind of a sound with a visual idea and a strongly aroused common emotional tone, may stamp an association so strongly in the memory that it easily gets recalled, whilst each recall makes it more habitual and fixed, so that at last it becomes, so to speak, organic.[10]

Echoing Helmholtz's sign theory of perception, James asserts that certain sounds call forth the emotional value of *other* sensations, and over time that association solidifies into an unconscious sign that we interpret as "organic." If there was any unity in the senses, it was a pragmatic fact of the human mind, not an objective fact of the physical universe.

The "long history of color in the West has always involved a productive tension . . . between utopian figurations of chromatic ecstasy and buttoned-up fears of colorful excess," Nicholas Gaskill observes, and the history of color hearing was no different.[11] In Jules Millet's 1892 dissertation, *L'Audition colorée*, he argued that color hearing constitutes "true progress in the perfection of our senses."[12] Austrian physician Max Nordau considered it just the opposite—a violation of the evolutionary process of physical and psychical differentiation as well as a symptom of degeneracy. In this vein, U.S. literary critic Irving Babbitt stated that color hearing "seems to give a definite physiological basis to that running together of all the different impressions, that mystical synthetic sense, of which the modern aesthete dreams—the sense that 'sees, hears, taste, smells, touches,' all in one," though he fairly considered it "a sign of a nervous disorder" that concerned not the "critic of art" but the "student of psychology and medicine, and in some cases the nerve specialist."[13] Those students typically attributed color hearing to "hereditary taint."[14] It was either a biological aberration or a sign of underdevelopment. Because of pervasive analogies between "the undifferentiated thinking of children and that of 'primitive' peoples," color hearing was considered a condition most prominent in the early stages of ontogenetic and phylogenetic development.[15] The newly invented figure of the homosexual, often aligned with underdevelopment or backwardness, was duly likened to the synaesthete. In their coauthored medical textbook *Sexual Inversion* (1897), psychologist Havelock Ellis and literary critic John Addington Symonds stated, "We may compare inversion to such a phenomenon as color hearing, in which there is not so much a defect, as an abnormality of nervous tracks producing new and involuntary combinations."[16] The sensory correspondence of sound and color seemed to beget further correspondences with the social world, as color hearing became a symptom of either a nervous disorder or degeneracy.

For these reasons, the fin de siècle effort to establish color music as an art was an uphill battle. Color music had developed partly as a way to experiment with the emotional effects of color hearing and partly to demonstrate that synaesthetic arts push us closer to human perfection, that they represent evolution rather than devolution. The dream of color music dates back to Isaac Newton, who claimed that music and color are products of physical vibration and therefore share a common law of harmony. Eighteenth-century mathematician Louis-Bertrand Castel endeavored to prove Newton right when he proposed an "ocular harpsichord." Technological innovations fueled this fantasy through the following century, such as U.S. artist Bainbridge Bishop's 1877 color organ, which used lighted attachments (designed for pipe organs) that could project color lights onto a screen in synchronization with a musical performance. British painter Alexander Wallace Rimington's 1893 color organ was the most successful invention in this field. He divided the color spectrum into intervals that were analogous to musical octaves and then attributed those colors to musical notes. Two years

FIG. I1.1 "Exterior of a Colour-Organ," from Alexander Wallace Rimington's *Colour-Music* (1912). Courtesy of the Huntington Library, San Marino, California.

later at St. James Hall in London, he debuted his own color organ, which used electric lamps to light up a screen of white drapery, while the performer controlled the light of the lamps in gradients of color tone, lightness, and saturation (figure I1.1). Like Bishop's color organ, Rimington's did not play music but was "played" alongside an organ that played musical sound. Nonetheless, the hope was to establish that color music, because its combination of color and sound could produce finer emotional feelings, was the art of the future—of society and of the species.

Along with other artists and inventors, Rimington insisted that color music was a fine art. The public viewed it instead as a popular fad. The "revolutionary art form kept regressing to the lowly craft of stage-lighting," Jonathan Rée remarks.[17] In *Littell's Living Age*, British statistician William Schooling defended color music using the same Darwinian principles that critics like Nordau had used to deride it. "The philosophy of evolution makes it clear that progress comes about by the differentiation of parts," he explained. "The highest organisms have highly specialized organs for the performance of very numerous functions, and close interrelations among the different organs.... Differentiation is a change from the simple to the complex, and the unraveling of the process leads us back to the simplicity of the early stages."[18] Whereas Nordau used this fact to argue that color music is as formless as the brain of the primitive mollusk—a synaesthetic creature that sees, hears, tastes, and smells all at once—Schooling insisted that color music secures the evolutionary process of differentiation. Mainly, it helps refine people's color sensitivity, defined as the "cultivated talent for feeling color harmonies, a talent that involved the cognitive powers of memory and association and that further invest color feeling with European hierarchies of class and ethnicity."[19] Indeed, two years after publishing *Physiological Aesthetics* (1877), science writer Grant Allen devoted his book *The Colour-Sense* to establishing the color sense as a metric of civilization. For artists like Rimington, then, blending color and music was not a return to the formless mind of the amoeba or mollusk but a mechanism of evolutionary advancement. Teaching audiences to differentiate within the harmonic systems of color and music was a matter not simply of cultural but biological progress. The synaesthetic arts stimulated rather than disintegrated civilized sensitivity. Color music doubled as sensitivity training.

Color musicians like Rimington aesthetically exploited synaesthesia to elevate the human race, but doing so required that they first invoke the established art of music to elevate the color sense. Schooling explained that color "seems to have every element necessary for exciting feelings as deep and as sympathetic as any that music calls forth, if only the appeal can be made and understood."[20] Philosophers from Berkeley to Hegel have conceded that although sound is more substantive than light, it is also "more ideal and subjective, closer to the inner soul and less involved with the 'outness' of an objective material world."[21] By "playing" light waves, artists extracted color from the viscous intervening body of paint; it now appeared a pure, immediate, ethereal feeling. In 1915, Edward Rice Doyle explained that color music "is mobile color that has no form. Like music, it is a harmony of tones, tinges, and hues in unisons, chords, or even orchestrations."[22] If music is "an abstract stimulus of emotional experience," then color music lets color absorb ideality from the seeming immateriality of sound and the legitimacy of music as an aesthetic system.[23] The 1915 Carnegie Hall performance of Alexander Scriabin's *Prometheus: Poem of Fire* featured a color organ (Preston Miller's chromola) that would secure the "possibility of our enjoying such an art as 'color music.'"[24] Color music transformed color into luminous abstraction, an outward manifestation of the internally transformative experience of color hearing.

The case was not entirely convincing to audiences; Scriabin's concert was both the apogee and the end of color music. Nonetheless, color music marked an effort to establish the synaesthetic experience of color hearing as a vehicle for social and biological progress. Indeed, the utopian potential ascribed to color music is perhaps clearest in Charlotte Perkins Gilman's "Dr. Clair's Place" (1915), the story of a doctor who uses sensory stimulation rather than S. Weir Mitchell's rest cure to treat her patients for nervous exhaustion. As narrated by the patient Octavia Welch, Dr. Clair's sanitarium offers homeopathic technologies such as a "moveable telephone, with a little megaphone attached to the receiver, and a long list of records. I had only to order what I chose, and listen to it as close or as far off as I desired," as well as "regulate the sound as [I] please."²⁵ For the "color treatment," Octavia is given a "little card of buttons, as it were, with wire attachments. I pressed one; the room was darkened, save for the tiny glow by which I saw the color list. Then, playing on the others, I could fill the room with any lovely hue I chose, and see them driving, mingling, changing as I played."²⁶ While these sensory treatments are distinct, their proximity is suggestive of color music—a synaesthetic binding signified in the doctor and patient's nominal relationship: the light-hued Dr. *Clair* and the musical *Octav*ia. Thus, if the era's new nervous disorders described "various weakenings and failures of the integrity of perception and its collapse into discarded fragments," as Jonathan Crary posits, then the color, music, and color music treatments mark a "union of the senses" that might remedy the civilized white woman's depleted and fragmented perceptions.²⁷

These experiments in color music decidedly failed, not surviving far past World War I, but the idea of a neat correspondence between sound and color "predetermined in the realm of the spirit" structured the era's broader fantasies of social harmony.²⁸ Although Helmholtz gave no reason to suppose an objective, universal system of correspondences, in his foundational study of acoustics, *On the Sensations of Tone* (1863), he offered another correspondence between color and sound: *klangfarbe*, or "sound color." The English word for klangfarbe is *timbre*, defined as the unique character of a musical instrument that distinguishes its sound from that of another instrument; timbre accounts for the qualitative difference between a violin's C note and a cello's C note, for instance. This "color" is not chromatic, but it captures the qualitative dimensions of sound that acoustics does not easily accommodate. In a chapter titled "Vowel Qualities of Tone," Helmholtz observed that the "vowel A . . . forms the common origin of all [other vowel sounds]."²⁹ The following decade, Rimbaud figured the vowel *A* as a sound that engulfs other sounds in darkness: as black. *A* was a chromatically black sound, but in the United States some sounds were "colored" as racially black. The idea of music as having a color is "based on mathematical and synesthetic principles derived in antiquity from the relationship between music and form, light, intervals, and timbre," musicologist Nina Sun Eidsheim explains. Yet when "colors are evoked in vocal descriptions, they are drawn upon specifically in order to create a sonic analogy with skin, and thus to racialize the sound."[30] In William Dean Howells's novella *An Imperative Duty* (1891), for instance, a white character locates Rhoda Aldgate's secret African ancestry in her vocal tone color: "I can hear it in her voice—it's a *black* voice!"[31] Rhoda's voice betrays her line of descent and, within the context of color music experiments, doubles as a chromola or color organ. This tension between the racial specificity of sounding bodies, as invoked by Howells, and the utopian ideal of music as a "treatment" for social ills, as invoked by Gilman, I further consider in the next chapter.

… { 2 }

Sound

THE ACOUSTICS
OF SOCIAL HARMONY

> There is, you might say, something peculiarly sociable about sounds: they only come into their own in each other's company. Although their impermanence may make them a natural symbol of transience, the way they mingle to produce fused unity makes them an emblem for companionable solidarity too.
> —Jonathan Rée, *I See a Voice*
>
> All forms of hearing are selective.
> —Paul Rodaway, *Sensuous Geographies*

Schoolteacher Mary Bradley Lane's utopian novel *Mizora: A Prophecy*, serialized in the *Cincinnati Commercial* newspaper from 1880 to 1881, describes Russian socialist Vera Zarovitch's journey into the interiors of Earth via a whirlpool in the Arctic Ocean. There she encounters a civilization called Mizora, notable for its all-female population and its socialist system of governance—but also for its people's harmonious voices and sensitive ears. Vera observes, "Their conversation [is] as musical to the ear as the love notes of some amorous wood bird to its mate."[1] Vera's utopian guide, Wauna, later explains, "Every sense we possess is of a higher and finer development.... Our appreciation of music, I notice, has a more exquisite delicacy than yours. You desire music, but it is the simpler operas that delight you. Those fine and delicate harmonies that we so intensely enjoy, you appear incapable of appreciating."[2] Vera admits to herself that she cannot "appreciate their mental pleasures any more than a savage could delight in a nocturne of [Frédéric] Chopin."[3] As the figure of the savage suggests, musical voices and auditory sensitivity are not ornamental features but the apotheosis of species progress. The Mizorans take no chances with this progress. In the cryptic syntax of the passive voice, Wauna explains that the "dark races" were "eliminated" and that with the help of new reproductive technologies, men were driven into "extinction."[4] This euphonic soundscape—songbird voices and sensitive ears—does more than literalize social harmony; it represents the end goal of selective reproduction, of socially engineered elimination and extinction. In Lane's socialist feminist utopia, differentiated musical sounds have replaced racial and sexual differentiation as an index of civilization.

Mizora models utopia on two seemingly oppositional acoustic principles: harmony, which blends subjects, and sensitivity, which differentiates them. These acoustic principles became central to postbellum utopian fantasies of social and evolutionary progress, and they derived from Hermann von Helmholtz's psychophysical study of hearing. Helmholtz spent the 1850s and 1860s researching not only the psychophysics of sight but also the psychophysics of sound. He drew on the field of physical acoustics, a branch of physics that since the seventeenth century has studied the quantifiable aspects of sonic vibration, including matter, force, and motion. Because most sonic vibrations exceed human audibility, physical acoustics does not take human hearing into account. The human sense of sound, as musicologist Benjamin Steege explains, occurs when "the energy of oscillating matter suddenly leaps into a new form, which is no longer just a figure of vibration but has become something beyond, apprehended via an altogether different modality—the aural."[5] In the 1840s, the field of physiological acoustics formed to study the interaction between sonic vibration and the human ear; its formation directly chronicles the first appearance of the word *aural* (pertaining to the organ of hearing) in writing.[6] In Helmholtz's widely popular and influential *On the Sensations of Tone* (1863), he used physical and physiological acoustics to assay the role of the human ear in defining sound qualities. Whereas Helmholtz's psychophysical optics diminished the epistemological value of seeing, his psychophysical acoustics strengthened the epistemological value of hearing. Rather than reduce the senses to strictly physical phenomena, science historian David Cahan writes, Helmholtz "maintained that there was a psychological component in auditory and visual perception, one that he vaguely referred to as being part of the 'soul' or the creative spirit in human beings."[7] As Helmholtz explains in the preface to *Sensations of Tone*, studying the psychical mechanism of hearing requires suturing two fields that "have hitherto remained perfectly distinct—*physical and physiological acoustics* on the one side and *musical science and aesthetics* on the other."[8] The "sensations of tone are the material of art," but art (music) is more than the sum of its material parts.[9] Helmholtz's *psychophysical acoustics*—I use this term to capture his synthesis of physical acoustics, physiological acoustics, and musical aesthetics—posits musical sound as an elastic "body" that makes manifest the creative spirit inhering in hearing itself.

Blending physics and physiology with aesthetics, psychophysical acoustics offered a model of universality that admits of subjective particularity: hearing a faculty common among human beings yet flexible enough to accommodate experiential and ethnological differences. As such, it convinced many thinkers that music is central to "the innermost drives and even evolutionary history of the species."[10] In *The Descent of Man* (1871), for instance, Charles Darwin argued that music is a primary arena of sexual selection, the evolutionary principle whereby aesthetics—that is, beauty and pleasure—drives an animal's reproductive decisions and ultimately species differentiation. The most attractive bird, the one that female birds will choose as their mate, is the one with the prettiest song, which must have "varied tones and cadences [that] excite the strongest emotions in his hearers."[11] In Edmund Gurney's treatise *The Power of Sound* (1880), the English psychologist similarly deployed Helmholtz's research to address the "position of Music, in relation to the faculties and feelings of the individual . . . and to society at large."[12] The affective capacity to register and respond to musical sound, as laid out by Helmholtz, now tethered the older liberal project of morally refining society to the eugenic project of biologically refining the species. Its founder, Francis Galton, described eugenics as a "utopian" project that aimed to improve the "national stock" by giving "the more suitable races or strains of blood a better chance of prevailing speedily over the less suitable than they otherwise would have had."[13] Once integrated into evolutionary discourse, psychophysical acoustics joined eugenics in conflating social progress with species progress, and the cultivation of the soul with the fitness of the body.

Grounded in the materiality and mechanics of sound yet elevated by the "creative spirit" of hearing, psychophysical acoustics offered a rich conceptual terrain for utopian speculations. Increasingly, these speculations constellated around an imagined universal sisterhood or sodality that could transcend embodied difference while claiming racial superiority. Utopian fiction reaches back to Thomas More's *Utopia* (1516), but following the abandonment of Reconstruction in 1877—an epoch that witnessed militant struggles for labor reform, the closing of the U.S. frontier, the rise of antiblack violence, and a massive influx of Asian and non-Protestant European immigrants—it became immensely popular. Between 1886 (the year of the Haymarket riot) and 1896 alone, more than one hundred works of utopian fiction appeared in the United States.[14] In response to this social turbulence and to the new sway of social Darwinist discourses, many writers subordinated the social, moral, and theological principles that had once undergirded utopian thought to biological ones. They viewed ideal society less in terms of shared ideals and more as a biological phenomenon (population) or an ethnological designation (civilization). What emerges in the post-Reconstruction United States, then, is an ideologically progressive ilk of utopian fiction: a preacherly and plotless genre that regards characters' biological perfection as evidence of the success of a particular social reform movement, such as white women's suffrage or racial uplift. Psychophysical acoustics played a significant role in these fantasies, as the concepts of *sensitivity*, *resonance*, and *sympathetic vibration* became central to meditating on the possibility of a public sphere that stripped subjects of their bodies while retaining their racial purity. Progressive utopian fiction, this chapter argues, mobilized psychophysical acoustics to imagine how subjects could be bound through the transcendent yet material properties of musical sound rather than bound to or bound as the "property" of the nation-state. The acoustics of social harmony proffered a utopian embodiment, one that consisted of a porous psyche and an impervious body.

Excavating the scientific underpinnings of this utopian experiment brings together media histories of sound and Americanist studies of sound. These adjacent critical fields have carefully documented the nineteenth century as the era of hearing's rationalization and racialization. Taking a cue from Friedrich Kittler, media history typically characterizes psychophysics as a positivist science—one that rationalized the sense of hearing, isolated auditory perception, and severed listeners from their social world. This important account is accurate but misses a larger point: Helmholtz's investigations posited hearing as a material but no less metaphysical experience. At the same time, such accounts risk isolating sonic experience from social constructions of human difference; this isolation has the effect of figuring sound as prior to race when in fact it is "always conducted from within history," as Gustavus Stadler reminds us.[15] Americanist sound studies has powerfully remediated this lacuna by tracking the formation of the "sonic color line," a term coined by Jennifer Stoever to describe the racialized listening practices consolidated through sound technologies, musical performances, and antinoise ordinances.[16] This chapter builds on these generative strains of sound studies scholarship by showing how psychophysical acoustics structured the sonic color line. Helmholtz's experiments provided U.S. writers with the vocabulary for exploring "audiotopia," the utopian potential of sonic experience to remap the social world for the purposes of survival.[17]

Progressive utopian fiction joined the broader project of *psychophysical aesthesis* by seeking to reconcile the "creative spirit" immanent to the auditory sense with reigning paradigms of human difference. Helmholtz was not inclined to Fechner's mysticism, but he upheld the psychophysical day view by describing the physical and the aesthetic as interrelated facets of the same experiential whole. This chapter builds on the epistemological, ontological, and aesthetic problems addressed in chapter 1, in which wartime grief could be mediated only through a mental fiction (the body image) that technically represented but "in spirit" accurately portrayed loss. It does so by tracking similar tensions in the speculative domain of utopia, as social harmony became newly mediated through auditory experiences that facilitated transcendent solidarity (à la Fechner's world soul) while maintaining racial distinctions. Because utopian fiction was the primary arena for experimenting with the political possibilities of acoustics, psychophysics acts in this chapter as the musical tonic organizing the relationship between the two novels under discussion: Edward Bellamy's *Looking Backward, 2000–1887* (1888) and Pauline Hopkins's *Of One Blood; Or, the Hidden Self*, first serialized in the *Colored American Magazine* (1902–3). Bellamy, described by Fredric Jameson as "a Thomas Edison ... of the industrial Utopia," might seem far afield of Hopkins, a race woman with interests in spiritualism.[18] Both, in fact, used acoustics as a model of social equality and considered it an apparatus of eugenics, which was "neither [an] inherently reactionary nor white" ideology.[19] There is no definitive evidence that either writer read *On the Sensations of Tone*; it was so widely reviewed and its concepts so saturated all discussions of music and sound, however, as to have fairly infused their thought. *Looking Backward* finds in auditory sensitivity a way to regulate the universal solidarity engendered by harmonic music, whereas *Of One Blood* turns sympathy into a vibratory vehicle of transpersonal black consciousness, a biomystical "world soul." Remaking social harmony into a mode of consciousness, these utopian fictions replace the nation-state with the dream state—far more fluid, though no less fraught—as the hallowed domain of social belonging.

RESONANT BODIES AND SENSITIVE EARS

In 1880, critic and Confederate veteran Sidney Lanier asked the readers of *Scribner's Monthly*, "Why has the immense development of music occurred in our particular modern age, rather than in some other?"[20] The answer to Lanier's question had appeared fifteen years earlier, when in the *Atlantic Monthly* Louis Gottschalk, America's first internationally recognized virtuoso pianist, declared, "Music is a psychophysical phenomenon."[21] This idea, likely learned while training in Germany, signaled to the reading public a positivist shift in music theory. Since antiquity, music theory had been based in mathematical abstractions such as ratio and proportion. But with the rise of empiricism in the seventeenth and eighteenth centuries—measuring and manipulating matter to arrive at truths—these theories were newly subject to experimentation. In the 1850s, Helmholtz began exploring the qualitative effects of this quantitative revolution, specifically by redirecting the physiological facts of hearing toward the psychical experience thereof. This work yielded an early iteration of his signature philosophical doctrine, the sign theory of perception, which argues that sense experience is a representation—not a reflection—of the object world. *On the Sensations of Tone* duly begins by describing hearing as a tripartite process of signification: the "*physical* part," when the external "agent reaches the nerves to be excited, as light for the eye and sound for the ear"; then "the *physiological*" part, when the "modes in which the nerves themselves are excited give rise to their various *sensations*"; and finally the "*psychological*" part, when "these sensations result in mental images of external objects."[22] The sign theory helped Helmholtz reconcile the objective phenomena of acoustics (the physical and physiological parts) with the subjective judgments of aesthetics (the psychological part). Profoundly reshaping acoustics and musical aesthetics, Helmholtz set forth a multipronged argument that sound is a relational phenomenon; that the human ear is a resonant organ that interacts with (rather than reacts to) the material world; and that music is a product of auditory sensitivity, a perceptual faculty unevenly developed among racial groups.

The cornerstone of Helmholtz's psychophysical acoustics is his resonance theory of hearing. Steege deftly breaks down the resonance theory into three parts: the "material ear" amplifies and mutes particular tones, the "mental ear" unconsciously synthesizes those tones into a sonic sign or "image," and the "third ear," which I call the *sensitive ear*, affectively responds to the different tones within that "sign."[23] Helmholtz determined that the first phase of hearing, the "material ear," results from the physical phenomenon known as *sympathetic vibration*. Every sound, comprising a range of frequencies, has upper partial tones and fundamental tones. Sympathetic vibration arises when two elastic bodies—one called the generator, the other the resonator—respond to each other at the same pitch. A familiar example is when a person (generator) sings into a piano with the pedal depressed, and the piano (resonator) reproduces the tonal quality of the vocal sound. To examine the role of the human ear in sympathetic vibration, Helmholtz slid a tuning fork (generator) along the string of a monochord (resonator) and found that the tone was barely perceptible except at a small point on the string that matched the fundamental tone of the tuning fork, which there swelled loudly. This revelation shifted epistemological weight away from the generator, from "the thing one normally thinks oneself as listening *to*," Steege explains, and toward the resonator, a "receptive and transformative object [that] isolates and enlivens" particular tones.[24] The resonator receives and responds to sound by isolating and amplifying certain tones. Helmholtz concluded that sound is not what emanates from the generator but what exists in the relay between generator and resonator. Sound, in other words, is relational—not a bounded object but an activity that draws elastic bodies (generator and resonator) together.

Helmholtz extrapolated acoustic resonance to auditory experience, arguing that hearing is "nothing less than a bodily form of sympathetic vibration."[25] If stringed instruments such as the monochord can discern the fundamental tones from the upper partial tones, then the ear should be able to do so as well. Citing anatomist Alfonso Corti's recent identification of hair cells in the inner ear or *cochlea*, Helmholtz posited that the ear is a resonant organ, with each nerve "tuned" like a piano string to respond to specific tones (either the fundamental or the upper partial tones) of a sound. He wrote, "Suppose we were able to connect every string of a piano with a nervous fiber in such a manner that this fiber would be excited and experience a sensation every time the string vibrated. Then every musical tone which impinged on the instrument would excite, as we know to be really the case in the ear, a series of sensations exactly corresponding to the peculiar vibrations into which the original motion of the air had to be resolved."[26] In this manner, the auditory nerves are "connected with small elastic parts" in the cochlea, which are set into sympathetic vibration by sound waves.[27] Like the piano, the cochlea is an elastic body that selectively resonates to the sounds that strike its nerves. Sympathetic vibration is the process by which the "material ear" differentiates frequencies or tones. Each auditory nerve responds only to the tones to which it is "hardwired" to vibrate, and this response amplifies that particular tone while muting all others. The material ear is a precise instrument that performs the work of what Stoever calls "sonic segregation."²⁸

The material ear is receptive and responsive to sonic vibrations, but the work of distinguishing different tones—the constant data analysis—threatens to overwhelm the perceiving subject. To account for how people synthesize these tones into a singular "sound," Helmholtz identified a second auditory process called the "mental ear." This psychological process simplifies and signifies on the complexity of what we hear for the practical utility of navigating the world. The first, material phase of hearing separates out sound waves into individual tones; the second, mental phase reverses course: it reattaches the fundamental and upper partial tones into a composite "image." For example, Helmholtz notes, "After the sound of a violin has ... constantly reproduced the same sum of partial tones in our sensorium, this sum of partial tones comes to be regarded as the compound sign for the musical tone of a violin. The oftener such a combination has been heard, the more accustomed we are to apprehend it as a connected whole, and the more difficult it is to analyze it by direct observation."²⁹ Repeated exposure—what we call experience—aggregates sonic data (the partial tones) into complexes (the compound sign), then assigns symbols to them (violin). The mental ear names an unconscious process that combines upper partials and fundamental tones to produce an auditory sign. "Partial tones are of course present in the sensations excited in our auditory apparatus, yet they are not generally the subject of conscious perception as independent sensations," Helmholtz clarified.³⁰ The sounds that we consciously register are not "natural" or unmediated; they are signs that smooth out tonal complexity. William James affirmed in *Principles of Psychology* (1890) that we "cannot dissociate the [upper partial] tones" because of an "inveterate habit we have contracted, of passing from them immediately to their import and letting their substantive nature alone."³¹ Regulating the exchanges between human body and sound waves, the "habitual" or mental ear (the ear with which we ambiently hear) settles the dynamism of the soundscape.

Even though the mental ear is useful for everyday life, Helmholtz viewed it as posing a distinctly "aesthetic problem" because it aggregates "sensible symbols of external objects without analyzing them"—and without analysis, there is no aesthetic feeling.³² The solution lay in the transcendent realm of sensitivity. As David Cahan points out, Helmholtz believed that awareness of upper partial tones "requires the soul [*Seele*] as much as the ear's nerves."³³

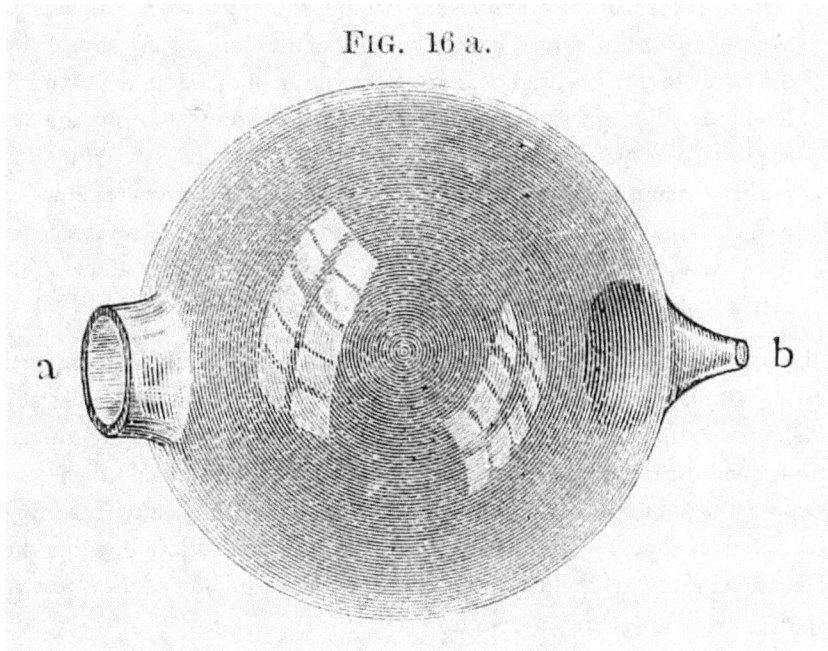

FIG. 2.1 Illustration of Helmholtz resonator from Hermann von Helmholtz, *On the Sensations of Tone* (1863).

Sensitivity to the minute similarities and differences among tones does not recover sensory immediacy. Instead it subjects the material ear to a kind of preconscious judgment. Unlike the material and mental ear, the "sensitive ear"—the psychophysical capacity to differentiate tonal sensations—is an educable rather than inborn "organ." It can only be cultivated. The Helmholtz resonator, which Helmholtz invented to study the material ear, proved useful for this cultivation. Because the mental ear is "naturally less selective," he explained, it is "impossible for the unarmed ear to recognize among several other stronger simple tones those which the resonator itself can fairly indicate."[34] The Helmholtz resonator is a glass bottle modeled on the cochlea: openings at both ends are covered with pigskin membranes, sized and shaped to resonate at a particular pitch, so that when inserted into the ear canal, the resonator mutes the tones of all frequencies except those to which it is tuned (figure 2.1).

On applying to the ear the resonator corresponding to any given upper partial of the compound c, such as g', this g' is rendered much more powerful when c is sounded. Now hearing and distinguishing g' in this case by no means proves that the ear alone and without this apparatus would hear g' as part of the compound c. But the increase of the loudness of g' caused by the resonator may be used to direct the attention of the ear to the tone it is required to distinguish. On gradually removing the resonator from the ear, the force of g' will decrease. But the attention once directed to it by this means, remains more readily fixed upon it, and the observer continues to hear this tone in the natural and unchanged compound tone of the given note, even with his unassisted ear. The sole office of the resonators in this case is to direct the attention of the ear to the required tone.[35]

The sensitive ear disaggregates the auditory sign produced by the mental ear. By attuning listeners to the material differences among tones, especially the upper partial tones eliminated by the mental ear, the Helmholtz resonator trained their "sensitive ear." And once trained, listeners could then consciously pick out upper partial tones from any number of sounds. Directing the resonant function of the material ear toward sense discrimination, the Helmholtz resonator validated sensitivity to tonal vibration as the "creative spirit" powering auditory experiences.

The sensitive ear initiated a newly "resonant" relationship to musical sound. No longer a passive body, the listener was now an active resonator shaping sound itself. An "uninstructed hearer is as little conscious of the reason of the connection of a clear and agreeable series of fluent chords as he is of the reason of a well-connected melody," Helmholtz wrote.[36] The sensitive ear, the barely conscious parsing of tonal arrangements, thus became a precondition of aesthetic feeling. Indeed, Alexandra Hui attributes the resonance theory not simply to Helmholtz's science but to his own aesthetic practices and preferences. As an amateur pianist and avid concertgoer who favored Haydn and Beethoven over "flashy virtuosic pieces and popular operas," Helmholtz was steeped in midcentury Germany's increasingly rationalized music culture, which lodged aesthetic value neither in the performance of music nor in emotional responses to music but in the material structure of the musical score.[37] It is unsurprising, then, that the sensitive ear scientifically validated critic Eduard Hanslick's argument that beauty resides in form, which is "the real *substance* of music."[38] Whereas the "sentimentalist" values "emotional revolutions," and the "musical enthusiast's [ecstasies] sink to the level of the crude emotion of the savage," he explained in *The Beautiful in Music* (1854), the rational listener who deploys "a calm but acutely sensitive ear" engages the "true and artistic method of listening."[39] Advancing Hanslick's position, an editorial writer for the *Atlantic* lamented that music had become "so thoroughly identified" with "emotional inspirations" that the public does not recognize the "fundamental principles underlying the entire structure, which involve physical, physiological, and psychological laws," and that an "understanding of its structure is essential to perfect appreciation of its truest beauty."[40] By tethering the physics of sound and the physiology of human hearing to the psychological domain of judgment, the resonance theory of hearing helped transform listening into "a way to worship at the temple of great art."[41]

Central to this new culture of listening, psychophysical acoustics framed music as a material structure that has a transcendent ability to affect listeners— but only if they are properly sensitized to tonal complexity. The sensitive ear originates in while remaining distinct from the universal regularities of the material ear and mental ear. It captures the experiential and even ethnological particularities of auditory experience. Therefore, Helmholtz further argued, the sensitive ear helps to account for the historical development and cultural varieties of musical systems. After all, one of the central questions driving *On the Sensations of Tone* is the tensile relation between the universal mechanics and the variable aesthetics of sound, between "natural phenomena [that] present themselves mechanically, without any choice," and musical systems that "have undergone multifarious alterations, not merely among uncultivated or savage people, but . . . among those nations where the noblest flowers of human culture have expanded."[42] Rather than reduce music to a strictly material structure, he acknowledged that music does not rest "solely upon inalterable natural laws" but is the "result of aesthetic principles, which have already changed, and will still further change, with the progressive development of humanity."[43] In this way, the sensitive ear reconciled the inalterable natural laws of sound with the historically and racially contingent principles of musical aesthetics. Helmholtz argued that to "distinguish small differences of pitch and intonate them with certainty requires a greater amount of technical musical power and cultivation of ear, than when the intervals [of tone] are larger. Hence among almost all uncivilized people we find the Semitones neglected, and only the larger intervals retained."[44] Complex musical structures, predicated on the layered arrangement of tonal elements, require a sensitive ear that can discern and separate out these elements. Hence, creating music built on small differences of pitch requires a sensitivity that "uncivilized people" lack. Conjoined in this way to discourses of human progress, auditory sensitivity not only reestablished the tonal differences of a given sound but also inserted human difference into the aesthetics thereof.

As the culminating phase of the resonant theory of hearing, the sensitive ear anchored Helmholtz's account of the development of musical systems. For although human beings have similar physiological and psychological processing capabilities, sensitivity is an "act of discernment" reflecting and shaping Western "social norms of discipline, culture, and value."[45] Accordingly, the trajectory that Helmholtz maps out in *On the Sensations of Tone* begins with the homophonic music (a melody accompanied by chords) of the "ancients and the Oriental and Asiatic nations," then the polyphonic music (two simultaneous melodies) of the Middle Ages, and finally the "harmonic or modern music" (multiple voices that are structurally concordant) from the seventeenth century onward.[46] What ostensibly makes harmonic music synonymous with modernity is its "clear characteristics of related combinations of tones," contra the simplistic music of the "Oriental and Asiatic nations."[47] Considered perfectly and fully developed, harmonic music was "the sole originating source of impressive musical effects in our age," Edmund Gurney wrote.[48] This impressive musical effect was entirely predicated on the auditory sensitivity that white European peoples had cultivated. The resonant theory of hearing managed to inaugurate hearing as a mechanical yet creative, material yet transcendent activity—and by extension music as a "psychophysical phenomenon" common to all human beings, yet with harmonic complexity specific to the so-called modern age. By valuing "tonal consonance and harmonic development" over other sounds, Helmholtz validated the "epistemological sensibilities of Western music theory," as musicologist David Novak argues.[49] In this fashion, psychophysical acoustics confirmed commonalities among humankind while asserting Western perceptual superiority. It went on to power progressive utopian fantasies of elastic bodies linked in sympathetic exchange yet individually regulated by the aesthetic activity of selective hearing.

SOLIDARITY AND SELECTIVE HEARING

Widely reviewed in both the scientific and the popular press, *On the Sensations of Tone* gave musical sound a quantifiable language that anchored postbellum fantasies of an egalitarian social order. Tone was an especially strong anchor. Helmholtz had attributed the superiority of harmonic music to its tonality—that is, music organized around a *tonic*, the chief tone in a musical score that connects all other tones by their relationship to it. He considered European tonal music, featuring classical harmonies and just intonation, superior to other musical systems because it demonstrated the "close and always distinctly perceptible relationship" of tones to one another.[50] In the *North American Review*, German physician Ernst Gryzanowski fleshed out the metaphysical dimensions of Helmholtz's claim by arguing that tonal music "binds notes together by giving them a common center. The center is to the plurality of notes what self-consciousness is to the plurality of sensations; it gives soul to music—not a soul in the sense of sentiment, but a soul in the sense of reason."[51] The tonic is the consciousness driving a musical score, the transcendent spirit that arranges distinct tones into something grander than the sum of its physical parts. The "binding and readjusting power of *tonality*, which in its widest sense is a world-compelling principle, [is] the spiritual rival of mechanism," he added.[52] Registering the day view of nature as comprising interrelated mental and material phenomena, the tonic orders without overdetermining the relations among individual elements. Further, as a "world-compelling principle," it yokes the cosmos to the polis, directing civic relations toward more transcendent possibilities. Because pleasure arises when "elements which differ in kind as well as in degree, forming a *variety*," coalesce, tonal music "must be a *unum e pluribus*" that balances "unity and plurality."[53] In transposing music theory into the U.S. national motto, Gryzanowski remakes harmony into a political structure—specifically pluralism, which at the time "became synonymous with democracy, liberalism, and Americanism."[54] Harmonic music, an arrangement of tonal multiplicity, modeled a solution to what his friend William James called "the problem of the one and the many."[55]

Edward Bellamy's utopian novel *Looking Backward, 2000–1887*, so popular that it spawned a cottage industry of imitators as well as the establishment of more than 165 Nationalist Clubs (also called Bellamy Clubs), envisions an ensouled civitas—or more precisely, a social harmony materialized through music. The novel notably brings eugenics and experimental science to bear on the socialist utopian experiments undertaken in the antebellum period: George Rapp's Harmony Society instituted a "universal citizenship," whereby people could "cede their individuality to a greater and more equitable whole"; Robert Dale Owen's New Harmony, Indiana, community was organized "around cross-class fantasies of a shared, free white manhood"; and the Brook Farm commune, which briefly counted Nathaniel Hawthorne among its members, practiced Charles Fourier's socialist concepts.[56] *Looking Backward* updates these earlier "harmony societies" by using tonality to model the "spiritual mechanism" organizing utopian subjects: *solidarity*. In his posthumously published essay *The Religion of Solidarity*, written in 1874, Bellamy first argued that "the harmony of universal life" lay in the "soul of solidarity within us," which puts the "personality of the subject in a state of suspense."[57] Further, because music "relax[es] the rigor of individual conditions, laying the petty, petulant instinct of the personality under a spell," it is a catalyst of solidarity.[58] Bellamy advances Helmholtz's claim that music has unconscious effects on the perceiver, that the "chief effects of the artistically beautiful proceed *not* from the part which we are able to fully realize."[59] Musical sound is to solidarity what "heavenly vision" is to the Fechnerian world soul: a stimulus connecting individuals below the threshold of consciousness. At first glance, of course, psychophysics has little to do with a novel as thematically and formally mechanistic as *Looking Backward*, powered as it is by the "inevitability effect" of its titular teleological frame.[60] Ensouling Bellamy's night view utopia, however, are mystical experiences of sound that dissolve psychical and, more threateningly, racial bounds. Looking inward as it looks backward, the novel limns the acoustics of social harmony, seeking to resolve the tension between solidarity and eugenics through the mystical states of consciousness activated by tonality and auditory sensitivity.

Propelling *Looking Backward* beyond its own narrative inertia is the internal drama of narrator Julian West's time travel. Fittingly, the vehicle of transport from 1887 to 2000 is a state of suspended consciousness. In response to the "never ceasing nightly noises" generated by Gilded Age Boston's ethnic tenements, Julian builds a subterranean chamber, from which "no murmur of the upper world ever penetrated."[61] There, once "surrounded by the silence of the tomb," he receives visits from "a Professor of Animal Magnetism," who hypnotizes him to sleep—but one night, that trance is so powerful that he enters "a state of animated suspension" that lasts 113 years.[62] Once discovered and revived by utopian residents Dr. Leete and his daughter Edith, Julian tours 2000 Boston with his guides, who teach him about the new social order: a global socialist military state that uses universal income, Taylorist mass production, and a labor force called the industrial army to mold citizens into a "monolith of gentility."[63] Julian's psychological tumult is what textures the otherwise frictionless social world. Throughout his stay, he finds himself unable to "regain the clew of my personality," failing to "distinguish myself from pure being any more than a soul in the rough" can before it has received "the individualizing touches which make it a person."[64] Sounding a lot like "larval" George Dedlow from S. Weir Mitchell's story, Julian laments the "moments when my personality seems quite an open question."[65] Although no longer physically asleep, "woke" Julian still exists in an occult state of consciousness.

Paradoxically, this egoistic displacement secures his place in the system, where pure being acts as the ontology or existential infrastructure of socialism—the below-threshold feeling of solidarity that governs civic relations.

Although transcendent solidarity might undercut the highly regimented utopia, it in fact serves as the "creative spirit" blending subjects' minds while leaving their bodies intact. The primary vehicle for balancing psychical interconnection and physical atomization is the novel's most famous fabricated technology, the musical telephone. (Charlotte Perkins Gilman's "Dr. Clair's Place" directly lifts the musical telephone from Bellamy.) When Edith shows Julian the "music room" in the Leete home, she explains that "all the really fine singers and players are in the musical service" division of the industrial army, and that their professional music is "so much grander and more perfect than any [amateur] performance."[66] The music room does not contain "new devices and musical instruments" that she will play for him. Instead it contains a music program featuring an "extraordinary range of vocal and instrumental solos, duets, quartets, and various orchestral combinations." The scene unfolds:

> "I am so glad you like the organ," said she. "I think there is scarcely any music that suits my mood oftener."
>
> She made me sit down comfortably, and crossing the room, so far as I could see, merely touched one or two screws, and at once the room filled with the music of a grand organ anthem; filled, not flooded, for, by some means, the volume of melody had been perfectly graduated to the size of the apartment. I listened, scarcely breathing, to the close. Such music, so perfectly rendered, I had never expected to hear.
>
> "Grand!" I cried, as the last great wave of sound broke and ebbed away into silence. "Bach must be at the keys of that organ; but where is the organ?"
>
> "Wait a moment, please," said Edith; "I want to have you listen to this waltz before you ask any questions. I think it is perfectly charming," and as she spoke the sound of violin filled the room. . . . When this had also ceased, she said: "There are a number of music rooms in the city, perfectly adapted acoustically to the different sorts of music. These halls are connected by telephone with all the houses of the city whose people care to pay the small fee."[67]

The music room houses the two acoustical components of socialist utopia: the musical telephone that unifies subjects through sympathetic vibration, and the harmonic music that it transmits, which yields solidarity. The device is, of course, modeled on Alexander Graham Bell's telephone. While studying at the University of London, Bell sought out *On the Sensations of Tone* to learn more about sympathetic vibration. Lacking an English translation, however, he had to make do with his imperfect grasp of German. He misread Helmholtz's claim that electrical tuning forks and resonators can produce vowel sounds; Bell thought that Helmholtz was claiming that vowel sounds can be transmitted electrically over wires. Based on this mistranslation, Bell tried combining electricity with the principle of sympathetic vibration, and in 1874, he invented a device that translated messages at different pitches (the material ear) into electricity, carried by one wire in the same direction (the mental ear), and then separated out into distinct messages (the sensitive ear). Bell initially called this device the "harmonic telegraph."

The purpose of the musical telephone is to regulate the utopian public sphere. By connecting isolated, privatized listener-subjects through a shared aesthetic experience, it realizes a disembodied public that is "all ears." At the same time, while the musical telephone reinforces this social atomization, the music it transmits facilitates a kind of transpersonal solidarity, the porous, boundless consciousness that the utopian state requires. As the conduit for harmonic music, the musical telephone has a distinctly spiritual function: to convert or transduce sympathetic vibration into the "sympathy of solidarity." In 2000 Boston, harmonic music (orchestral combinations, symphonic scores, waltzes) replaces Gilded Age mesmerism as the means of suspending "personality," of awakening the "passion for losing ourselves in others." It acts as the tonic that binds individuals together by readjusting their "personality." Music critic John Sullivan Dwight, erstwhile director of the school at Brook Farm, certainly felt this way. He claimed in the *Atlantic Monthly* that music "prompts each to fill his place cheerfully and unobtrusively, forgetting the self in the harmonious whole, weaving a sympathetic bond," and that it "unites and blends and harmonizes all who may come within its sphere."[68] Dwight partakes of the "utopian liberal belief in the elevation of the masses through culture and education," explaining that music is a means not simply of cultivating the soul but of civilizing a multiracial citizenry.[69]

> Consider its civilizing agency, so far as it may become part of the popular, the public education. We, as a democratic people, a great mixed people of all races, overrunning a vast continent, need music even more than others. We need some ever-present, ever-welcome influence that shall insensibly tone down our self-asserting and aggressive manners, round off the sharp,

offensive angularity of character, subdue and harmonize the free and ceaseless conflict of opinions.... This rampant liberty will rush to its own ruin, unless there shall be found some gentler, harmonizing, humanizing culture, such as may preface whole masses with ... a sweet sense of reverence for something far above us.... We need to be so enamored of the divine idea of unity that that alone shall be the real motive for assertion of our individuality.... What can so quickly magnetize a people into this harmonic mood as music? We blend in joyous fellowship when we can sing together; perhaps quite as much so when we can listen together.[70]

Music culture is a way to cultivate sympathy in a diverse population, a means to promote national unity, because in harmonic music the "divine idea of unity" manifests as a "humanizing culture" that "subdues" individualism and racial conflict. The purpose of the musical telephone is not simply to "magnetize" isolated subjects but to "tone down" their egoistic impulses, and thereby realize a more placid social arrangement. The musical telephone equalizes subjects through what social reformer Edith Brower identified as the "transcendental realm of harmony."[71] It is, in other words, an acoustic mechanism of emotional sympathy or solidarity.

Auditory experiences in Bellamy's novel facilitate this bourgeois project by converting harmonic tonalities into "socially constructive tonalities," as Nick Yablon has argued.[72] After all, Helmholtz considered harmony not simply a "modern" musical structure but one that has been "essential and indispensable" to "Western Europeans during the last three centuries."[73] This is the problem with harmonic music: it is a vehicle of transcendence that sets resonant subjects into sympathetic vibration yet potentially renders them overly labile. Dissolving personality, it might dissolve physical particularity. And so the aesthetic faculty of selective hearing is required to regulate the excess resonance or elasticity of the utopian body. When Edith Leete plays orchestral combinations for Julian in the music room, there are not two but three auditory processes at work: the musical telephone is the material ear that separates sound from the generator ("But where is the organ?"), harmonic music is the "mental ear" that spiritually connects the resonators (listening subjects), and the music room is the "sensitive ear" that reasserts racial differences. The name "music room" is not a descriptor but a performative, a locution that constitutes any sound that fills that space *as* music—and all other sonic matter as noise. Addressing the deleterious effects of urban noise on the impressible white body, physician John Girdner warned readers of the

North American Review that when "poured in the auditory canals," the city's "Babel of discordant sounds and noises" produces neurasthenia.[74] Within the context of the era's many antinoise ordinances, the 2000 music room duplicates Julian's 1887 soundproof sleeping tomb; both are time capsules meant to preserve the white body by muting outside noise. The musical telephone is the material infrastructure of transpersonal consciousness, but that consciousness is predicated on an originary distinction between musical and nonmusical, "good" and "bad," sound.

It is by now axiomatic that noise is a construct; it does not exist in itself but only "in relation to the system within which it is inscribed"—namely, the "harmonic system," which "functions through rules and prohibitions," in the words of philosopher Jacques Attali.[75] That noise is the constitutive other of music is the very premise of *On the Sensations of Tone*, which addresses noise only to dismiss it. In the first chapter, Helmholtz claims that "non-musical sound" is made of "nonperiodic" waveforms that are "irregularly mixed up and as it were tumbled about in confusion," and musical sound made up of "periodic" waveforms that "strike the ear as perfectly undisturbed, uniform sound."[76] German physiologist Julius Bernstein advanced this music/noise binary when he argued in *The Five Senses of Man* (1876) that "irregular vibrations" cannot be "taken up" by the cochlea because its nerve fibers, "which seem to be adapted to tones of definite pitch," can only be "thrown into sympathetic vibration by tones which approach its fundamental tone."[77] If the ear is physiologically unequipped to receive irregular waveforms, then noise is sound that exceeds sympathetic vibration. Noise is a construct that "renders certain sounds—and the bodies that produce and consume them—as Other," but it does so by constructing racial bodies as nonelastic, as necessarily incapable of sympathetic vibration and, by extension, solidarity.[78] Located in the Leete family's bourgeois home, the music room architecturally structures racial distinctions; music is what happens "inside," experienced by bodies resonant—relational, lively, orderly—enough to correspond with their sonic environs. All else is mere noise: "static," inchoate, external, and insufficiently elastic for resonance. This distinction between noise and music, part of the novel's dual commitment to universal brotherhood and white supremacy, qualifies the "pure being" of solidarity as a racially pure being.

Bellamy's novel thus presents the sensitive ear as the psychophysical mechanism driving selective hearing. And selective hearing, in turn, is an evolutionary mechanism that ensures racial futurity. Citing Helmholtz, Darwin argued in *The Descent of Man* that noise differs from music "only in the want of continuity of [regular] vibrations, and in their want of harmony.... Thus an ear, to be capable of discriminating noises, must be sensitive to musical notes."[79] Our emotional responses to sound serve an evolutionary purpose: to propagate the species. Auditory sensitivity, which "discriminat[es] noises" from "musical notes," is instrumental to sexual selection. English psychologist Havelock Ellis extended this Darwinian formulation in *Sexual Selection in Man: Touch, Smell, Hearing, Vision* (1905). He claimed that the senses are an erotic stimulus of sexual selection: "When a man or a woman experiences sexual love for one particular person from among the multitude by which he or she is surrounded, this is due to the influence of a group of stimuli coming through the channels of one or more of the senses. There has been a sexual selection conditioned by sensory stimuli."[80] Given that American interpretations of evolution "fused faith in science with a commitment to continual improvement and progress," it follows that the music room is the setting for sexual selection.[81] It is an acoustic space that doubles as a space of white heterosexual courtship and as such protects white racial futurity—as promised by the marriage plot between Julian and Edith—from the biological rigidity of ethnic "noise."

What unfolds in the Leete family's music room is a particular kind of selective hearing: what we might call *sexually* selective hearing, in which auditory sensitivity ensures the whiteness of the listener. "Sexually selective hearing" becomes instrumental to strengthening the most desirable traits of the fittest (white, nondisabled) subjects over time. Bellamy considered sexual selection essential to the improvement of humanity and joined eugenic feminists like Charlotte Perkins Gilman—a frequent speaker at Bellamy Clubs—in arguing that female choice of sex partners facilitates species progress. Indeed, as the marriage plot progresses, Edith Leete explains to Julian that the "principle of sexual selection, with its tendency to preserve and transmit the better types of the race, and let the inferior types drop out, has unhindered operation," and that "more important than any of the causes I mentioned as tending to race purification has been the effect of untrammeled sexual selection upon the quality of two or three successive generations."[82] Edith's argument is that when women are no longer forced to marry out of economic necessity they are free to pursue their natural impulse, which is to find the male partner with the best traits. Over time, women's choices precipitate "race purification." Bellamy's follow-up novel, *Equality* (1897), clarifies that the race being purified is the white race. In it, Dr. Leete describes an "industrial regimen," modeled on Booker T. Washington's Tuskegee Institute, that "educates, refines, and elevates" those who need it "as a civilizing agent" more than the "white population, which had been relatively further advanced."[83] Socialism has supplanted capitalism but not racial capitalism; it is easier for Bellamy to imagine a world without corporations than without segregation. "The new system involved no more commingling of the races than the old had done," Julian explains in the mistitled sequel.[84]

The sensitive ear required for aesthetic transport represents a specific kind of listening practice—sexually selective hearing—that mutes the racialized sounds too rigid for sympathetic vibration. Solidarity becomes, then, a component of rather than a counterpoint to white supremacy. As "the only living representative in the direct line," Julian is shadowed by the possibility of race suicide.[85] Edith represents an ideal match. Not only does his surname index an allegedly superior civilization and hers "an 'elite' social status," but their elastic bodies promise to work in harmonious relation toward progress.[86] This marriage directs whiteness toward the future but does so by conjuring a problem from the past, a problem produced by excess resonance or relationality: incest. As goes the climactic reveal, Edith is the great-granddaughter of Julian's 1887 fiancée, Edith Bartlett, who, after presuming Julian dead, had "made a marriage of esteem, and left a son who had been Mrs. Leete's father. Mrs. Leete... gave her [daughter] the name of Edith."[87] Julian and Edith Leete's courtship barely skirts incest, as Julian now feels that Edith Bartlett "had been re-embodied for my consolation," and when embracing his new fiancée, "the two Ediths were blended in my thought, nor have they ever since been clearly distinguished."[88] It is difficult to ignore the fact that Edith Leete *would have been* Julian's great-granddaughter had he not, however preposterously, spent the last 113 years buried underground in a state of suspended animation. Julian marries his own kin not in blood but certainly in spirit. This particular marriage plot accords with Walter Benn Michaels's provocative claim that in the early twentieth century, incest served as a eugenicist technology of "prevent[ing] half-breeds."[89] Upholding the white supremacist status quo, Julian and Edith's nearly incestuous sexual selection guards the utopian body against racial mixing, which would "spell disharmony—disharmony of physical, mental and temperamental qualities," according to U.S. biologist and eugenics movement leader Charles Davenport.[90]

Incest resolves the biological crisis of race suicide and the ontological crisis of pure being. In short, it preserves the whiteness of the utopian population while dissolving differences of consciousness into a collective world soul. Crucially, Edith's ancestry activates her own crisis of pure being. She tells Julian, "What if I were to tell you that I have sometimes thought that her spirit lives in me, that Edith Bartlett, not Edith Leete, is my real name. I cannot know it; of course none of us can know who we really are; but I can feel it."[91] Edith's inability to tell herself apart from her foremother echoes Julian's own existentially fraught moments. For him, "habits of feeling, associations of thought, ideas of persons and things" frequently break loose as he sinks below the threshold of consciousness into the spiritual domain of solidarity, the "idea that I was two persons, that my identity was double" registering his interpellation.[92] Incest makes it impossible for Edith and Julian to "know who [they] really are" and for this reason represents a kind of biological corollary of solidarity, described by Bellamy as the "passion for losing ourselves in others or for absorbing them into ourselves."[93] Yet because the affianced couple lose themselves not in each other but in their individual pasts—2000 Julian in 1887 Julian, Edith Leete in Edith Bartlett—incest largely prevents solidarity from yielding too much displacement of the personal. "Everybody is part of a system, with a distinct place and function," but "there is no place for me anywhere. I was neither dead nor properly alive," Julian bemoans.[94] Constantly pulled into "pure being," Julian suffers from excess solidarity, which puts the resonant white body in an eternal state of suspended consciousness, neither alive nor dead. Incest redirects the outward pull of solidarity—the porous psyche resonating with others—backward in time, so that becoming absorbed in one's own past, rather than becoming absorbed in other people, becomes part of the eugenic project of future purity.

Predicated on the exclusion of noise, harmonic music facilitates solidarity, a psychical state that props up racial purity. The psychophysical acoustics underwriting the eugenic body politic is clearest in a spectacular scene, when, after applying a "clockwork combination" to the musical telephone that will awaken him at a specific time, Julian has a dream that transports him to the Alhambra in medieval Spain:

> A band of Nautch girls, round-limbed and luscious-lipped, danced with voluptuous grace to the music of brazen and stringed instruments. Louder and louder clashed the cymbals, wilder and wilder grew the straining, till the blood of the desert race could no longer resist the martial delirium and the swart nobles leaped to their feet; a thousand scimitars were bared, and the cry "Allah il Allah!" shook the hall and awoke me, to find it broad daylight, and the room tingling with the electric music of the "Turkish Reveille."
>
> At the breakfast table, when I told my host of my morning's experience, I learned that it was not a mere chance that the piece of music which

awakened me was a reveille. The airs played at one of the halls during the waking hours of the morning were always of an inspiring type.[95]

Julian's dream makes manifest the unconscious longings—for sex, for death—that the utopian order represses. Crucially, though, it is a dream orchestrated by composer Theodor Michaelis's popular march "Turkish Reveille." Julian's dream imbues the song with an Orientalism that, beyond the title, the musical score does not actually have. The original score featured no clashing cymbals, "noisemaking percussion instruments" historically associated with the "less meaningful musical structures" of non-Western cultures.[96] The "Turkish Reveille" dream dissolves music into noise, whiteness into ethnic alterity. Clearly, then, the music meant to "inspire" has unexpected effects on utopian subjects, for whom the music stimulates feelings not of universal brotherhood but instead of erotic desire for nonwhite women—or, as a counterpoint to incestuous kinship, a desire for exogamy. Mechanically transmitted and musically induced, the Orientalist dream demonstrates that pre- or subconscious states of being are the safest arena in which a person might feel the "sympathy of solidarity," might become "passionately absorbed" into others, without diminishing their own racial purity or committing social taboos. The dream state, an "elastic" domain where racial and sonic segregation do not hold, is the apotheosis rather than an aberration of utopian solidarity. Using harmonic music and sexually selective hearing to materialize the internal drama of solidarity—a drama in excess of the rationalized and regimented infrastructure of civic life—*Looking Backward* fantasizes socialism as an impossible arrangement of psychically porous yet racially particular subjects.

GOOD SYMPATHETIC VIBRATIONS

Bellamy's socialist utopia turned harmonic music into a medium of solidarity and selective hearing into a mechanism of sexual selection; together these acoustic principles set the white body on a trajectory of historical and evolutionary progress. But in this moment, ethnographic fieldwork was pressuring the reigning logic that the European musical scale is the universal standard and nonwhite people's musical systems are meaningless noise. In phonetician Alexander Ellis's 1885 English translation of *On the Sensations of Tone*, he argued that there is no single musical scale and supported this claim by adding to the book's appendix an analysis of non-Western scales. Hui observes that this emergent cultural relativism was "taken seriously" but "did not lead to an immediate collapse in the belief in a universal musical aesthetic that just so happened to be Western."[97] Upholding Helmholtz's theory that the European tonal system meets the "natural" requirements of the ear and is "more harmonically complex and emotionally subjective" than "folk songs," critics, ethnographers, and social reformers used the "disciplining strategies" of Western music to revalue "savage" sounds as music.[98] For instance, composer Antonín Dvořák proposed that African American song could be the foundation of American symphonic music, but as Nancy Bentley observes, this allowed "white classical musical authorities to recognize the powerful appeal of black 'folksongs' while still remaining certain that African Americans themselves were 'not inherently musical' and retaining their ignorance of or indifference to accomplished choral groups."[99] Slave spirituals now counted as music but only to the extent that they remained stylistically subordinated to Western musical systems.

Psychophysical models of tone sensation contributed to the construction of black music as a lesser art, but it also provided African Americans a way to champion black music as a force of racial progress. Twenty years after Pauline Hopkins's turn as a star singer, she took to the *Colored American Magazine* in 1901 to track the careers of "phenomenal vocalists" Elizabeth Taylor Greenfield, Anne Pauline Pindell, and the Hyers sisters (Anna Madah and Emma Louise). These women, she argued, prove that the "genius of music, supposed to be the gift of only the most refined and intellectual of the human family, sprang into active life" among African Americans, and since emancipation, "Negro song" has "become a part of the classical music of the century."[100] In *Of One Blood; Or, the Hidden Self*, serialized in the magazine one year later, Hopkins creatively exploited critic John Sullivan Dwight's assertion that symphonic music activates social harmony. "If I sing to you," he wrote, "a vibration of my soul, my feeling, imparts itself to the atmospheric medium, traveling on until it becomes the vibration of *your* soul, your feeling. The spiritual fact of music answers to this physical fact."[101] Hopkins adopted Dwight's psychophysical theory that sympathetic vibration is the "physical fact" powering music's affective transmissions. Psychophysical acoustics lubricated her efforts to imagine black music as a medium of transpersonal racial consciousness—a consciousness that organizes kin rather than citizens. This acoustic experiment required the concept of timbre, a term developed around 1840 to name the unique tonal quality of an instrument (such as the flute or the human voice) that exists below the threshold of audibly distinct pitches. In *On the Sensations of Tone*, Helmholtz identified timbre (*klangfarbe*, or tone color) as the reason "why sounding bodies show great differences."[102] He determined that timbre is a function of upper partial tones; pitch owes to the frequency of sound waves, whereas timbre "owes to wave form, more specifically to the series of upper partials that a compound wave carries."[103] In European and North American culture, vocal timbre accounted for the biological differences among "sounding bodies"—that is, it manifests racial essence. What emerged was a "micropolitics of timbre," characterized by musicologist Nina Sun Eidsheim as the "process of discernment involved in listening to and naming voices that locates the black body in tonal quality."[104] Rather than shy away from this auditory micropolitics, Hopkins used vocal timbre to racialize sympathetic vibration, and ultimately to claim a black diasporic world soul where black kinship, fractured by the transatlantic slave trade, can be restored.

Shifting the acoustic basis of social harmony from tonality to timbral vibration, *Of One Blood* authorizes the female-sung slave spiritual as a biomystical conduit of racial consciousness. It thus partakes of a black tradition that precedes and exceeds the Bellamite school of utopian fiction, as Dohra Ahmad writes, by refusing the "totalitarian impulses of that canonical strain" and replacing "natural and inevitable evolution" with unfinished futures.[105] Like Sutton Griggs's *Imperium in Imperio* (1899) and Edward A. Johnson's *Light Ahead for the Negro* (1904), *Of One Blood* focuses on the process of "ideological change that would lead to utopia rather than on the accomplished perfection of utopia itself."[106] The book is organized by a bifurcated plotline—one American, the other African—and a dual commitment to the biological theory of monogenesis, or shared ancestry (of one blood), and the psychological theory of a "hidden self," a term directly lifted from the title of William James's *Scribner's* essay on double consciousness. These conceptual and thematic crossings spin a web around the novel's love triangle: Reuel Briggs, a telepathic doctor (based on James) passing as white; Dianthe Lusk, a black soprano, a spirit medium, and a tragic mulatta; and plantation heir Aubrey Livingston. After Reuel and Dianthe fall in love and marry, Aubrey forces Reuel on an expedition to Ethiopia, where he reconnects with his "hidden" blackness in the hidden city of Telassar. Meanwhile, Aubrey takes Dianthe as his mistress and to his home in Maryland, where she learns that she, Reuel, and Aubrey are all siblings, born of the deceased clairvoyant slave Mira and her enslaver, Aubrey Livingston Sr. In the end, Aubrey kills Dianthe and then himself, and Reuel, revealed to be of ancient royal lineage, returns to Telassar to fulfill his racial destiny as an African king. Marked by rape, incest, and murder, the novel is unlikely to appear utopian—but its aspirations for black music operate in precisely that key. As a singer of spirituals, Dianthe is a (spirit) medium of racial consciousness, her sounding body vibrating across time and space to bring African peoples into sympathy with one another. The "phenomenal" black female vocalist underwrites the novel's utopian potential, her voice binding black people together through affective resonance rather than biological essence.

Reuel has layers, but Dianthe is elastic. He triumphantly excavates utopia—ancient African civilization—but she is the novel's proverbial unsung hero. A member of the Fisk Jubilee Singers, Dianthe gives a virtuosic performance of the slave spirituals that spurs Reuel's geographic and spiritual journey from New England to Ethiopia. Indeed, it is while Reuel reads *The Unclassified Residuum*, a Jamesean book about "supernatural phenomena or *mysticism*," that his Harvard classmate Aubrey Livingston—who as a southerner claims to "know and understand Negro music"—invites Reuel to a "jubilee concert."[107] In the "new era in the life of the nation" initiated by the "passing of slavery," the Fisk Jubilee Singers prove that the "Negro possessed a phenomenal gift of music," and further, that those "fortunate enough to listen once to their matchless untrained voices singing their heartbreaking minor music with its grand and impossible intervals and sound combinations" are "eager to listen again and again."[108] The description of the singers' voices as "untrained" yet virtuosic in the "grand and impossible intervals and sound combinations" of their music speaks to a distinctly "black" version of the European classical mode. As Daphne Brooks points out, when the Fisk Jubilee Singers formed in 1871, their director George White "steeped [them] in classical training."[109] The singers negotiated these two aesthetic modes, having perfected a "crisp and sonorous interpretation of the 'sorrow songs' of slavery, a combination of exquisite four-part harmonies and double pianissimi" that "refined" the spirituals into classical arrangements—all the better to set their "black" sound apart from minstrelsy.[110] At the same time, Eidsheim underscores, audience preferences for "spirituals paired with classical repertoire" were based on general attitudes that black people's "natural aptitude for the spirituals" would invest their "interpretation of classical music" with "emotional capital."[111]

That emotional capital lay in vocal timbre. In listening "again and again" to the "heartbreaking" music of "untrained voices," the white audience is listening for the unmediated sound of black subjectivity—that is, for the "gift" of natural expressiveness. As the raw material index of race, vocal timbre acoustically structures *ethnosympathy*, defined by sociologist Jon Cruz as a nineteenth-century mode of cultural reception informed by the "humanitarian pursuit of the inner world of distinctive and collectively classifiable subjects."[112] In the postbellum period, ethnosympathetic listening valued the slave spirituals for their authentic testimony and emotional expressiveness rather than for their actual political expression. Timbre naturalizes the myth of the black voice as more "affective, truthful, and expressive than other voices," as an inherently musical sound that remains "mired in the past and colored with the whip-crack of subjection."[113] A *Washington Post* article, "Negroes as Singers" (1903), claimed that "the most striking results are obtained from negroes on the plantation" because cultivation lessens the "peculiar vibrating quality" of the black voice.[114] The emotional authority ascribed to the nonwhite person's voice constitutes a "chronobiopolitical" formation, Dana Luciano argues, in which the "evocative" voice of Native Americans places them outside of historical time—and likewise the "peculiar" timbre of African Americans situates black life in the historical past.[115] According to the *Post*, after all, the black voice retains "its original savagery, and when sung with the peculiar timbre which is the special attribute of the negro's voice it produces an effect which gets the nerves tingling."[116] Euro-American music is notable for its harmonic system, and African American music for the harmonic substrate called timbre, the immediate tonal quality that hits a nerve rather than stimulates the mind. Vocal timbre underwrites the ethnosympathetic listening practices that naturalize "the untrained voice as an expression of 'essential identity,' an unmediated expression of black interiority."[117] Artlessness authenticates the Fisk Jubilee Singers' "minor music" while validating the white bourgeois listener's sentimental "heartbreak."

Within this ethno-acoustic context, the two black ensemble performances that bookend *Of One Blood*—the Fiske Jubilee Singers in the Boston concert hall and the otherworldly "Ethiopian pageant" in Aubrey's plantation house—together denature the timbral mechanics propping up the habits of ethnosympathetic listening. In these scenes, the black person's "sounding body" exploits sympathetic vibration to dislodge vocal timbre from the "black-sounding" body, thereby refusing self-disclosure. In the Boston concert hall, when men and women "dark in hue, and neatly dressed in quiet evening clothes," file onto the stage, the "old abolitionists in the vast audience felt the blood leave their faces beneath the stress of emotion." The scene continues:

> The opening number was "The Lord's Prayer." Stealing, rising, swelling, gathering, as it thrilled the ear, all the delights of harmony in a grand minor

cadence that told of deliverance from bondage and homage to God for his wonderful aid, sweeping the awed heart with an ecstasy that was almost pain; breathing, hovering, soaring, they held the vast multitude in speechless wonder.

Thunders of applause greeted the close of the hymn. Scarcely waiting for a silence, a female figure rose and came slowly to the edge of the platform and stood in the blaze of lights with hands modestly clasped before her.... There fell a voice upon the listening hear, in celestial showers of silver that passed all conceptions, all comparisons, all dreams; a voice beyond belief—a great soprano of unimaginable beauty, soaring heavenward in mighty intervals.

"Go down, Moses, way down in Egypt's land, Tell ol' Pharaoh, let my people go," sang the woman in tones that awakened ringing harmonies in the heart of every listener.

"By Jove!" Reuel heard Livingston exclaim. For himself, he was dazed, thrilled; never[,] save among the great artists of the earth, was such a voice heard alive with the divine fire.

Some of the women in the audience wept; there was the distinct echo of a sob in the deathly quiet which gave tribute to the power of genius. Spellbound they sat beneath the outpoured anguish of a suffering soul. All the horror, the degradation from which a race had been delivered were in the pleading strains of the singer's voice. It strained the senses almost beyond endurance. It pictured to that self-possessed, highly-cultured New England assemblage as nothing else ever had, at the awfulness of the hell from which a people had been happily plucked.[118]

At the outset of the performance, sonic activity—*stealing, rising, swelling, gathering, thrilled, told, sweeping, breathing, hovering, soaring,* and *held* crowd a single sentence—undercuts the ethnosympathy displayed by the "old abolitionists." The "improvisational and interactive" event transforms the concert hall into a "terrain of exchange and struggle" between the "pleasures of the performative agent" and the "engaged yet disconcerted spiritual pathos of the audience," as Brooks persuasively argues.[119] Shifting emphasis from the "heartbreaking" melancholia of black performance to the "spectacle of white ethnosympathy for suffering and black art," the scene privileges the "complexity of the black performative *experience*" over the complexity of black music—the "grand and impossible intervals" first described by the narrator.[120] The Fisk Jubilee Singers are not passive objects of the audience's sympathy but instead active performers for their own pleasure (and for the funding of Fisk University). Nor do the listeners passively receive the "innate" sorrow of the slave spirituals; they are as actively engaged as the singers in the production of the music and the meaning thereof. The acoustic interaction between singers and listeners does not entirely flatten the racial power dynamics, but it does expand the "performance" of black interiority beyond pathos and into the domain of pleasure.

This fictive performance signals what might be called *ethno*sympathetic vibration, by which I mean a musical practice that uses acoustic resonance to pressure ethnosympathy's play of power. Hopkins uses sympathetic vibration to counter the racial timbre embedded in ethnosympathy. If, as Dwight argued, music transforms sympathetic vibration from a physical fact into a spiritual one—an emotional as well as physical resonance between two vibrating bodies—then the "spiritual fact of music" infuses the jubilee concert, as the "soul" of the singers vibrates with the audience's "soul." In the material exchange of emotion between singers and listeners, the "harmony in a grand minor key" that "falls upon" the "listening ear" resounds in the audience's "weeping" and "sobbing." Dianthe's classical singing voice is especially resonant, as it "soars heavenward in mighty intervals," which causes the audience to match that frequency through their heightened feelings of "awe," "wonder," and "ecstasy." African American music unlooses the "New England assemblage" from its "self-possession." The soprano sings in "tones that awakened ringing harmonies in the heart of every listener," like a glass that has shattered itself in sympathetic vibration with an opera singer's high voice. Shifting from object to action, the "pleading strains" of Dianthe's voice "strain the senses" of shattered listeners like Reuel, who is ecstatically "beside himself." The audience's emotional "ringing" represents the "spiritual fact" of music that answers to its "physical fact." Manipulating the resonant and non-localizable body of sound, the singers transform race from a rigid "being" into a being-in-between.

Here, then, black musical acoustics enacts a vibratory sympathy that counteracts cross-racial ethnosympathy. By staging auditory experience as a dynamic relation between two elastic bodies—the singers as generators, the audience as resonators—the Boston concert hall scene transforms African American music from mere "folk" song into an artful activity that undercuts the racial politics of emotional sympathy. The singers, in short, engineer acoustic resonance to free black interiority from the burden of authenticity that their vocal timbre is forced to carry. When, later, Dianthe gives a private performance of the slave spirituals in the home of Reuel's friend Molly Vance, her voice is described as "beyond belief" and "alive with divine fire"; it draws white women like Molly into "an irresistible bond of sympathy."[121] These sympathetic vibrations set in motion a series of sonic vibrations that thwarts ethnosympathy but equally if not more importantly leads to "the formation of a Pan-African community capable of collective resistance and change."[122]

The forming of this diasporic community is a far from secular affair. Following a series of sensational events (some of which include: Dianthe dies in a train wreck while in the employ of a mesmerist; Reuel uses animal magnetism to bring her back to life; she suffers amnesia, but Reuel does not remind her that she is black because he wants to marry her), Dianthe slowly finds her way back to singing and, by extension, back to her blackness. When the newlyweds visit a friend's house, Dianthe sits down at the piano and intuitively begins singing "Go Down, Moses."

> Scarcely was the verse begun when every person in the room started suddenly and listened with eager interest. As the air proceeded, some grew visibly pale, and not daring to breathe a syllable, looked horrified into each other's faces. "Great heaven!" whispered Mr. Vance to his daughter, "Do you not hear another voice beside Mrs. Briggs?"
>
> It was true, indeed. A weird contralto, veiled as it were, rising and falling upon every wave of the great soprano, and reaching the ear as from some strange distance. The singer sang on, her voice dropping sweet and low, the echo following it, and at the closing word, she fell back in a dead faint. Mr. Vance caught her in his arms.
>
> "Mrs. Briggs has the soul of an artiste. She would make a perfect prima donna for the Grand Opera," remarked one man to Molly.[123]

Dianthe's performance delivers the "audibility of slave resistance" and sets her on a journey toward assuming the "role of mystic performer" in the novel's "vision of New Negro transnational identity."[124] Indeed, her song moves not only the audience but her unconscious black self as well. Resonating through Dianthe's elastic body, sympathetic vibration is a utopian mode of connection. It reconfigures kinship, typically organized around blood, as a "mysterious mesmeric affinity," in Hopkins's words.[125] In short: sympathetic vibration turns black kinship into a transpersonal mode of consciousness.

As a spirit medium and virtuosic singer who embodies the spiritualist potentiality of the slave spirituals, Dianthe is a doubly resonant body. Every sonic vibration is a spiritual one too. The scene, literalizing the "spiritual function" that Helmholtz and music critics had ascribed to sympathetic vibration, suggests that blackness is not a fixed property but an occult consciousness vibrating across space and time. Her self is "another"; her voice is its own "weird" echo. That Dianthe's voice becomes in this scene contrapuntal—the highest (soprano) and the lowest (contralto) range of the classical female singing voice—bears out the resonance of black embodiment. When Reuel journeys to Ethiopia and discovers there the hidden city of Telassar, Dianthe's generating contralto finds its resonator in the Ethiopian queen Candace, whose "flute-like voice" Reuel mistakes for Dianthe's. Through the vibration of her voice between high and low frequencies, Dianthe connects with her African sister/self. A vehicle of transport to Telassar, where the "well-known tones of [her] voice" communicate to Reuel and seem "ever calling to him through space," sympathetic vibration dislodges vocal timbre from the body, pushing Dianthe's hidden self beyond itself and toward a transpersonal consciousness that can reassert kinship ties.[126] Remade into a spiritualist practice, the slave spirituals present vocal timbre as the "unclassified residuum" of musical sound—which is to say, the racial excess rather than the racial essence of auditory experience.

Dianthe's contrapuntal voice spiritualizes the mechanics of sympathetic vibration. It engenders a transpersonal black consciousness that connects her not simply to her black self but to her black family. Sympathetic vibrations connect generations of generators and resonators, of daughters and (fore)-mothers. When held captive in Aubrey's southern home, for instance, Dianthe seeks out her grandmother Aunt Hannah, the "most noted 'voodoo' doctor or witch in the country," to help her kill Aubrey. As she treks through the woods, "a low sound, growing gradually louder, fell upon [her] ear; it was the voice of the old woman crooning a mournful minor cadence, but for an instant it set a chill about the girl's heart. It was a funeral chant commonly sung by the Negroes over the dead. It chimed in with her gloomy, despairing mood and startled her." Much like the white listeners at the jubilee concert, whose hearts "ring" with Dianthe's voice, here Dianthe "chimes" with the chant's "minor cadence." The "peculiar" sound—vocal timbre—reconnects the two women and, in turn, connects them to their ancestors. When, after Aubrey makes Dianthe drink the poison she had intended for him, she hears on her deathbed "strains of delicious music, rising and falling in alternate cadence of strong martial measure, floating in waves of sound down the corridor."[127] Aunt Hannah's "low" voice grows "gradually louder," and so too does the volume of the funeral chant:

Louder it grew, first in low and wailing notes, then swelling, pealing through arch and corridor in mighty diapason, until the very notes of different instruments rang out as from a vast orchestra. There was the thunder of the organ, the wild harp's peal, the aeolian's sigh, the trumpet's peal, and the mournful horn. A thousand soft melodious flutes, like trickling streams upheld a bird-like treble; whilst ever and anon the muffled drum with awful beat precise, the rolling kettle and the crashing cymbals. . . . Louder and yet more loud the music swelled to thunder! The unseen mass must have been the disembodied souls of every age since Time began, so vast the rush and strong the footfalls. And then the chant of thousands of voices swelling in rich, majestic choral tones, joined in the thundering crash. It was the welcome of ancient Ethiopia to her dying daughter of the royal line.[128]

The extended description of the funereal orchestration—its *low and wailing* notes; its *swelling, pealing* and *mournful* timbre; its *diapason*, or burst, of harmony; the *peals* and *sighs* of various instruments; its rhythmic beats—rebuts general attitudes that harmonic music is a European aesthetic. Hopkins exploits sympathetic vibration to assert a bidirectional correspondence between Aunt Hannah's morose sorrow song and the mystical "birthplace" of civilization, populated by the "souls of every age since Time began." The ancient collective chant of "thousands of voices" responds to and amplifies the conjure woman's solo "Negro" chant. Dianthe's death becomes a moment of high performance that displaces the ethnosympathetic reduction of the sorrow songs to black melancholy with a musical system that makes a voluble pan-African claim to ongoing liveness.

The rich complexity of African American music, its multilayered tonal arrangement and diversity of instrumentation, instantiates a heterogeneous cultural identity formation. Traces of this heterogeneity appear in Reuel's association of Ethiopian music with the song of "Venetian gondoliers, possessing as it did the plaintive sweetness of the most exquisite European airs. There was generally a leading voice answered by a full chorus." And when Dianthe recalls her "hidden" African American identity upon singing "Go Down, Moses," she simultaneously recalls her classical training, her "intimate companionship with Beethoven, Mozart, and Hayden [sic]."[129] The entangled lineage of African and European music is clearest in the orchestral performance that accompanies Dianthe's death. After taking in the "vast orchestra" and its choral accompaniment, she cries:

"I see them now! The glorious band! Welcome, great masters of the world's first birth! All hail, my royal ancestors—Candace, Semiramis, Dido, Solomon, David and the great kings of early days, and the great masters of the world of song. O, what long array of souls divine, lit with immortal fire from heaven itself! O, let me kneel to thee! And to thee, too, Beethoven, Mozart, thou sons of song! Divine ones, art though come to take me home?"... The pageant passed, or seemed to pass, from her whose eyes alone of all the awe-struck listeners, with mortal gaze beheld them. When, at length, the last vibrating echoes of the music seemed to die away in utter vacant silence to the terrified attendants, Dianthe still seemed to listen.[130]

Composed of the ancient kings and queens of Western civilization as well as European composers of "modern" harmonic music, the "glorious band" is an ensemble coextensive with the jubilee concert that had put Dianthe and Reuel in each other's orbit. No longer a performer but a listener, Dianthe is animated by the "vibrating echoes of the music" even as it—and she—"dies away." The orchestral funeral chant does not flip so much as dismantle the ethnosympathetic script rehearsed in the jubilee concert. Corresponding to the monogenetic theory advanced by the novel, the "glorious band" and its ancient instruments, from organ to flute, manifest shared aesthetic ancestry. Black music directs its past toward the establishment of a physically and geopolitically decentralized but spiritually unified civilization that, as with Bellamy's utopia, comprises psychically porous yet racially distinct subjects.

The novel's radical rethinking of racial subjectivity by way of psychophysical acoustics, however, is at least partly limited by its insistent appeal to biological essentialism as a principle of social reordering. Even as her utopia diverges from Bellamy's by constructing "a discourse around blood and purity that stands as a response against racialists of previous decades," *Of One Blood* nonetheless joins *Looking Backward* in advancing the notion of blood "as the basis for racial superiority or bland social harmony."[131] Hopkins frames harmonic music as a medium of psychical commonality between "ancient" Africa and "modern" America, but implies that marriage among the "talented tenth" is the only way to protect black life. Although *Of One Blood*'s matrilineal kinship ties unspool *Looking Backward*'s vision of universal brotherhood, the two novels cleave to fantasies of racial purity. Hopkins agrees with Bellamy's eugenic feminist argument that patriarchy hinders sexual selection by hampering women's innate desire to select the sexual partners likeliest to provide "fit" offspring. The difference is that Hopkins homes in on slavery as the patriarchal source of sexual selection's perversion. It is not simply that slavery prohibits black women from selecting male "mates," but that it allows white men, their owners, to rape them; slavery is an institution that, well after its abolition, engenders mixed-race children. The novel's biologism is readily apparent in its incestuous plotline: the revelation that married couple Reuel and Dianthe are siblings (children of slave Mira and her master, Aubrey Livingston Sr.) and that Aubrey is their brother as well. In the same way that *Looking Backward* concludes with a quasi-incestuous marriage between Julian and his "could have been" great-granddaughter, *Of One Blood* concludes with Reuel's marriage to his sister-wife's African double, Queen Candace. This plot development is incest without incest: a way to ensure racial purity without committing social taboos. Candace may not physically be Dianthe, but she represents a sibling affinity that otherwise reproduces slavery's genealogical corruptions. *Of One Blood* effectively pushes monogenesis to its logical ends: if we are all of one blood, then all sex is incestuous. The marriage of African American royalty (Reuel) to African royalty (Candace) evacuates incest of its impurities while securing the futurity of the black race.

Although Dianthe is a tragic mulatta, doomed to die so that racial purity and progress might be secured, her exceptionally sounding body—connecting "real" and occult worlds, modern and ancient civilizations—acts as a conduit for this progress. The social and familial possibilities of resonance are specific to the *female*-sung slave spiritual because it manifests the evolutionary development of the race. According to an *Atlantic* essay, "Parlor Singing" (1869), "as any race of mankind is cultivated and civilized, the difference in the physical power of the two sexes is widened," which is why, although there is "a twang peculiar to the race," when "I heard a negro man and a negro woman singing together, and, as I did not see them, I could not determine whether the duet was performed by two of the same sex or otherwise."[132] According to this logic, black men and women sound alike because they are less evolved, less sexually differentiated. *Of One Blood* takes pains to resex the black woman's voice, as Dianthe's soprano and Candace's flute-like voice reverse the Western-facing and forward-facing "course of empire" by reasserting kinship ties. Black women's vocal timbre acts as a creative reservoir for channeling past glory toward a more promising racial future. Indeed, the echo of Dianthe's virtuosic performance of "Go Down, Moses" can be heard in the "Harp of David" advertisement that accompanied the novel's serialized installments in 1902 and 1903 (figure 2.2). By drawing on the biblical iconography of the harp—an instrument associated with Judeo-Christian worship—the ad-

FIG. 2.2 "Harp of David" advertisement in *Colored American Magazine*, November 1902.

vertisement secures the sacred nature of harmonic music. Within the pages of *Colored American Magazine* (the magazine's cofounder, Harper S. Fortune, was a trained violinist), it encodes the sacred nature of racial uplift, signaled by the woman harpist whose apparent whiteness sanctions the respectability of black musicianship. In this way, musicianship becomes an aesthetic mechanism of black womanhood.

The harp's "tone quality" and its "embodiment of Perfect Harmony" aligns timbre and harmony with white femininity. The advertisement thus underscores the utopian change in consciousness that musical acoustics and aesthetics can serve to effect. And by indexing an enslaved civilization—the Old Testament being central to the slave spirituals—within the pages of *Colored American Magazine*, it partakes of an African American tradition of "appealing to biblical and classical sources both to challenge exclusive Euro-American claims to a Greco-Roman heritage and to advance the notion of African and Asian civilizational precedence."[133] The citation of biblical antiquity, in other words, buttresses Hopkins's case—or rather, Hopkins's novel helps to recontextualize the advertisement by elaborating on the black musical aesthetics that underlie the white woman's musicianship. Presented alongside *Of One Blood*, the advertised harp becomes an instrument of black respectability and, at the same time, a site of black origination. It also joins *Of One Blood* in suggesting the difficulty of ensuring the continuation of black royalty without racial intermingling—a difficulty glimpsed in Reuel's description of the descendants of the ancient African civilization as "ranging in complexion from a creamy tint to purest ebony," with hair that varies in texture from "soft, waving curls to the crispness of the most pronounced African type."[134] Pure blood is an impossibility even in utopia; life in the hidden city, even though fortified by incestuous attractions, is never entirely cloistered from the traumatic afterlife of slavery. What remains and what retains the potential for living otherwise are the sympathetic vibrations, the "embodiment of Perfect Harmony," activated by the "unclassified residuum" of Western acoustics: vocal timbre.

....

In the utopian fantasies that flourished in the Progressive era, psychophysical acoustics helped remodel kinship as transpersonal consciousness, as a feeling labile enough to bring people into attachment across time and space while simultaneously securing the supremacy of racial civilizations. The transcendent solidarity that the resonant "body" of sound makes possible remains perpetually crosscut by the eugenic discourses reasserting racial purity. These metaphysical and eugenic impulses—one directed toward pure being, the other toward racially pure being—remain in fruitful if irresolvable tension. *Looking Backward* and *Of One Blood* experiment with psychophysical acoustics to imagine how subjects might open up to each other without negating the hereditary principles that order them. But whereas *Looking Backward* looks forward to the white supremacist future secured by sexual selection, *Of One Blood* looks backward to the African "cradle of civilization" as a blueprint for renovating the present. In these divergent yet not dissimilar texts, musical sound and sensitive ears constitute an entry point into the mystical world soul necessary for above-threshold experiences of idiomatic social harmony. As such, they extend psychophysics by delineating the alternate worlds in which mind and body become entwined but never reducible to each other. In this fashion, literary utopian experiments parlayed psychophysical acoustics into modes of sexually selective hearing and timbral vibration that forge universal connectedness without forgoing racial particularity.

Oriented around the hearing ear, psychophysics helps account for the conservatism of progressive utopias, specifically the reliance on biology as a basis of social order. In Eidsheim's analysis of twentieth- and twenty-first-century musical practices, she provocatively argues that the key modality of sonic experience is not audition (hearing) but vibration (movement). The study of sound through physical acoustics (vibration) rather than physiological acoustics (audition) denatures racial identity, specifically the idea that a person's race is encoded in the tonal quality of their voice. Defining sound as "a vibration of a certain frequency in a material medium rather than [as] vibrations in the ear" also denatures the link between sound and hearing—highly important given the long history of deafness as the impetus and occasion for sound technologies (most notably Bell's telephone) that benefit the hearing.[135] While I agree with these scholars, it is worth emphasizing that however essentializing and ableist the oto-centric model of hearing is, the resonance theory afforded postbellum writers a new language for describing the metaphysical circuitry of social and historical progress. Grounded in Helmholtz's research, psychophysical acoustics underwrote wider efforts to turn musical experiences, which bring the perceiving subject into transcendent communion with others, into a mode of racial cultivation. Novels like *Looking Backward* and *Of One Blood* thus take their place within a broader *psychophysical aesthesis* that bridged the physiological laws and evolutionary principles governing the body and the psychical processes governing the soul.

Tone sensation, we have seen, historically has been tied to fantasies of race as a kind of impersonal structure of relation, constituted through the (sympathetic) interaction of differently sounding bodies. Psychophysics therefore has implications not simply for utopian fiction but more broadly for current theories of tone and other "low affect" categories. A sonic quality and a literary device, tone has been theorized as nonproprietary, as a circuit of action. Sianne Ngai's compelling analysis of tone as an "ugly feeling," for example, draws on Silvan Tomkins's theory of affect-as-amplification to argue that tone is an aesthetic category involving affective transference, translation, and interpenetration among bodies. Ngai usefully leverages acoustical terms such as resonance and feedback; her claim that tone is a "global or organizing affect" can in fact be traced back to *On the Sensations of Tone*.[136] In Helmholtz's discussion of musical aesthetics, he wrote, "The motion of tone surpasses all motion of corporeal masses in the delicacy and ease with which it can receive and imitate the most varied descriptions of expression. Hence it arrogates itself by right to the representation of states of mind, which the other arts can only indirectly touch by showing the situations which caused the emotion."[137] Music conveys no precise feelings but only "states of mind" that listeners necessarily interpret according to their own subjective experience. Rather than express love, music activates the ambient mood that might produce it. Attending to the sensory dimensions of literary tone helps us engage the materiality of a most diffuse and disembodied affect, this nonlocalizable feeling that "slips in and out of subjective boundaries," in Ngai's words.[138] Understood as the all-pervasive force field within which specifiable feelings come into being, tone constitutes the "unclassified residuum" of affect itself. Drawing on Hopkins in particular, we might speculate that contained within a psychophysical account of tone is the dream of a vibratory subjectivity organized around inflection rather than intentionality, amorphousness rather than agency.

{ INTERVAL 2 }

Notes on Scent

The Mizorans in Mary Bradley Lane's *Mizora* (1881) are not only known for their sensitive ears; they are known as well for their olfactory refinement. "The sense of smell was exceedingly sensitive with the Mizoran people," Vera explains. "They detected odors so refined that I was not aware of them."[1] With their psychophysical capacity to respond to and reflect on olfactory sensations, the Mizorans have surpassed Vera, herself limited to the mere physiological ability to receive olfactory sensations. Darwinian thinker Grant Allen had elaborated on this evolutionary distinction between what I call "sense ability" and sensitivity in *Physiological Aesthetics* (1877). He attributed the "low place of Smell in the aesthetic hierarchy of the senses" to the remoteness of the olfactory lobe from the cognitive faculties—hence the "relatively large emotional waves, and the relatively small intellectual information" the sense yields.[2] As a species evolves, it relies less on smell for survival. For civilized human beings, then, the sense "is a mere relic, which has outlived its principal uses," and thus "has come to be almost purely a source of pleasure and pain. This peculiarity helps to raise it almost to the aesthetic level."[3] Almost. Civilization evacuates the olfactory sense of any use value, thus freeing it up for aesthetic feeling. Yet because of its close ties to instinctive rather than reflective emotion, the sense of smell can never offer access to truly aesthetic feelings. Olfactory sensitivity, unencumbered by irrationality and corporeality, was the domain of the Mizorans—a utopian fantasy.

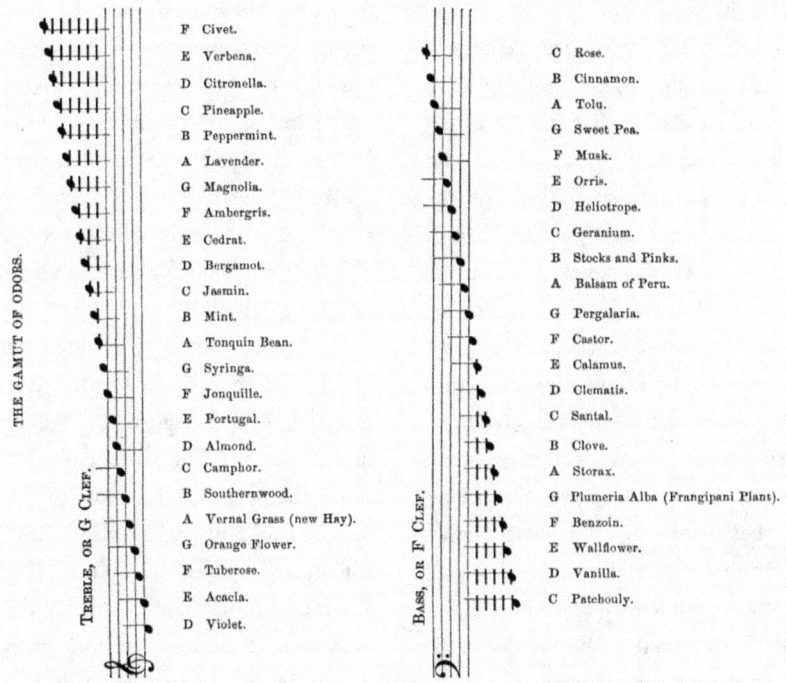

FIG. 12.1 Scent correspondence to musical notes. From G. W. Septimus Piesse, *The Art of Perfumery*, 3rd London ed. (1867).

Notable efforts were made to realize this fantasy by transforming the sense of smell into a medium of artistic expression. "Shall we take them [odors] up into the regions of science and art, and make them ... educators in the process of cultivating the imagination and refining the tone of society?" painter and poet C. P. Cranch asked in 1869.[4] One way to use odors to cultivate the imagination and refine society was by exploring their acoustical properties. Philadelphia perfumer Richard Cristiani claimed, "If refinement consists in the knowledge of the best mode of enjoying the higher faculties we possess, we must learn to distinguish the melody of perfumes."[5] The idea of melodic perfumes can be attributed to English perfumer G. W. Septimus Piesse, who in the third edition of his perfume manual *The Art of Perfumery* (1867) added a "gamut of odors," a schema that classified scents based on their correspondence to musical notes (figure 12.1).

The gamut of odors—Piesse's son Charles Henry Piesse renamed it *odophone*—expanded eighteenth-century naturalist Carl Linnaeus's taxonomy of smells from seven to fifty, and it attached each smell to a sound. The elder Piesse was the first to use musical terms like *note*, *chord*, *harmony*, and *progression* to name particular scents and combinations. "There is," he explained, "an octave of odors like an octave in music; certain odors coincide, like the keys of an instrument."[6] The purpose of the odophone was to produce more artful perfumes. "Perfumes blend harmoniously when combined according to a scale," *Scientific American* explained.[7] Charles Henry Piesse offered specifics. "On the odophone, santal, geranium, acacia, orange-flower, camphor, corresponding with C (bass 2d line below), C (bass 2d space), E (treble 1st line), G (treble 2d line), C (treble 3d space), constitute the bouquet of chord C."[8] Music furnished the system that authorized perfume as a fine art.

Over time, the odophone's synaesthetic correspondences shifted from the associative to the empirical. Belletristic nature essays by abolitionist Thomas Wentworth Higginson described the "air [as] perfumed music" and hands "wandering over the moss as over the keys of a piano, bringing forth odors for melodies."[9] But following Helmholtz's psychophysical acoustics, artists pursued more material links. "Smelling and hearing are essentially the same acts," claimed the *New York Times* in 1882. "Science has already succeeded in converting nearly every gas into a solid and nearly every solid into a liquid. We may, therefore, hope that it will in time succeed in converting smell, sight, and hearing from one state into another. We could then enjoy Wagner's music through the sense of smell, and could have it put up in small and dainty vials."[10] No one managed to convert Wagner's music into perfume, but "a sort of smell piano, or instrument for producing harmonies and contrasts of odors," was proposed more than once.[11] Avant-garde artists experimented with smell precisely because it activated both delight and disgust. The "scented harmonies" and "fragrant orchestrations" that Jean Des Esseintes invents in Joris-Karl Huysmans's 1884 novel *À Rebours* (*Against Nature*) exploit air as a medium that blends sound and scent. For the dramatic performance of *Salomé* (1893), Oscar Wilde initially planned to replace the orchestra with "braziers of perfume" that would emit scented clouds corresponding to particular emotions.[12] The odophone began as a conceptual device for authorizing perfumery but was reimagined as an instrument for delivering mood-altering aromas. It offered a model for cultivating aesthetic appreciation of smell but also inverted the sensory hierarchy, as artists valued the olfactory sense not despite but because of its primal link to the irrational, the emotional, and the extravagant.

Working within the symbolist tradition, poet, critic, and former secretary to Walt Whitman Sadakichi Hartmann devoted much time to experimenting in the olfactory arts. In the art journal the *Forum*, he wrote, "Smell is the most emotional of all senses in man, and is able to arouse sentimental [and] intellectual associations more swiftly than any other one, furnishing momentary reliefs from the prosaic duties of life and calling forth sensations of immediate and disinterested pleasure."[13] The problem with the odophone was that it did not accept scent on its own terms. The "Octophone [*sic*]" systematized odors in relation to "note[s] on the piano," but for "aesthetic experiments, [it] is of but little value. The affinity between sounds and odors is purely speculative."[14] For perfume to stir the imagination, its emotional effects had to be based on "the physiological characteristics of smell itself" rather than borrowed from another art. Aesthetic possibility lay in the composition and behavior of odor molecules: the "moment of contact with an odor is always the acutest one," the "most persistent smells become imperceptible to the olfactory surface after a few minutes' exposure (contrary to the visual and aural sensibilities)," and different odors are "subject to their specific gravity and the prevailing motion of the air."[15] The success of perfume concerts would depend on the relation between quality and duration as well as between the medium and motion of air, which affects felt intensity. Smell shared with music the potential to excite mental impressions but its physical "acoustics" had yet to be properly harnessed.

To prove that the "sense of smell is capable of artistic and intellectual functions," Hartmann undertook a series of "private tests and occasional experiments" that formed the scientific basis of his perfume concerts. Adopting the methods of Fechner and Helmholtz, he quantified olfactory sensitivity by spraying scents into the air at regular intervals. "By various experiments I found that it was impossible to distinguish clearly a succession of ten or eleven perfumes, produced at intervals of two minutes each." Based on his findings, Hartmann composed a perfume melody that would inspire a distinct series of mental images, "analogous to a 'musical thought.'"[16] A succession of juniper, civet, violet, strawberry, new-mown hay, and crabapple "readily suggested a stroll in the woods." Another series of "peau d'espagne, incense, patchouli, and carnation" failed to convey his operatic idea of "some Carmen kneeling in the darkened aisles with red carnations in her hair" because it was "too subtle and too literary a conception to be conveyed by odors." To physically convey such stories or mental pictures, Hartmann used a system of giant electric fans that swept currents of air across large perfume-drenched cheesecloths and out into the auditorium. He then practiced these sequences under "different conditions of ventilation," with friends placed around the auditorium shouting "Now!" the moment they perceived the scent.[17] A psychophysical practitioner himself, Hartmann used physics to test scent's potential to be "revelatory in an abstract or figurative way, evoking certain moods or ambiences, existential states and intuitive, pre-lingual understandings."[18]

These experiments developed into a smellscape that could convey the unique character of place. In 1902, Hartmann composed *A Trip to Japan in Sixteen Minutes*, featuring a succession of eight scents: "White Rose, to suggest the departure from New York, large bunches of roses brought to the steamer to the departing tourists; Violet told of a sojourn on the Rhine; Almond of Southern France; Bergamot of Italy; Cinnamon of the Orient; Cedar wood of India; and the Carnation of the arrival in Japan."[19] Using scent to transport subjects to foreign inner worlds (memory and desire) and to foreign outer worlds (the Orient, India, Japan), *A Trip to Japan* spectacularly entwined the individual and cultural mediation of smell. In September of that year, the *Times* announced that Hartmann, "an aesthete and an odorist," planned to "excite impressions on the human mind" with the "perfumes of Japan worked into a song" while "soft Japanese airs [are] played and a geisha girl dances."[20] A month later, it exclaimed, "The training of the Public's nose has begun! . . . Any Nose that pays for his, her, or its seat will be wafted from New York by successive puffs of perfume until . . . arrival in Yokohama, no matter in what region that dull clod the body may have been left behind!"[21]

The perfume concert doubled as a "magic carpet ride" fueled by Orientalist codes of olfactory signification. Born in Japan, raised in Germany, and later naturalized as a U.S. citizen, Hartmann artistically exploited his racial ambiguity. In his unpublished memoir, he wrote of embracing both his identity as "Eurasian" and the Western appreciation of Japanese aesthetics in order to fashion himself into "a kind of living impression of this sentiment."[22] Affirming the function of Orientalism as a burden and an opportunity for Asian American artists, following Josephine Park, *A Trip to Japan* shows Hartmann participating in the aesthetic arts movement as a "native" representative of *japonisme*, the bold aesthetic style that the West associated with Japan.[23] As simulated "air travel" to a land of exotic pleasure, *A Trip to Japan* activated an inner smellscape that was distinctly Orientalist. The psychical world to which it transported audiences was as touristic as it was transcendental.

That was the plan at least. The perfume concert was, in Hartmann's words, "a complete failure."[24] Travelers did not get very far before disembarking; *A Trip to Japan in Sixteen Minutes* lasted four minutes, cut short by the jeers of the crowd. (In 2014 the Institute for Art and Olfaction saw through Hartman's composition by organizing a tribute performance, *A Trip to Japan in Sixteen Minutes, Revisited*.)[25] Hartmann blamed the sudden change of venue. After arrangements with the Carnegie Lyceum fell through, his concert ended up at the rowdy New York Theatre, following Edward E. Rice's Sunday night program of minstrelsy performers and the Rossow Midgets. The audience wanted "the vulgar tendency of a Sunday 'pop.'"[26] Instead it got an "effete man accompanied by two geishas using electric fans to waft the smell of flowers towards their seats."[27] The air as well thwarted Hartmann's plans. It was especially thick that night, having collected the crowd's tobacco smoke and the city's rainwater: "It was a rainy night with an unusual amount of moisture in the air."[28] The synaesthetic art fell short of training the public nose or revolutionizing the arts. If Hartmann's goal was to determine if perfume concerts can be "raised from an amusing, but rather expensive, parlor entertainment to a more popular artistic expression," he had his answer—although it wasn't the one he wanted. Hartmann insisted that the concert required an audience "of a more intellectual order," but he realized that the deeper problem was the subjective nature of the sense itself.[29] Cedar wood recalled to him "the moldering smell peculiar to houses which have remained uninhabited for years," but to another "the shipment of Oriental goods, and [to] another of a pencil factory in Long Island."[30]

By presuming that his highly personal associations were held in common, Hartmann towed the Kantian line of universal taste. But with smell, so tied to individual emotion and memory, universal feeling is an impossibility.

Regardless of audience or air, the perfume concert was a disaster because the sense of smell could not move beyond the personal to the impersonal world of disinterested judgment. When cultural critics Max Nordau and Irving Babbitt were not deriding color music as degenerate, they were mocking Hartmann's perfume concert as laughable at best and a social threat at worst. Denouncing aestheticism and "confusion in the arts," Babbitt asked:

> Can the same perfume be counted on to suggest the same vision to any two persons? This is the crux of the whole matter. In 1902 there was given at New York in the Carnegie Lyceum [sic] the first experimental perfume concert in America.... But any attempt ... to have a whole audience respond in a similar manner to olfactory suggestiveness is foredoomed to failure. It is likely to appeal not to the audience's sense of smell, but a far more wholesome sense—its sense of humor. And this I understand is what happened in the New York experiment.[31]

By privileging the sense of smell, the perfume concert defied Enlightenment rationalism and the evolutionary primacy of sight and sound. "If confusion has crept into the arts, it is merely a special aspect of a more general malady, of that excess of sentimental and scientific naturalism from which . . . the occidental world is now suffering," Babbitt remarked.[32] As its name implies, of course, *A Trip to Japan in Sixteen Minutes* was explicitly Orientalist. But Babbitt's screed shows that regardless of olfactory content or semantics, the perfume concert as such was implicitly "Oriental" because smell manifests the allegedly irrational, childlike, and emotional nature of East Asian peoples. From Babbitt's perspective, to blend sound and smell was to blend an advanced civilization with a primitive one. Perfume concerts "Orientalized," and thereby undermined the modernity of, the Occident. Nordau took a more alarmist tack, suggesting that perfume concerts set Western people back to their prehuman origins. Because of the vestigial status of the olfactory lobe in modern human beings, he argued, it is impossible for smells to awaken complex mental activity. "A 'symphony of perfumes' in the Des Esseintes sense can no longer give the impression of moral beauty" because it does not "inspire a man with logical sequences of ideas and judgments" and represents "an atavism going back . . . to the primeval period of man."[33] The aesthetic project of cultivating the primitive sense of smell was an atavistic one—a violation not simply of the laws of "moral beauty" but more pressingly of the "natural" progressive trajectory of humankind. To train the individual and public nose was not simply to dabble in the "Oriental" but to devolve.

As *A Trip to Japan in Sixteen Minutes* demonstrates, perfume concerts went the way of color music. Hartmann never staged another public performance, although he did orchestrate smell concerts as after-dinner entertainment. Such private performances advanced the "intrinsic artness of odour" by formalizing its mysterious affective potency.[34] Directly rebutting Grant Allen's Darwinian account of the *almost* aesthetic value of smell, Hartmann argued, "Smell is not a 'mere relic,' but, aesthetically speaking, an undeveloped sense, similar to the sense of hearing in those pre-historical times when monosyllabic chants were the only expression of music."[35] What began with a luxury perfumer's effort to legitimize scent by adapting it to the musical scale transformed into a series of experiments that yielded an affectively powerful correspondence between smell and sound. If people and populations could cultivate their sense of hearing over time and thereby progress from monosyllabic chants to complex harmonies, then there was hope yet for an outlier like the olfactory sense—though, as the next chapter reveals, the revaluation of smell was predicated on a crucial, if fragile, distinction between biological and chemical "essences."

{ 3 }

Smell

PERFUME, WOMEN, AND
OTHER VOLATILE SPIRITS

> At the pivotal point between the "outer" senses of sight and hearing, which rely on some outside stimulation, and the "inner" senses (taste and touch), which react in conjunction with the body, the sense of smell is ambivalent, neither one nor quite the other.
> —Annick Le Guérer, *Scent*

> Our sense of smell slides from knowledges to memory and from space to time—no doubt from things to beings.
> —Michel Serres, *The Five Senses*

When Sadakichi Hartmann performed his perfume concert *A Trip to Japan in Sixteen Minutes* in 1902, he endeavored to turn the olfactory sense into a medium of geographic and affective transport. "The delicate aroma of Magnolia blossoms will take us to the magnolia swamps on the Mississippi River. Rosemary conjures up in every mind, acquainted with New England scenes, an old homestead with its flowerbeds before the front porch," he wrote.[1] The concert's novelty was not simply the synaesthetic correspondence of sound and smell but the pastoral scents it featured. A glib *New York Times* reviewer wondered if Hartmann's "smell machine" might be put to more practical uses, such as converting the city's noxious odors into, say, bergamot. After all, anyone "who has ever wandered through the Gowanus Canal district of Brooklyn ... take[s] in at least half a dozen odors at once," from refuse disposal sites to "the bursting of a gas main in the vicinity of an eastside slaughter house."[2] However laudable Hartmann's intentions, the "smell machine" remained fairly laughable—an amusement unlikely to prevail over the olfactory plague visiting most U.S. cities. Indeed, one year later and 850 miles away, Atlanta congressmen led an "olfactory crusade" against workers. They proposed an ordinance that would allow train conductors to ban anyone from whom "emanates a smell offensive to any other passenger," especially those "who work in factories."[3] The para–Jim Crow ordinance did not pass but did suggest that what made industrial smells so threatening was less their disagreeableness and more their ability to cross color and class lines. In an environment newly populated by foul pollutants and working-class bodies acting as their "carriers," magnolia and rosemary offered a transient flight of fancy—a potpourri but not a robust vehicle for art.

Together, the would-be olfactory crusade and Hartmann's perfume concert encapsulate general attitudes about smell as a sensory experience to be both reviled and revered. The sense had long been dismissed as "an orphan and an outcast," as the "very pariah of the five senses," according to one of Hartmann's reviewers.[4] Kant, for instance, considered the sense of smell "contrary to freedom" because "taking something in through smell" is too ephemeral to provide a consistent stimulus of thought, thereby compromising the civilized subject's reason and will.[5] And its ephemeral character stymied empiricist protocols. "Until you can measure the likeness and the differences you can have no science of odor," Alexander Graham Bell declared.[6] Chemist Robert Duncan, in his book *The Chemistry of Commerce* (1907), added that odor "can be measured only by the nose," a device of "small utility as a quantitative measure of one smell as against another."[7] Unlike the optic and tonal differences analyzed by Helmholtz's ophthalmoscope and resonator, the nose can detect only qualitative differences. Because the nose is an imprecise instrument, *Harper's Weekly* observed, "physicists, physiologists, and psychologists are at a loss to account satisfactorily for the manner in which the sense [of smell] is excited."[8] Critic Henry T. Finck went further, lamenting in "The Aesthetic Value of the Sense of Smell" (1880) that "psychologists and physiologists have so persistently and universally undervalued and misrepresented the sense of smell that men have come to feel ashamed of having it."[9] Similarly, psychologist Joseph Jastrow's "A Plea for the Sense of Smell" (1886) in *Science* affirmed, "The division of the five senses into higher and lower has carried with it both a moral and an aesthetic implication. Sight and hearing have been the aesthetic educators of our race, yet at various times have attempts been made to rescue one or other of the remaining senses from the aesthetic degradation to which they have been consigned."[10] Having recently joined his mentor C. S. Peirce at the National Academy of Sciences to present on Fechner's psychophysical law, Jastrow well knew the lacuna in psychophysical research: olfactory and gustatory experience. The experimental study of embodied consciousness systematically ignored the senses that resisted quantification.

Too subjective even for the science of sense experience, the olfactory sense became the object of another experimental field: the commercial branch of chemistry known as perfumery. In the eighteenth century, chemistry "evolved out of alchemy to become an Enlightenment science," but perfumery—with its secret concoctions going back centuries if not millennia—retained an aura of mysticism.[11] Following Friedrich Wöhler's discovery of chemical reaction in 1828, perfumers began using chemical synthesis to make synthetic odor molecules. This development helped them remake their occult practice into a legitimate science. In keeping with the professionalization of the sciences, perfumer Hyppolite Dussauce declared in his manual *A Practical Guide for the Perfumer* (1868) that perfumery had freed "itself from the old beaten path of quackery," and that with "its present scientific character, it is worthy of the consideration and support of rational people."[12] The perfumer's goal was not to reveal universal truths but to use the "oppositional and affinitive power of chemical reaction" to monetize pleasure.[13] Once synthesis made olfactory materials cheaper and opened up the luxury goods market to the middle-class consumer, perfume became "a thing entirely of the present [nineteenth] century," according to the *Manufacturer and Builder*.[14] That perfumery constituted a commercial industry does not negate the fact that perfumers were, I argue, psychophysical practitioners: exploring the psychical, experiential, and even spiritual facets of olfactory sensation. Again and again perfumers sought to isolate and test out the immaterial emotions, memories, and desires that their products stimulated. However devalued smell was in the domains of aesthetics and the empirical sciences, perfumery made it a sense that the U.S. public could no longer afford to neglect.

Picking up where Fechner and Helmholtz left off, perfumers explored the correspondence between odor molecules and inner life. By this point, it was well known that odorous materials "emanating from bodies, and coming into contact with the olfactory nerves, produce the sensation of smell. Substances to be odorous, need, therefore, to be volatile to a certain extent."[15] This chemical volatility accounts for why "odors impregnate all bodies," Dussauce explained.[16] Volatile impregnation is, in today's critical parlance, a "transcorporeal" relation between the human world and the more-than-human world of molecules.[17] In fact, the transcorporeal interrelation of bodies and odors inheres in the word *smell*, which, as Holly Dugan points out, has a "linguistic reflexivity" that reflects the "material instability of olfaction."[18] *Smell* is a lexical Möbius strip that dissolves subject and object: as an intransitive verb, it refers to a body that exudes odor ("She smells like roses"), and as a transitive verb, it denotes perceiving another body's odor ("She smells the roses"). This transcorporeality and material instability, furthermore, operates at the level of affect. As Teresa Brennan has argued, "imbibing smells" is a mode of "affective transmission," a means by which we "feel the atmosphere or . . . pick up on or react to others."[19] To smell and be smelled is to affect and be affected. Or in Dussauce's terms, when odors impregnate bodies, they do so psychically as well as physically. "Who has not experienced the delightful sensation caused by inhaling a fresh breeze loaded with the spoils of the flower tribe? An indescribable emotion invades the whole being," Franco-English perfumer Eugène Rimmel wrote in his 1867 treatise *The Book of Perfumes*.[20] European and North American perfumers like Dussauce and Rimmel further tested smell's transcorporeal entanglements by harnessing the psychophysical correspondence between chemical and emotional volatility—between material scents and the evanescent feelings they catalyze.

Attuned to these correspondences, writers turned their attention to the risks posed by a sense that depends on "proximity, on chemical contact, [and] on physical infiltration."[21] They focused in particular on unnatural scents, especially those newly thickening the air: fetid industrial toxins and synthetic perfumes. In the late nineteenth and early twentieth centuries, Hsuan Hsu explains, foul pollutants were turning the air into "a biopolitical medium of life and death."[22] A genre known for its preoccupation with the environmental forces and irrational impulses that determine human behavior (decidedly for the worse), naturalism became an important arena for navigating this new biopolitical medium. What emerged in U.S. fiction were "naturalist smellscapes," following Hsu, that materialized the uneven effects of foul-smelling air—a sign of toxic matter—on different people and groups. Alongside and aslant these naturalist smellscapes, synthetic perfumes saturated the more cosmopolitan air of the fin de siècle city, the epicenter of "art for art's sake" symbolism and decadence. While unnatural toxins befouled the slums, urbane perfumers advanced a "desire to improve on nature."[23] They vaunted the art of their chemistry by creating synthetic scents that flaunted their status as concoctions with no link to nature. Take, for instance, the "*ur*-scene of synthetic poesis": aesthete Jean Des Esseintes, the antihero of Joris-Karl Huysmans's 1884 novel *À Rebours* (*Against Nature*), inventing a perfume that mixes nature and industrial waste, specifically jonquil and gutta-percha with coal tar.[24] Not the opposite but the obverse of the naturalist smellscape, synthetic perfume was an aesthetic commodity that turned the foul into the basis of erotic, imaginative, and mystical experiences. To be sure, social critics like Max Nordau considered those who revel in the dark beauty of synthetic perfume, who prefer "the odors of putrefaction to the perfume of flowers," degenerates.[25] Psychophysical paradigms underwrote this dialectical push and pull between decadent and naturalist accounts of smell: perfume as both an atmospheric spirit and a chemical material capable of arousing those feelings that insistently flirt with humanity's more primordial passions. Amid preoccupations with the mind's environmental entanglements, the psychophysics of smell suggested a human ontology beholden more to synthesis than to nature, more to chemistry than to biology.

Moving from the transpersonal consciousness generated by the resonant "body" of harmony to the transcorporeal affects catalyzed by manufactured "spirits," this chapter brings into focus the evanescent environments shaping consciousness at the turn of the twentieth century. With the rise of evolutionary accounts of smell (both the ability to smell and having a body that smells) as a "corporeal, animalistic, primitive, and therefore degraded sense," perfumery refashioned itself as an experimental science that, by studying the psychological component of the olfactory sense, could expand the reach of aesthetics.[26] This systematic effort dramatically changed what perfume was and did: a scent that began as biological material derived from flora or fauna was remade into a synthetic chemical "spirit" that re-created nature and then, when perfumers began creating odor molecules that moved beyond or "against nature," a spirit meant to affect (rather than reflect) the world. By century's end, the purpose of perfume was not to cloak the body in nature but to activate people's inner nature—their deepest desires and memories. Perfumery was therefore fundamental to a particular kind of *psychophysical aesthesis*, one that sought to explore the full-bodied but short-circuited longings of white women and black men. With its artificial contents and increasingly abstract style, synthetic perfume became crucial to mediating the experiences of women whose sexual and economic freedoms were inseparable from the "recognition of all human life, public and private, as entailing an ongoing attempt to work with and manage the facts of our experience as embodied beings," in Jennifer Fleissner's words.[27] Tracking the relays between perfume and womanhood, Kate Chopin advanced a psychophysical aesthesis to describe the atmospheric currents that both sustain and constrain the New Woman.

Favoring an aesthetic sensibility "located in neither any one place nor any one self," *The Awakening* (1899) and "Lilacs" (1896) deploy olfactory pleasure to remake the air into a diffuse yet decisive medium of intimacy—one that floats illicit desires while failing to free women of a life that feels like a death sentence.[28] James Weldon Johnson's *Autobiography of an Ex-Colored Man* (1912), however, shows that these pleasures do not temper so much as temporalize the racial perils of detachability, as the unnatural but not artificial stench of burned black flesh forces an uneasy resemblance between pleasure and peril.

THE PSYCHOPHYSICS OF PERFUME

In 1869, writer and artist C. P. Cranch—best known for his playful depiction of Ralph Waldo Emerson as a transparent eyeball—issued "A Plea for the Sense of Smell" in *Putnam's Monthly*. As Joseph Jastrow would do fifteen years later in his own appeal in *Science*, Cranch bemoaned the devaluation of the olfactory sense. He did so through a startling, if timely, conceit:

> While Seeing, Hearing, Tasting, [and] Feeling are honored and privileged and educated, poor Smelling must . . . stand out in the cold oftentimes, like the servant of others, when he is fairly entitled to equal suffrage, and equal rights, privilege, [and] education. . . . The other four senses have clubbed together since Adam's fall, and formed a sort of oligarchy, and the fifth sense is like a third estate—nay, worse; he is in some respects treated as the descendants of Ham are treated by the Caucasian. And in spite of any declaration of independence, which declares him the equal of his brothers, he is laughed at or treated in silent contempt as an inferior. And yet the Nose is of the same color and blood as the rest of the family.[29]

Published during U.S. Reconstruction, "Plea" likens the denigration of a sensory modality to the ongoing denigration of an entire population. Despite their citizenship and equality before the law, African Americans remain outcasts. Likewise, the sense of smell is considered inferior to its sensory brethren. While this metaphor provocatively fuses sensory and social orders, nonetheless Cranch is making a plea on behalf of the sense of smell, not on behalf of African Americans. And in a strange twist, Cranch pivots from using African Americans to garner sympathy for smell to alleging that they will benefit from the aesthetic revaluation of smell. Only "after the African has moved forward to his rightful place in the scale of humanity; after woman has all that she needs to take her fitting place beside man in society . . . will the long-neglected olfactory be educated and mankind be lifted to new aesthetic heights by perfumes cultivated or created expressly for the age."[30] In this liberal fantasy of cultivation, training the olfactory sense yields a more democratic, egalitarian social order. Perfume, then, is an art and a civilizing project—a training device that by sensitizing the material and metaphorical "nose" will improve social relations.

The rhetorical slipperiness of Cranch's plea, moving between ethnological claims about African Americans and aesthetic claims about smell, neatly encapsulates the place of perfume in U.S. culture. Perfumers legitimated their work as a science by styling perfume as an engine of social progress. Perfume civilized people, they maintained, because it "sensitized" their primitive noses, stimulating finer reflections instead of base desires. Publicizing what perfumes do (civilize the masses) entailed explaining what perfume is: a chemical essence extracted from a floral or faunal body. Over the course of the century, this chemical essence served to mask the biological "essence" called racial odor, the idea that particular races have a distinct odor inhering in their bodies. Limning consciousness in the language of chemistry, perfumers offered a psychophysical account of smell that required ethnological and evolutionary discourses. The nineteenth-century transformation of perfumery into a culturally pervasive and commercially successful industry shows the sense of smell being remade or "uplifted" into an aesthetic experience—one that secured racial distinctions both by attuning the nose to fine gradations of scent and by transforming the human body into a barely perceptible olfactory spirit.

Because of smell's reputation as a bodily sense tied to instinct rather than to intellection, it was a sense that largely fell under the purview of physiology. In mapping out the inner circuitry of smell, German physiologist Julius Bernstein explained that olfactory nerves connect the nose to "the anterior portion of the cranium in a bulbous swelling, the *olfactory ganglion*, which is strongly developed in lower animals."[31] In this fashion, the physiology of smell supported evolutionary accounts of species change. That olfactory nerves lead to the ancient core of the brain (the *rhinencephalon*—literally "nose brain"), which processes emotion and which rules "lower animals," validated smell as a sense bound to primitive animals. As a result, the main practitioners of psychophysics never bothered with it. E. H. Weber, for instance, mentioned that "in many animals [it] seems much more acute than in man, because the membrane containing the olfactory nerves is much larger."[32] Fechner said only that we do not smell some "odorous substances in the air . . . because they are too diluted, yet the dog or the savage with his sharpened sense organ smells the trail which we can no longer smell, though we could smell it just as well, were it but stronger."[33] These dismissals are entirely the point. Smell is not worth studying because it is a savage "sense-ability," a strictly physical ability to receive olfactory sensations. In *Littell's Living Age*, English physiologist Edward Dillon argued, "The greater importance of the sense of smell to the lower animals than to man, and to man in past ages and remote countries than to the western European of the present day" explains why "in civilized man, this sense remains merely the vestige of a vestige," like an appendix.[34] As a species evolves, this Lamarckian account goes, it uses its nose less and less for survival, and thus its olfactory sense diminishes. Olfactory sense-ability proves the developmental belatedness of savages and the modernity of white people, for whom the outcome of evolutionary advancement is a weak faculty of smell. Conversely and tautologically, primitives—thought to represent "ancient" man—have a strong olfactory sense-ability because smell is an "ancient" sense.

Although innate, primitive people's olfactory sense-ability was not immutable. In physician William Ogle's clinical study *Anosmia, or Cases Illustrating the Physiology and Pathology of the Sense of Smell* (1870), for instance, he cites a case reported in 1852 about an enslaved black child who developed a white patch of skin that spread until it "extended over the whole external surface of the body: so that, but for his woolly hair, the body might have been taken for a fair European.... At the same time that the boy began to change his color, he also began to lose his sense of smell, and by the time he had become white, his smell was . . . completely lost."[35] The anecdote proposes that becoming visually "white" entails becoming nasally "white": anosmic, or unable to smell. Race is not merely skin color but sensory capacity. Far from a fixed biological determination, it is a designation subject to change according to acquired physical or pathological conditions. If illness or disability can make a savage person white, this medical case suggests, then so too it can make a white person savage. In "The Aesthetic Value of the Sense of Smell," Henry Finck stated, "It has been proved by repeated experiments that Indians and negroes can recognize persons in the dark by their odor, and tell what race they belong to. The case of Julia Brace, a deaf and blind mute in the Massachusetts Asylum for the Blind, shows that this power may be regained by the Caucasian, when it is needed."[36] In short, pathological conditions and environmental circumstances shape the human body's sensory capacities. Enforcing biological distinctions among racial groups while allowing for individual flux, smell was an animalistic sense that nonetheless revealed the plasticity of racial material.

With the cultural ascendance of ethnological and evolutionary accounts of human difference, olfactory sense-ability went "hand in hand with crudity."[37] Importantly, "the average civilized man," Finck stated, "has as yet no serious occasion for looking down on the savage for his indifference to noisome odors."[38] He further asked, "Can odors, like sounds and colors, be made to serve as the basis of an art?"[39] How, in other words, could civilized people's sense of smell be recuperated without sliding back down the evolutionary ladder? How can it be safe for white people to use their noses? According to Finck, Charles Darwin was onto something when he observed in *The Descent of Man* (1871) that a strong sense of smell among the "dark-colored races of men" does not "prevent the Esquimaux [*sic*] from sleeping in the most fetid atmosphere, nor many savages from eating half-putrid meat."[40] Finck further added that although in "savages the physical acuteness of the sense is very high the *aesthetic* sensibility is at the minimum, and accordingly they are indifferent to, or even enjoy, what otherwise must be repulsive to them."[41] If sense-ability names the raw physical ability to receive olfactory sensations, then *aesthetic sensibility* (Fechner called this "sensitivity") names the psychophysical capacity to discern the quality of olfactory sensations. In sum, a racial population is either sense-able or sensitive, depending on their biological development: people either can smell many odors but not discern their quality or cannot smell many odors but can discern their quality. Finck claimed the aesthetic value of the olfactory sense by splitting it into two inversely related parts: primitive sense-ability and civilized sensibility, or sensitivity. To become the basis of an art, the olfactory sense had to transform from unthinking sensation to finer feeling.

Perfume effected this transformation. An apparatus of sensitivity, it pushed the stubbornly material sense of smell beyond the body and into a more transcendent order of experience. Taking up Darwinian discourses, perfumers legitimated their olfactory products as products of civilization, on par with painting and music. "The history of perfume is, in some manner, the history of civilization," Eugène Rimmel asserted.[42] With chapters on "The Egyptians," "Uncivilized Nations," and "Modern Times," Rimmel's *Book of Perfumes* set perfume along a linear trajectory beginning with ancient rites and rituals and ending with the modern toilette. European and North American perfumers followed this teleological script. Part recipe collection, instruction book, and ethnology, the nineteenth-century perfume manual adheres to the following conventions: first, a lament that the olfactory sense is not taken seriously, then an encomium to the delicate and pleasurable olfactory sensations supplied by nature, and finally the affirmation of perfume as the apotheosis of evolution, an art "met with among all people possessed of any degree of civilization," in the words of English perfumer George Askinson.[43] In the preface to the manual *Perfumery and Kindred Arts* (1877), Philadelphia perfumer Richard Cristiani acknowledged that perfume is "practiced among barbarous and savage nations," but took recourse to Darwin in rationalizing that "to them a rancid smell may be the most pleasant."[44] More than the bearers of good taste, perfumers performed the crucial role of training the public in olfactory sensitivity, which would, Cranch and others hoped, further refine the species. An art that doubled as an engine of progress, perfume made the primitive act of smelling into a civilized activity. It allowed civilized white populations to use their sense of smell without risking atavism.

Within these racial discourses, critics sought to "psychologize" the physiological sense of smell by distinguishing between savage sense-ability and civilized sensitivity. Perfume was an engine of civilization at the biological level of population, but also an art at the chemical level of composition. In short, it was a transcendent body that stimulated transcendent feelings. "Let us be thankful to science that she has discovered a means of separating the rose's spirit from its leafy body, and securing for the former a stoppered immortality," a writer for *Harper's Monthly* stated.[45] The means of this separation was distillation, an age-old process that perfumers like G. W. Septimus Piesse meticulously described in their treatises. In the 1860s, *Scientific American* printed excerpts from Piesse's *The Art of Perfumery* (first published in the United States in 1857) that described the distillation process: "The odor of flowers is owing to a minute portion of a volatile oil being constantly generated, and thrown off by the plant. This perfume is termed an *essential oil* by chemists. When the flowers are distilled with water, the essential oil rises with the steam, and is condensed with it in the still-worm," and finally is combined with alcohol to form a concentrate called the "spirit."[46] Moving from solid to gas to liquid, distillation dematerializes then rematerializes an odorous substance or body. It is a process that extracts pure "essence" from the body producing it—and then discards that body. In the language of *spirit* and *essence*, distillation suggests that consciousness might be a chemical compound, embodied yet atmospheric. A liquid substance made all the more ethereal by its absorption of oxygen, perfume embodies the figure around which aesthetic feeling constellates: the pure inviolable spirit. By mixing chemistry with metaphysics, perfumers severed the olfactory sense from fleshy embodiment.

Perfume, then, made manifest the psychophysical dimensions of smell in two related ways: to smell perfume is to psychologize the otherwise physical sense of smell (sensitivity), and to wear perfume is to "spiritualize" the body, a kind of transubstantiation. *Essence* and *spirit* were not new terms; they have been defined since the seventeenth century as liquid extracts from substances obtained through distillation. What was new in the nineteenth century was the biological essence called "racial odor" that the chemical-cum-metaphysical essence of perfume now served to neutralize. With the rise of racial science in the eighteenth and nineteenth centuries, as Khalil Gibran Muhammad observes, body odor was added to "the holy grail of racial difference."[47] This inclusion began with Thomas Jefferson's assertion in *Notes on the State of Virginia* (1785) that black people "secrete more by the glands of the skin, which gives them a very strong and disagreeable odor."[48] In 1842, the *U.S. Democratic Review* similarly attributed the "strong and offensive smell of the African Negro" to their "peculiar secretions."[49] No longer something all human beings have, body odor was now a biological trait specific to primitive racial groups. "In nineteenth-century American culture, to smell bad was to exhibit invidious social inferiority," historian Peter Hoffer writes.[50] At century's end, a *New York Times* article on "racial odor" discussed the possibility that a "particular fragrance belongs to each of the races of mankind."[51] The racial odor attributed to African and African American people in particular was musk. "Musk odor ... most nearly approach[es] the odor of sexual secretions," English psychologist Havelock Ellis alleged, before asserting that the "smell of the negress is musky in character."[52] Whereas racial odor was a biologically transmitted essence locked within the primitive body, perfume was a chemically produced essence divested of the body, on par with the civilizationist narrative of scent that perfumers had spun. Racial odor made perfume appear all the more aesthetic—a spirit *of* but no longer *in* the natural world.

Perfume was promoted as a chemical essence, a bodiless scent, over and against the ethnological concept of racial odor. The last half of the nineteenth century duly bore witness to a dramatic change in its function and style. Up until this point, the most popular perfumes for men and women were those derived from animals (ambergris, civet, musk, etc.) because they were heavy enough to cloak body odor. But in the eighteenth century, alongside the emergent concept of racial odor, an "olfactive revolution" installed odorlessness as the bourgeois ideal, mainly through the implementation of hygiene codes and the deodorization of public space.[53] Animal perfume fell into desuetude. An odorless body needed no olfactory drapery; only those who had something to hide (moral licentiousness, poor hygiene, poverty, and so forth) wore animal perfume. And in any case, if the purpose was to telegraph one's odorlessness, then perfumes derived from animal glands were entirely counterproductive. Unsurprisingly, reporter Lucy Hooper declared in the *Ladies' Home Journal* that musk is "too powerful for European tastes at the present day."[54]

The new purpose of perfume was, paradoxically, to publicize the odorless (hence clean, respectable) body. What emerged was "a schema of perception based on sweetness," as historian Alain Corbin has argued, that invested floral perfumes—light, subtle, airy—with aesthetic value.[55] Insofar as the flower embodies "an arc between the material and immaterial," floral scents better fit the chemical term *spirit*.[56] By "setting the seal on the image of a diaphanous body that simply reflected the soul," they transform the wearer's body into one so fragile that it flirts with its own abstraction.[57] But equally if not more important are the disciplinary strategies floral scents require. The perfume wearer's body must already be odorless because otherwise pungent body odors or "racial odor" will overpower the light scent, and the perceiver must have a sensitive nose, attuned to the subtlest notes. The popularity of floral perfume thus instantiates a distinctly psychophysical aesthetics: the taste for the just-noticeable difference between odorless and scented air. To wear floral perfume is to become dematerialized into a "spirit" and thereby enhance the body's seeming universality. Floral perfume, a spirit distilled from the least material natural specimen, reconstituted whiteness as but the faintest whiff of embodiment—breezy.

Within this perceptual schema, floral perfumes took their place as the most aesthetic class of smells. In *The Toilet and Cosmetic Arts in Ancient and Modern Times* (1866), English chemist Arnold Cooley wrote that "musk, ambergris, and civet are obtained from the animal kingdom; but the aroma of none of these is comparable in sweetness and freshness to that of the rose, or in delicacy to that of the orange blossom."[58] Finck likewise asserted that "vegetable life" constitutes the "aesthetic treasures of perfumery."[59] Further, given that the "explosion of popular interest in flowers" in the nineteenth century buttressed bourgeois gender ideologies, to aesthetically elevate smell was also to feminize it.[60] "Floral femininity" emerged as a disciplinary practice that combined the true woman's purity and domesticity with the flower's simple beauty and implied fertility; it taught white middle-class women to "becom[e] a human flower for the aesthetic consumption of others," argues art historian

Annette Stott.[61] The angel in the house was also a hothouse flower. Whereas for centuries men and women had worn (animal) perfume equally, this "floralization" of the perfume market produced a highly gendered cultural sphere. Floral perfumes became objects of aesthetic consumption that identified the female consumer as herself an object of aesthetic consumption. In fact, floral femininity goes some way in explaining how Cranch manages in his "A Plea for the Sense of Smell" to transfer the burden of elevating the olfactory sense—thereby uplifting African Americans—to white women:

> The rose in a lady's hair, the bouquet she holds in her hand, the faint perfume of her dress, will carry one's thoughts not only to the flower garden and the conservatory, but to all the amenities of refined female society. She will move about among those of the coarser sex like the sweet south. She will bring with her everywhere a suggestion of refined culture and Christian civilization.... How can there be wrath and harsh words and brutal deeds in a room where flowers are breathing out the perfume which seem so naturally absorbed by woman that they may be called feminine, adding the last touch of beauty to her person by their odors as by their forms and colors?[62]

This schema advances the "myth of the perfumed sex," the belief that women naturally "smell of nothing stronger than the flowers with which they are associated."[63] If, according to magazines like the *Continental Monthly*, "the *soul* of the flower" is its "evanescent odor," then the perfumed sex is that soul.[64] For Cranch, white Protestant women *are* that evanescent odor—an odor extracted, more specifically, through *enfleurage*, a process whereby flowers too fragile for distillation are pressed into lard until their essential oils saturate it, yielding a pomade. Rose in hair, bouquet both in hand and in clothes: flowers impress the "lady" to the point of unctuous absorption. Remade into a distinctly "feminine mode of expression," perfume constituted white womanhood as a kind of chemical essence.[65] That it was now the "fashion for ladies to adopt some perfume, which becomes identified with them as surely as their favorite flower," according to the *Times*, reframes perfume as elemental rather than ornamental to bourgeois femininity.[66] Walt Whitman's *Democratic Vistas* (1870), for instance, exalts the "physiologically sweet" wife-mother whose "charm, the indescribable perfume of genuine womanhood, attends her, goes with her, [and] exhales from her."[67] At base, the perfumed sex is a means of differentiating bourgeois women from men while securing their whiteness: it directs body odor away from the biological essentialism of "racial odor" and toward the immaterial domain of chemical essence.

The twinning notions of racial odor and the perfumed sex were steeped in a perfume culture dramatically transformed by psychophysics. Now what mattered were the faintly sweet body and the sensitive perceiver capable of registering such fine-grained scents. Boston perfumer Frank Sanford Clifford's self-published novel *A Romance of Perfume Lands; or, The Search for Capt. Jacob Cole, with Interesting Facts about Perfumes and Articles Used in the Toilet* (1875) crystallizes this development, with the sense of smell operating as an agent of civilization because it was the basis of an art. Clifford's story is nominally about the efforts of the narrator, his unnamed wife, his sister-in-law Susie, his friend Brad Cole, and a French chemist named Jean to rescue a missing captain. But the search is really an ecotour of the global perfume trade. The narrator is a perfumer who wants to "make a collection of each and every kind [of flower], with a view of forming a conservatory, to study all the methods of extracting and manufacturing, and to obtain all new ideas about which would advance the intersection of the perfumery business and teach others the value and the benefits accruing from the use of perfume."[68] Their yacht, *Cynthia*, is outfitted with equipment for distillation: "an assortment of vials, a set of percolators and receivers, a small copper still, ... and bottles which were to contain samples of ottos, essences, oils, and extracts, that we expected to collect."[69] The purpose is not to collect but to extract resources from "perfume lands" in and around the Global South, places inhabited either by "light-hearted denizens" or "ferocious looking savages."[70] But crucially, neither the narrator nor the chemist Jean does the colonial work of "collection." Sally, an amateur botanist, does it. Considered a "ladylike pastime [fitting] the mold of acceptable activities for true women," botany was an amateur science for most of the nineteenth century.[71] Presented by Clifford as a mere female hobby, botany domesticates the imperial violence of the perfume trade, while the distilling laboratory aboard the *Cynthia* represents a "clean, rational space occupied by male scientists" that effaces women's labor.[72] *Romance of Perfume Lands* takes its place in a transnational brand of plantation fiction that maps the agrarian world of the "Old South" onto the Global South.[73] Acutely modern yet drenched in nostalgia, perfume is a civilizing project that papers over the violence of the trade's gendered and colonial infrastructure. Equally if not more important, the novel leverages the perfumed sex to tether the psychophysics of perfume—the transcendent spirit inhering in the flesh—to the evolutionary discourses of racial odor enshrining it.

The popularity of floral perfume was a matter of olfactory quality: a light and airy scent that spiritualized the body contra the heavy scent that enfleshed it. When in the 1830s scientists began isolating and reproducing the chemical structures of natural substances, the physical structure of scent became important as well. As perfumers began to use synthetic molecules in place of flowers too expensive to buy or too fragile to distill, Cranch issued a plea to women: wear perfumes that are not only "so subdued as to be just perceptible" but that also "suggest fields and gardens rather than the perfume-shop. . . . A naturally lovely character is better than a church-manufactured saint."[74] Transposed into a familiar debate about women's innate character, perfumes rooted in nature and those born of the laboratory alternately registered female docility and deception. Distilled perfumes have *terroir*, a unique quality specific to the plant (and place) from which it was extracted. The relocation of perfumery from the land to the laboratory deracinated scent. Perfumers now traded essence for mimesis; instead of capturing the "real thing," they replicated it. The *New York Times* article, "Chemical Perfumes," revealed that violet essence is actually an "extreme dilution of a constituent part of the oil of lemon and lemon-grass."[75] Thus, if the "soul of the flower resides in its perfume," as poet Edith Thomas declared in the *Atlantic*, then synthetic perfumes constituted a class of spirits with no soul.[76] Cheap imitations of nature, synthetic perfumes can "never yield the same pure and delicious fragrance as natural flowers and fruits. There is always a sickly tinge to their sweetness," declared science writer Grant Allen.[77] Within this context, and given the "growing tendency of American women to make use of perfumery," according to the *Times*, it was all the more imperative that women smell *of* rather than *like* nature, lest they too lose their essential purity.[78]

As major consumers of perfume, women were especially vulnerable to the risk of artifice that chemical synthesis posed. Unlike the simple floral essences extracted through distillation, synthetic perfumes are compounds that blend synthetic and natural elements. Some correlated this complex material structure to a more complex, hence more aesthetic, olfactory experience. Chemist Robert Duncan argued that a perfume "must have persistency of staying power; it must have intensity, and it must be superlatively agreeable. These qualities are obtained only by the most artful combination."[79] The one element fundamental to the staying power and intensity of these artful combinations was musk. The *New York Times* stated, "Musk is introduced much more than is generally known. It gives strength to a composite perfume, but after the more delicate scent has vanished it is objectionable to many."[80] Despite objections, musk was necessary to synthetic perfume because it is a *fixative*—a large heavy molecule that evaporates slowly and therefore can equalize the volatility of essential oils. Fixatives hold and boost the strength of light scents. As the last odor in a perfume to be perceived, the one lingering the longest after others have faded, musk gives floral scents the "body" needed to be just perceptible. Made possible by an animal scent—and one signifying a racially black odor, no less—synthetic perfumes were not as "against" nature as was supposed. Botanist Arthur Stace observed, "Scarcely anybody will acknowledge that he likes the smell of musk, but nevertheless the perfumers regard it as a principal source of profit."[81] Perfumers like Rimmel instructed women to avoid wearing synthetic perfumes because "these compounds generally contain musk."[82] The link between the chemical content of perfume and the biological content of the wearer is evident when, in William Dean Howells's novella *An Imperative Duty* (1891), "tragic mulatta" Rhoda Aldgate sends her white suitor Edward Olney a handwritten note that diffuses "a perfume which was instantly but indefinitely memoriferous" and that reflects a "young lady . . . so full of character, so redolent of personality."[83] Rather than reflect virtue, the scent artfully masks Rhoda's black ancestry. The purpose of musk is to chemically bind lighter volatile odors, but here it amplifies rather than fixes what Tavia Nyong'o calls the "mutable and even volatile category" of race.[84] By deracinating perfume, chemical synthesis de-essentialized embodiment; the racial odor at the base of perfume set floral femininity afloat.

A combination of floral and animal, natural and artificial materials, synthetic perfume contained not simply a chemical but a social volatility. By century's end, perfumers increasingly refused to hide their artificial and animalic ingredients. They instead exploited the raced and gendered entanglements of nature and synthesis, plant and animal, spirit and flesh, by abandoning fidelity to nature. Initially, chemical synthesis facilitated olfactory mimesis; Rimmel argued that the perfumer's goal is to "copy nature. He strives to imitate the fragrance of all flowers. . . . Is he not, then, entitled to claim also the name of an artist, if he approaches even faintly the perfection of his charming model?"[85] But as chemistry yielded odor molecules with no known equivalent in nature, perfumers started to create nonreferential bouquets. Citing a set of perfumes manufactured by Lundborg Perfumes, chemist John Snively wrote in *Harper's*, "Inventive art creates perfumes by compounding which are unknown in nature. Few persons at all familiar with perfumery

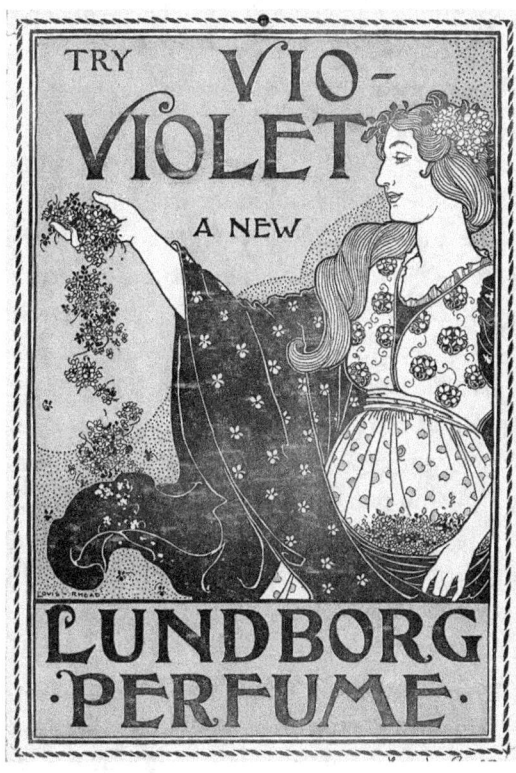

FIG. 3.1 Louis J. Rhead, *Try Vio-Violet, A New Lundborg Perfume* (1895). Color lithograph, 17 15/16 × 12 inches. Image copyright © The Metropolitan Museum of Art. Image source: Art Resource, New York.

are unacquainted with 'Jockey Club,' 'West End,' 'Mousselaine,' and 'Millefleurs,' which have no counterpart in the flower garden or spice grove. These bouquets have attained a popularity which has perhaps even exceeded the simpler odors."[86] Perfume houses such as Lundborg adopted an abstract style that staged the artifice of their materials—free-floating signs redouble free-floating synthetics (figure 3.1). Especially well known for their hybridity were Houbigant's 1882 perfume Fougère Royale (the first to use synthetic coumarin) and Guerlain's 1889 Jicky, a mixture of artificial (vanillin) and natural (amber), floral (lavender) and animal (civet) ingredients, meant to elicit both clean and fleshy feelings. These "decadent perfumes," as I call them, advanced a chic cosmopolitan style that fin de siècle artists and consumers embraced. And crucially, they were unisex perfumes, renouncing the myth of the perfumed sex by playing up the olfactory ambiguity between men and women. Neither extracted from the natural world nor seeking to represent it, perfume became an art of subjective experience—its new purpose to stimulate mood, desire, and memory. Decadent perfumes traded the simple refinement of floral extraction for the material intricacies and intimacies of abstraction, and in so doing remade the scented body into an evanescent atmosphere that unsettled without upending biological essence.

More so than others, Kate Chopin—with her evocative style and daring depiction of "sexual taboos in the name of delightful aestheticist pleasures"— merged perfume's new substance and stylization with the sexuality of the New Woman.[87] That Chopin's stories circulated alongside perfume advertisements in the new women's (and New Woman's) magazine *Vogue* rendered the "sensory impressions and erotic feeling" that she brought into "the purview of high fiction" indistinguishable from those activated by the synthetic commodity itself.[88] These sensations were both marketed to and constellated around the New Woman, a figure that emerged around 1890 to designate middle-class white women who pursued higher education, a career, and consumer ephemera and who either delayed or rejected marriage and motherhood; she plays the counterpart to the effete male dandy who spurns a life of productive industry for one of self-indulgent leisure. According to the era's social Darwinian logic, if evolutionary development leads to sex differentiation (physical differences between the sexes), then by hewing closer to masculine behaviors, the New Woman represents degeneration rather than social progress. This logic helps to account for why early reviewers praised Chopin's controversial novel *The Awakening* (1899) for its regionalist depiction of "the sensuous atmosphere of life in New Orleans" while denouncing heroine Edna Pontellier as an aesthete "confined entirely to the senses."[89] One reviewer compared the novel to British illustrator "Aubrey Beardsley's hideous but haunting pictures with their disfiguring leer of sensuality," adding that "when she writes another book it is to be hoped that she will choose a theme more healthful and sweet of smell."[90] The invocation of smell, albeit idiomatic, connects Chopin to Huysmans's antihero Jean Des Esseintes, the aesthete who invents perfume from coal tar. The crucial difference, though, is that the perfumes that Chopin invents do not call to the wildness of base human urges but rather materialize the Jamesean "wild facts" of the bourgeois woman's lived experience.

The Awakening arrives at several artificial perfumes by either extracting scents from nature or inventing them wholesale, and then compounding both into a scent that mediates bodies and saturates minds. (In 2012, *The Awakening* was adapted into a perfume, a "complex, unisex, warm, slightly sweet, but earthy fougère.")[91] Interested not in what perfume is but in what it does once the bottle is unstoppered, the novel charts the alchemical effects of perfume on bodily consciousness. Cultural historian Richard Stamelman explains, "Rubbed into the skin, a perfume blends with the odor molecules of the body; the combined fragrances of flesh and scent then vaporize into the atmosphere. Through the medium of perfume the body becomes an airborne essence.... Scent transforms the body into an altogether different, less substantial, more ethereal, and invisible incarnation of being."[92] Wearing perfume catalyzes a kind of mutual transubstantiation: the wearer enfleshes the perfume while the wearer herself evaporates, misty if not mystical. Attentive to this relay, Chopin's perfumes thicken the space between people; they produce affective environments that do not elicit pleasure so much as mediate illicit pleasures. *The Awakening* reroutes what Fleissner calls the New Woman's "stuckness in place," her inertia and inability to move forward, through the perfumed atmospheres that body forth desire, intimacy, and longing.[93] For even as the novel tracks the forward movement of Edna's "awakening" from a state of metaphysical slumber to one of wakefulness, it is an enlightenment that entraps, a birth of consciousness leading to bodily death. This awakened consciousness cannot be extracted from, but is also not wholly confined to, the body. As Edna's internal changes push her out of sync with Creole gender norms, scented atmospheres enflesh the air with her heavily charged longings. In its physical composition and ontological implications, perfume captures the paradox of the New Woman's stuckness: she is racially and economically privileged yet sexually oppressed, free to circulate but moving only in circles. And so by turning perfume into a *style*—a specifically decadent one—*The Awakening* limns the ambient pleasures and pervasive ambivalences of a life floated by certain freedoms yet held in abeyance, ever hanging in the air. With perfume now a synthetic material untethered to any particular person or place, the New Woman arrived as a figure defined not by her biological essence (floral femininity) but by her chemical volatility: those nonnormative desires detachable from but ever "fixed" by, and fixated on, blackness.

Chopin uses synthetic scents to deracinate intimacy, to make it a distributive rather than possessive relation. As such, *The Awakening*'s ambient zones of pleasure initiate multidirectional rather than bidirectional attachments. In an early scene when Edna joins her friends Robert Lebrun and Mme. Adèle Ratignolle on the beach at Grand Isle, she sketches Adèle, who had never "seemed a more tempting subject than at that moment, seated there like some sensuous Madonna." The picture, however, "bore no resemblance to Madame Ratignolle," who is "disappointed to find that it did not look like her."[94] The portrait refigures rather than represents its subject—as Mlle. Reisz's piano recital does later, a performance that "arouses" for Edna "the very passions themselves" rather than invoking "mental pictures."[95] Edna's portrait joins perfume in eschewing figuration in favor of provocation. Indeed, upon finishing the sketch, a "breeze soft and languorous... came up from the south, charged with the seductive odor of the sea."[96] The oceanic odor that moves among the three close friends redirects the circuitry of an already nebulous desire. It charges the air with triangulated seductions: Robert rests his head on Edna, who beholds Adèle, whom Robert had courted once. A kind of distributive intimacy is apparent as well when Edna and her husband, Léonce, join other couples in a walk along the beach. She inhales "strange, rare odors [from] abroad—a tangle of the sea smell and of weeds and damp, new-plowed earth, mingled with the heavy perfume of a field of white blossoms somewhere near."[97] Like the decadent perfume Fougère Royale, which used synthetic molecules to evoke the smell of hay, Chopin's salty-sweet-earthy bouquet condenses space and disperses mood. Irreducible to any one thing, it is a migratory agent that detaches and reattaches couples in novel assemblages, that stimulates just-perceptible intimacies by trading mimesis for osmosis.

Lacking an identifiable origin point, these hybrid scents offer an avenue for female expression by advancing an expansive diffusion of libidinal affect freed from its confinement in matrimony. Free-roaming scents redouble this promiscuous mobility, as when Edna visits Mme. Antoine's home on the Gulf Coast island of Chênière Caminada. In a pivotal scene of "awakening," just before Edna takes a nap, she lies on the absent hostess's bed:

> How luxurious it felt to rest thus in a strange, quaint bed, with its sweet country odor of laurel lingering about the sheets and mattress! She stretched her strong limbs that ached a little. She ran her fingers through her loosened hair for a while. She looked at her round arms as she held them straight up and rubbed them one after the other, observing closely, as if it were something she saw for the first time, the fine, firm quality and texture of her flesh. She clasped her hands easily above her head, and it was thus she fell asleep.[98]

Here, Edna's "firm" flesh resembles the "firm, elastic flesh" of the Cajun beauty Calixta in Chopin's story "The Storm" (1898); Calixta's body is likened to a "creamy lily that the sun invites to contribute its breath and perfume to the undying life of the world."[99] Like the lily, laurel emits a sweet country odor. But whereas the lily's sweetness materializes heterosexual desire, the laurel's does not. In fact, laurel does not even have a sweet country odor; it is a plant classified as a *chypre* (French for Cyprus), a family of high-end perfumes known for their mossy, animalic, and spicy notes. The unnatural scent of female self-pleasure emerges in the gap between laurel's fictive and factual odor. Duly enveloped by a synthetic scent that is and is not laurel, Edna becomes both the subject and the object of her desire. As such, the laurel cuts against another woman's supine body, this time splayed out on the marital bed: Adèle in labor. Sitting "on the edge of a little low couch next to the bed," she endures contractions that seize Edna "with a vague dread" and that recall "the heavy odor of chloroform, a stupor which had deadened sensation. . . . With an inward agony, with a flaming, outspoken revolt against the ways of Nature, she witnessed the scene of torture."[100] Figuring birth as against nature (*à rebours*), Chopin invokes an anesthetic that leaves the mind vulnerable in a way that shuts down intimacy. Both chloroform and laurel are soporifics, but whereas the latter suffocates women, the former lets them stretch. This olfactory juxtaposition reveals the ease with which the pleasures that travel under the threshold of consciousness transpose into peril: the woman unable to feel herself.

The unsettling conversion of female pleasure into female torture, in turn, suggests the ease with which life might shade into death. Once her own charged relations with men have faded, Edna realizes that she can only be a wife or a mistress, and that love, like perfume, is intoxicating but transient. Her life ends with the determination—perhaps spontaneous, perhaps not—to remain at sea. Swimming in the Gulf of Mexico, she "did not look back now, but went on and on, thinking of the blue-grass meadow that she traversed when a little child, believing that it had no beginning and no end. . . . Edna heard her father's voice and her sister Margaret's. . . . The spurs of the cavalry officer clanged as he walked across the porch. There was the hum of bees, and the musky odors of pinks filled the air."[101] The "musky odors of pinks" is an animal-floral hybrid that marks racial odor and floral femininity, respectively. Edna's father is, after all, a former Confederate officer who enjoys retelling "amusing plantation experiences."[102] But further, the musky pink collates the intangible configurations of sexual pleasure and the diffuse forms of racial contact that underwrite Edna's aesthetic awakening. "If perfume is connected to memory," critic Laura Frost writes, then "the reminiscences triggered by the new synthetics included the primal, the infantile, the bestial, and the excremental."[103] The musky pinks reverse ontogeny and phylogeny; Edna is infantile, Edna is primitive. Musk becomes a temporal knot that recalls the infant's "great blooming, buzzing confusion" of the senses, in the words of

William James, and resuscitates a slave past marked by the patriarchal clang of the Confederacy.[104] The musky pink duly gestures toward modes of intimacy that float rather than flee the violence that saturates postbellum social life.

But in addition, this scent's musky fixative retroactively assigns a "racial odor" to the quadroon who takes care of Edna's sons. One morning Edna stands on the veranda of her home after Léonce has left for work: "She inhaled the odor of the [jessamine] blossoms and thrust them into the bosom of her white morning gown. The boys were dragging along the banquette a small 'express wagon,' which they had filled with blocks and sticks. The quadroon was following them with quick little steps, having assumed a fictitious animation and alacrity for the occasion."[105] This scene typifies important claims that the function of black women in the novel is to affirm Edna's "class position and allow her to critique the sexual constraints associated with it."[106] Edna's whiteness is secured—literally, by affixing jessamine to her bosom, à la Cranch's fantasy of woman as enfleurage. She is the perfumed sex, whose naturally fragrant body is her very "essence." Even though the novel catalogs several racial types, perfume renders Chopin's racial schema a far more volatile than fixed configuration. Racial odor might enhance Edna's floral femininity; it might represent the exotic sexuality Edna seeks to appropriate; it might also be the unspoken yet potent force that binds the quadroon's "fictitious animation" to Edna's own fictitious "alacrity" for her maternal and wifely duties. The implied musk acts as the hidden fixative binding together the two reluctantly domestic women. As such, it paradoxically reveals the volatility of Creole racial configurations. Read with perfume's racialized substances, the jessamine scent turns racial particularity into a kind of atmospheric contingency; it dislodges the racial and gender forms that, under the signs of fixity and purity, are always available for consumption. By story's end, inhaling the musky pink, Edna has done more than absorb the quadroon's "impermeable selfhood"; she has sunk into it.[107] Her fixity, or stuckness, is materialized through the synthetic scents that mark diffuse relations, but it cannot help but circle back to essentialist notions of human difference. Embodied but not fleshy, atmospheric but not transcendent, the jessamine musk bouquet captures the pleasures and perils of being in between.

The Awakening transforms its sensualist potencies into a distinct style that registers the ineffable intimacies and contingencies surrounding the New Woman, whose desires can only take an evanescent form. Far from a stable index of race and gender, perfume acts as an affective force field that deracinates even as it differentiates bodies. But it also underscores the correspondences and crucial differences between the New Woman and another female type that Anne Anlin Cheng identifies in this era: the "yellow woman," adorned with orientalist ornaments like silk and porcelain. Cheng argues that Asiatic femininity is constructed through artificial materials, and that this "ornamentalism" reveals a "politics of human ontology indebted to commodity, artifice, and objectness."[108] Because of the New Woman's proclivity for decadent perfumes—synthetic scents that play up their artifice—she has an asymptotic relation to the "yellow woman." This proximity is further borne out in the East Asian artistic styles appropriated by the aesthetic arts movement (e.g., japonisme). As presented in Edna's atmospheric body, the New Woman exploits the artificial materials that constitute the Asian woman's flesh but shrinks these aesthetic commodities from the scale of the object (e.g., porcelain) to that of the molecule (i.e., perfume). The very being of the New Woman is a "spirit," and, further, one predicated not on thingness as such but on dissolving distinctions between things: between the animal (musk) and botanical (pink), the natural (laurel) and the synthetic (chloroform). Absorbed into the skin and carrying the body into the air, perfume constitutes the New Woman as an assemblage of detachable racial referents. After all, it is when smelling musky pinks, a scent operating at the nexus of the elemental and the ornamental, that Edna decides to confront the oceanic horizon of her own stuckness. In between the black woman's ontology of "musky" flesh and the yellow woman's ornamentalist ontology, the New Woman's olfactory ontology gestures toward the experiential and existential inertia that whiteness can lubricate but not fully dislodge.

RECURSIVE REMINISCENTS

Perfume creates new spheres of intimacy and, as Edna's final moments imply, of recollection. As Hyppolite Dussauce had written, the purpose of perfume is "to fix the most fugitive odor," to capture and contain living matter's fleeting scent by transforming it into a liquid substance.[109] Chopin's experiments with perfume, however, teach us that memory, like desire, is impossible to localize or fix. Time, after all, is a crucial element of the olfactory sense. The more we imbibe a particular smell, the more we fail to notice it. As the odor "impregnates" us, as Dussauce would say, we adapt to it, so that this external stimulus now appears entirely internal and, as a result, undetectable. This is the psychological effect of our physical entanglement with smells: the more we receive and respond to olfactory stimuli, the less sensitive to them we become. In psychophysical terms, duration sinks olfactory sensation below the threshold of consciousness. But, the musky pinks suggest, a countervailing force is at play as well with smell and time: olfactory sensations can resurface the past. Perfume activates not only mood but also memory. Indeed, when composing his perfume concert, Sadakichi Hartmann remarked, "The feelings aroused by odors alone are ... *reminiscent* in their effect.... The reminiscent impressions are infinite in their variety, are absolutely a matter of individual taste, and can in no way be analyzed."[110] Decadent perfumes circle around while circumscribing the New Woman, whose detachability marks her stuckness, but they also dramatize scent as a time apart—a reminiscent feeling that brings people into nonnormative structures of attachment. In an era of mass consumerism and industrialization, decadent perfumes commingled nature and synthesis as well as pleasurable intoxication and perilous toxicity. This commingling materialized the stuckness experienced by those positioned not simply "against nature" but against time, not simply the New Woman but the lesbian and the "ex-colored" man too.

It is entirely fitting that *The Awakening* concludes with an "ancient" sense that, more than any other sense, "calls up ancient memories with a wider and deeper emotional reverberation," in the words of Havelock Ellis.[111] Smell was considered a primitive sense that made legible the emotionally unsettling and temporally vertiginous experiences of recollection. In this historical moment, the notion of a deliberative memory was giving way to a more disjunctive model of consciousness. After picking up *Elements of Psychophysics* in a used bookstore, Hermann Ebbinghaus decided to extend Fechner's study of the psychological effects of sense experience into the domain of time. His 1885 dissertation on the psychology of memory (published in the United States in 1913) explored the subjective effects of physical stimuli that persist after those stimuli have disappeared. He arrived at the notion of "involuntary memory," wherein everyday sensory stimuli unconsciously evoke the past. Embodied consciousness interacts with the world not only in the present but also (and simultaneously) in the past. Under Ebbinghaus, memory took its place as an inner feeling that the material world could stimulate. And odors were the materials that most stimulated memory, pushing it above the threshold of consciousness. Of course, thinkers had long been interested in the power of odors to stir memory. In the 1850s, Oliver Wendell Holmes declared that memory "is more readily reached through the sense of smell than by almost any other channel"; a half-century later, his anecdotal observation was an empirical fact.[112] Psychologists Alice Heywood and Helen Vortriede reported in

1905 that the "observation that smell possesses a great power to revive past experience is so frequently made in every day life that it seemed worthwhile to attempt a laboratory test of its correctness." They concluded that smells do in fact "derive their associative power from their power to reproduce affective states of mood."[113] Smell was a sense that physiologically opened onto the ancient past of the species as well as opened up a person's psychical past. Having primitive olfactory sense-ability puts people in touch with their ancestral past, while having civilized olfactory sensitivity puts them in touch with the deepest recesses of their soul.

Published three years before *The Awakening*, Chopin's story "Lilacs" (1896) proleptically picks up where the novel leaves off—with the temporal recursions opened up by the olfactory sense. But whereas *The Awakening* presents perfume as a formless cloud that diffuses states of longing, "Lilacs" presents it as temporally diffuse: evanescent yet excavating deep-seated memories. The story moves between cosmopolitan Paris, where the widow Adrienne Farival lives a scandalous life as a chanteuse, and the rural convent where she had been raised and which she visits each spring. During one such visit, Adrienne reminisces with Sister Agathe about her first pilgrimage: "Always shall I remember that morning as I walked along the boulevard with a heaviness of heart—oh, a heaviness which I hate to recall. Suddenly there wafted over me the sweet odor of the lilac blossoms. A young girl had passed me by, carrying a great bunch of them. Did you ever know, Sister Agathe, that there is nothing which so keenly revives memory as a perfume—an odor?" Agathe answers affirmatively, as "the odor of fresh bread" instantly conjures her aunt's "great kitchen." Adrienne responds:

> "Well, that is how it was with me, Sister Agathe, when the scent of the lilacs at once changed the whole current of my thoughts and my despondency. The boulevard, its noises, its passing throng, vanished from before my senses as completely as if they had been spirited away.... And through all I could see and could smell the lilac blossoms, nodding invitingly to me from their thick-leaved branches.... I became like an *enragée*; nothing could have kept me back. I do not remember now where I was going; but I turned and retraced my steps homeward in a perfect fever of agitation: 'Sophie! My little trunk—quick—the black one! A mere handful of clothes! I am going away. Don't ask me any questions. I shall be back in a fortnight.' And every year since then it is the same. At the very first whiff of a lilac blossom, I am gone! There is no holding me back."[114]

The women are describing what today is called *odor memory*: when a specific scent stimulates an emotionally intense, involuntary memory. Notably, the emphasis on smell reflects daily experiences marked not by a forward-moving, evolving consciousness but one fractured and split by competing temporalities. For Adrienne, the scent of lilac blossoms yields weighty memories from the depths of personal time. To borrow Walter Benjamin's formulation, the lilac scent "deeply drugs the sense of time."[115] As crystallized by Adrienne's instant transformation into an *enragée*, the lilac scent is a sudden event that itself suspends, delays, and anesthetizes time. It takes hold of the "whole current" of her thoughts, as she forgets where she is going and yet, by dint of the accretion of indefinite intuitions prompted by "the very first whiff," she knows exactly where she must go. The women know that odor enters through the nose, but that odor memory goes straight to the heart.

Tethered to early psychological theories of time as an affective experience, the sense of smell materializes a personal yet shared relation to a present drugged, as it were, by moments of recursion and suspension. The unpredictable paths of these reminiscent feelings are queer because scent engages the body with past and present bonds rather than reproductive futurity. After all, Havelock Ellis's theory of homosexuality, or "sexual inversion," involved claims about the role that "odors and perfume play in the emotional life of women. . . . In the majority of inverted women, the odor of the beloved person plays a considerable part. Thus, one inverted woman asks the woman she loves to send her some of her hair that she may intoxicate herself in solitude with its perfume."[116] When Adrienne is at home in Paris, she "snuffles the air and exclaims, 'What do I smell?' She espied the flowers . . . held them up to her, burying her face in them for the longest time, only uttering a long 'Ah!'" The lilac scent hits her "like a thunder clap"—an ecstatic event that transposes the temporal lag between light waves and sound waves into a lag between the secular "now" of the cosmopolitan city and the sacred "then" of the pastoral convent.[117] Her face buried in flowers, Adrienne's reminiscent feeling is a queer phenomenon. Set against the clock that Agathe dutifully watches while Adrienne lives in Paris, the lilac's scent registers a labile temporality built around seasonal and affective returns. Adrienne "never announced her coming" because she never had to. The "nun knew very well when to look for her. When the scent of the lilac blossoms began to permeate the air, Sister Agathe would turn many times during the day to the window."[118] In this way, "lilac time" makes manifest an unspoken love ("never announced"), itself the unspoken reason why the Mother Superior bans Adrienne from future visits.[119]

In the wake of this untimely passion, Agathe's "face was pressed deep in the pillow in her efforts to smother the sobs that convulsed her frame. A lay sister came out of the door with a broom, and swept away the lilac blossoms which Adrienne had let fall upon the portico."[120] The lilac emits a scent whose intoxicating effects are precisely what condemn the women to solitude, as evidenced by the juxtaposition of Adrienne's face ecstatically buried in flowers and Agathe's face sobbing into a pillow. In addition to circulating the New Woman's illicit desires, scent allows the "inverted" woman, ever out of sync, to circle back in time.

Bodying forth an altered relation to time, scent works in "Lilacs" to "confer value on still unrecognized lives and unacknowledged affective bonds," as Nancy Bentley argues.[121] Whereas Chopin's story describes a singular instance of the queer pleasures and temporal shocks that scent galvanizes, James Weldon Johnson's *Autobiography of an Ex-Colored Man* (1912) orchestrates a series of narrative shocks that channel racial violence through the mnemonic power of perfume. The novel presents itself as the unnamed black narrator's account of his life moving across regions, continents, and color lines; he records a series of events leading up to and explaining his decision to pass as white. Johnson's incorporation of music and performance into the depiction of black social life is well documented, but he also uses perfume to "keep time," to track the violent acts that disrupt any feeling of historical continuity. *Ex-Colored Man* duly shows that although perfume functions as an aesthetic arrangement of subjective time, its transformative effects are in fact an uncanny reproduction of white supremacy. The cosmopolitan pleasures moving through the fin de siècle market were coextensive with "black life at the nadir," as the cultural and aesthetic rise of perfume directly overlapped with new forms of racial terror, most notably lynching. "If a substance is to act upon the olfactory nerve it must be volatile," chemist Samuel Sadtler wrote.[122] *Ex-Colored Man* experiments with the volatility of a "spirit" that is neither extracted from flesh nor simulated via synthesis but that is *only* flesh. It delineates the extralinear temporality of the extralegal terror of lynching—something Johnson well knew, having survived a near-lynching in Jacksonville, Florida—by tracing the circuitous route along which perfume morphs into its foul other: smoke. Behind every perfume cloud transporting a New Woman to illicit realms of feeling is an unnatural yet nonsynthetic scent: the black man's body set afire, vaporized, up in smoke.

Far from yielding equality for the "descendants of Ham," as Cranch had hoped in his "A Plea for the Sense of Smell" a half-century earlier, the elevation of the olfactory sense resulted in scents that cloaked certain horrors. Johnson investigates the bodies that perfumery discards in the quest for pure essence. Rose water may be ethereal, but what of its original flesh, the rose that had once exuded the scent? What of the bodies that perfumery discards as so much detritus? How do we make sense of perfumery's fetid byproducts? These questions are posed early on, when the novel's narrator recounts his childhood love for a fellow orchestral player, a white girl "who had moved me to a degree which now I can hardly think of as possible." In trying to pinpoint why he had been overcome with love during a concert performance, he recalls:

> [There] was just the proper setting to produce the effect upon a boy such as I was; the half dim church, the air of devotion on the part of the listeners, the heaving tremor of the organ under the clear wail of the violin, and ... her slender body swaying to the tones she called forth, all combined to fire my imagination and my heart with a passion though boyish, yet strong and, somehow, lasting. I have tried to describe the scene; if I have succeeded it is only half success, for words can only partially express what I would wish to convey. Always in recalling that Sunday afternoon I am subconscious of a faint but distinct fragrance which, like some old memory-awakening perfume, rises and suffuses my whole imagination, inducing a state of reverie so airy as to just evade the powers of expression. She was my first love, and I loved her as only a boy loves.[123]

Retrospective narration reproduces the perfume that it describes: both catalyze the affective intensity of reminiscence. The "faint but distinct fragrance" brings the force and lived immediacy of love—a word repeated three times in one sentence—into the present, but in a way that "evades the powers of expression." The perfume-induced memory can only be expressed and experienced "partially," in lexical and temporal fragments. This ineffability trope, the narrator's insistence on the impossibility of describing the feelings and memories solicited by perfume, does more than invoke Romanticism's preoccupation with art's transcendence of language. It links the "memory-awakening perfume" to the novel's climactic event: the lynching that the narrator witnesses and that the novel can only partially express through metonymic reproduction, as Jacqueline Goldsby has powerfully argued.[124] In its overlaying of past and present, the fragrance portends the disturbing alchemy of love between a black boy and a white girl: its conversion into the "murder! rape!" charges that fuel the lynching.[125] The scent that suffuses the boy's imagination and bodies forth the past also gestures toward the peril of perfume's sensuous atmospheres.

While fragrances conjure inexpressible or partially expressible memories, this inexpressibility tethers scent to the color line that separates the girl from the narrator. Smell is, as a writer for *Harper's* had noted, "the poorest of all the senses in the point of language."[126] In Georg Simmel's essay "Sociology of the Senses" (1907), he went so far as to attribute Jim Crow segregation to the status of smell as an ante- and antilinguistic sense:

> Smell . . . remains, as it were, captive in the human subject, which is symbolized in the fact that there exist no independent, objectively characterizing expressions for fine distinctions. . . . The impressions of the sense of smell resist description with words; . . . they cannot be projected onto the level of abstraction. And there is that much less resistance from thinking and volition to the instinctive antipathies and sympathies that are attached to the olfactory sphere surrounding people, and which, for instance, often have significant consequence for the sociological relationship of two races living in the same territory. The reception of the Negro in higher social circles of North America is out of the question by reason of the body odor of the Negro.[127]

Simmel argues that smell is a sense "captive" in the person, trapped within the strictly physical body, unable to move into the psychical domain of abstraction. Smell is a "fleshy" sense, opposed to reason and therefore opposed to representation. It is so involuntary, so resistant to thought that it resists signification altogether. As a result, white North Americans have an instinctive antipathy to the "olfactory sphere surrounding people"—and more specifically to black people's "racial odor"—that their rational faculties cannot override. Under the racial "sign" of its linguistic signlessness, then, the sense of smell buttresses the color line. Were the sense of smell more amenable to "expressions for fine distinctions," the domain of sensitivity and judgment, then black people's body odor would not so viscerally repulse "higher social circles." Within this frame, then, the just-perceptible sensation—the "faint but distinct fragrance" of the Sunday concert—stimulates a just-expressible memory (the memory of the lynching, also featuring a primarily white audience) hovering around the threshold of the narrator's consciousness. Johnson transforms race from a sociological fact into an imaginative, ineffable force.

The reminiscence sparked by particular scents, as this early scene suggests, radically disrupts the narrator's internal clock. Such temporal drifts are materialized in the fragrances, and with them the memories, that waft in the air. Perfume is not simply a temporal drug, à la Benjamin, but a "temporal drag," following Elizabeth Freeman, whereby history's throwaway "objects" drift into the present.[128] After attending a black church meeting one night, the narrator is swept up in a crowd of white people who lynch a black man by burning him at the stake. He watches the flames "crouch" then "leap," and he hears the man's "cries and groans . . . choked off by the fire and smoke," and then confesses: "I was fixed to the spot where I stood, powerless to take my eyes from what I did not want to see. It was over before I realized that time had elapsed. Before I could make myself believe that what I saw was really happening, I was looking at a scorched post, a smoldering fire, blackened bones, charred fragments sifting down through coils of chain, and the smell of burnt flesh—human flesh—was in my nostrils."[129] Lynching is a largely visual spectacle (a ritual performance, a modern entertainment, a photographic genre) as well as a sonic event, recorded with early phonographic technology. Yet given the narrator's insistence on the smell of burned human flesh that flashes forth in the present moment of his writing, the novel suggests that "to witness a lynching was also to smell it."[130] The irony, historian Linda Tucker points out, is that although "whites often commented on what they perceived as the distasteful smell of blacks," in the lynching by fire, they "took the tortured black body into themselves through smell."[131] Sociologist Orlando Patterson similarly considers "being suffused with the odor of the lynch victim's roasting body" an act of cannibalism.[132] Smell not only decenters the eye from the act of witnessing but also reveals the impossibility of distance for the witness. Once the victim's burned flesh is in the nose, incorporated into the perceiver's body, the victim has become internal to the witness. Lynching is "encoded forever, through the overwhelming odor of his roasting body, on the memories of all who participated."[133]

The lynch mob (consisting of white people and people either passing or mistaken for white, such as the narrator) takes into itself a body that, once rendered bones, ash, and a foul odor, is no longer racially black. For once in touch with fire, all flesh and all bones have the same charcoal color and exude the same stench. Lynching reduces all organic material to racially and sexually undifferentiated flesh. And in abstracting the African American man to the point of unidentifiability, it reveals the violence that subtends the myth of the perfumed sex, as obliquely referenced by the "faint fragrance" that suffuses the narrator's memory of the white teenage girl he had loved. Here, the status of the perfumed sex as a delicate "spirit" that can be both extracted from the body and synthetically abstracted is predicated on the foul stench of the black person's charred remains—the black person prohibited from transcending their body, held captive to their body. Lynching and perfumery begin to appear less distinct; fiery decomposition is, in its own way, not unlike aqueous distillation. The central difference is whose bodies are made vulnerable, and for whom detachability is more toxic than intoxicating. As Hartmann explained of his perfume concert, his aim was to "excite aesthetic feelings and not elemental ones like . . . fear," which can be produced "by the burning of meat."[134] Perfume aestheticized the sense of smell through a process of extraction (essential oil from flesh) and then through the process of abstraction (synthetic simulation). This process also resulted in a discarded body, a throwaway object: the natural specimen evacuated of its olfactory essence. As the affective circuit between the fragrant concert and the fetid lynching demonstrate, this chemical conversion of flesh into spirit is predicated on, and is an uncanny inversion of, the reduction of flesh not into spirit but into the deadening elements of ash and dust. Perfume is the biopolitical technology of "making live" that succeeds only to the extent that smoke "lets die."

The stench of human flesh activates a surfeit of memory; smell is a sense that remembers too much. That the victim dies before the narrator realizes "time had elapsed" shows the disjuncture between the event's external duration and his inner feeling of its instantaneity. Detaching the stench from the event itself, odor memory sets past, present, and future adrift. The reminiscence of the lynching disperses throughout personal and narrative time, as though diffused by an atomizer—an application device for spraying perfume around the body (rather than dab liquid onto wrist and neck), thought to enhance personal "aura" (figure 3.2). But the "smell conveyed by a spray is too fugitive," Hartmann observed, because the skin does not directly absorb it.[135] The fugitive "spray" of the lynching produces a perverse kind of perfume cloud. The smell of burned flesh tethers the "devoted" audience in the "half dim church" that "fires" young love to the big church meeting, where the "possibilities of electrified collectivity" then get converted into the "shock of racial terror" that is "the very wiring of modern life," as Lindsay Reckson persuasively argues.[136] In addition, the smell that hangs around the lynching filters into the "smoky" Atlanta restaurant, which exudes the "rancid odor of

FIG. 3.2 Raphaël Kirchner, advertisement featuring an atomizer. "Les Parfums Lubins, Mettent l'âme en fête [Lubin Perfumes, celebrate the spirit]." From *L'Illustration*, March 16, 1912.

fish fried over several times, which almost nauseated me."[137] It also lives in the "heavy odor of the tobacco [that] almost sickened me" at the Jacksonville cigar factory, where the narrator once worked.[138] Caught in a chain of deferred signification, the decadent trope of cigarette smoke that typically displaces the "naturalist smellscape" of industrial smoke is itself displaced by the overdetermined symbolism of cigar smoke: the black phalluses frequently sold as lynching memorabilia. Burned bodies—animal, plant, human—travel as olfactory traces that rupture historical and novelistic time through the antiblack violence they repeat and compress. The charred black body is a simultaneously natural and unnatural substance, one revealing the naturalist smellscapes that belie the decadent perfume cloud (figure 3.3). The burning smell marks death, yet once it has infiltrated the nostrils and entered into the psyche refuses to die. In tracking the temporal volatility of reminiscent feelings, Johnson shows that the intoxicating pleasures of perfume—that breezy whiff of whiteness—might at any point turn toxic.

As an aesthetic object, a feminized commodity, and a biopolitical medium that distributed intimacies and fragmented temporalities, perfume saturated

FIG. 3.3 Jane Atché, *Papier à cigarettes JOB* (1896). Color lithograph, 31 × 42 cm. Musée des Arts Decoratifs. © RMN-Grand Palais. Image source: Art Resource, New York.

turn-of-the-century accounts of varyingly wayward lives. Within *The Awakening*, "Lilacs," and *Autobiography of an Ex-Colored Man*, the olfactory sense unmoors time and causation from the sequence of daily life; it is where analepsis and prolepsis commingle. Insofar as they are volatile, plotless, and reliant on the whims of air currents, odors manifest the tenuous relationality and nonlinear temporality of those gendered, raced, and sexualized subjects whose stuckness—to different degrees and to different ends—is as psychological as it is social. Exploring stuckness by exploiting the possibilities of synthetic perfume and its affective returns, Chopin and Johnson query the pleasures and perils of detachability: the free-floating attachments that suffuse the life of diaphanous yet deviant white women and the metonymic violences that circle around black life. Flowers and flesh exude scents that are both evanescent and reminiscent, that let loose expansive desires and recursive interiority. Read with perfume's changing style, substance, and uses, these stories orchestrate the always-tenuous relation of differentiated subjects to abstraction. To know and to feel different orders of scent becomes one way to maneuver within and around a social order that differentially manages "life itself" through not only biological reproduction but chemical reproduction as well.

....

The characterization of the olfactory sense as anterior to evolution and antithetical to transcendence contributed to its designation as primitive—hence, positioned as conceptually and historically other than the psychological, spiritual, or aesthetic. Attempts made by mid- to late nineteenth-century perfumers to elevate their products to the status of art involved refashioning perfume as the psychophysical dimension of the olfactory sense, both in what it is and what it does: a chemically pure and refined "spirit" that has been successfully extracted from its material home, and an olfactory material that stimulates instinctual but no less beautiful emotions, memories, and pleasures. As it changed in production method (distillation to synthesis), in substance (essence to artifice), and in style (realism to abstraction), perfume increasingly shed its biological function as an index of inner racial or gender identity. Instead it was an aesthetic arrangement of feeling—one that secured social hierarchies and challenged the violence thereof. Kate Chopin and James Weldon Johnson in particular harnessed perfume's synthetic stylization, atmospheric embodiment, and temporal diffusions to describe the experiences of differentiated subjects (the white woman ambivalent about marriage and motherhood, the man ambivalent about his blackness) in moments of impasse, when living feels like a state of suspension at best or a kind of dying at worst. By describing as well as concocting scents that entirely undo any distinction between what is natural and what not, what is internal and what external, they folded perfume into the project of psychophysical aesthesis. Consequently, the chemical relays between the just-perceptible whiff of white womanhood and the just-expressible stench of lynching became affective relays too. Musky pinks circulate pleasure while orbiting the toxic odor of burned black flesh.

This psychophysical aesthesis dramatizes a tension inhering between the biological and the chemical, perhaps clearest in a brief aside made by Thomas Wentworth Higginson in his Civil War memoir, *Army Life in a Black Regiment* (1869). In it, Higginson, an abolitionist who helped train and lead the first regiment of ex-slaves, peppers his war stories with belletristic descriptions of the coastal South, at one point reflecting, "It seemed to me that the woods had not those pure, clean, innocent odors which so abound in the New England forest in early spring; but there was something luscious, voluptuous, almost oppressively fragrant about the magnolias, as if they belonged not to Hebe, but to Magdalen."[139] Whereas "pure, clean innocent odors" reflect the moral righteousness of the North, the "luscious, voluptuous, and oppressively fragrant" magnolia bears out the sinfulness of the slave system. The flower's full-bodied scent encodes slavery into the South. Racial oppression is, quite materially, in the air. But as Higginson's reference to Magdalen suggests, the magnolia's "cloying fragrance" registers not only as racial exoticism—its scent so robust as to be musky—but also as vulgar sexuality and gendered artifice. Odor molecules are entirely detachable from the biological organism exuding it (the magnolia) but are perpetually pulled back toward biological configurations of race and sex. In Higginson's own psychophysical account of the warring regions, olfactory sensations of "clean" or "voluptuous" odors correspond to the "spirit of place" and, at the same time, are irreducible to— entirely detachable from—those places.

The olfactory sense attunes us to a tension arising in the late nineteenth century between the biological as entirely material and the chemical as a kind of spiritual matter. This tension between the material and immaterial has been transposed into debates about mediation and experience. There is, after all, an ongoing critical tendency to pit smell against language. Scholars have described smell as a sense that lacks "grammatical discipline," has "no synonyms," and "cannot be named."[140] It is "incapable of transcending its physical matrix," writes philosopher Annick Le Guérer. "Indeed, the emotional relationship is generally deemed responsible for our lack of a suitable olfactive vocabulary."[141] The formal innovations of the writers I have considered challenge this perspective. Indeed, for Higginson smell is poetic because of, not despite, its immediacy and indescribability. In "The Procession of Flowers" (1862), he writes:

> If in the simple process of writing one could physically impart to this page the fragrance of this spray of Azalea beside me, what a wonder it would seem! And yet one ought to be able, by the mere use of language, to supply to every reader the total of that white, honey, trailing sweetness, which summer insects haunt and the Spirit of the Universe loves. The defect is not in language, but in men. There is no conceivable beauty of blossoms so beautiful as words—none so graceful, none so perfumed.[142]

More than heighten the wonder of fragrances, language creates new spheres of attachment. Indeed, much as Bruno Latour has found that the training of noses in today's perfume industry teaches the perceiving body "to be affected by hitherto unregistrable differences," likewise articulation does something to the scents themselves.[143] When read with and within rather than outside the literary, smell offers a point of entry into stories about the experiential and emotional undercurrents of the biological "facts" of human difference. It thus remains crucial to consider the pull of olfactory experience within and against biological embodiment as such—a pull that places just-perceptible and just-expressible feelings at the center of challenges to technologies of extraction and abstraction, and a pull that radically reconfigures familiar forms of differentiation. Rather than show what the sense of smell does to language, writers like Chopin and Johnson, working aslant naturalist and decadent figurations of the primal body, inverted the terms of the relationship; they stressed what language does to the sense of smell. To return to this chapter's second epigraph, then: in attending to the olfactory experiences that slide from things to beings (and that constitute certain beings as things) we might take a cue from our authors by engaging language as always more and other than sensation, a material that unravels the very bodies with which it is spectacularly entangled.

Olfactory Gusto

In *Food and Flavor: A Gastronomic Guide to Good Living* (1913), critic Henry T. Finck set out to teach Americans the importance of flavor. In a section called the "Psychology of Eating," he paused to recount his career as the music editor of the *New York Evening Post* and as the epicurean editor at the *Nation*. As the story goes, when Finck entered Harvard University in the 1870s, he decided to study "the phenomena of the senses in man and animals," having delighted since childhood "in the pleasures of the senses of sight, hearing, and smell." He then spent a few years in Germany to study the senses "not as an amateur but as one prepared to make original researches." But, as with most youthful adventures, things did not go according to plan:

My most ardent desire was to work in the laboratories of the University of Berlin under Professor Helmholtz, whose monumental books on the sensations of tone and on the phenomena of sight had revealed so many secrets to the world of science. Unfortunately he was not lecturing on those subjects at that time. Moreover, re-perusal of his books made me feel as if he had covered all the most interesting ground. I therefore looked about for a region in which I could do some exploring on my own account, and soon found it in the functions of the sense of smell and taste.[1]

Finck's reminiscence points to the privileged status of sight and sound in psychophysical research—a status in keeping with the empiricist preference for the material stimulants, such as light waves and sound waves, that can be measured and manipulated. (Touch, as I show in chapter 5, was considered subjective yet uniquely capable of "filling in" for sight and sound when needed.) By devoting himself to the senses of smell and taste, Finck was able to carve out a space for himself in the experimental study of subjective experience. From student of psychophysics to art critic, Finck's career—bookended by "The Aesthetic Value of the Sense of Smell" (1880) and *Food and Flavor* (1913)—neatly tracks the alternate routes through which the excessively subjective (too emotional, too corporeal) senses of smell and taste were explored. Perfumers were the primary researchers of the psychical experiences that scent solicits, while working-class and middle-class women experimented with the "spiritual" heights of gustatory sensation in the kitchen.

The scientific neglect of smell and taste goes some way in explaining why these senses were not taken up in the synaesthetic arts as systematically as sight and sound (color music) and even sound and smell (perfume concerts). Piesse's odophone, for instance, forged a correspondence between smell and sound in order to legitimize the olfactory sense, so that it might absorb aesthetic authority from music. If it were hard enough for the public to take seriously color music or a perfume concert, then it would be nearly impossible to forge a new art from taste and smell. Signaling instinctive and irrational faculties, these senses were linked not to perceptual sensitivity, the affective substrate of aesthetic judgment, but instead to nervous sensitivity, considered the basis of medical disorders like neurasthenia. The psychologist studied sight and sound (and touch) but smell and even taste fell under the purview of the nerve specialist. As characterized by George Miller Beard, the era's most famous nerve specialist, neurasthenia is a debilitating condition of fatigue suffered by genteel white people; their overly receptive nerves render them vulnerable to stimulating urban environments. In 1906, Havelock Ellis wrote that "odors are powerful stimulants to the whole nervous system, causing . . . an increase of energy which, if excessive or prolonged, leads to nervous exhaustion," and that "aromatics containing volatile oils" can in "large doses produce depression. . . . It is doubtless on this account that it is among civilized peoples that attention is chiefly directed to perfumes, and that under the conditions of modern life the interest in olfaction and its study has been revived."[2] Given the decadent perfumes flooding the market, Ellis's remark usefully distills the paradox of scent in this moment: a sensual intoxicant and a toxin that depletes "nerve force," threatening the vitality of the civilized white body. Perceptual sensitivity shades into nervous sensitivity, as the very commodity marking the aesthetic heights of civilization also activates the neurasthenic process of degeneration.

It is unsurprising that Ellis deemed a "great many neurasthenic people peculiarly susceptible to olfactory influences," including "eminent poets and novelists" Charles Baudelaire and Joris-Karl Huysmans.[3] He forgot to name Charlotte Perkins Gilman, who received treatment for neurasthenia (actually, postpartum depression) from S. Weir Mitchell. In the 1880s, Mitchell applied the insights gained from his earlier studies of nerve injuries to bourgeois nervous diseases. So doing, he developed the rest cure for neurasthenic women—effectively a "house arrest" that mandated bed rest and mindless domestic work punctuated by periods of forced feeding. Gilman knew firsthand the deleterious impact of patriarchal medicine on women's sanity and, ultimately, on their racial vitality. "The Yellow Wall-Paper" (1892) famously tells the story of a new mother suffering from nervous exhaustion. Her physician-husband John uses the rest cure to treat her, which only makes her sicker. Presented as a series of journal entries, the story tracks the woman's intensifying obsession with her bedroom's wallpaper, which commits "every artistic sin" with its ever-shifting yellow hue and peripatetic pattern.[4]

She even begins to see a woman creeping underneath the wallpaper. Unlike this trapped figure, however, the wallpaper is not confined to the bedroom; it exceeds its own material properties. "There is something else about this paper—the smell!" the woman writes in her journal. "It creeps all over the house. I find it hovering in the dining room, skulking in the parlor, hiding in the hall, lying in wait for me on the stairs. It gets into my hair." The smell's nonlocalizable body and its nonidentifiable quality captivate her. "Such a peculiar odor, too!" she declares. "I have spent hours in trying to analyze it, to find what it smelled like ... but the only thing I can think of that it is like is the *color* of the paper! A yellow smell!" This breakthrough is a breakdown. The woman rips off the wallpaper, and then *becomes* the odor: she "creep[s] smoothly on the floor," then "creep[s] just the same" despite her husband's protestations, and finally when he faints, she must "creep over" his body (figure 13.1).[5] Restless rather than well rested, she is on the move.

The story's conclusion—the narrator crawling like an animal, a child, an invalid (in the era's locution)—limns the dire consequences of patriarchal oppression: the suppression of white racial progress. The synaesthetic "yellow smell" registers what it feels like to devolve. The color yellow has long been associated with sickliness and decay, but at the turn of the twentieth

FIG. 13.1 Illustration from Charlotte Perkins Gilman, "The Yellow Wall-Paper," *New England Magazine*, January 1892.

century it saturated accounts of white civilization under siege from below (e.g., the sensationalist "yellow press" that catered to the masses), from afar (e.g., the "yellow peril" posed by Asian immigrants), and from within (e.g., the sensual decadence spread by the British literary journal the *Yellow Book*). Yellow acquired an evolutionary charge as well. In a *Popular Science Monthly* article, "The Psychology of Yellow," Ellis claimed that "savages" and children "share a love of yellow" because of their underdeveloped minds.[6] The narrator's feeling for and fascination with the wayward color yellow indexes her slide back in developmental time to the unrestrained emotion of the child or primitive. And her response to the wallpaper's smell slides her back even further. Physician and critic Max Nor-

dau's bestselling screed *Degeneration* diagnosed European civilization's alleged decline on the basis of its art and literature, which he considered overly fixated on synaesthesia—and the sense of smell. For a scent to strongly affect a civilized person, he claimed, "their front lobe must be depressed and the olfactory lobe of a dog substituted for it. . . . Smellers among degenerates represent an atavism going back, not only to the primeval period of man, but infinitely more remote still, to an epoch anterior to man."[7] The following century, Sigmund Freud used this evolutionary logic to align normate sex with visual perception: the "assumption of an upright gait made his [man's] genitals, which were previously concealed, visible," hence the "diminution of olfactory stimuli" in sexual arousal.[8]

And so when at story's end the woman abandons bipedalism in favor of all fours—eyes on the ground, nose level with genitals—domestic entrapment appears as a kind of lobotomy, the human brain swapped out for that of a dog. Taken together, "yellow smell" resembles the olfactory hallucinations attributed to neurasthenic women, which were "very difficult to characterize due to some ill-defined synaesthetic quality," medical historians Anne Harrington and Vernon Rosario explain.[9] This particular color-smell combination evinces what it feels like to lose your grip on an already tenuous claim to civilization. As a white person, after all, the narrator can agentially respond to stimuli, but as a woman, she is overly susceptible to those stimuli. Routed through nervous sensitivity rather than perceptual sensitivity, *yellow smell* is not an aesthetic stimulant of civilization but the pathological substrate of white womanhood's "atavistic tendencies."[10]

The narrator's synaesthetic experience tethers the gendered condition of neurasthenia to the racial and sexual degeneracy with which "art for art's sake" male writers such as Huysmans were charged. But because of its conceit as a woman's journal, and therefore its narration in the subjective mode of the first person rather than the observational mode of the third, "The Yellow Wall-Paper" has more to say about what synaesthesia produces rather than what it diagnoses. We are invited into the internal drama of discerning what is actually internal to (i.e., a sensation) and external to (i.e., a stimulus) the narrator. Is the trapped woman in the wall or in her head? Did the smell that got into the narrator's hair already go to her brain? The narrator's determination that the smell "is like the *color* of the paper! A yellow smell!" amplifies and answers these questions. When the senses collapse into one another, anything resembling "objective" reality also collapses. The color-odor mixture yields ontological indeterminacies about what is real and unreal—or, as turn-of-the-century psychologist June Downey explained in her study of synaesthesia, what is "true" and what is literary. "I have spent hours trying to analyze it, to find what it smells like," the woman writes, before disclosing that it is a "yellow smell." By identifying what the odor is *like* rather than identifying what it *is*, she refashions the search for meaning as a search for metaphor. Rather like the unpacking of a nesting doll, her analysis of the wallpaper engenders more rather than less figuration. Refracted through this scene of pathological womanhood (neurasthenia, hysteria), synaesthesia operates in the discursive key of *like*, as an experience not endowed with preformed meaning but as one that only "makes sense" as a metaphor—as a mode of relation. The yellow smell discloses that all feeling is a feeling like. Color and scent become biological markers of human difference in the same moment that they become literary events mediating the lived experience of that difference.

Gilman was not the only one to consider how women's racial precarity turns synaesthetic experience from a vehicle of aesthetic transport into a case of nervous prostration. One year prior, William Dean Howells's novella *An Imperative Duty* told the story of Rhoda Aldgate, who belatedly learns from her aunt Mrs. Meredith that she is one-sixteenth black. In its effort to capture the lived experience rather than the legal or biological facts of the color line, the story limns the feelings that escape quantitative analysis. Accordingly, Rhoda likens the "loss" of her whiteness to a phantom limb, and Mrs. Meredith claims that her niece's vocal timbre betrays her blackness. But in a story preoccupied with the precarity of white womanhood—Mrs. Meredith suffers bouts of nervous exhaustion that require the care of "nervous specialist" Dr. Edward Olney—it is a synaesthetic encounter with black people that motivates the "tragic mulatta" to forgo her legally mandated racial identity. When Rhoda seeks out her new community at a church meeting, she tries to "intensify the fact to her outward perception; she wished . . . to reconcile herself to it [blackness] by owning it with every sense."[11] Church is a site of fellowship and, for Rhoda, of racial conversion, where she might be reborn an African American and perhaps a race woman (à la Frances Harper's 1892 novel *Iola Leroy*). Rather than own blackness with every sense, however, it is through the senses that blackness owns her—and that she disowns her blackness.

> The night was warm, and as the church filled, the musky exhalations of their bodies thickened the air, and made the girl faint; it seemed to her that she began to taste the odor; and these poor people, whom their Creator has made so hideous by the standards of all his other creatures, roused a cruel loathing in her, which expressed itself in her frantic refusal of their claim upon her. In her heart she cast them off with vindictive hate. . . . But when she shut her eyes, and heard their wild, soft voices, her other senses were holden, and she was rapt by the music from her frenzy of abhorrence.[12]

The scene charges the religious sentiment that synaesthesia had generated with a fragmented racial sentiment. The musky taste becomes part of "a range of involuntary acts, including unusual sensory experiences" specific to popular religious practices that had become pathologized at century's end.[13] Rhoda's taste of the musky black bodies embodies the otherness of black Protestantism, given the "putative physical excess of [black people's] lived relation to worship."[14] More so, with the musky "racial odor" of black bodies in worship—the force of persons exercising extravagant emotion and devotion to each other and God—lodged in her mouth, Rhoda's gustatory-olfactory experience crystallizes what Kyla Wazana Tompkins calls "racial indigestion," the colonial dialectic of alimentary desire for and repulsion of blackness.[15] The gustatory-olfactory-aural experience of blackness is at once a neurasthenic faint and a synaesthetic swoon; synaesthesia is both mystical transport and pathological symptom. By submitting to clinical discourses of race, Rhoda disavows the claim that the synaesthetic excess of black embodiment makes on her. Indeed, she flees the church and opts to marry Dr. Olney, who "treats" her blackness in the same way he treats Mrs. Meredith's neurasthenia: as an illness to be overcome. The difference is that passing, not rest, is what cures her. (Unable to imagine interracial union in the United States, *An Imperative Duty* ends with their marriage in Italy, where Rhoda "blends in.") To disavow synaesthetic black embodiment is to assert one's white nervous sensitivity.

In tracking the countervailing movements of two precariously "white" women—one who abandons her whiteness in favor of primitive creeping, another who uses nervous sensitivity to cloak her blackness—yellow smells and musky tastes articulate how women embodied the tenuous distinction between neurasthenia and synaesthesia, between a pathological condition that debilitated the civilized body and a mystical experience coded as wayward. These scenes attune us to a shift in the affective regime of womanhood. For nervous sensitivity denoted receptivity to the world without emotional reflection or regulation, and thus it fell short of the moral sentiment with which it traditionally had been associated. Treated by nerve specialists rather than taken up by social reformers, nervous sensitivity was the underbelly not simply of synaesthesia but of sentimentality: white women's heightened receptivity to the environment produces anxiety rather than sympathy, nervous exhaustion rather than righteous enthusiasm. And yet the postbellum era is known for its derision of sentimental modes of expression, anything that might appear overly cloying. "The most inane thing ever put forth in the name of literature is the so-called domestic novel, an indigestible, culinary sort of product, that might be named the doughnut of fiction," *Atlantic Monthly* editor Charles Dudley Warner proclaimed.[16] Trading doughnuts for cakes and fiction for recipes as domesticity's primary genre, the following chapter tracks the women cooks who lodged the gustatory sense at the core of aesthetic taste and in so doing ascribed blackness a flavor that was not disgustingly musky (as it was for Rhoda Aldgate) but daringly, decadently sweet.

{ 4 }

Taste

SCRIPTS FOR SWEETNESS,
MEASURES OF PLEASURE

> By carefully following the same recipe, two experienced cooks will obtain different results because other elements intervene in the preparation: a personal touch, the knowledge or ignorance of tiny secret practices, an entire *relationship to things* that the recipe does not codify and hardly clarifies.
> —Michel de Certeau, Luce Giard, and Pierre Mayol, *The Practice of Everyday Life*

> I am the sugar at the bottom of the English cup of tea.
> —Stuart Hall, "Old and New Identities, Old and New Ethnicities"

Thus far we have seen how psychophysical feeling—signs born of the interrelation of mind and matter—moved with and athwart biological frameworks of human difference. In turn, the project of psychophysical aesthesis remade these signs into lived genres: the five senses are modes of affective relation that mediate the tensile entanglement of self and social world and that assert the primacy of lived experience to configurations of power. Across these projects the material circuits of sensory activity (not-seeing, resonant hearing, olfactory essences) structure impossible desires for social attachments that transcend embodied consciousness while securing the body's heritable but not immutable particularity (phantom limbs, socialist solidarity, atmospheric intimacy). In this chapter, I shift focus away from these invisible, elastic, and evanescent relations and toward a mode of feeling so contained as to be seemingly self-enclosed: the sense of taste. It is in fact ironic, philosopher Carolyn

Korsmeyer observes, that the sense of taste has furnished the "metaphor for aesthetic sensitivity" while being excluded from the domain of aesthetics. "Taste directs attention 'inward' to the state of one's own body. When one tastes a flavor, that flavor is positioned phenomenologically in one's mouth, nose, and throat; the sensation is perceived to be an alteration of the body."[1] That taste's inwardness was of a visceral rather than psychical type—aimed at the innards rather than activating interiority—explains why psychophysics entirely neglected the sense, even though Fechner had formulated sensitivity as the perceptual substrate of judgment and developed an "aesthetics from below." In perhaps the clearest distillation of psychophysical aesthesis, women cooks ventured to go where professional scientists would not. They drew on their culinary expertise to experiment with the psychical dimensions of taste, ultimately determining that the self-enclosed sense stimulates extravagant pleasures and that these pleasures dilate what counts as aesthetic feeling.

In the nineteenth century, the experimental sciences radically upended entrenched ideas about the senses—except that of taste. Physicists grappled with the behavior of light waves, physiologists applied acoustics to human hearing, and chemists invented their own odor molecules, but theories of the gustatory sense remained unchanged. In botanist C. J. Sprague's *Atlantic Monthly* essay "What We Feel" (1867), he attributed this lacuna in scientific research to the difficulty of isolating flavor from food. Sugar has "certain chemical constituents which go to make up a saccharine compound," but its "sweetness is not measurable in the chemist's scales. [Sugar] can be analyzed, and its constituent elements accurately defined. But sweetness is not one of those elements."[2] Chemists can analyze the properties of food and physiologists the effects of food on the human body (both contributed to the nineteenth-century reform movement of dietetics), but neither can analyze the felt experience of food, called flavor or taste. Physiologist Julius Bernstein explained, "Observations are very difficult to make, and uncertain in their result, because substances placed upon a certain spot of the tongue will not readily remain isolated but spread very rapidly."[3] Odor molecules are evanescent, but they can at least be contained in a bottle. Taste sensations arise when soluble matter dissolves in the mouth. It is impossible to observe flavors that emerge only in inverse relation to matter's dissolution. A further problem was the organ of feeling itself: the tongue. Smell has air as its medium, a writer pointed out in *Scientific American*, but taste has "no medium that conveys its impressions; the communication of such impressions must . . . be immediate, that is, the tongue must touch the thing tasted."⁴ As a corporeal, immeasurable, and immediate sensation, taste proved elusive to science and useless to aesthetics. In *Physiological Aesthetics* (1877) Grant Allen flatly stated, "Properly speaking no sensation of Taste can be classified as aesthetic."⁵

Taste was a sense even more scientifically and philosophically neglected than smell. In a revised edition of *The Senses and the Intellect* (1902), Scottish thinker Alexander Bain argued that all five senses have an "intellectual" and "emotional" character. He criticized Fechner for studying only "the purely intellectual property of sensation—namely [sense] discrimination" while ignoring the "emotional states as, for example, pure pleasure."⁶ Smell and taste were the senses most aligned with emotional states like "pure pleasure," in contrast to the discriminating senses of sound and sight. Perfumers explored the sensuous atmospheres that their olfactory products generated, pleasures that circulate freely among bodies. All the while, domestic women—the sisters, mothers, wives, daughters, and workers (enslaved, indentured, underpaid) cooking daily in the kitchen—investigated gustatory pleasures entirely material in their sensuousness and experienced only in a single body, the eater. These women worked at the nexus of two new civilizing projects: gastronomy, which purported to turn eating into an art, and culinary science, which regarded flavor as incidental to nutrition, the real purpose of eating. In the preface to *Food and Flavor* (1913), critic Henry T. Finck observed that "schools, women's societies, and society women have taken up the matter [of cooking] in England as well as in America, and great changes are impending—changes which, it is hoped, this volume, coming at the 'psychological moment,' will help to accelerate."⁷ Although refused entry into the art of gastronomy—practiced by professional chefs (i.e., men)—women tested out a full-bodied aesthetics, assaying the pleasures that unfold in the flesh, on the tongue. Rather than produce delicate foods that might elicit finer feelings, rather than elevate sensory taste by modeling it on abstract notions of beauty, they instead set to reconstituting taste as the aesthetic pleasure immanent in the bodily act of eating. With the home kitchen replacing the university laboratory as the site of psychophysical experimentation, women cooks investigated the point at which consciousness becomes carnal.

Whereas body image, tonality, and perfume were "creative spirits," flavor was a *soul*—a term that was not synonymous with airy "spirit" but instead conjured the unseemly twin of aesthetics: bad taste. Food takes a linear path (down the hatch), but flavor moves in a lateral direction; it yields pleasures that are contained within the body yet socially uncontainable. Flavor was considered the psychological component or "soul" of food and sweetness the soul most closely approaching the aesthetic. Eighteenth-century philosopher Edmund Burke had declared "sweetness the beautiful of taste."[8] Yet by dint of its link to the colonial sugar plantation, sweetness was also a fleshy, ungovernable soul. General attitudes held that sweetness, the flavor most "beautiful" for civilized gourmands, was irresistible for white women and people of color, whose irrational cravings required the intervention of culinary science. Within the context of what Kyla Wazana Tompkins calls "racial indigestion"—the twinning desire for and disgust at the black body—sweetness became a kind of dialectic, pitched between fine-grained feeling and instinctual appetite.[9] Alongside and in response to this dialectic, a range of women undertook a project of psychophysical aesthesis that remade their ungovernable "sweet tooth," their bad taste, into the basis of culinary expertise. To explore the affective rather than digestive demands that sweetness makes on the feeling body was, for them, to track the contingencies and contradictions of aesthetics. Nineteenth-century women's culinary writing (including recipes, poems, and letters) reveals a systematic effort to measure sweeteners like sugar and molasses against the immeasurable effects thereof—and, in so doing, uncover the racial and gendered surplus of aesthetic taste at the level of affect and embodied action.

Whether "amateur" or professional cooks, white or black, northern or southern, many women endeavored to plumb the depths of embodied consciousness into the flesh. Recipes powerfully illuminate these experiments. Bearing a direct link to food preparation, the recipe is a discursive genre with distinct formal features—a list of ingredients followed by a series of imperatives—and it gives coherence to the culinary event. But the recipe is perhaps best understood as a "scriptive thing," defined by Robin Bernstein as a material artifact that structures "a performance while allowing for agency and unleashing original, live variations that may not be individually predictable."[10] A recipe is a script that implies but does not codify action; it leaves room for improvisation (to varying degrees of culinary success). If the kitchen is a space of everyday performance, then the recipe is a kitchen tool you can do things with and do things differently each time. Equally important, it is a "peculiarly female form of writing" that historically has made it possible for women to share knowledge and construct community.[11] As Tompkins writes, "Scribbled into family bibles or onto envelopes, cut from newspapers and stuffed into other books, recipes (and cookbooks) are often discarded as marginalia and ephemera, left behind as the archival traces of labor that is both minoritized and quotidian."[12] Located at the nexus of text and performance, recipes appear not all that different from poems, which in the nineteenth century were also memorized, recited, copied, collected, edited, and exchanged.[13] Far from a merely evidentiary document and far from an isolated discursive form, recipes were scriptive materials that moved among folkways and that brought people, mainly women, into intimate community and fellowship.

This project of psychophysical aesthesis flourished as an archive of the commensal, of the everyday: the culinary documents either orchestrating particular tastes (recipes and epistolary correspondences) or meditating on particular tastes (poems) among real and imagined people. This chapter reads two interlinked archives of taste: variations on a single confection—the Caribbean dessert black cake—in the recipes of freewoman Malinda Russell, ex-slave Abby Fisher, writer Emily Dickinson, and social reformer Fannie Farmer; and the various culinary writings (recipes, letters, poems) that comprise Dickinson's singular oeuvre. Whereas women's recipes make intuitive sense to the project of psychophysical aesthesis, Dickinson's place might require a brief explanation. The stylistic similarities between a recipe and a Dickinson poem (economy of form, staccato rhythm) call attention to a deeper truth: that Dickinson practiced writing and cooking as interrelated aesthetic activities. This practice is evident in the materiality and sociality of her writings, her nonnormative relationship to domesticity, and her culinary flair (sending family and friends baked goods; winning a prize at a local fair for her Rye and Indian bread; composing poems on the back of recipes). Building on the instructive scholarship of Virginia Jackson and Alexandra Socarides, this chapter is attentive to the material contingencies and "surplus of literal context" that help us rethink what lyric, a poetic form concerned with the experiential moment, can mean.[14] When placed in the company of both well-known and lesser-known cooks and when taking into account the charges of bad taste that her first critics leveled against her, Dickinson's writings clarify the stakes of women's gustatory experiments: to reorganize aesthetics around racialized experiences of lawless pleasure.

The relation between these two archives is meant neither to lyricize recipes nor to contextualize lyric poems. It is, rather, to recover the everyday materials that various women used to meditate on the intimate community of taste—a gustatory sensus communis—made possible through the interanimation of culinary and poetic measures. Together, the black cake archive and the Dickinson archive advance the project of psychophysical aesthesis by opening up the self-enclosed sense of taste to its own radical alterity. A sense so internally oriented as to appear foreign or external to the self, taste—especially sweet flavors, at once beautiful and robust—becomes the means by which women pressed racial blackness into a more illicit state of gendered feeling. Practicing an "aesthetics from below" that not even Fechner dared to imagine let alone implement, these cooks tested out the relation between physical magnitude and psychical sensation—food and pleasure—with the goal of revaluing the carnal appetites that aesthetic experience does not regulate so much as require.

THE SOUL OF FOOD

The "psychology of eating" laid out in Finck's gastronomic guide *Food and Flavor* assigns an aesthetic function to food. Finck argued that flavor, the gustatory quality of food, is the "guiding principle to the *science* of cookery. Strange to say, there are cookbooks in which the word Flavor is not found! The recipes given in such books may be correct, but to follow them mechanically is like playing the notes of a piano piece without knowing anything about expression marks. Flavor is the soul of food as expression is the soul of music."[15] Finck's criticism of flavorless cookbooks came at a moment when cooking was considered a means to an end: fuel machinelike bodies with the energy (vitamins and minerals) needed for productive labor. In response, and in keeping with his interest in psychophysics, Finck proposes that flavor is the subjective quality that "ensouls" cooking. In so doing, he opens up a day view of eating as a material but not strictly mechanistic activity. Taste sensation—flavor—was that aesthetic component. Cooking may be an exact science, but to make it an art the cook must bend or "transcend" the laws of chemistry and physics according to her personal taste. Flavor became to cuisine what the body image was to the body, tonal harmony to music, and perfume to smellscapes: the spiritual principle governing the interrelation between matter and mind. But unlike body image, tonal harmony, and perfume, flavor was the most corporeal aspect of food consumption. It was the soul that made aesthetic pleasure possible and, paradoxically, was an irrational faculty thought to dominate women and nonwhite peoples. Through flavor, taste became a sense with a uniquely embodied kind of soul—a raced and gendered one.

This paradox emerged through two opposing yet related civilizing projects: gastronomy, the "science of good eating" that made flavor a central feature of cuisine, and culinary science, which taught immigrant and working-class women to use nutrition (i.e., the chemical and physical analysis of food) rather than flavor as a guide to food preparation. Established in France by lawyer and self-professed epicure Jean Anthèlme Brillat-Savarin, gastronomy aimed to retrofit aesthetic judgment to sensory taste. It did so by encouraging a purposeful rather than libidinal relationship to food. In *The Physiology of Taste* (1825), he asserted that gastronomy "classifies [foods] according to their different qualities, indicates those agreeable in combination, and which, by measuring their various degrees of edibility, separates those which can form the basis of our meals from those which are no more than accessories."[16] Gastronomy styled itself as the "art" of taste, as painting was the art of seeing, and it accordingly defined "good food" based on preparation and presentation, grounded in the aesthetic principles of balance and harmony. A half-century later, Grant Allen rebutted Brillat-Savarin's claim; he argued that gastronomy was "not aesthetic" because human beings had developed cooking to make food digestible, not palatable. Furthermore, gustatory sensitivity—the ability to discern gradations of flavor—was a survival mechanism, not a means of lofty reflection. The purpose of the tongue's "highly discriminative nervous structures" is to alert the eater to the presence of substances that would "produce disastrous results upon the stomach."[17] Because the tongue's assessment is based on immediate intuition rather than disinterested intellection, and because it directs feeling inward to the state of one's body out of vital necessity (will this kill me or not?), whatever feelings that sensory taste generates are rooted in evolutionary principles. In short, sensory taste is anything *but* a universal value judgment. Allen did allow that in its "highest developments the practice of cookery ... almost rises to the dignity of an art."[18] Many late nineteenth-century thinkers, aiming to support the new art of gastronomy, used Darwinian logic to make the opposite argument: that gustatory sensitivity is entirely aesthetic because it facilitates species development, and even social progress.

In the effort to cultivate the public palate, gourmands emphasized that gustatory sensitivity and good food were mutually reinforcing. The problem with modern cooking was that it was unstructured. According to a *New York Times* article entitled "Good Cookery a Flower of Evolution" (1884), "few simple and uncompounded tastes [are] still left to us; everything is so mixed together" that it is nearly impossible "to realize the distinctness of the elements which go to make up most tastes as we actually experience them."[19] As a result, added *Scientific American*, most people "cannot distinguish the delicate natural flavors of food, and therefore lose a large share of that gustatory enjoyment which they should experience." Bad cooking blunts people's sensitivity, so that they "cannot relish the delicious peach without peppering and spicing it highly," while only "to an unperverted taste [is] water the sweetest and most agreeable of drinks."[20] Gastronomy promised to lower the public's high gustatory threshold. As with the women who douse themselves with heavy animal scents versus those who spray themselves with a whiff of floral essence, a low sensitivity threshold signals delicacy of feeling. Hence, the least refined eaters require higher intensities of spice to consciously register flavor, while the most refined eaters can detect trace flavor in the plainest foods. Gastronomy lets you relish food and claim refinement for it. In deriving maximal sensation from minimal stimulation, a gourmand experiences pleasure while asserting his low sensitivity threshold. Who else could find water sweet? Good cooking disciplined the tongue, Charles Henry Piesse explained, so that the "real gourmet" could "distinguish between various differences of flavors."[21] Akin to dietetic fads like Fletcherism, which instructed eaters to enjoy meager portions, gastronomy blurred the distinction between the epicurean and the ascetic, for in both cases, as Jennifer Fleissner argues, "so much is made of so little."[22] But unlike Fletcherism, gastronomy entailed taking disproportionate pleasure in discerning trace qualities (flavors) of food rather than in consuming trace quantities of food. The gourmand's gustatory sensitivity secured flavor as the civilized and civilizing component of physical eating.

This gastronomic cultivation, bringing the mind to bear on food, gained more urgency as Darwinian evolution undermined the idea of human exceptionalism. In *The Descent of Man* (1871), Charles Darwin observed, "Monkeys have a strong taste for tea, coffee, and spiritous liquors," which "proves how similar the nerves of taste must be in monkeys and man."[23] Because the act of eating and the physiology of taste bring humans and nonhumans close together, gustatory sensitivity—the psychological aspect of food consumption—is a capacity that reasserts species as well as racial difference. "Man has been called a cooking creature, to distinguish him from other animals, and the designation is both persistent and just," a writer for the *Times* noted.[24] In the periodical *Galaxy* as well, America's first celebrity chef, Pierre Blot, declared,

> The more civilized the man, and the higher his place in the human species, the more scientific and tasteful his cooking.... The savage falls on what is set before him, and proceeds to gorge himself.... The civilized man, the gastronomer, observes fixed laws in the order of his dishes: he never overloads his stomach and dulls his palate by partaking too much of one dish or set of dishes; but always so arranges the succession of dishes that the taste is constantly diverted and stimulated by variety.[25]

Gastronomy elevated taste by submitting it to aesthetic protocols, thereby civilizing the appetites otherwise indistinguishable from those belonging to savages, who "eat without thought of or care for relish, only to support life."[26] It became a crucial means of asserting human superiority and white supremacy. The gourmand finds pleasure not in consuming food but in tasting it, not in the feeling of satiety but in the finer feelings orchestrated by a dish. Gastronomy reassured white bourgeois eaters that no matter how primitive the sense of taste, their gustatory sensitivity certified their human and racial superiority.

Whereas gastronomy took aim at the mouth, culinary science went for the gut. The former civilized taste by transforming food from a practical utility into a medium of aesthetic pleasure, but the latter did the reverse: it returned food to the status of practical utility, and in so doing it excised taste entirely from the act of eating. Culinary science was a Progressive-era reform movement that originated in domestic science, first advanced in social reformer Lydia Maria Child's manual *The Frugal Housewife* (1829) and Catharine Beecher's *A Treatise on Domestic Economy* (1841); both framed household management as a pillar of republican womanhood. Culinary science advanced this bourgeois gender ideology, but its purpose was population management rather than family management. The "angel in the house" governed now the physiological as well as moral health of her family. Religious instruction combated spiritual ailments, while proper food preparation combated the digestive ailments thought to lead to poverty, alcoholism, criminality, and "worker discontent." In settlement houses, cooking schools, and women's magazines, culinary science taught women "every aspect of food except the notion of taste."[27] It spoke a language "based on chemical analysis and experimental physics," and it used concepts and formulas "no longer tied to sensorial experience," as Massimo Montanari explains. "Who knows the flavor of carbohydrates or the taste of vitamins?"[28] Ella Kellogg's *Science in the Kitchen* (1893), for instance, billed itself as bringing "order from out of the confusion of mixtures and messes . . . by the elucidation of the principles which govern the operations of the kitchen, with the same certainty with which the law of gravity rules the planets."[29] Feminists like Mary Bradley Lane viewed this order as necessary for the progress of civilization; her utopian novel *Mizora* (1881) features "schools where cooking was taught as an art," so that every cook is "a chemist of the highest excellence" and seasoning is "done by exact weight and measure, and there [is] no stirring or tasting."[30] This fantasy demonstrates that, contra what its name suggests, culinary science remodeled the kitchen into a factory, not a laboratory (where hypotheses are tested and particular outcomes are not guaranteed). "Indulgence and pleasure had no place in domestic scientists' recipes for workers, immigrants, and poor farmers," food historian Donna Gabaccia writes.[31] Home scientists did try out new tastes but followed recipes to a tee, with the aim of maximizing bodily energy.

Culinary science replaced matrilineal knowledge with universal laws, thereby refashioning women into home scientists who prepared food according to empirical procedures rather than inherited customs.[32] It was a doubly civilizing project that regulated both the eater and the cook, ensuring the productivity of the men and children eating home-cooked food while disciplining the women themselves, who were not to be trusted as cooks. Cultural authorities were "deeply suspicious of women's ability to make good food choices," especially given their alleged penchant for sweets.[33] In the *Galaxy*, diplomat Albert Rhodes attributed indigestion to women's bad cooking and waxed nostalgic for the bygone era when the "daughter worked with the mother, and was thus trained in the accomplishment of the culinary department, as the daughter is now trained to thrum on the piano."[34] Culinary science corrected course by teaching the angel in the house chemistry and physiology. In 1876, *Godey's Lady's Book and Magazine* praised cooking schools as a way to combat the "prevalence of dyspepsia among Americans." On the one hand, "Chemistry has analyzed the constituents of our food, and shown the effect of each upon health and bodily habits. . . . Schools of cookery . . . will lead her [every girl] directly to chemistry and physiology; on the other, it will fit her to be the mistress of a household."[35] Reformer Fannie Farmer, called the "mother of level measurements," advanced this ethos by insisting on scientific terminology and standardized cooking equipment (such as measuring spoons), both of which would yield an infinitely replicable final product and, more broadly, turn everyday cooking into an activity in step with progress. Farmer also formally reorganized the cookbook; her bestselling *Boston Cooking School Cook Book* (1896) was structured not around the social ritual of the meal (breakfast, lunch, dinner) but around organic compounds such as oils, starches, and "vegetable salts." Culinary science contained women's sweet tooth and controlled their folk knowledge by replacing subjective taste with objective units. These tools and methods made domestic women and domestic workers both the objects and the subjects of the civilizing mission of taste.

With cooking rebranded a culinary science, the civilizing power of bourgeois womanhood converged with racist stereotypes about black people's unrestrained appetite. As Tompkins argues, the kitchen remained a central space "where the threatening porosity between bodies—most specifically between ruling-class and subaltern bodies—is most apparent. As a practice, the intimacy of everyday nineteenth-century middle-class life necessarily took place across categories and spaces of social difference within the home."[36] By disciplining taste, a sense bound up with the "unruly flesh" and a "pleasure that did not submit to objective laws," culinary science reeled in the excess bodily pleasures to which ruling-class women and subaltern bodies were unevenly susceptible.[37] In an 1876 essay on the philosophy of frying, for instance, Confederate veteran Randolph Harrison declared that the "overweening love of darkey cooks for 'fat'" is hard for "them to resist," and so "the mistress will have to superintend the operation."[38] The purpose of professionalizing cookery was not to elevate white women and people of color into gourmands but rather to teach them the rules and regulations of cooking, especially given their intimate position as both caterers to and proxies for the mouths of their superiors. Culinary science brought the taste of differentially irrational persons in line with the white men they served.

Vilifying ethnic foodways as unhealthy and praising New England cuisine for providing the simple, plain taste their "students" needed for social belonging, culinary reformers "elevated a set of nationally applicable standards over local practice."[39] In combination with the homogenization of food, the standardization of food preparation threatened to render flavor extinct. Culinary science aimed to rationalize food preparation while neglecting flavor, whereas gastronomy "aestheticized" taste by inculcating a sensitivity for flavors. What emerged from these competing efforts to alternately elevate and excise flavor was the valuation of black cooks as the purveyors of a gustatory soul that could delight without diminishing the civilized palate. These entangled culinary projects were woven into the plantation nostalgia that saturated the public sphere at century's end. Fond remembrances of slavery were disseminated through Lost Cause myths as well as foodstuffs, as white southerners praised the flavorful dishes that slaves had once prepared for them. In the consumer market, Aunt Jemima pancake mix (established in 1890) served as "the extension of a slave woman" and "contributed to the widespread naturalization of black women's culinary abilities," Doris Witt argues.[40] The Jemima Code names the cultural script that the white appetite for the exotic other typically follows, whereby black women cooks are figured as "simply born with good kitchen instincts" and therefore "incapable of creative culinary artistry."[41] The gastronomic value of black culinary artlessness was inscribed in Creole politician Charles Gayarré's local history, "A Louisiana Sugar Plantation of the Old

Regime" (1887), printed in *Harper's Monthly*. He declares, "The negroes are born cooks," then continues:

> The African brute, guided by the superior intelligence of his Caucasian master, in the days of slavery in Louisiana, gradually evolved into an artist of the highest degree of excellence, and had from natural impulses and affinities, without any conscious analysis of principles, created an art of cooking of which he deserves to be immortalized.... Who knows how to roast? Who knows how to season *just à point*? And the flavor?—the flavor! Whither has it evaporated? How many delicious dishes have vanished forever of which the best cooks of France have never dreamed!... Black Pierrot or yellow Charlotte... is not within the comprehension of anyone born since the firing of the first gun against Fort Sumter.... The creole cook could not survive the acquisition of his own liberty in Louisiana.[42]

Gayarré was far from alone in contending that black cookery had become a "dying species" now that African Americans were without a benevolent "Caucasian master" to guide their gustatory instincts. Indeed, in neurologist S. Weir Mitchell's introduction to Célestine Eustis's cookbook *Cooking in Old Creole Days* (1903), he linked "the surrender at Appomattox" to the "calamity" of the "disappearance of the colored cook," and asked, "What other black art there was in the kitchens where the dark mammys reigned, who now can say?"[43] In the preface to *The Creole Cookery Book* (1885), African American cooking signified not only as a "black art" but also as an "occult science" that was "the hereditary lore of our negro mammies."[44] Bemoaning the loss of the "occult" magic of the meal prepared in bondage, these descriptions of slave cooking distance African Americans from modern civilization while framing flavor as a kind of vocal timbre: the material element that indexes racial authenticity. The secret to seasoning *just à point* has nothing to do with any particular property of food and everything to do with the status of the cooks as legal property. Southern cookbooks advanced the gastronomical art of flavor by insisting that the plantation was the best cooking school of all, the one that guided black people toward refined ends rather than—as culinary science did—effacing their instincts altogether.

With the rise in prominence of gastronomy and culinary science at the end of the nineteenth century, black people's instinctive "taste" both required rationalization and represented the "soulful" mechanism guiding the palate. More so than white women, black men and women were said to be driven by flavor, hence the occult "spirit" of their foods. Black Appalachian poet Effie Waller Smith wrote against this paradox in "Apple Sauce and Chicken Fried" (1903):

> You may talk about the knowledge
> Which our farmers' girls have gained
> From cooking schools and cookbooks
> (Where all modern cooks are trained):
> but I would rather know just how,
> (Though vainly I have tried)
> To prepare, as mother used to,
> Apple sauce and chicken fried.
>
> Our modern cooks know how to fix
> Their dainty dishes rare,
> But, friend, just let me tell you what!
> None of them can compare
> With what my mother used to fix,
> And for which I've often cried,
> When I was but a little tot—
> Apple sauce and chicken fried.[45]

A sort of ode to the inherited skills lost ("vainly I have tried") in the gaining of scientific knowledge of cooking, Waller's poem emphasizes the imagination and intimacy, the affect and memory, bound up with home cooking. This encomium to black maternal taste shows how gastronomy turned ascetic moderation into an aesthetic experience ("dainty dishes"), while culinary science outsourced the affective labor of retaining the gustatory "soul" of food to the very people too primitive to become "modern cooks." Thus, when Finck complained that the "nutritive aspects of food" were overshadowing the gustatory pleasures that it offered, he could not help but exclaim, "Flavor! In that word lies the key to the whole food problem. Undoubtedly the nourishing property of food is also of importance; without it we could not live. Yet if we eliminate palatability, it is no more than medicine."[46] Within the context of the dueling art and science of eating, Finck's praise for palatability establishes the "food problem" as a problem about the uncivilizable trace of race. It would be fair to say that gastronomy and culinary science allowed white Americans to have their proverbial cake and eat it too—a way to regulate black bodies while relishing the flavor that their cooking offered, a way to experience flavor, the uncouth "soul" of food, while reasserting their own superiority. (The post–World War II African American culinary style called soul food can be viewed as a reclamation of this "spiritual" component.) In this fashion, bourgeois women became the purveyors of food's racialized "soul," thereby making taste an *almost* aesthetic experience.

SWEETNESS AND POWER AND FLOUR

Combined with the postbellum era's plantation nostalgia, the projects of culinary science and gastronomy reconstituted flavor as the peculiarly embodied soul of food. Furthermore, sweetness was the specific flavor that excited this psychophysical soul. Although Allen argued that gastronomy was "almost" an art, he admitted that "sweet and bitter tastes form the real crux of the present question" as to whether taste sensations, as Burke had stated, can be beautiful.[47] The crux of sweetness was that it is as delicate as it is uncivilized. Insofar as the "pure gustatory nerve has been specifically modified in the course of our development so as to be chemically stimulated by certain absorbed substances," Allen stated, those substances that gustatory nerves register as "sweet" also "stimulate the flow of saliva, and mechanically [facilitate] the act of swallowing," as evidenced by the diet of "man, especially in an uncivilized state," being composed of fruits.[48] Survival hinges on sustenance, which is why people thought to exist in or close to a state of nature (i.e., primitives, women, and children) have an innate predilection for sweetness. Although the evolutionary purpose of sweetness might discount the sensation from aesthetic feeling according to a certain Kantianism, Allen nonetheless detected "a faint approach to the aesthetic level in tastes of the pure gustatory class" because they do not convey "the idea of grossness and bodily functions."[49] The taste buds located on the tip of the tongue—as far as possible from the visceral depths of the alimentary tract—are the ones that register sweetness. Mapping the physical distance from tongue to gut onto the cerebral distance needed for judgment, Allen allows that sweetness can become a "flavor of the higher sort," and sweet foods "*delicate,* a word at which once implies aesthetic discriminativeness."[50] Sweetness approaches the beautiful because it is a "pure gustatory" sensation that is evolutionary but not alimentary, stimulating salivation rather than more vulgar bodily functions.

Allen's physiological assessment of the aesthetic value of taste encapsulates how sweetness came to intensify the paradox of flavor: the most delicate taste sensation and simultaneously linked to unrestrained craving. Further, if the surfeit of bodily experience was not enough to jeopardize the aesthetic value of sweetness, the foodstuff that aroused this sensation certainly did: sugar, a slave crop. In his foundational account of "sweetness and power," Sidney Mintz argues that global racial capitalism—specifically, transatlantic slavery—powered the transformation of sugar from a luxury into an everyday necessity.[51] From the sixteenth to the nineteenth century, the triangular trade involved the export of sugar and molasses from Caribbean plantations to New England, where it was sold to distilleries for rum production, the profits of which went to purchasing Africans for slave labor on Caribbean sugar plantations. So entwined were sugar products and slavery that in the early nineteenth century, British abolitionists advanced the "blood sugar topos"; this trope figured sugar as the material trace of the enslaved body in order to convince consumers that when they drank sweetened tea they had blood on their tongues.[52] John Weiss adopted this logic of transubstantiation—sugar into blood—in his history of the Haitian Revolution (1791–1804), written in response to "questions connected with emancipation."[53] Weiss's "The Horrors of San Domingo," serialized in the *Atlantic Monthly* from 1862 to 1863, emphasizes that French colonizers did not realize "the dreadful paradox that sugar and sweetness are incompatible, and [France] could not taste the stinging lash as the crystal melted on her tongue."[54] Here, sweetness is not an objective fact but a subjective sensation, entirely dependent on the social position of the perceiver—whether they are a commodity or a consumer. Within this conceptual framework, the aesthetic pleasure of sweetness cannot be experienced apart from the "culture of taste and economies of pleasure" that slavery makes possible.[55] However delicate and dainty, sweetness cannot shake its material origins and relation to the (slave) market; the soul of food smacks of violent oppression.

In combination with culinary science and reformist efforts to curb unhealthy appetites, the profound "impact of the Haitian Revolution on dominant nineteenth-century Western ideologies about the 'negro's' capacity for republican governance" meant that in the postbellum era, sweetness no longer sparked sympathy for enslaved black people. Instead it prompted disgust with black citizens.[56] As historian Laurent Dubois writes, Haiti had become "an object of scorn and openly racist polemic" through stories about "the barbarity of the slave insurgents," the resulting "descent into laziness and lawlessness," and ultimately "the disastrous consequences of freedom."[57] That the United States imported raw sugar and molasses from Haiti and other countries with nonwhite populations rather puts too fine a point on the sugar-refining process: that it is a whitening project (as it is with flour and cotton). Sugar arrives from "Porto Rico, Brazil, Manila, Jamaica, San Domingo, and Barbadoes" in a "black, dirty, 'raw' state," mixed with "dirt, mud, sticks, niggers' shoes, old hats, pipes, bones, undissolved newspapers, and sleeveless shirts," the *Chicago Daily Tribune* salaciously asserted in 1873.[58] Molasses was even more barbarous. According to the *Manufacturer and Builder*, countries in the West Indies ship "dirty dark brown and almost opaque molasses" that puts U.S. grocers "in danger of finding a well-preserved dead cat or negro baby left in the barrel."[59] And then there was the symbolism of the product itself: the "color always suggested an affinity for black snakes and negro labor," the *Tribune* further stated.[60] In the United States, sugar refineries separated out "impurities" first by crushing and heating sugarcane, then boiling down the remaining juice and solidifying it into brown sugar, then dissolving the brown sugar, boiling it, and finally filtering it into granulated white sugar; the drainage from boiling is molasses (which, if distilled, yields rum). The finished product took on a "clean" crystalline form. It is little surprise that from 1880 to 1915, the sale of white sugar doubled and that of brown sugar and molasses dramatically sank. The sweetness of raw sugar and molasses no longer conjured tortured black bodies but instead stimulated fears about racial contamination.

Materially inseparable from black people's labor, sweetness became a site of deep contradiction. Not only was sugar laced with traces of the black body, but it was also the substance that stimulated the baser instincts of black people. In T. B. Thorpe's antebellum sketch "Sugar and the Sugar Region of Louisiana" (1853), written one year prior to his anti-Tom novel *The Master's House*, he suggested that the "peculiar labor, the constant indulgence in eating the juice of the cane, produces unwonted health, and consequently the highest flow of animal spirits [in slaves]."[61] The accompanying illustration depicts the joyful entanglement of sugarcane and a black baby, bearing out a climatological theory of racial difference (figure 4.1). Here, black people's childish sweet tooth is innate but also a result of their tropical environment. They have a sweet tooth partly because they are less evolved and partly because of their intimacy with sugarcane—as a kind of occupational hazard. The cultivator becomes the juicy crop. After the Civil War, as new technologies made sugar cheaper to refine and purchase, and as "economic devaluation coincided with cultural demotion," sweets became "feminized, and women were sweet."[62] The racialized sweet tooth came to underwrite a gendered relationship to sweetness—which is why culinary science targeted women. Women "have more natural difficulty" cooking than men do, Albert Rhodes asserted:

There is a sweet tooth running through her sex which affects her taste and renders her less trustworthy. She is less exact ... and does not reason as the man does.... He gives pounds and ounces as to quantity where she gives approximative handfuls. The man is more particular about the food which he consumes himself, which makes him more careful about what he prepares for others. Many women are content provided they have ice cream and sweet cake.... If the women at a table were not under the eye of the stern sex, they would begin dinner with dessert.[63]

Like the African Americans whose "occult" culinary art flourishes under the gentle guidance of the plantation mistress, women—dealing in approximations—require the "stern sex" to ensure that the dinner they prepare isn't actually dessert. Their consumption of sugar obfuscates the "peculiar" structures inhering in sugar production. The sweet tooth that black people allegedly had developed as a result of their labor in the sugarcane fields now takes hold in the bourgeois white woman. In turn, the bourgeois woman's sweet tooth acquires a domesticating function: to sublimate and perpetuate racial dominance by embodying the irrational appetites and drives that prove her inferiority to white men. If sweetness was a delicate aesthetic feeling indulged by delicate women, it was one that bore an uncanny resemblance to the bodily cravings attributed to black people.

The material production, symbolic significance, and innate predispositions associated with sweetness marked a kind of tipping point between soul and body, the moment when taste yields a pleasure as dainty as it is corporeally excessive. Although designated as in-home chemists, women did not distance themselves from their racialized sweet tooth or "bad taste." The popularity of black cake in this period, a dessert as old as slavery that nonetheless did not appear in print in the United States until the nineteenth century, certainly suggests as much. In its geopolitical history and in the symbolic weight of its darkness and density, black cake became a generative site for experimenting with the affective economy of sweetness. Black cake is a Christmas dessert born of the sugar plantation; Caribbean slaves adapted English plum pudding and fruitcake to regional resources: brown sugar, molasses, and rum. As the cake migrated to North America, and later as black cake recipes circulated in print cookbooks, the U.S. version came to differ from the original in one central way: it used brandy (from English fruitcake) in place of rum. Because this substitution yields a chromatically lighter black cake, molasses was crucial in distinguishing American black cake from its English relatives. If you

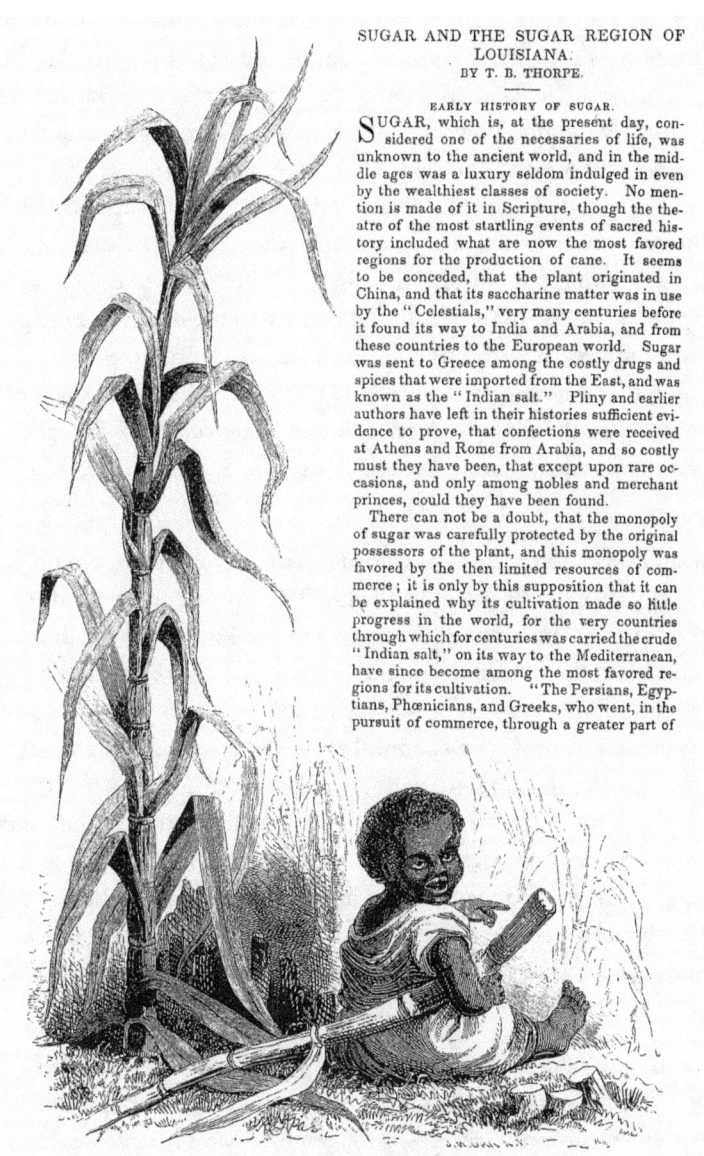

SUGAR AND THE SUGAR REGION OF LOUISIANA.

BY T. B. THORPE.

EARLY HISTORY OF SUGAR.

SUGAR, which is, at the present day, considered one of the necessaries of life, was unknown to the ancient world, and in the middle ages was a luxury seldom indulged in even by the wealthiest classes of society. No mention is made of it in Scripture, though the theatre of the most startling events of sacred history included what are now the most favored regions for the production of cane. It seems to be conceded, that the plant originated in China, and that its saccharine matter was in use by the "Celestials," very many centuries before it found its way to India and Arabia, and from these countries to the European world. Sugar was sent to Greece among the costly drugs and spices that were imported from the East, and was known as the "Indian salt." Pliny and earlier authors have left in their histories sufficient evidence to prove, that confections were received at Athens and Rome from Arabia, and so costly must they have been, that except upon rare occasions, and only among nobles and merchant princes, could they have been found.

There can not be a doubt, that the monopoly of sugar was carefully protected by the original possessors of the plant, and this monopoly was favored by the then limited resources of commerce; it is only by this supposition that it can be explained why its cultivation made so little progress in the world, for the very countries through which for centuries was carried the crude "Indian salt," on its way to the Mediterranean, have since become among the most favored regions for its cultivation. "The Persians, Egyptians, Phœnicians, and Greeks, who went, in the pursuit of commerce, through a greater part of

FIG. 4.1 Illustration accompanying T. B. Thorpe, "Sugar and the Sugar Region of Louisiana," *Harper's Monthly*, November 1853.

combine then bake flour, butter, sugar, eggs, spices (cloves, nutmeg, mace), dried fruits (raisins, currants, citron), and brandy but forget molasses, then you have made a fruitcake. Molasses, the treacly dregs of sugar refinement, was a culturally devalued sweetener, thought to materially contain and chromatically semaphore black bodies. But it was highly valuable to the American black cake—a kind of test case for the limits of sweetness's aesthetic bounds.

If the recipe is a text that archives culinary repertoires, then black cake recipes bring into focus not only the physical labor but also the racialized extravagance embedded in the feminized domain of the delicate. They produce and distribute sweetness through the unruly black body, thereby asserting the pleasures rather than the horrors of San Domingo, the island of sugar production and successful slave revolution. Take, for instance, one of the earliest U.S. print recipes for black cake, in Lettice Bryan's *The Kentucky Housewife* (1839):

> BLACK CAKE.
> Pick and wash two pounds of whortleberries; spread them out on a cloth, dry them and dredge them with flour. Prepare two pounds of currants in the same way. Seed, cut in half and flour two pounds of raisins. Wash the salt from a pound of butter, and *work it to a cream* with two pounds of sifted brown sugar; add half a pint of molasses, two powdered nutmegs, a spoonful of powdered mace and a large glass of brandy. Sift a pound of flour, beat a dozen eggs to a froth, and stir them in turn into the butter, &c.; then stir in alternately the fruits, beat it very hard at the last, bake it in a large deep pan with moderate heat. Make an icing of powdered white sugar and beaten white of eggs, in the proportion of four ounces of sugar to one white of egg; flavor it well with oil of lemon or extract of roses. Color it a little with some dark thick preserve juice, and put a thick coat of it over the cake.[64]

This black cake reflects native foodways, such as the use of whortleberries (relatives of blueberries) in place of citron. But what distinguishes it from other nineteenth-century recipes is its emphasis on physical work: picking, washing, spreading, drying, dredging, seeding, cutting, flouring, creaming, adding, sifting, stirring, beating, stirring, baking, making, flavoring, coloring, coating. That sticky dried fruits must be chopped, butter "work[ed] . . . to a cream," and fruits bound together in a heavy batter, beaten "very hard at the last," incorporates the female body—more specifically, the black woman's body—into the recipe. Bryan's is the rare southern cookbook to mention the people who actually do the cooking in the plantation kitchen. Her preface states: "Have established rules for domestics and slaves to be governed by, and fail not to give them such advice as is really necessary to promote their own welfare as well as your own."[65] Insofar as the antebellum kitchen was a marker of class division that housed potential "domestic insurrection," the acknowledgment of slave cooks in a cookbook that features an Afro-diasporic recipe—for a dessert no less—can be a way to reassert white governance, to cut against the potential fervor inhering in the cake itself.[66] Yet the presence of slaves in the cookbook and in the recipe's sweet ingredients (brown sugar, molasses) instantiates the black life that the mistress cannot entirely manage.

After the Civil War, sweetness becomes a sense of subjection, one that binds the racialized pleasure of gustatory excess to the precarity of black freedom. In many ways Malinda Russell's self-published *A Domestic Cook Book*—printed in 1866, when black people were free though not yet citizens—crystallizes the dialectic of sweetness as both a vital necessity (as Allen had claimed) and a spiritually "pure" feeling. In addition to being one of the first cookbooks, if not the first, authored by an African American woman, *A Domestic Cook Book* is notable for two reasons: it is devoted almost entirely to desserts, and it rejects the cookbook's impersonal conventions by using the author's life story to set a sentimental framework for the recipes contained within. As narrated in the preface, Russell was born to a freewoman in Tennessee, became a cook in Virginia, married, had a son "who is crippled, having the use of but one hand," became widowed, then moved back to Tennessee to run a pastry shop.[67] But in January 1865, a "guerilla party" stole her money and forced her out of town; she writes from Michigan, where she will "try and recover at least part of my property. This is one reason why I publish my Cook Book, hoping to receive enough from the sale of it to enable me to return home."[68] Russell invokes her life story again in the following section, "Rules and Regulations of the Kitchen," which briefly states, "The Kitchen should always be Neat and Clean. The Tables, Pastry Boards, pans, and everything pertaining to Cookery, should be Cleaned," then returns to her deservingness:

> Being compelled to leave the South on account of my Union principles . . . and having been robbed of all my hard-earned wages which I have saved; and as I am now advanced in years . . . I have put out this book with the intention of benefiting the public as well as myself. I learned my trade of FANNY STEWARD, a colored cook, of Virginia, and have since learned many new things in the art of Cooking. I cook after the plan of the "Virginia Housewife."[69]

The paratextual apparatus is where sentimentality sells the pastry cookbook. Further, the citation of Mary Randolph's popular cookbook *The Virginia Housewife* assures white women readers that Russell too is a bourgeois woman with comprehensive culinary knowledge. The reference to her tutelage under a "colored cook" both asserts her knowledge of the "occult" art of black cookery and establishes her as a worthy object of white sympathy. Every confection is a supplication.

A collection of dessert recipes published to bring the author financial security and autonomy, *A Domestic Cook Book* equates freedom with sweetness. In "Rich Black Cake," Russell bends sentimental conventions to invite sympathy while demonstrating her own sovereignty of taste:

RICH BLACK CAKE.

Two cups sugar, one and a half cup molasses, two cups butter, one cup sour cream, four cups unsifted flour, eight eggs, one and a half lb raisins, one lb citron, one lb currants, one tablespoon mace, one do. cloves, one do. cinnamon, one wine glass brandy, one do. rose water, extract of lemon.[70]

Although the narrative form of "Rich Black Cake" is highly orthodox, it is more a collection of nouns: objects and amounts. The refusal of verbs removes directives from the event and negates authorial presence or voice. This stylistic choice affirms that, as Doris Witt suggests, "preserving one's heritage or proving one's racial authenticity" was less important to black culinary writers "than achieving the rights and benefits of American citizenship."[71] With no narrative arc or sequential action, the recipe opens up the black cake to a wide range of potential performances. At the same time, Russell's self-effacement might be a strategy for hiding her blackness behind or even *in* the cake. The recipe's sparse prose, after all, heightens its only real luxury item, which is where Russell's personal taste asserts itself: *rich*, a quality that exists between the formal properties of flavor and texture. The adjective cites Mary Randolph's recipe "Rich Fruit Cake," but given its author's aims and aspirations, *rich* also aligns blackness with material extravagance: the cake thickened with unsifted flour, moistened by the sour cream's fat content, and punctuated with a tanginess (the sour cream and lemon extract) that "bites back" at the cloying sweetness of sugar and molasses. *Rich* redirects the sentimental frame of delicate sweetness away from sympathy and toward sumptuousness, even as the author presents the pastry cookbook as a dire matter of survival.

While Russell's recipe gives sweetness a fleshy feel, Abby Fisher's recipe explicitly signifies on the sensation's racial properties. Abandoning the search for sympathy, Fisher's cookbook *What Mrs. Fisher Knows about Old Southern Cooking* (1881) dramatizes the tension between culinary science and the "occult science" of plantation cuisine. The title telegraphs this tension: "Mrs. Fisher" dispels slavery's specious kinship claims (she is married but she is not Aunt Abby) and "knows" underscores learned (rather than magical) cooking skills, while "old southern cooking" pulls readers into the fantasy of a Stowian "Aunt Chloe," happily and intuitively cooking for her kind owners. Fisher's authorial persona is that of "a complete instructor," in her words, who selectively deploys the aura of the mammy minstrelsy figure.[72] As Rafia Zafar argues, had Fisher disclosed her own life story of being born into slavery, readers might have been "less willing to accept her authority as an expert."[73] And so Fisher moves between the two models of cooking available to her—the mammy and the culinary scientist—to capitalize on the white appetite for southern food. This goes some way in explaining why she presents black cake as fruit cake:

FRUIT CAKE.

One pound of flour sifted and browned in stove, one pound of citron sliced into very small pieces, one pound of raisins cut in small pieces, one pound of currants well washed and dried with clean towel, one teacup of almonds chopped fine, one tablespoonful of powdered cinnamon, half a teaspoonful of mace, one tablespoonful of allspice, half a teaspoonful of ground cloves, one pint of black molasses strained before using, one wineglass brandy, one pound of butter, one pound of sugar, one dozen eggs. Beat whites and yelks [sic] separate, light, before adding to cake.[74]

Fisher's cake appears more bourgeois than Russell's because it prescribes scientific measurements—pounds and teaspoons over pinches and dashes. But Russell's black cake is more anglicized, more fruitcake-like, because of its brown color (due to the sour cream). Fisher's cake is intensely black. In calling for two cups of "black" molasses—likely blackstrap molasses, an inkier and denser version of "true" molasses—this fruit cake is quantitatively blacker and qualitatively sweeter than Russell's. Bending the Jemima Code until it breaks, Fisher materializes southern blackness in abundance under the guise of the more reserved English fruitcake.

The U.S. social life of this Caribbean dessert demonstrates the various ways in which women cooks intensified the aesthetic possibilities of sweetness through (rather than apart from) the racial politics of sugar products. Emily Dickinson's 1883 manuscript recipe for black cake nicely distills this intensification. Sent to her friend Nellie Sweetser with the cake itself, the recipe stages the tension between the orthodoxy of the recipe form and the more revolutionary possibilities that its contents imagine.

> Dear Nellie
>
> Your sweet beneficence of Bulbs I return as Flowers, with a bit of the swarthy Cake baked only in Domingo.
>
> Lovingly,
> Emily
>
> BLACK CAKE—
> 2 pounds Flour—
> 2 Sugar—
> 2 Butter—
> 19 Eggs—
> 5 pounds Raisins—
> 1½ Currants—
> 1½ Citron—
> ½ pint Brandy—
> ½—Molasses—
> 2 Nutmegs—
> 5 teaspoons
> Cloves—Mace—Cinnamon—
> 2 teaspoons Soda—
>
> Beat Butter and Sugar together—
> Add Eggs without beating—and beat the mixture again—
> Bake 2½ or three hours, in Cake pans, or 5 to 6 hours in Milk pan, if full—[75]

Fisher makes a bolder claim to the "swarthiness" of sweetness than the poet, who referred to her kitchen as Domingo; Fisher's fruit cake is half the size of Dickinson's black cake but calls for double the molasses. Nonetheless, the quantities of the listed ingredients in Dickinson's recipe seem to hew toward the hyperbolic, as if to conjure the sensuous excess of blackness; when fully assembled, the cake weighs about twenty pounds.[76] Although Dickinson's recipe is a marked departure from Fisher's, Russell's, and Bryan's formal style, the black cake itself is socially conventional. Its massive size was likely modeled on Mary Randolph's "Rich Fruit Cake" (which called for four pounds each of flour, butter, and currants; two pounds each of sugar, raisins, and citron; and no fewer than thirty eggs) and, given that black cake is a holiday dessert, meant to make enough for gifting to friends and family.[77] Which is to say: Dickinson's cake is measured. In sharing with the aptly named Sweetser a recipe that partakes of the gift economy, Dickinson establishes blackness as a sweetness that—doled out in pounds and pints—moves not inward to the body but outward, as a mode of sociality.

Indeed, even the black cake recipe that would seem the most restrained still constitutes a "counter-archive of pleasure," following J. Michelle Coghlan.[78] Credited with standardizing the recipe into a vertical list of ingredients followed by narrative instructions, reformer Fannie Farmer included in her *Boston Cooking School Cook Book* a recipe for dark fruit cake that modulates but does not excise the "occult" sweetness inhering in its Caribbean materials.

DARK FRUIT CAKE.

½ cup butter.
¾ cup brown sugar.
¾ cup raisins seeded and cut in pieces.
¾ cup currants.
½ cup citron thinly sliced and cut in strips.
½ cup molasses.

2 eggs.
½ cup milk.
2 cups flour.
½ teaspoon soda.
1 teaspoon cinnamon.
½ teaspoon allspice.
½ teaspoon mace.
¼ teaspoon clove.

½ teaspoon lemon extract.

Follow directions for mixing butter cake mixtures. Bake in deep cake pans one and one-quarter hours.[79]

Farmer's cake is notable both for what it lacks (liquor) and for what it specifies (brown sugar). The omission of brandy underscores the purpose of culinary science, to reform society from the inside out—the soul by way of the stomach. Farmer's recipe registers the indebtedness of culinary science to the temperance movement. It also reframes the respectability politics of Russell's sentimental "Rich Black Cake" recipe. After all, with the exception of brandy and brown sugar, the two recipes are nearly the same. Both include a dairy component for moisture and lemon extract for a slight tang that textures sweetness. Perhaps most importantly, both are relatively small in their proportions. Reduced to amounts that do not reach a full cup, Farmer's is the smallest of the American black cakes. Where Fisher and Dickinson use molasses to enhance the "swarthiness" of sweetness, Russell and Farmer satisfy the "dark" sweet tooth while reigning it in. This tension plays out through quantity and quality: Farmer sweetens and darkens the cake by using brown sugar in addition to molasses while modulating that sweetness and darkness to mere half-cups. Far from a triumph of culinary homogenization, "Dark Fruit Cake" gestures toward a certain irrepressibility of flavor that not even level measurements can temper.

As with the scriptive-ness of the recipe, the racial meanings embedded in black cake are highly contingent. Recipes, following this chapter's first epigraph, can clarify but not codify embodied practices and performances. The uneven and often contradictory interactions of race, gender, region, and class across recipes for Caribbean black cake neither wholly contest nor entirely concede to wider efforts to limit the parameters of sweetness to the dainty and the delicate. Through their own formal and culinary innovations, these recipes perhaps unexpectedly reveal that white and black women's experiments with sweetness were also an experiment in racial embodiment. The dessert itself—so deeply tethered to racial capitalism, black sociality, and slave insurrection—becomes a way to recalibrate the quotidian "science" of cooking. In other words, sweetness comes to matter more and to matter differently in this epoch because it was the most "soulful" aspect of food yet deeply rooted in past and ongoing forms of enslavement, as well as in the racialized cravings that women were supposed to control. In the teeth of the transatlantic slave trade's history and afterlife, these recipes dramatically stage a psychophysical account of sweetness as an aesthetic feeling so subjective as to be social, so corporeal as to be a collective experience, and so incalculable in its effects as to unsettle distinctions between female domesticity and racialized lawlessness.

THE WOMAN IN WHITE IN DOMINGO

From Lettice Bryan to Fannie Farmer, recipes for black cake constituted an experiment in the racial surplus of sweetness, as cooks sought to determine the point or threshold where carnal appetite transposes into aesthetic feeling. In the psychophysics of sweetness, Emily Dickinson takes her place among several women who assayed the racial properties of the dainty. Her archive—poems, letters, recipes, foodstuffs, flowers, scraps, fascicles, and more—uniquely brings into focus the power of sweetness to racialize and enflesh finer feeling. More specifically, it lingers in the ungovernable gustatory pleasures inhering in delicacy, and that so doing dissolves distinctions between aesthetic sensitivity and the appetitive sweet tooth. Although the brain often acts as the organ of finer feeling in Dickinson's world ("The Brain—is wider than the Sky—"), Domingo signals the visceral cravings that course through if not constitute our very consciousness.[80] In the Dickinson archive, *Domingo* is the abbreviated name for the French colony Saint-Domingue—a word that compresses the Caribbean island's history as the first slave colony in the New World and its notoriety as the first nation-state born of successful slave revolution, when Haiti declared independence in 1804. A central site of psychophysical aesthesis, *Domingo* is shorthand for a racialized lawlessness, sensuous excess, and revolutionary politics that, set alongside nineteenth-century black cake recipes, provokes a set of larger questions about the convergence of the gourmand and the savage in the process of culinary and poetic world making.

The culinary science movement reached its height in the 1890s, the same decade that witnessed the publication of the first three collections of Dickinson's poems (in 1890, 1891, and 1896), as edited by her friend Thomas Wentworth Higginson and the writer Mabel Loomis Todd (whom Dickinson knew as her brother's mistress). Perhaps as a result of this convergence, Dickinson's personal taste—her gustatory proclivities and culinary prowess—anchored her initial reception. In Higginson's *Atlantic Monthly* essay "Emily Dickinson's Letters" (1891), he describes his first meeting with Dickinson in 1870, when she insisted that "'people must have puddings,'" as though sweetness is not a privilege but a right.[81] British literary critic Andrew Lang rebutted, "She could make a pudding though she had little sympathy with the luxurious taste which calls for such dainties. Poetry is a thing of many laws. . . . Miss Dickinson in her poetry broke every one of the natural and salutary laws of verse."[82] Lang further asked if Dickinson's writing was "poetry at all? . . . One must urge that lawless poetry is skimble-skamble stuff, with no right to exist."[83] Thus did a writer's sweet tooth, her penchant for puddings, become the basis for evaluating her verse. Dickinson's poetic body collapses distinctions between aesthetic taste and sensory taste; her failure to regulate her tongue constitutes a failure to regulate imagination. The *Literary World* considered Dickinson's poems "wrong in their excess."[84] She prepared her poems as she did her puddings: unthinkingly so. The *Chicago Journal* called her a "literary freak" whose verse has a "piquant flavor" and could tickle "a jaded palate but [could] have no permanent influence over a sane mind."[85] Arlo Bates similarly cautioned that Dickinson's poems "violated the canons of both [meter and rhythm]. There is a barbaric flavor often discernible."[86] Librarian Harry Lyman Koopman attributed these violations to the fact that "woman is more lawless than man."[87] Bodily craving drives the woman whose poetics is not unlike the "occult science" of flavor practiced by black cooks. Critics used Dickinson's primitive palate to explain her refusal to conform to poetic law, hence her overly flavorful and uncivilized verse.

But Dickinson proved elusive as ever. When not a lawless poet of flavor, she was an eccentric poet of sparseness. Helen Knight Wyman, on the twentieth anniversary of her cousin's death, published her personal essay "Emily Dickinson as Cook and Poetess" (1906) in the *Boston Cooking School Magazine of Culinary Science and Domestic Economics*. As befitting the premier periodical of the culinary reform movement, Wyman made a case for the poet's gender normativity by describing Dickinson's dedication to household management. Although we might think of Dickinson "as all soul and voice," and although Dickinson's "mind might be occupied with 'all mysteries and knowledge,' including meteors and comets, her hands were often busy in the most humble household ways," Wyman clarified. For evidence, she supplied readers with Dickinson's corn cake and rice cake recipes, which had been found pinned into "a favorite cookery-book belonging to my mother." The former was "copied by my youngest aunt [Lavinia], but signed 'Emily Dickinson,'" and the latter "given by a New York aunt and the words added, 'Both are delicious.'"[88]

EMILY DICKINSON'S CORN CAKE.
Wheat flour, two tablespoonfuls.
Brown sugar, two tablespoonfuls.
Cream (or melted butter), four tablespoonfuls.
Salt.
Eggs, one.
Milk, one-half pint.
Indian meal, to make a thick batter.

EMILY DICKINSON'S RICE CAKE.
One cup of ground rice.
One cup of powdered sugar.
Two eggs.
One-half cup of butter.
One spoonful of milk with a very little soda.
Flavor to suit.
   Cousin Emily.

The holograph recipes bespeak a commitment to the bland New England fare that culinary science called "American." This is a bourgeois, not a barbaric, Dickinson—the Emily Dickinson whose protestant New England family owned and frequently consulted Child's *The Frugal Housewife*. Unlike Dickinson's black cake recipe, the rice cake and corn cake recipes feature judicious measures and punctuation. In content, form, and print context, they temper her poems, deemed "ungovernable in form," with plain and simple taste.[89] Working against two competing ideas of Dickinson as all body ("literary freak") and all soul (the ascetic woman in white), Wyman's Dickinson appears a humble home scientist adhering to the laws of the kitchen.

Culinary science helps account for the gustatory idioms that critics deployed to dismiss Dickinson's verse as well as Wyman's use of recipes to defend it: for the former, her "piquant" poems stray beyond aesthetic laws, and for the latter, her bland dishes prove her disciplined domesticity. But perhaps more than culinary science, Dickinson's writings—spectacular entanglements of the concrete and the abstract—go furthest in explaining the culinary frame that detractors and devotees alike used to read her verse. They are a "*minimalist* text, through their internal economy, their conciseness and their minor degree of equivocation."[90] Here, Luce Giard is describing recipes but could be describing Dickinson's poems, known for words "boiled down to the core."[91] The resemblance between the two is clearest not in the rice cake and corn cake recipes—likely edited by Wyman for standard punctuation and to conform to the impersonal style of culinary science recipes. Stylistic affinity instead is clearest in the manuscript black cake recipe, which features spare diction measured out in dashes. Of course, Dickinson was not the only one to forge a correspondence between recipe and lyric. Lydia Sigourney's *Lucy Howard's Journal* (1858) is a "recipistolary novel," following Doris Witt, that features recipes such as "Apples and Cream," written in the epic rhythm of trochaic tetrameter à la Henry Wadsworth Longfellow's "Hiawatha."[92] What differentiates Dickinson here is that she is always questioning "the economy according to which poems are written, as she is also always questioning the economies within them, endlessly raising questions of relation and magnitude," in Sharon Cameron's words.[93] Recipes too are an art of compression; they make the most of every word. More than formally resembling recipes, Dickinson's poems moved in the same social circuit as recipes. Sharing poems with friends and arranging them into fascicles is no different than copying and pinning recipes into a cookbook. Like most middle-class women, Dickinson treated recipes and poems almost interchangeably—notably so when she copied Fr1564 ("The Things that never can come back, are several") onto the back of a friend's coconut cake recipe. In ways both stylistic and substantive, taste underwrote Dickinson's poetics.

Alongside the many cooks who experimented with the racially embodied surplus of sweetness, Dickinson assayed the "refined" feelings that sugar activated by collapsing aesthetic taste and sensory taste. Domingo in particular serves as a figure of gustatory pleasure that authorizes Dickinson's lawless style—in keeping with the commodification of racial difference to "enhance the white palate," which bell hooks famously calls "eating the other."[94] Dickinson's Domingo suggests a romantic racialism, but it is not merely reactionary. The island's first appearance in her early poems tethers lawlessness to a primitive state of nature rather than to black revolution:

> Butterflies from St Domingo—
> Cruising round the purple line—
> Have a system of aesthetics—
> Far superior to mine[95]

Domingo constitutes an edenic world, existing in a time prior not only to slave revolution but also to slavery. A similar trope unfolds in Fr726, in the speaker's declaration, "I could bring you Odors from St Domingo / Colors—from Vera Cruz—/ Berries from the Bahamas—have I." These early poems evoke the innocuous riches and pleasures of nature, and they establish the superiority of nature over the written word. However, during the American Civil War, Domingo comes to constitute a more racially than naturally lawless aesthetics. It is worth briefly noting here the mediating role of the *Atlantic Monthly* in this development. It is well known that in April 1862, following Higginson's *Atlantic* essay "Letter to a Young Contributor," Dickinson sent Higginson some poems and he swiftly responded with praise and perhaps light criticism. It is less known that the following June, the *Atlantic* ran the first installment of John Weiss's "The Horrors of San Domingo" and that shortly thereafter, Dickinson wrote to Higginson, "Your letter gave no Drunkenness, because I tasted Rum before—Domingo comes but once."[96] Having likely read the first installment of Weiss's serialized history, Dickinson relocates Domingo. It is no longer outside history but now a colony linked to New England by way of the sugar plantations and the byproducts, molasses and rum, manufactured at home. The sweet liquor intensifies the association of blackness with pleasure but, perhaps more importantly, casts Dickinson's poetics *as*

Domingo, as a racially intemperate, wayward, and uncontrolled "system of aesthetics."

Once filtered through the Civil War and the specter of the Haitian Revolution, Domingo signifies a lawless aesthetics infused with carnal desire—a cultivated taste immanent to the body. In 1863, after Higginson had moved to the South Carolina Sea Islands to train and lead a regiment of ex-slaves, she wrote him: "I trust you may pass the limit of War, and though not reared to prayer—when service is had in church, for Our Arms, I include yourself—I, too, have an 'Island'—whose 'rose and Magnolia' are in the Egg, and it's 'Black Berry' but a spicy prospective."[97] Here, Dickinson coyly references the Sea Islands. By invoking the racial connotation and "spontaneous and uncultivated nature" of the "Black Berry," she suggests that her "berries" have not yet sprouted, while Higginson's work of "'cultivating' black people" is well underway.[98] This racial "spice" reappears around 1865 in Fr1064, an ominous poem about craving. Domingo compounds the berry's blackness:

> As the Starved Maelstrom laps the Navies
> As the Vulture teazed
> Forces the Broods in lonely Valleys
> As the Tiger eased
>
> By but a Crumb of Blood, fasts Scarlet
> Till he meet a Man
> Dainty adorned with Veins and Tissues
> And partakes—his Tongue
>
> Cooled by the Morsel for a moment
> Grows a fiercer thing
> Till he esteem his Dates and Cocoa
> A Nutrition mean
>
> I, of a finer Famine
> Deem my Supper Dry
> For but a Berry of Domingo
> And a Torrid Eye—

The poem is about spiritual and political hunger, and these appetites are interwoven in the Crumb and Berry, compressed icons of the ritual components of sacrament: bread and wine, Christ's flesh and blood. But transubstantiation unfolds through the art of the "deconstructed" meal, which defamiliarizes the sacrament by breaking it down into its component parts: the lone crumb broken from the loaf, the lone berry severed from the vine. As a result, the Tiger ends up consuming (chewing? drinking? both?) a "Crumb of Blood." The Crumb and Berry register the uncontainable pleasures of what is unobtainable, and in a more specifically Christian key, the salivation in the hope for salvation. At the same time, "Domingo" invites an allegorical reading, in which the tiger represents the enslaved black person who, starved for freedom and humanity, hungers "for revenge," and the speaker represents the white person who hungers "for an emotional intensity that she imagines the slave has and she lacks."[99] Incorporating the enslaved black person's craving for political recognition into the speaker's spiritual craving for communion with God, the Berry of Domingo is a small "dainty," a Morsel, that entangles the outsized desire for the presence of the divine other with the outsized desire for the presence of the racial other.

Taste becomes a feeling that is all out of proportion. Sensitivity names the capacity to experience enormous pleasure from the daintiest morsel—a pleasure so intense as to be indelicate. The poem stages the untoward drama of gustatory pleasure, of the savage surplus at the heart of aesthetic sensitivity. And this drama unfolds at the level of meter, which is, in quantitative terms, both too much and too little. In addition to the political urgency conveyed by trochaic rhythm, the lines proceed in alternating sequences of nine and five syllables; the poem is either a half-foot more or a half-foot less than the prosodic norm (9/5/9/5), the common measure—alternating lines of iambic tetrameter and iambic trimeter (8/6/8/6)—that Dickinson typically used. As the poem's wayward rhythm accumulates and intensifies, the starved tiger, a figure of ravenous and predatory desire, develops a taste for the human. The dash between "partakes" and "Tiger" compresses eating into a momentary pause, a structural hinge that transforms the beast into a gourmand. Locating pleasure in quality rather than in quantity, a finer morsel rather than a "mean" cornucopia satisfies. "A little bread—A crust—a crumb—/ A little trust—a demijohn—Can keep the soul alive."[100] Desire turns fulfillment into famine; the entrée is now an appetizer. But desire reverses course: the "Morsel" of flesh packs a mean punch.

The bodily pleasures of the ascetic aesthete come to fruition in the poem's structural turning point, "I, of a finer famine." The speaker, neither in nor of the scene being described, occupies a precarious position that redoubles her precarious relation to the large tropical cat. Here, appetite does not draw a clear distinction between the presumptive human speaker and the beast; it instead brings them close to each other. Having consumed finer foods, they are both spoiled for "Nutrition Mean." The juicy human flesh and the Berry of Domingo that the Tiger and speaker now dine on, respectively, become less and less distinct. "What chemistry!" Walt Whitman exclaimed, "That blackberries are so flavorous and juicy."[101] According to the alchemical logic of transubstantiation, the tropical berry *is* juicy human flesh. Once the Tiger gets a taste of Man, it wants more; in getting a taste of his own humanity, the insurrectionary black person desires only freedom. "I, of a finer famine" does not turn away from the animal to the human but rather turns toward the impossibility of separating the appetites of the two. The violent scene of the Tiger's meal comments not on its savagery but on the carnal appetite that the civilizing project of taste cannot fully tame. By "deeming" her supper "dry," the speaker presents passion as rational judgment, as evaluative connoisseurship. But who exactly is savage, and who civilized? After all, "to eat animals is not to master animals but to betray one's own intimacy with them," Anne Anlin Cheng writes.[102] In eating the Berry of Domingo—as juicy as Man—the speaker begins to look a lot like the Tiger, even as she might become its next meal. With the collapse of Man and Tiger, citizen and slave, the savage who would rather starve than deign to eat menial food becomes the gourmand, while the gourmand comes face to face with the savage appetite at the core of her finer famine.

This torque—the turning of aesthetic and sensory taste into each other—offers a powerful meditation on the uncanny intimacy of the savage and the gourmand, figures that are so like each other as to be each other. Dickinson's first critics thought her a savage; her cousin considered her a gourmand; Higginson knew she was both. "Wayward and unconventional in the last degree; defiant of form, measure, rhyme, and even grammar; she had yet an exacting standard of her own, and would wait many days for a word that satisfied," he wrote in the *Christian Union*.[103] Higginson elaborated that Dickinson "wrote verses in great abundance; and though curiously indifferent to conventional rules, had yet a rigorous literary standard of her own."[104] Dickinson is an exotic beast crouched in the wilds of her home, patiently but ravenously awaiting the thrill of the chase and the deeper satisfactions of the Tongue. The rigor of Dickinson's poetic lawlessness, the cornucopia of lyrical morsels contained within her archive: these paradoxes mark a sustained effort to open up aesthetics to its ungovernable sensuality. In 1870, she told Higginson, "You speak of 'tameless tastes'—a Beggar came last week—I gave him Food and Fire and as he went, 'Where do you go,' / 'In all directions.'"[105] Tameless taste becomes a model for the poet as a "subversive figure," which Domingo renders inseparable from "Dickinson's furtive Africanist concerns," in the variant Fr1488B.[106]

> One of the ones that Midas touched
> Who failed to touch us all,
> Was that minute domingo
> The blissful oriole.
>
> . . .
>
> A Pleader, A Dissembler
> An Epicure, a thief,
> Betimes an oratorio,
> An ecstasy in chief;
>
> The Jesuit of orchards
> He cheats as he enchants
> Of an entire attar
> For his decamping wants.

The black and gold bird figures the poet as a trickster, but one with a tameless taste that proliferates possibilities, enchanting rather than explaining the world. Crucially, the bird is a *minute* domingo—an image that enjoins diminutive femininity to racial lawlessness. Unlike the large cat that dines on dainty flesh and berries, the minor bird has an oversized appetite, eating things "entire." Dickinson's poetics move between the "tameless taste" signaled by the Tiger and by the minute domingo, between the exacting standards of the savage and the wildness of the whimsical Epicure. The revolutionary blackness that Domingo semaphores, then, becomes a resource for turning finer feeling into its sensuous opposite.

Reorienting aesthetics around carnal and culinary activity, "tameless tastes" is less a figure for Dickinson's poetic project than it is that project's disorderly organizing principle. If Dickinson's poems are preoccupied with the feral pleasures immanent in finer feeling—that is, the excessive pleasures of gustatory discrimination—then her culinary practices (recipes, baking, and serving food) explore the inverse: the aesthetic potentiality of barbaric indulgence. According to her niece Martha Dickinson Bianchi, while the family attended church on Sundays, Aunt Emily would escort her to the cellar and give her "such lawless cake and other goodies, that even a child of four knew it for excess.... There was an unreal abandon about it all such as thrills the prodigality of dreaming."[107] The cake is lawless because of its sweet contents and the time of its consumption, the Sabbath. That it replaces the fragile sacramental wafer heightens the "excess" and "unreal abandon" of the pleasure it already affords. The lawless cake may not have been black cake, but its lawlessness carries a trace of Domingo.

Further, this fugitive consumption occurred around the summer of 1883, when Dickinson sent Nellie Sweetser the black cake recipe. While Dickinson's recipe takes its place among gendered efforts to experiment in the racial properties of sweetness, it is now worth texturing that account by reading the recipe within her decade-long preoccupation with "bad taste." Notably, Dickinson's recipe arrived in Sweetser's hands along with "a bit of the swarthy cake baked only in Domingo." With the substitution of "swarthy" for "black," Dickinson converts chromatic blackness into racial blackness. The cake's "swarthiness," in turn, corroborates another conflation: of island and kitchen. The violence of the sugar plantation is obfuscated now by the Amherst kitchen, where Dickinson baked alongside her mother, her sister Lavinia, and the family's "black" Irish housekeeper, Margaret Maher, described by Dickinson as "warm and wild and mighty"—*torrid*, we might say.[108] To be sure, Dickinson considered home a world entire; she named one hallway the Northwest Passage. And yet Domingo is striking not simply because it describes the tropical climate of a poorly ventilated room where a cake has been baking for three hours on a summer's day. Equally if not more important, it racializes the heart of the bourgeois home, the site where lawless pleasures—not revolutionary but also not regulated—infuse everyday domestic activities.

Dear Nellie
    Your sweet beneficence of Bulbs I return as Flowers, with a bit of the swarthy Cake baked only in Domingo.
    Lovingly,
    Emily

BLACK CAKE—
2 pounds Flour—
2 Sugar—
2 Butter—
19 Eggs—
5 pounds Raisins—
1½ Currants—

1½ Citron—
½ pint Brandy—
½—Molasses—
2 Nutmegs—
5 teaspoons
Cloves—Mace—Cinnamon—
2 teaspoons Soda—

Beat Butter and Sugar together—
Add Eggs without beating—and beat the mixture again—
Bake 2½ or three hours, in Cake pans, or 5 to 6 hours in Milk pan, if full—

Domingo is the scene of the black cake's preparation, and it is something like the mise-en-scène of the recipe's many meanings. At the juncture of contemporaneous black cake recipes and of Dickinson's culinary archive, the poem joins Fr1064 in staging racial difference as the gastronomic play of relation and proportion. The recipe may resemble the disciplined poetic measures of its lyrical counterparts, but in aesthetic thrift lies gustatory excess; Dickinson's culinary measures are lawless. In contrast to the crumbs and morsels scattered across her poetic archive, this recipe befits a woman who "stood for *indulgence*," according to Bianchi.[109] The copious amounts in "Black Cake" can be attributed to it being a Christmas specialty shared in a celebratory, lavish, and openhanded spirit. But the affective responses that lyric poems solicit hold as well for the recipe, as its accumulation of ingredients generates a feeling of fullness, even as the dash that punctuates "full" registers less a mark of finality than a pause for meditating on fullness as always incomplete, on fullness as a feeling that, over time, fades away and ever so recursively turns back into wanting more. This desire for more hinges on the juxtaposition of the recipe's lyric economy and the surplus value of its materials. And these materials embody racial lawlessness: raisins and currants incarnate the (Black) Berry of Domingo, and they are recontextualized by the sugar and molasses, which sweeten and darken the "berries" and reconstitute blackness as that which, like the recipe, exceeds itself. "Vinnie [Lavinia] says the dear would like the rule. We have no statutes here, but each does it as well, which is the sweetest jurisprudence. I enclose Love's 'remainder biscuit,' somewhat scorched perhaps in the baking, but 'Love's oven is warm.' Forgive the base proportions," Dickinson wrote in a letter, sent with a packet of the caramel chocolates she had made and the recipe or "rule" for them.[110] Her kitchen had no laws, which made its "biscuits" all the sweeter. Outside the prescriptions of the recipe, Domingo offered up "base" proportions that reconfigured what refinement feels like.

Read as constitutive of, rather than simply adjacent or ancillary to, Dickinson's poetic project, black cake, lawless cake, puddings, and other confections epitomize the centrality of sensory taste to what Fred Moten calls the "feminized locus of the culinary transaction, in the interest of a pleasure that is neither productive nor reproductive."[111] Renouncing print publication as well as marriage and motherhood, Dickinson experimented with alternative economies of womanhood, specifically the social reciprocity (etymologically linked to the word *recipe*) built into the culinary transaction. "You are a great poet—and it is a wrong to the day you live in, that you will not sing aloud. When you are what men call dead, you will be sorry you were so stingy," writer Helen Hunt Jackson told Dickinson.[112] But stinginess generates more fugitive economies of taste. In 1891, Amherst native Macgregor Jenkins recalled "play[ing] gypsy" as a child and raiding "neighboring pantries" with his friends; at one point they "besiege[d] the pantry window" at the Dickinson Homestead, "when unexpected help came. A window overlooking our camp was raised and Miss Emily's well-known voice called softly to us. To our amazement and joy, a basket was slowly lowered to us. It contained dainties dear to our hearts. Such gingerbread, such cookies and cake, no gypsies ever dreamed of! Many times afterwards our pressing needs were supplied by means of that fascinating basket. We adored our unseen deliverer!"[113] Poised at the windowsill, Dickinson appears a minute domingo, an epicurean accomplice to the children's game of food piracy. "We have all heard of the Boy whose Constitution required stolen fruit, though his Father's Orchard was loaded—There was something in the unlawfulness that gave it a saving flavor," she had written to her nephew Ned.[114] "Dainties" lowered in a basket from a window, much like lawless cake furtively shared with a girl on a Sunday morning, materialize the extraordinary pleasures of the everyday. Illicit intimacies cleave around taste: giving sweets to children outside the regulated kitchen (in the cellar, out the window) and publishing poems through the mail rather than in print constitutes a "system of aesthetics" bent on turning "stinginess" into hospitality, a morsel into a feast.

Yet the kitchen was not the lawless Domingo that Dickinson's recipes, cakes, and caramels suggest. Bianchi elaborated that her aunt was rather *precieuse* about it [baking]—using silver to stir with and glass to measure by. Her utensils were private.... An imaginary line was drawn all about her 'properties' which seemed to protect them against alien fingers—lent a difference in taste to the results.... She never trusted to her imagination there—never gave herself a chance to get a quart or a teaspoonful of Eternity in by mistake, as she gravely explained, though I caught a twinkle in her eyes, when she was concocting that wine-flavored delight she called 'Homestead Charlotte Russe.'"[115]

Like her "defiant" verse, to borrow Higginson's descriptor, Dickinson's indulgent dishes were in fact made possible by exacting standards and meticulous precision. Bianchi's description verifies Wyman's characterization of Dickinson; she was, apparently, a proper home scientist, a woman who used the methods advanced in the pages of the *Boston Cooking School Magazine*. This kitchen is *not* Domingo but instead a quasi-laboratory space of measurement, of method, and of prohibitions against any "alien fingers" spoiling the final product. This anecdote is entirely in keeping with a woman relentlessly pressing on the scalar tension of the body-mind relation—small stimulus, extravagant sensation—through the interplay of lawful restriction and lawless potentiality. The difference between Dickinson and Fannie Farmer, then, is that whereas for the culinary reformer, regulation tempers flavor, for the poet, regulation amplifies it. In Fr626:

> Undue significance a starving man attaches
> To Food—
> Far off—he sighs—and therefore—Hopeless—
> And therefore—Good—
>
> Partaken—it relieves—indeed—
> But proves us
> That Spices fly
> In the Receipt—It was the Distance—
> Was Savory—

The recipe is well suited to describe the mundane uneventful event, as it archives the lawless joys and longings that flourish in between the lines. Food relieves starvation, but it has a short shelf life. A more lasting pleasure is located not in the act of eating but in the recipe, where spices—like a minute domingo—fly. A couple months after sending Sweetser the black cake, Dickinson wrote her again: "Sweet Nellie, Blossoms, and Cakes, and Memory!

'Choose ye which ye will serve'! *I* serve the Memory. Blossoms will run away / Cakes reign but a Day / But Memory like Melody / Is pink Eternally."[116] Closer to a poem than to the cake it scripts, the recipe serves up Memory, archiving the tastes that so quickly dissolve in the mouth. It brings indulgent aesthetics and ascetic self-discipline close to each other. After all, it is not the food but the recipe that is savory, a word that has its etymological origins in the Latin word *sapere*, meaning "to be wise." *Savor* alerts us to a "dual relation to food, one in which necessity and extravagance, animal need and human desire, are literally rendered inseparable from one another," Fleissner explains.[117] Dickinson's savory recipes underscore how sensory taste, the "psychological" dimension of eating, became an object of home experimentation that allowed women to explore the uncouth pleasures of aesthetic feeling at the interface of raced and gendered embodiment. Across differences of race, class, and region, women exploited the fungibility of culinary and poetic measures to meditate on the corporeal excess at the core of consciousness. What emerged was a kind of gastronomic praxis of intimacy, one that remade delicacy of feeling into an undomesticated pleasure—one that unsettled more than it upheld the home.

....

Across an idiosyncratic if understudied archive of cookbooks, recipes, poems, letters, and desserts, and poised both with and against the reform projects of gastronomy and culinary science, a psychophysical aesthesis emerged that actively blended aesthetic taste and sensory taste. It was a project that elevated the gustatory sense not by proving that the base tongue has lofty reaches but instead by showing that aesthetic feeling requires the tastings of the tongue. Sweetness, the most refined feeling and yet entirely racialized because of its colonial history, was a symbolic and material intensifier for these experiments. It dramatically staged the deeply corporeal cravings, pleasures, and violences inhering in the most beautiful of flavors. And in the black cake recipes that moved among women, sweetness crystallizes the irresolvable tension between distinction and dissolution, between the aesthetic and the political, and between food's finer feelings and its material circuits. Crosscutting the universalized notion of food and civilizationist imperatives forged by culinary science and gastronomy, the black cake recipes authored by nineteenth-century U.S. women such as Bryan, Russell, Fisher, Dickinson, and even Farmer constitute an inquiry into the place of sensory taste in the role of conscious feeling. What does saliva have to do with the soul? In the process of dissolution, a new aesthetics is born. Dickinson's archive usefully demonstrates that this aesthetics or taste is not self-enclosed or solipsistic but highly social. Taste was a sense that escaped empirical capture, but this made possible new models of aesthetic taste organized around intimacy rather than disinterest, a community in which the extravagant potentialities inhering in the ordinary act of eating abound. "A modest lot—A fame petite / A brief Campaign of sting and sweet—/ Is plenty! Is enough!"[118]

Embracing a sense activated by chemical dissolution means practicing a "dissolute" aesthetics. Bookended by its raw brown state and the dark dregs of its refinement (molasses), sugar production traffics not only in pleasure but also in *disgust*, a word that means "bad taste." As Sara Ahmed observes, brown sugar and molasses were perceived as dirty not because the racial other is dirty but because the "other is already seen as dirt, as the carrier of dirt, which contaminates the food that had been touched."[119] Molasses in particular literalizes the discursive process and affective economy that Ahmed calls "stickiness," whereby a sign or object accumulates affective value through iteration and repetition. When "the body of another becomes an object of disgust... then the body *becomes* sticky."[120] Stickiness is the affective as well as the material quality of molasses, a thick syrup—a liquid veering into solidity—that becomes disgusting in the process of its production, but that, when binding other ingredients like flour and fruit together, becomes its opposite: pleasurable. As figuratively "sticky" qualifiers, *dark* fruit cake and *rich* black cake are the viscous trace of the incorporation of the black body—connected with raw materiality as well as waste—otherwise expelled from the technological and colonial production of refinement, or "good taste." These byproducts of white sugar perform attachments, bound up in power relations, experienced as disgust and desire. The black cake is not simply a contact zone of different cultural foodways, but perhaps more importantly a foodstuff that actively blurs subject and object, need and desire, good taste (the delicate) and bad taste (the dissolute). And the recipe is the genre that scripts its historically situated affective intensifications. In the culinary repertoires that leave sensory taste open to an ongoing aesthetic stickiness, then, we might attend to the possibilities that black cake proposes for consuming otherwise.

{ INTERVAL 4 }

Mouthfeel

Shortly after the American Sugar Refining Company (ASRC) trust formed in 1887 to restrict price competition in the sugar industry, it mounted a smear campaign "to denigrate brown sugar, whose refining it did not completely control."[1] Exploiting the equation of darkness with filth and whiteness with cleanliness, this campaign insisted on the dangers of consuming raw brown sugar and the health benefits of consuming refined white sugar. The brand name that the ASRC chose for its product played up the visible resemblance between sugar cubes and dominoes, but this name was lexically shadowed by the racial trace of the raw: Domin(g)o. According to one muckraking exposé on sugar production, brown sugar arrived at the Domino Sugar refinery in Brooklyn in "filthy bags" containing "cigar stubs, dead rats, negro babies, [and] bilge water." All this detritus was "washed off" in a vat, and then "a greasy old Dutchman stirred it up occasionally, expectorating tobacco juice here and there, and scrap[ed] his Williamsburg mud into the future frosting of our wedding cake."[2] Sweetness—linked here to middle-class matrimony—ever proffered the underbelly of sugar production, namely fears that the refining process further contaminated sugar with the animal, racial, and working-class bodies through which it passed along its route from the plantation to the palate.

One hundred forty years after the *Chicago Daily Tribune* exposé, multimedia artist Kara Walker confected the installation *A Subtlety, or the Marvelous Sugar Baby* (May to July 2014) in the abandoned Domino Sugar refinery as an "Homage to the unpaid and overworked Artisans who have refined our Sweet tastes from the cane fields to the Kitchens of the New World."[3] In the months prior to the refinery's scheduled demolition for redevelopment, Walker coated white polystyrene blocks with refined sugar, and from these blocks—sugar cubes, really—built a monumental sculpture, 75.5 feet long and 35.5 feet wide: *Sugar Baby* (figure 14.1). A mammy, she sports the minstrelsy aesthetic of the Aunt Jemima kerchief. A sphinx, she is crouched like a giant cat in both submissive aggression and aggressive submission, beaten down yet defiantly making the obscene *figa* gesture (its meaning varies from "good luck" to "fuck you") with her left hand. Her biological kin and culinary byproducts surround her: life-sized worker boys (carrying either baskets or bunches of bananas) made from sugar and cast in molasses. *A Subtlety* is named after the edible toys that seventeenth- and eighteenth-century European aristocrats consumed, though this title calls attention to one starkly clear interpretation: white sugar is white supremacy; black lives continuously feed capitalism. *Sugar Baby* is, after all, a classical ruin housed within an industrial ruin—the Domino factory an "example of the kind of wreckage the progress of capital has historically left in its wake," as John Levi Barnard notes.[4] Walker's art tracks the historical continuity of the white consumption of blackness, from taking in the "blood sugar" of decorative confections to taking up and taking over gentrified urban spaces like Brooklyn.

A Subtlety enters the past and present of slavery through the culinary, which makes its claim to the aesthetic through sweetness, a gustatory sensation that Enlightenment philosopher Edmund Burke described as "the smooth of taste." He cited breast milk as an example of how "water, oil, and a sort of sweet salt, called the sugar of milk" combine to give a "great *smoothness* to the taste."[5] With the bodily fluids of motherhood already "baked into" the aesthetic concept of the smooth, *Sugar Baby*'s two corporeal excesses combine, as the sheer magnitude of sugar that comprises her maternal body redoubles the outsized sexual body parts (breasts, buttocks, vulva) that she serves up. Here Walker recalibrates the culinary "as an effect of an evacuation of reason that's bound to a certain giving up of, which is to say, giving oneself up to, the body and its base or basic (or bassic) functions," in the words of Fred Moten.[6] This giving up of oneself to sensual corporality has been constructed as anterior to or in excess of the intellection that aesthetic feeling requires. Although her voluptuous curves are smooth, *Sugar Baby* is granular; her sugary body cuts against the aesthetics of smoothness. She proposes a new aesthetic, one realized

FIG. 14.1 Kara Walker, *A Subtlety, or the Marvelous Sugar Baby* (2014). Polystyrene foam, sugar, 35.5 × 26 × 75.5 feet. Artwork © Kara Walker, courtesy of Sikkema Jenkins & Co., New York.

through the *syn*aesthetic of the body's "base or basic (or bassic)" functions: mouthfeel, a sensation that enjoins the taste of something to its tactile consistency. As philosopher Carolyn Korsmeyer writes, "Touch nearly always accompanies the sensation of taste ... especially if one extends tasting beyond the isolations of laboratory experimentation and considers actual eating, including biting, chewing, and swallowing."[7] *Sugar Baby* torques the civilizing project of taste into the uncivilizing project of mouthfeel.

Sugar Baby also demands a gesture specific to mouthfeel: licking. Here, I borrow from Moten's theorization of the jazz lick, an improvisatory pattern or phrase described as a "culinary-musical pleasure" that is "always tempt[ing] and sometimes fill[ing] in the open possibility of social life that attends the instrumentality to which such impure means consent."[8] *A Subtlety* meditates on the historical pain behind that synaesthetic pleasure, a pain articulated through a different kind of improvisatory, synaesthetic lick: that of the lips (taste) and that of the whip (touch). The lick is, after all, an erotic and aesthetic act of servility: a stylized gesture that conveys libidinal desire by overperforming the pleasure of tasting. The lick is less about ingestion or consumption than it is a drawn-out moment of encounter. It plays the eroticized counterpart of the savoring that the gourmand performs;

licking slows down time to linger, pause, and let things move (dissolve, moisten, coat) at their own speed. But where savoring twins the slow time of a food particle's dissolution in the mouth to the slow time needed to process and reflect on that physical activity, the lick is less contemplative. It draws out the act of tasting for the sake of taste itself—we might call it a decadent act. As Mel Y. Chen explains, licking is a notably queer gesture that constitutes a "physically and emotionally intimate, pleasurable, and desirous" scene, but because it demonstrates the "interconstitution of people and other people, or people and other objects," it always threatens to transform erotic intoxication into actual toxicity.[9] *Sugar Baby* is sweet yet monumental, composed of refined yet grainy particles, her pose regal from the front yet crude from the back. She demands to be licked and threatens to bite back.

An improvisational gesture that makes contact with an object (its flavor, its texture) without necessarily consuming that object, licking moves the black woman's body outside the constrictive frame of the abject sexualized object. Walker's *Sugar Baby* represents "bad taste" because, as Moten reminds us, with dessert "there is no question of nourishment or necessity"—and the bad taste she represents exposes the "bourgeoisie's self-consuming jones."[10] This staging of the desire for the black body *as a crav-*

ing or "jones" has an antecedent in the autobiographical sketch that precedes William Wells Brown's novel *Clotel* (1853). This sketch includes an anecdote about how Brown came to learn the alphabet. While a fugitive slave on the run, Brown purchased sticks of barley sugar and used that sugar to coerce a Quaker boy in Ohio to teach him how to read. "I thought I had better give him a taste ... so I called him to me, and got his head under my arm, and took him by the chin, and told him to hold out his tongue; and as he did so, I drew the barley sugar over very lightly. He said, 'That's very nice; just draw it over again. I could stand here and let you draw it across my tongue all day.'"[11] The homoerotic (bordering on pederastic) exchange doubles as gustatory inscription. The fugitive draws the sugar across the boy's tongue, so that his own tongue eventually will draw sounds from written signs. In soliciting a lick—a "mouthfeel" that plays on the tongue—Brown suggests that white people's consumption of the racial other is, both materially and metaphorically, a sugar craving. The fugitive and the sphinx are purveyors of "bad taste" that convert white people's sugar craving into capital.

But mouthfeel has a multitiered history. Foundational to Brown's scene of sugary transaction is Antiguan abolitionist Mary Prince's declaration in her slave narrative *History of Mary Prince* (1831), "To be free is to be sweet."[12] Her statement seems clear and simple, but it obscures subject and object to powerful effect. Is to be free to be *the* or *a* sweet, or is to be free to taste sweetness yourself? This syntactical obfuscation reproduces the insurgent potential of sweetness. Alexander Weheliye argues of Prince's narrative, "The (almost) unlimited capacity for opiate-inducing syrupy tastes and textures frees the potentiality of subjugated subjects ... since they, deprived of both sugar and liberty, know the hunger that moves in survival as freedom."[13] Bearing out the insurrectionary potential of tasting the sweets that the law denies you, Prince's assertion frames sweetness as a quality that represents the opposite of the sugar plantation: freedom. But the gustatory lick of sugar cannot be experienced apart from the tactile lick of the whip. As the transatlantic slave trade took hold in the seventeenth century, *lick* acquired an additional meaning: "a smart blow (c.f. to lick on the whip), a beating."[14] When two enslaved boys are subjected to repeated punishment, Prince writes, "Lick—lick—they were never secure one moment from a blow."[15] At another moment, a slave owner flogs a woman "as hard as he could lick ... till she was screaming with blood. Her shrieks were terrible."[16] A lick: a quick pass of the tongue, coating an object with saliva, and a quick application of the whip, coating a body in pain and blood. Further, Prince's history tracks another "lick" applied to the black body, one that compounds the lick of the whip: salt. Prince had been forced to harvest salt in bogs, where "our feet and legs, from standing in the salt water for so many hours, soon became full of dreadful boils, which wear down in some cases to the very bone, afflicting the sufferers with great torment."[17] Salt eats at her black body, which in turn becomes the salt that she mines. Salt was tortuous labor and torture device: Prince was subjected to "seasoning," the practice of rubbing salt into the whipped slave's bleeding wounds.[18] Behind every lick of the lips is a sequence of other licks—the whip, the salt—that in fact consume the enslaved woman's body, leaving her barely intact.

Refiguring these culinary histories, *A Subtlety* quite literally textures sweetness with the lick that it solicits—a lick that materially produces the impossibility of *not* consuming the black body. Its sugary excess cuts against the "lick—lick" of the whip as well as the salt that licks the enslaved woman's body dry, while reducing sentimental readers to the brackish waters of their own tears (a *Torrid Eye*, as Emily Dickinson might say). The *Sugar Baby*'s proportions assert the black woman as a site of white consumption, the lick of the lips never far removed from the lick of the whip. But like the declaration "To be free is to be sweet," the monument refuses objecthood (slave) and liberal subjectivity (self-possession),

activating what Moten considers the "necessary relation between enjoyment, flight, and resistance that the culinary brings to life."[19] The *Sugar Baby* refuses to give herself over to capitalist valuation, and this refusal comes alive through its mouthfeel. Under the summer heat, the molasses-covered skin of *A Subtlety*'s worker boys softened and melted (figure 14.2). The melting was the point; Walker describes molasses as having "this kind of tar resonance. There is this feeling that things don't just go away, and that this molasses has been oozing down these walls for a hundred years or so. It never dries completely, and it stays alive."[20] The boys appear mutilated, as though they have been licked by the whip—or by white consumers. Their bright amber "juice" (a mixture of resin and molasses that is suggestive, in both color and texture, of the juicy berry of Domingo) drips off their bodies and pools around their feet. Exposure to time and sunlight makes each a New World Venus de Milo. Yet the syrupy surface of the molasses "skin" that makes them so vulnerable to decomposition is what allows them to resist objectification; the boys are objects in the process of unbecoming. The same goes for *Sugar Baby*. The molasses dripping from the factory ceiling "licked" or stained the monument, while *Sugar Baby* was subject to constant erosion because the sugar granules themselves did not bind. Glistening and granular white purity

FIG. 14.2 Detail: Kara Walker, *A Subtlety, or the Marvelous Sugar Baby* (2014). Artwork © Kara Walker, courtesy of Sikkema Jenkins & Co., New York.

needed, as white supremacy does, constant reinforcement. In this fashion do the mammy-sphinx and her worker boys stand as "profane fragments"—tempting a tongue lick while evoking the whip lick—that dissolve subject and object.[21]

A fragile installation that daily decomposed and, no less, was scheduled for demolition, *A Subtlety* is a "counter-monumental site," following Dana Luciano, that resists the willful amnesia of slavery and empire encoded in national monuments.[22] Walker exposes monumentality as a mode of sugarcoating, which is to say, she turns sugarcoating from an act of euphemistic cover into an act of exposure. The whiteness of refined sugar makes explicit the black woman's body that historically "bears the traces of bareness," in Moten's words.[23] This mouthfeel advances a tempting pleasure experienced outside objecthood and subjectivity, in part by using taste-texture to trouble distinctions between surface and depth, as well as oppression and resistance. In soliciting a lick that both tickles and penetrates, *Sugar Baby* turns dispossession from abjection into a refusal of the logic of possession. In this way, the lick thwarts the distribution of the sensible—the injunction not to talk with your mouth full, not to speak and eat at the same time—and thereby turns the palate into a source of what Davide Panagia calls "inevitable political disorder."[24] Walker's *A Subtlety* refuses white consumption by exploiting the aesthetic and temporal fragility of its material properties. The synaesthetic mouthfeel it betokens opens up sweetness to the tactile consistencies and cultural inconsistencies of our historical present, all while offering up a model of consuming otherwise: licking. "Numerous usages in our languages indicate that people who have five senses find it difficult to keep their functions distinct. I understand that we hear views, we see tones, taste music. I am told that voices have color. Tact, which I have supposed to be a matter of nice perception, turns out to be a matter of taste," Helen Keller explained.[25] Walker powerfully upends the "matter of taste" through appeal to "tact," though as the next chapter illustrates, in Keller's case, the tactile is also a sense that establishes the impossibility of subjectivity as the very condition of being.

Touch

{ 5 }

LIFE WRITING BETWEEN
SKIN AND FLESH

> Though forced to touch and be touched, to sense and be sensed in that space of no space, though refused sentiment, history and home, we feel (for) each other.
> —Stefano Harney and Fred Moten, *The Undercommons*

> Touch has its ecstasies.
> —Helen Keller, *The World I Live In*

In 1888, a brief notice appeared in the philosophy journal *Mind* announcing a new edition of Gustav Fechner's *The Little Book of Life after Death*, printed "just after the aged man had gone to discover what truth there was in his bright speculation of half a century ago."[1] Immediately preceding that notice was one about "a second Laura Bridgman" named Helen Keller, blind and deaf since infancy.[2] The intellectually precocious eight-year-old girl, the notice stated, was following in the footsteps of Bridgman, reformer Samuel Gridley Howe's celebrated deaf-blind student at the Perkins Institution for the Blind. The next year, Bridgman died and Keller matriculated at Perkins. Keller was a subject of sympathy, as Bridgman had been, but as one coming of age during the rise of the New Psychology, she was also an object of study. Bridgman's death secured Keller's status as a noteworthy "fund of psychological interest," in the words of *Mind*'s editor, George Croom Robertson.[3] Psychologists might learn how consciousness, in the absence of visual and auditory stimulation, develops through tactile sensations. The brief contact between Fechner and Keller—the deceased psychophysicist and the newly born psychological subject, rather like two ships passing in the night—registers a transitional moment when feeling was drifting away from broader metaphysical questions but had not yet landed on positivist shores.

The New Psychologists studied Helen Keller in her youth, but Keller had her own ideas about the tactile surfaces and interfaces that compose human consciousness—and, in a more psychophysical key, about what it means to *be* and what disabled being means. Keller brings us full circle from the psychophysics of sight to that of touch, shuttling us in this chapter toward the inverse of the body image (i.e., the psychical reality governing physical reality): the tangible matter governing psychical reality. Keller inverts the question posed by amputee soldiers during the Civil War, *What happens when inner feeling drives the physical body*? In the early twentieth century, she asks, *What happens when external touches constitute interiority?* Nerve specialist S. Weir Mitchell claimed that the physically incomplete amputee's phantom limbs disclose a mind too rigid to adapt to new bodily configurations; experimental psychologists claimed that the touches constituting the mentally incomplete deaf-blind girl suggest a mind so plastic as to have no metaphysical configuration, no *I*, at all. Limning an expansive notion of selfhood or "soul life" at least partly indebted to Emanuel Swedenborg's mysticism, Keller spent most of her life showing that touch expands rather than contracts what *I* is.

That touch could render consciousness so porous as to be amorphous—no clear division between inside and outside, mind and matter, sensation and stimulus—has much to do with the amorphousness of touch itself. Aristotle designated touch the most primitive sense not because it is crude but because it is primal: a holistic or "common" sense. The persistent question of whether touch is a sense in itself or the precondition of sensing led physicist John Le Conte to note in 1885 that "metaphysicians and physiologists [differ] in relation to the services that ought to be attributed to the sense of touch" because the "same tactile nerves are cognizant of several distinct kinds of sensation," including "pain, temperature, [and] titillation."[4] Despite the shortcomings of its circuitry, touch was the "most important [sense], for by it alone is the first impression of matter made upon man, and without it he would not be able to truly and fully commune with the outer world," a writer for *Harper's* explained.[5] Pushing the Lockean view of touch as the "first impression" through which we acquire knowledge, psychologists transformed the epistemological Molyneux problem (Can a man who lacks a sense acquire the idea pertaining to that sense?) from a thought experiment into a laboratory experiment. But now the question was not only how we know through the senses; it was also how what we know through the senses shapes who we are. Hence psychologist Joseph Jastrow's claim in his "Bridgman, Laura and Helen Keller" entry in the *Dictionary of Philosophy and Psychology* (1901) that a "psychological study of the blind deaf-mute may contribute largely to an understanding of the relation of the senses to one another, and of the relation of sense endowment to intellectual achievement and general mental development."[6] In the *American Anthropologist*, John Hitz—superintendent of the Volta Bureau, Alexander Graham Bell's research institute for deafness—argued that Keller's responsibility was to disprove the "pedagogical limitations heretofore supposed to prevail in regard to the educational ability of those bereft of what so far have been considered the most essential organs of perception in attaining academic distinction." Keller acquired academic distinction through "the manual or finger alphabet" and thereby "[entered] into conscious life."[7] Only through a regulated touch can a deaf-blind person have any kind of meaningful existence.

In her writings, Keller frequently discussed the textures of her conscious life. "The sense [of touch] is the chief medium between me and the outer world," she explained.[8] Keller explored touch as an embodied genre and as a literary genre: as autobiography, the genre of interiority, of selfhood. Given that touch is a sense of surfaces, the question follows, here asked by critic Sidonie Smith, "What might skin have to do with autobiographical writing and autobiographical writing with skin?"[9] One answer lay with Susan Stewart's observation that touch is "a threshold activity—subjectivity and objectivity come quite close to each other."[10] In a similar vein, Judith Butler has proposed that touch "is given form through an autobiographical account" but requires "openness to the outside that postpones the plausibility of any claim to self-identity."[11] In these critical accounts, touch is an autobiographical sense not because it constitutes the self but because it stages the drama of a self occasioned by alterity, a self in a state of perpetual deferral. As a "narrative discourse in which 'I' is both subject and object," autobiography reproduces the split, or dual, self of touch.[12] In Keller's oeuvre, the lived genre of touch and the literary genre of autobiography dramatically merge. Not only her physical but also her literary corpus are demonstrably autobiographical, forced as she was to write memoir after memoir for a public eager to access a mind mediated solely through contact. Autobiography at once amplified and muted Keller's public voice. She lamented the forced solipsism:

> Every book is in a sense autobiographical. But while other self-recording creatures are permitted at least to seem to change the subject, apparently nobody cares what I think of the tariff, the conservation of our natural resources, or the conflicts which revolve about the name of Dreyfus.... Until they [publishers] give me opportunity to write about matters that are not-me... I can only do my best with the one small subject upon which I am allowed to discourse.[13]

By the age of twenty-eight, Helen Keller was already exhausted with the autobiographical subject "Helen Keller." Although most disabled persons were excluded from narratives of self-formation, Keller was entirely trapped within them. An author of eight autobiographies—*The Story of My Life* (1902–3), *Optimism* (1903), *The World I Live In* (1908), *Out of the Dark* (1913), *My Religion* (1927), *Midstream: My Later Life* (1929); *Journal* (1938); and *Teacher: Anne Sullivan Macy* (1955)—she lived a life that she had been narrating since childhood. Most knew Keller's life story anyway. As early as 1896, when Keller was sixteen years old, *Harper's Monthly* editor Charles Dudley Warner reminded readers, "The story of Helen Keller is too well known to need repetition"—and then proceeded to repeat it.[14] The public appetite only grew: Doubleday issued ten reprints of *The Story of My Life* in its first year of publication. Autobiographical touch made Keller's *I* possible even as it foreclosed other possibilities. In Keller's sense of touch, lived experience and the literature of experience entirely fused.

Deeply interlaced with the bodies of other people and things, Keller's life writings elucidate the tactile feelings that unsettle post-Enlightenment fictions of autonomous selfhood. After all, G. Thomas Couser explains, because the autobiographical *I* is "typographically identical with the Roman numeral *I* and phonemically identifi[ed] with the word *eye*," it encourages us to "conceive of the first person as unique, integral, and independent."[15] The autobiographical *I* also homophonically suggests that the self is a visual being (*eye*). Keller's life writings, with their intimate depiction of touches that yield a relational self, remake autobiography from a narrative of independence into one of interdependence. Keller exploited autobiography to claim rational autonomy while "exposing [its] lie of the age-old masculine fantasy of singularity," or *Bildung*, mainly by revealing how "people with disabilities find their live[s] so inextricably tethered to the lives of others."[16] To be sure, even though Keller was an outspoken socialist and feminist, her politics were not consistently radical (and in any case first-wave feminism was itself a highly racist and classist project). Kim Nielsen has revealed that Keller did not "see herself as part of a minority or oppressed group, only as an individual who had difficulties."[17] Keller's first autobiography, *The Story of My Life*, the first time a disabled person had told their story to a mass audience, bears out her conservative disability politics. It reifies the "dominant script of disability as individual tragedy" and certifies Keller as a "supercrip" who "overcame" personal adversity despite her limitations.[18] As Georgina Kleege writes, *The Story of My Life* "set the standard" for disability autobiography as "a quintessential 'triumph over adversity' story."[19] While it is undeniable that *The Story of My Life* portrays disability as an individual obstacle to be overcome, it is equally the case that its thematic and material deployment of touch undoes the very concept of the individual, ultimately in the service of remaking *I* from a fixed entity into a collaborative activity. Revealing Keller's radical exteriority rather than her possessive interiority, *The Story of My Life* pushes at the limits of the genre that confined its author. Indeed, Keller's psychophysics of touch goes some way in explaining why *The Story of My Life* was reviewed in *Good Housekeeping* as well as in *Popular Science Monthly* and *American Anthropologist*. For some, it played at the heartstrings; for others, it disclosed a person who wore her mind on her skin.

Keller limns consciousness as a contact zone, a meeting place between two or more bodies. I thus read her as a psychophysical researcher in her own right—in this case, she was her own test subject—as well as an early phenomenological theoretician. Here, I amend Diana Fuss's insightful claim that Keller's writings "resemble exercises in phenomenology" to argue that her writings *were* exercises in phenomenology.[20] Keller's life writings advance the psychophysical model of touch as relational and use that relationality to explore the ontological reversibility of subjectivity—that is, the self as other, and the subject as object. This concept anticipates mid-twentieth-century phenomenologist Maurice Merleau-Ponty's notion of *double sensation*: "My body is recognized by its power to give me 'double sensations': when I touch my right hand with my left hand, my right hand, as an object, has the strange property of being able to feel too.... The body ... tries to touch itself while being touched."[21] The idea of touch as a chiastic relation of reversibility between self and world has been foundational to current feminist, queer, and disability theories of embodied difference. Brought into being by the outside, by otherness, touch is a "queer orientation," Sara Ahmed argues, because what "touches is touched, and yet the toucher and the touched do not ever reach each other; they do not merge to become one."[22] This intimacy without synthesis allows touch to "cross boundaries rather than create distance," Janet Price and Margrit Shildrick claim, and thereby register the everyday interdependencies that disability brings into focus.[23] In the critical tradition that Keller helped inaugurate, touch is a double sensation that activates a "fleshy engagement with material bodily variation"—an engagement that has less to do with attachment and more to do with immersion in difference.[24]

While Keller's literary corpus contributes to the phenomenological traditions advanced across today's critical fields, equally if not more important, her formulation of touch as a double sensation, as the lived condition of an intersubjective consciousness, had direct bearing on her historical moment. Keller's touch constituted something like the limit case of white racial impressibility, the Lamarckian theory that acquired sense impressions stimulate species progress. Insofar as impressibility protected the "refined, sensitive, and civilized subject" from the "coarse, rigid, and savage elements of the population suspended in an eternal state of flesh," Kyla Schuller argues, in Keller's white disabled body, skin and flesh became close.[25] To be unimpressible is to be assigned to the raced and desexed state of "flesh" that, in Hortense Spillers's seminal account of transatlantic slavery, names a wounded bodily state, the condition of rupture that turns black life into the raw material from which profit and culture are extracted.[26] Flesh is the carnality of being, the corporeal substance too rigid to absorb sensations and adapt to the world. Skin, however, is the impressible surface seemingly hardwired to the nervous system, itself a "differentially pliable and agential entity in continuous interplay with its environment."[27] Unlike flesh, skin routes embodiment through "the aesthetic history of 'surface' and the philosophical discourse about 'interiority' [that] provide the very terms on which modern racial legibility in the West is limned."[28] It functions as "a threshold, a point of contact, a site of intersubjective encounter, between the inner and outer self and between the self and the other," as Michelle Stephens writes.[29] In Keller's autobiographical body, skin and flesh touch. Although her mind was a skin that absorbed external data, the dominance of touch suggested to many that her mind was only external data. Keller's disabled female body turns racial impressibility in on itself, showing how a person can be imagined as so intersubjective as to be no subject at all, rather flesh-like.

Describing a mind that many found illegible if not unintelligible, Keller delineated a mode of consciousness mediated almost solely through touch. Her sensory experiments unfolded alongside and influenced the psychologists who studied her. Joseph Jastrow and William James drew on E. H. Weber's psychophysical studies of tactile sensitivity to investigate touch as the switch point between the conscious self and the hidden self—as a vector of double consciousness. In her autobiographies, however, Keller remade double sensation from a disorder into a gift, expanding consciousness beyond the bounds of the singular. This chapter, attentive to the fact that Keller's *I* emerges only in the company of others, tracks the psychophysical aesthesis of touch through Keller's physical and aesthetic entanglement with her teacher Anne Sullivan and her ally W. E. B. Du Bois. These queer pairings reveal a kind of ontological reversibility; in *The Story of My Life* (1903), Keller and Sullivan's dyadic self turns the skin into a zone of psychical contact, and when *The Story of My Life* keeps company with Du Bois's autobiography of a people, *The Souls of Black Folk* (1903), the black person's mind appears to have a skin, a physical surface. If autobiography proffers the "idea of the self as other," then Keller's and Du Bois's autobiographies point to touch as the sensation of double consciousness—one arising from exclusionary practices.[30] Taken together, the life stories told by "gifted" or "talented" people studying their own experiential doubleness reveal the interdigitation of raced and disabled being. As skin and flesh fold in on each other, interiority becomes external to itself and bodily difference transforms from a biological fact into a genre of feeling—touch—shared by two friends inhabiting proximal cultural locations.

SELVES BELOW THE THRESHOLD

As a child, Helen Keller recalled, she "was told that nine tenths of the human being's impressions came to him through his eyes and ears, and I wondered if my friends and I would ever be able to understand each other."[31] Touch, it seemed, trapped her "in a form of epistemological narcissism" and "an essentially infantile relation to herself."[32] According to John Le Conte, the "eagerness with which the infant examines by touch every attractive object within its reach" proves that mental development entails a shift away from tactile toward visual and auditory epistemologies.[33] The deaf-blind person's mind had not developed past "infantile receptiveness."[34] Although touch was considered an infantile sense, it had new purchase for psychologists interested in how the perceptual faculties shape thought. In a *Popular Science Monthly* article on "the diversity of various minds," Joseph Jastrow established three types of thinkers: the "eye-minded" person who absorbs more "what he reads than what he hears"; the "ear-minded" person for whom a "lecture impresses him more deeply than a review article"; and the "motor-minded" person (which means "muscular and tactual sensations") who would be "aided by writing what he [had] read."[35] Classified as a "motor-minded" type, Keller "provided clear evidence of the possibility that one could think in a variety of 'material'"—not just images and tones but objects.[36] Studies of Keller's tactile mind were part of the broader rise of lived experience's epistemological currency, which psychophysics had helped to launch. Around this time, the "object lesson" took hold in North American and European education systems; using material objects as the basis for instruction served the purpose of "training children's perceptive abilities" and "giving a child experiences ... in order to shape them into a reasonable being."[37] Notably, Maria Montessori developed a "plan of tactile education that made use of touchable 'didactic material' to hone the discriminatory capacities of schoolchildren" in the hopes that students "would understand their fingertips as vital instruments for knowing and encountering the world."[38] Education reformers sought to nurture self-formation through a cultivated touch. Psychologists, however, found that touch in fact is a substrate of consciousness that deforms the self.

The idea that touch is an occult experience of the self's own otherness began with Fechner's doctoral adviser turned colleague E. H. Weber, whom E. B. Titchener considered "the foundation stone of experimental psychology."[39] Weber's 1834 book *De Tactu* (*Concerning Touch*) and his 1846 book *Der Tastsinn und das Gemeingefühl* (*The Sense of Touch and the Common Sensibility*) marked a germinal moment in not only the history of touch but also natural science. They were the first studies to produce a body of knowledge about human sensation based on experimental methods for measuring subjective experience. Weber had set out to reveal the inner structures of touch by measuring the relationship between tactile stimuli and feeling subjects' mental experience thereof. His first innovation was to differentiate touch from pain on the basis that our "sense-organs are directed outwardly not inwardly, in order that the mind may receive impressions from the external world: it would become very confused if internal processes were persistently demanding its attention. One intestinal canal touches and rubs against another, lungs rub against the skin of the pleura covering the chest cavity, muscles press and rub against each other: but we have no sensations of these."[40] Pain, much like the sense of taste, is a feeling that directs the subject inward to the state of their own body. Conversely, the surface feelings of the skin orient the subject outward to others, to the world. For Weber, Mark D. Paterson explains, any measure of touch "entails a conscious attention to sensation from the outside," as opposed to the bodily interior.[41] To access the nervous structure mediating this consciousness, Weber blindfolded his laboratory subjects and then applied a tool with two movable compass points, called a caliper, to various parts of their bodies, at every point asking them to report if they felt one or two contacts. This design allowed Weber to determine the smallest distance apart that the compass points could be placed for subjects to still perceive them as distinct. He called the minimum distance at which subjects perceived the points the "two-point threshold—e.g., the threshold of consciousness." As a result, touch become "understood . . . as purely psychophysiological."[42]

Weber was the first to empirically determine that touch has a psychological component. At midcentury, the calipers were redesigned into an instrument called the *aesthesiometer*, which pushed this experiential dimension into a more pathological domain (figure 5.1). In the 1880s, Jastrow made some improvements to the aesthesiometer, and soon after, educators like Montessori began using it to train children's tactile sensitivity. Outside the school and in more clinical settings, however, tactile sensitivity was not a faculty to be cultivated but a symptom of nervous sensitivity. When Wilhelm Wundt used Weber's two-point method in his 1858 dissertation on the touch sensitivity of hysterics, he inaugurated the aesthesiometer as a tool for diagnosing abnormal minds. William James secured this link between tactile responsiveness and mental states in his *Principles of Psychology* (1890). While discussing the plasticity of the mind—how it adapts to the environment—James asserted that "nervous tissue" is endowed "with a very extraordinary degree of plasticity" and thus "the phenomena of habit in living beings are due to the plasticity of the organic materials of which their bodies are composed."[43] The skin, organic material composed almost entirely of nerves, was an appropriate object for determining "to what outward influences the brain-matter is plastic."[44] Hence, whereas insensitive or coarse skin cannot absorb sense impressions that would modify the brain, sensitive and pliable skin facilitates the modification of the mind, an important process for evolutionary development. By way of Weber's psychophysical research, the material surface of the body became at century's end a key vector of neuroplasticity—and of civilization.

When James reviewed French psychological studies of hysteria in his essay "The Hidden Self" (1890), the skin had become an overly plastic material. He argued that an unconscious and a conscious life coexist and that trances can be used to reach the unconscious. James linked the unconscious self to touch: "If touch be the dominant sense in childhood, it would thus be explained why hysterical anaesthetics, whose tactile sensibilities and memories are brought back again by trance, so often assume a childlike comportment."[45] The return

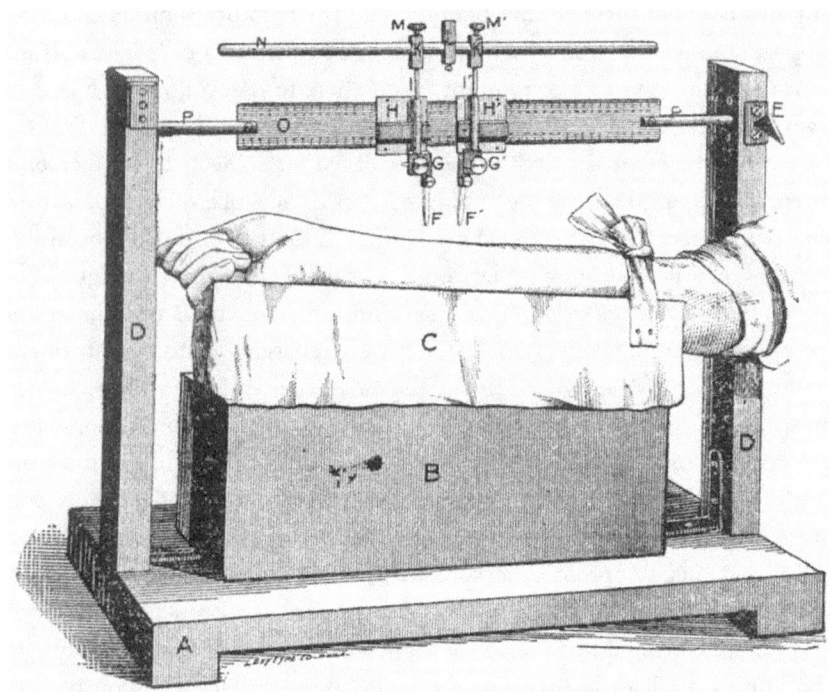

FIG. 5.1 Diagram from O. T. Mason, "Notes: A New Aesthesiometer," *American Journal of Psychology* (1888).

of the infant mind in the entranced hysteric explains her tactile sensitivity. Touch, then, is the modality through which the "hidden self" manifests. Various "pricks, burns, and pinches" on the skin that go "unnoticed by the upper self" are "complained of as soon as the under self gets a chance to express itself by the passage of the subject into hypnotic trance."[46] The means of proving this distinction between the eye-minded "upper" self and the tactile-motor-minded "under" self was the aesthesiometer:

> Doctors measure the delicacy of our touch . . . by the compass-points. Two points are normally felt as one whenever they are too close together for discrimination. A certain person's skin may be entirely anaesthetic and not feel the compass-points at all; and yet this same skin will prove to have a perfectly normal sensibility if the appeal be made to that other secondary or sub-consciousness. . . . M. Binet, M. Pierre Janet, and M. Jules Janet have all found this. The subject, whenever touched, would signify "one point" or "two points," as accurately as if she were a normal person. But she

would signify it only by these [hand] movements; and of the movements themselves her primary self would be as unconscious as of the facts they signified, for what the submerged consciousness makes the hand do automatically is unknown to the upper consciousness, which uses the mouth.[47]

The aesthesiometer discloses that touch is the "secondary" self. Repressing tactile sensibilities makes possible the conscious rational self. Touch is how the self's otherness surfaces; it is the sense of contact between self and self-as-other. Even though the aesthesiometer was developed to rationalize touch, it ended up revealing something irrational about the sense: its close connection to occult dimensions of consciousness. To measure the surface-level sensitivity of the skin was to register the unquantifiable depths of the self.

In medicine and psychology, touch was the sense of a hidden self, a kind of psychical substrate inhering in all humans that pathologically "motor-minded" people (e.g., hysterics and epileptics) could not contain. The hidden self's uncontainability manifested in physical symptoms that included "contractions of the hands, convulsive tics, violent contortions of the extremities, extravagant poses and chaotic gesticulations."[48] In one striking example in "Notes on Automatic Writing" (1889), James describes a case of "hand consciousness" in a "hystero-epileptic" woman named Anna Winsor.[49] He found in Winsor a subject whose consciousness was "split into two parts, one of which expresses itself through the mouth, and the other thorough the hand. The mouth consciousness is ignorant of all that the hand suffers or does; the hand-consciousness is ignorant of pin-pricks inflicted upon other parts of the body" and carries "its own peculiar store of memories with it."[50] Hand consciousness and mouth consciousness coexist but are strangers to each other. Winsor's hand, like a phantom limb, did not belong to her. "It is clairvoyant," James stated, and it "endeavors to prevent her from injuring herself... when she is raving. It seems to possess an independent life."[51] In their search for the boundaries between body and mind, and between unconscious and conscious life, psychologists lighted on a theory of the self as divided into higher and lower faculties. Reason, will, and judgment constitute the "visual self," manifested in "mouth consciousness," while instinct, affect, and reflex govern the "tactile self," manifested in "hand consciousness." This division applied to all people but was most pronounced in those groups or individuals considered too impressionable—not to external stimuli but to one's own inner, primal depths—to prevent this hidden self from dominating their personality. In abnormal subjects, the conscious self is subordinated to the excessively lively and agential hidden self. James thus viewed double consciousness as involving split personality, a condition in which the perceiving subject is "partly known and partly knower, partly object and partly subject."[52]

The deployment of the aesthesiometer in clinical studies of pathological (and pathologically female) types rendered tactile sensitivity a literal metric of rationality that could be applied to other groups, specifically disabled people. In an essay on Laura Bridgman written for *Mind* in 1879, psychologist G. Stanley Hall claimed that the aesthesiometer revealed that "Laura has in her hands and face a sensitiveness to ordinarily imperceptible and sometimes imaginary dust which very closely resembles, save in degree, that described by [Jean-Martin] Charcot and Westphal as one of the characteristics of incipient mania."[53] Here, the manic's abnormally developed mind and Bridgman's unevenly developed mind circulate under the sign of disability. And as with Bridgman, Keller's status as a "supercrip" was perpetually shadowed by deviance. In the inaugural issue of the *Psychological Review*, Jastrow reported on his study of Keller at the 1893 Chicago World's Fair. There he had set up a psychological laboratory in the Anthropology Building to determine the "relative functions of the senses, and the faculties that interpret and assimilate the facts of sensation in the economy of the mental life."[54] For this public experiment, Jastrow used an aesthesiometer to determine Keller's tactile threshold, which he then measured against the threshold of sighted and hearing audience members. "Helen's fingertips and the palm of her hand (a region interesting because it is here that the impressions of the manual finger alphabet which she 'reads' are in part received) are decidedly more acute than in the average individual," Jastrow revealed.[55] Keller later rebutted this claim, arguing that her tactile sensitivity was not innate but learned, because the "only superiority there is comes with use and intensive training."[56] Although the experiment falsely found that Keller was hypersensitive, it did reveal that she had been turned into an aesthesiometer—her body itself a means of determining the point at which the hidden self crosses the threshold of consciousness. Keller was not entranced, and in no way suggested mania. For the disabled girl, contra the hysterical woman, the occult potentiality of tactile sensitivity hewed closer to the oracular than the pathological. "She has learned so well what movements people make under the influence of different feelings that at times she seems to read our thoughts," the *New York Times* declared in 1889.[57] Many assumed that Keller, all touch and no sight, necessarily wore her hidden self—a kind of sixth sense—on her skin.

Proximal to clinical discourses of hysteria, psychological studies of touch help clarify the stakes of heated postbellum debates about whether deaf and deaf-blind people should communicate with their hands or with their eyes and mouth. Scientific thinkers remanded touch to an early stage of ontogenetic development, figured by the infant, as well as to an early stage of phylogenetic development, figured by the racial primitive. The educational philosophy of manualism and that of oralism marked two different responses to the problem of disabled embodiment. Whereas manualists such as Edward Gallaudet "destabilized the hegemony of hearing" by advocating for sign language and deaf-specific institutions, oralists "reasserted the power of normalcy" by championing lip reading and oral speech with the aim of assimilation.[58] Although his work is best known for benefiting the hearing ear, Alexander Graham Bell was a zealous oralist, and in fact he had first invented the telephone to make speech visible to deaf people. Bell considered sign language akin to the "hand consciousness" of hysterics and to the manual communication of primitive races, especially Native Americans. For eugenicists like Bell, if lip reading fostered a rational mind, then "to sign was to step down in the scale of being," writes historian Douglas Baynton.[59] Sign language also encouraged intermarriage among deaf people, which Bell feared would lead to the formation of "a deaf variety of the human race." At the National Academy of Sciences in 1884—there, that same year, C. S. Peirce and Jastrow presented on the law of psychophysical parallelism—he insisted, "We do not find epileptics marrying epileptics.... It is reasonable to suppose that the continuous intermarriage of persons possessing congenital defects... would result after a number of generations in the production of a vigorous but defective variety of the race."[60] Lip reading encouraged marriage (hence, sex) between deaf and nondeaf people, which would biologically dilute the "defect." (Holding fast to his principles, Bell married a former pupil from the Horace Mann School for the Deaf.) More immediately, it forced deaf-blind people to "overcome" their tactile sensitivity and ensure normativity relative to the pathologized others linked to hand consciousness.

Given Bell's commitment to biological models of human difference, it is unsurprising that "Charles Darwin" was the first word that he spelled into Helen Keller's hand. Since the age of six, Keller had found in Bell a lifelong friend and benefactor; she dedicated *The Story of My Life* to him. In 1890, she received her first speech lessons from educator Sarah Fuller, who had learned her pedagogical methods from Bell. But because Keller was blind as well as deaf, oralism was for her profoundly manual. To lip read, according to Keller's

FIG. 5.2 Anne Sullivan holds open a book and reads aloud to Helen Keller. Keller's left hand touches Sullivan's lips to feel the vibrations of Sullivan's words (c. 1894). Courtesy of the Perkins School for the Blind.

biographer Joseph Lash, she placed her "hand lightly on the lower part of [the speaker's] face and the fingers of her other hand in [the speaker's] mouth so that she could sense the position of the tongue," as well as feel the articulatory movements and vibrations that accompany specific sounds, which she learned to vocally imitate.[61] "Sometimes the flow and ebb of a voice is so enchanting that my fingers quiver with exquisite pleasure, even if I do not understand a word that is spoken," Keller admitted.[62] Far more sensual than it was ever meant to be, lip reading entangled bodies: hands on throat, fingers in mouth, the handling of tongue and lips. Oralism aimed to overcome the disabled body's difference and produce an autonomous subject, but Keller's disability made that project impossible. Oralism could not restrict the touches that directed her consciousness toward plurality. In fact, it ended up further plasticizing her. With Anne Sullivan, who had acted as prosthetic eyes and ears since Keller was eight, in the intimate feedback loop between lip reader and lip speaker, the two women dramatically embodied Jamesean double consciousness: the sighted Sullivan the above-threshold self and the tactile Keller the below-threshold self (figure 5.2).

The link between touch and consciousness that James first explored in studies of hysteria and hypnosis resurfaced in his *Atlantic Monthly* essay "Laura Bridgman" (1904). In it, he asked why Bridgman was intellectually superior to other deaf-blind people in her midcentury moment and why Keller was intellectually superior to Bridgman in her turn-of-the-century moment. James admitted that the "mental material of which it [Keller's reality] consists would be considered by the rest of us to be of the deadliest insipidity," and yet her "thought is free and abundant in quite exceptional measure. What clearer proof could we ask of the fact that the relations among things, far more than the things themselves, are what is intellectually interesting, and that it makes little difference what terms we think in, so long as the relations maintain their character."[63] In this elaboration of radical empiricism, what is less important is the avenue of experience (e.g., sight or touch) than how mental life maps out the transitive relations among those avenues. Jastrow similarly remarked that although the "deprivation of the two most intellectual of the senses leaves an indelible impress upon the habits and manners of the mind, yet the community of mental economy . . . is by far the more notable factor in comparison."[64] He arrived at this conclusion based not on his 1893 laboratory experiment but on Keller's *The Story of My Life*. Likewise, in response to Keller's *The World I Live In* (1908), James wrote directly to Keller, "I have found the book extraordinarily instructive."[65] While Jastrow measured the tactile contours of Keller's consciousness and James used clinical studies of "motor-minded" hysterics to study double consciousness, determining that touch is the sensation of the hidden self, together their research lit upon a larger truth: that the self is plural and plastic, not singular and fixed. In the twentieth century, Keller abandoned the aesthesiometer as a tool for assaying the experiential multiplicity of surface contact; she replaced it with autobiography. "With my hand I seize and hold all that I find in the three worlds—physical, intellectual, and spiritual."[66] By exploiting the self-undoing properties of touch to describe a life of holding and being held by others, the motor-minded writer got a hold of herself.

THE STORY OF MY, HER, THEIR LIFE

At one point Keller "wonder[ed] if any other individual has been so minutely investigated as I have been by physicians, psychologists, physiologists, and neurologists."[67] At the root of nineteenth-century discussions about touch was the question of whether it alone could form a fully developed psyche, and ultimately an agential self. Hence, Catherine Kudlick argues, at the root of all discussions about Keller was "the question of whether she was a thinking person in her own right."⁶⁸ *The Story of My Life*, Keller's first and most popular autobiography, endeavored to resolve this question with a resounding *yes*. This complete self was not unitary, however; its thematic and material engagement with touch replaced the self-possessive individual with a pluralistic model of being. Touch was less the sense Keller lived by and more the web in which she lived. Because her claim to personhood hinged on her linguistic abilities, she devoted significant space in *The Story of My Life* to describing how manual language—the tactile repertoires of finger spelling, lip reading, sign language, and reading raised-print type—sensitized her. In the course of sketching out the autonomy that manual language grants, touch emerges in Keller's narrative as a double sensation, following Merleau-Ponty, that renders her simultaneously subject and object, self and other. Deploying the haptics of her "disabled body [to] change the process of representation itself," Keller explodes the Western self by transforming autobiography, the genre of the self par excellence, into a mode of relation and a manner of collectivity.⁶⁹ Through its descriptions of her tactile subjectivity and in its collaborative production, *The Story of My Life* stages the epidermal drama of an interiority that comes into being through others, that is formed from the outside.

For the reading public, the novelty of *The Story of My Life* was not simply that it shed light on Keller's seemingly impenetrable mind, but that she was capable of writing it at all. In fact, Keller felt compelled to publish *The Story of My Life* to combat the charges of plagiarism shadowing her every accomplishment. Questions about the originality of Keller's thought stemmed from the fact that touch formed her consciousness. Whereas the sense of taste was suspect because it was too immediate, the sense of touch was suspect because it was too mediated. The skin was too thick a medium. How could a mind that relied on other sources for self-knowledge possibly generate its own thoughts? Anything Keller wrote had to be incomplete at best and fraudulent at worst. In a review of her autobiography, the *New York Times* stated that Keller had narrated "her life as far as she can know it."⁷⁰ To be sure, the qualifying phrase "as far as she can know it" is demeaning. Yet the text seems to anticipate if not affirm this condescension toward disability authorship, for it supplements Keller's life story with other people's stories of Keller's life. *The Story of My Life* is a thrice-told story: part 1 is Keller's own narrative; part 2 is a curated selection of Keller's correspondences, written from age seven to twenty-one, and introduced by her editor John Macy; and part 3 is Macy's "Supplementary Account of Helen Keller's Life and Education," which includes Anne

Sullivan's recollections, letters, and reports. This schema submerges Sullivan's substantial presence in Keller's life—and submerges the author herself. Keller's narrative constitutes 140 pages of a 400-page book, which makes two-thirds of "my life" *her* life. Tellingly, a review in the *Los Angeles Times* classified *The Story of My Life* as a "biography."[71] The paratextual apparatus meant to validate Keller's agency and autonomy ended up decentering her from her own story. But it also pluralized her, nicely reproducing what Keller's narrative, part 1, discloses: that her "my" is both a first- and third-person, singular and plural, designation. My is also her/their/our.

The impetus for *The Story of My Life* was a charge of plagiarism. In 1892, at the age of twelve, Keller wrote a story called "The Frost King" as a birthday present for Michael Anagnos, Samuel Gridley Howe's son-in-law and his successor as the director of the Perkins Institution for the Blind. Anagnos enjoyed the child's story and printed it in the Perkins alumni magazine, which in turn the weekly publication *Goodson Gazette* reprinted. Some of the *Gazette*'s readers discerned an uneasy resemblance between "The Frost King" and Margaret Canby's children's story "Frost Fairies" (1874), which prompted the *Gazette* to print matching phrases and paragraphs that pointed to plagiarism. A public controversy ensued, resulting in Perkins conducting a trial to determine whether Sullivan had falsified Keller's writing abilities. Impugning both the originality of Keller's thought and Sullivan's pedagogical legitimacy, the event put "consciousness on trial."[72] Keller and Sullivan were cleared of any charges; the judges determined that Sullivan likely had manually read Canby's story to Keller and that the girl had unwittingly reproduced elements of it in her own writing. Nonetheless, Anagnos was humiliated, and although he initially defended student and teacher, he later reversed course and publicly shamed the women. Sullivan was hounded by charges of wielding Svengali-like mesmeric influence over the credulous girl, and Keller by public skepticism about "the basic elements of her personhood."[73] The plagiarism trial left the young celebrity "with a deep uncertainty about the provenance of her ideas and the autonomy of her consciousness—doubts few adults ever have to grapple with," writes Georgina Kleege.[74] So deeply woven together were reading, writing, and feeling—all mediated through the sensitive hand—that what most disturbed Keller was that the plagiarism had been unconscious. Were her experiences her own, or were they reports she had so absorbed and internalized that her mind mistook them as its own? This question opened up the possibility that Keller was an impossible subject, a person whose very consciousness was a copy, not an original.

The anxiety of inauthentic consciousness caused by this ignominy expressed itself as an anxiety of inauthentic authorship. *The Story of My Life* begins not in the mode of self-assertion ("I was born.") but with trepidation about exposure: "It is with a kind of fear that I begin to write the history of my life. I have, as it were, a superstitious hesitation in lifting the veil that clings about my childhood like a golden mist."[75] If the plagiarism trial had taught her anything, it was that the public viewed disability as a kind of negative ontology, a lack or deficiency at the core of being. What if, she seems to wonder, lifting the veil only reveals that there is nothing underneath? But touch materializes disabled being as more of an ontological surplus—as multiple being(s). Tactile sensitivity was first woven into the fabric of Keller's life through finger spelling, a manual mode of linguistic notation in which specific hand configurations are used to represent specific alphabetic letters. In an early scene in *The Story of My Life*, Sullivan, shortly after relocating from Boston to Alabama to teach the child, gives Keller a handmade doll to teach her how to fingerspell. "When I played with it a little while, Miss Sullivan slowly spelled into my hand the word d-o-l-l. I was at once interested in this finger play and tried to imitate it.... I stood still, my whole attention fixed upon the motions of her fingers."[76] Whereas a deaf person can see these manual signs, Jim Swan explains, for the deaf-blind person, the hand "is the material surface on which someone else's fingers imprint a sequence of tactile signs ... with letters, words, and sentences all spelled one after the other onto the same surface."[77] When speaking, Keller's fingers inscribe letters into the palm of Sullivan's hand; when listening, the palm of her hand is written on and over by Sullivan's fingers. If the alienation of subject and object is traditionally thought to inaugurate the Lacanian speaking subject, Diana Fuss points out, then finger spelling suggests otherwise: "Subject and object occupy the same epistemological frame, in which the very term 'subject' and 'object' refer to both the world of matter and the world of grammar."[78] In *d-o-l-l*, Keller and the doll—human and thing—are caught in the process of becoming each other. Finger spelling turns the speaking subject into an object.

D-o-l-l marks Keller's plaything at the very moment that it marks her as an autobiographer. More than simply describing touch in an autobiographical format, Keller suggests that touch is experientially autobiographical. Because finger spelling transforms the body into the very material of language, all communication becomes life writing. This vibrant embodiment of language is perhaps why Keller had trouble distinguishing her ideas from what she read: because for her touch was both an experiential sign (à la Helmholtz)

FIG. 5.3 Portrait of Helen Keller and Anne Sullivan seated side by side, with Sullivan reading a book and finger spelling into Keller's hand (c. 1899). Courtesy of the Perkins School for the Blind.

and a linguistic sign. She acknowledged, "It is certain that I cannot always distinguish my own thoughts from those I read, because what I read becomes the very substance and texture of my mind. Consequently, in nearly all that I write, I produce something which very much resembles the crazy patchwork I used to make when I first learned to sew."[79] Absorbing words and worlds, skin is an imaginative tissue. When reading a book in Braille print type, Keller could physically trace the origin of particular ideas, could revisit particular phrases or chapters. In the diachronic temporality of fingerspelling, however, each word does not simply succeed the prior word but physically replaces it. The impressible flesh of the hand becomes a palimpsest of prior markings that the mind absorbs and incorporates. Once internalized, the ideas carried in words are nearly impossible to locate in time or space because they constitute Keller's very being. Further, because books printed in Braille were rare and expensive, Keller typically read through Sullivan's hand: Sullivan visually read a book while manually signing it, word for word, into Keller's hand—every tale twice-told (figure 5.3).[80] In the tightly closed circuit produced by the two women's hands, there is no material distinction between Shakespeare's verse, the news, and idle chitchat. Ownership becomes moot. Touch, then, is a sensation of chiastic reversibility: ideas are tactile, and texture is ideational. Language is a lived experience.

Keller read, conversed, and oriented herself in the world through the same medium: skin. Her phenomenological descriptions of manual language serve to discredit the idea that one's consciousness can be plagiarized. Rather than prove that her thoughts are her own, *The Story of My Life* delegitimizes the very premise of originality, arguing instead that all ideas are borrowed because to be a sentient creature is to be in contact with outside "sources." Indeed, the performance of finger spelling enacts the bidirectional becoming of self and world. In the famous water-pump scene—a scene that Keller and Sullivan would re-create in the silent film adaptation *Deliverance* (1919) and then in the 1920s on the vaudeville stage—Keller first learns to attach ideas to tactile impressions. When Sullivan places the girl's hand under a waterspout while spelling into her other hand *w-a-t-e-r*, Keller suddenly feels "a thrill of returning thought; and somehow the mystery of language was revealed to me.... I left the well-house eager to learn. Everything had a name, and each name gave birth a new thought. As we returned to the house every object which I touched seemed to quiver with life. That was because I saw everything with a strange, new sight that had come to me."[81] Water and *w-a-t-e-r* baptize Keller as a feeling person. Matter and mind converge to deliver her from infantile solipsism. From this point onward, manual language acts as the oracular "strange, new sight" that stimulates conscious feeling.[82] When tied to language, tactile sensitivity marks her as a thinking subject. Yet it also breaks the grip of the subject-object paradigm. Finger spelling intensifies openness and otherness; it is a way of being subject and object.

By describing her hands as a simultaneous agent and recipient of sensation, then, Keller establishes the sense of touch as a phenomenologically double sensation, as an experience of sensing and being sensed. In *Midstream: My Later Life*, Keller elaborated on the embodied consciousness that this double sensation yields: "The tactual sense reigns throughout the body, and the skin of every part... becomes extraordinarily discriminating. It is approximately true to say that every particle of the skin is a feeler which touches and is touched, and the contact enables the mind to draw conclusions regarding... the vibrations which play upon the surface of the body."[83] Described as "a feeler which touches and is touched," skin demonstrates the ontological continuity between subject and object. Skin is a dynamic exchange between the sensing body (Keller) and the sensed others (dolls, water, Sullivan) that bring both into being. As the primary scene of double sensation, skin makes bodily copresence essential to the experience of selfhood. Because Keller's experiences were so deeply lodged in touch, self-recognition had to come from the outside—a fact crystallized by her manner of reading, which is not a solitary activity that cultivates interiority but a social activity that unfolds through epidermal exposure. Mediated through touch, the autobiographical self is a figure internally split into subject and object yet radically coextensive with others.

The centrality of language acquisition to Keller's life story cannot be divorced from the touches that double Keller's autobiographical *I*. Even as tactile language heralds the author's triumph over her bodily "deficiency," and thus positions her as an autonomous subject, Keller is at pains to emphasize that her success is not self-made but entirely due to Sullivan, her lifelong companion. Touch splits Keller in half, but it also doubles her. "Before my teacher came to me, I did not know that I am."[84] Sullivan was the double(-goer) that touch gave Keller; she had to be handled by Sullivan before she could become an *I*. Keller's selfhood comes into being by being acted on, not by acting on the world. As an individual who could not "have a self before she had a double," in critic Jodi Cressman's words, Keller argues that interiority requires outside intervention.[85] For instance, after describing her rebirth as a speaking subject, Keller reflects, "My teacher is so near to me that I scarcely think of myself apart from her. How much of my delight in all beautiful things is innate, and how much is due to her influence, I can never tell. I feel that her being is inseparable from my own. . . . All the best of me belongs to her—there is not a talent, or an aspiration or a joy in me that has not been awakened by her loving touch."[86] Here, Sullivan is at once internal and external to Keller. Double sensation suggests a "queer orientation," following Ahmed, which "by seeing the world 'slantwise' allow[s] other objects to come into view."[87] This queerness proffers a slant theory of consciousness: the women, with fingers and lips interlaced, cannot but share a mind. Doubled, touch not only others but queers the self. Sullivan's "loving touch" makes Keller's "plagiarized" consciousness a collaborative one. *The Story of My Life* is the story of an individual who developed into a couple—or rather, the story of two women who functioned as two halves of a single being.

Touch's queer orientations are perhaps most apparent in part 3 of *The Story of My Life*, when John Macy describes the Keller/Sullivan dyad as "an unanalyzable kinship."[88] He knew this well, having lived with the women from 1905, when he married Sullivan (Keller accompanied them on their honeymoon), to 1914. But what is perhaps most unanalyzable about their kinship is their constant contact; the subjects "Helen Keller" and "Anne Sullivan" were formed by a (double) sensation that belonged to no one, not even themselves. Combined with their interdependent lifestyle, this collaborative consciousness meant that neither had an identity apart from the other (hence I consider Keller's *Teacher: Anne Sullivan Macy* an autobiography). Keller wrote that Sullivan "strove to supply" the "stimulating contacts of life," and that she was "ever at hand to keep me in touch with the world of men and women, and did everything she could to develop ways by which I myself could communicate directly with them. During the four years I was in Radcliffe College, she sat beside me in the classroom and with her supple speaking hand spelled out the lectures to me word by word. In the same way she read many books to me."[89] Keller could not pinpoint where her body ended and her teacher's body began. "In all my experiences and thoughts I am conscious of a hand. Whatever moves me, whatever thrills me, is a hand that touches me in the dark, and that touch is my reality."[90] A hand was most often *the* hand of Sullivan, who was Keller's reality. In *Teacher* (1955), written twenty years after Sullivan's death, Keller noted, "To this day I cannot command the uses of my soul or stir my mind to action without the memory of the quasi-electric touch of Teacher's fingers upon my palm."[91] To the extent that touch is an indeterminate exchange, "a trace, always deferred, always leading toward another moment," in Erin Manning's words, then Keller's life writings extend that indeterminacy into her relationships.[92] Touch becomes a queer double sensation that orients *my* life toward *our* life together.

In limning an elastic subjectivity shaped by physical touch, Keller risked writing a self whose interiority was so open to the world, so absorptive of external stimuli, that it was unrecognizable as such—a kind of chameleon. *The Story of My Life* posits touch as a double sensation that both splits the self in half (Keller as subject/Keller as object) and doubles it (Keller/Sullivan). But more so, *The Story of My Life* actually reproduces this relational consciousness at the level of textual production. The tactile processes of self-recognition described in *The Story of My Life*, in other words, are inseparable from the tactile processes of self-representation that shaped *The Story of My Life*. The text's composition and production, as much as its contents, obfuscate the unitary self by giving the first-person singular *my* multiple referents. Notably, Keller's life story began as a series of essays for a literature professor at Radcliffe College, who had instructed her to write about herself. Sullivan persuaded Keller to publish the essays as a memoir, and Macy helped Keller and Sullivan revise the story; it was serialized in the *Ladies' Home Journal* in 1902, then printed as a book in 1903. The first installment in *Ladies' Home Journal* featured two titles: "Helen Keller's Own Story of Her Life, Written Entirely by the Wonderful Girl Herself," and "The Story of My Life." Preceding Keller's "my," an editorial foreword stated:

> As the feat may seem almost incredible, it may be in order to say at the beginning that every word of this story as printed in THE JOURNAL has actually been written by Helen Keller herself—not dictated, but first written in "Braille" (raised points); then transferred to the typewriter by the wonderful girl herself; next read to her by her teacher by means of the fingers; corrected; then read again to her, and in the proof finally read to her once more. It is the editor's hope to be able to publish at the conclusion of Miss Keller's own story a supplementary article by one of her friends [Macy], explaining, in detail, exactly how this marvelous work was done.[93]

In its form as a printed book as well, *The Story of My Life* is about Keller's life but also about *The Story of My Life*. Because of the pervasive skepticism about the originality of Keller's thoughts, Macy's editorial explanations serve to bring transparency to Keller's compositional process. These explanations also heighten the novelty of the text, a narrative "incredibly" written by a disabled woman. This paratextual apparatus was required of many minoritized writers. Slave narratives and mendicant street literature (memoirs written and sold by disabled beggars) are performative acts of self-authorship that "established the life-writer as, at bare minimum, someone capable of self-reflection and self-representation," but that also required the testimony of privileged subjects.[94] Macy aimed to amplify Keller's authority but ended up muting it.

In conjunction with Macy's testimony, what served to both validate and vex Keller's authorship were the writing machines she used. In part 3, Macy emphasized that Keller "read from her braille copy the entire story, making corrections as she read, which were taken down on the manuscript that went to the printer. During this revision she sat running her finger over the braille manuscript, stopping now and then to refer to the braille notes on which she had indicated her corrections."[95] Here, the manual dexterity involved in writing—typing, finger spelling, touch reading—is where Keller's authority lies. The physical trace of her hand was so important to Keller's public authorship that *The Story of My Life* begins not with her typewritten words but with two facsimile reproductions: one of a letter she had handwritten to Boston clergyman Phillips Brooks and the other of a manuscript page typed on a Braille writer (figures 5.4 and 5.5). Tellingly, the reproduced manuscript

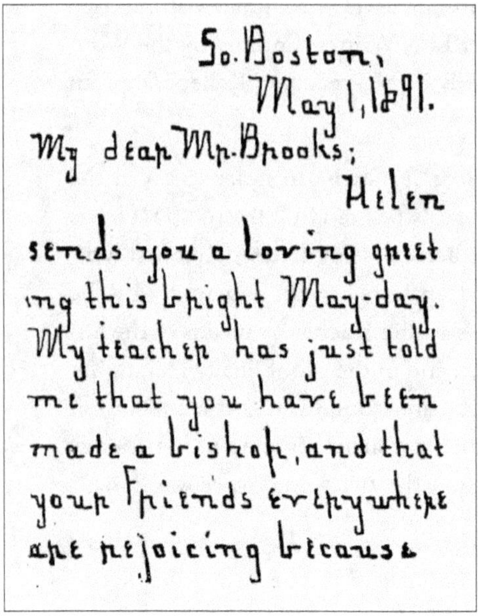

So. Boston,
May 1, 1891.
My dear Mr. Brooks;
Helen sends you a loving greeting this bright May-day. My teacher has just told me that you have been made a bishop, and that your friends everywhere are rejoicing because

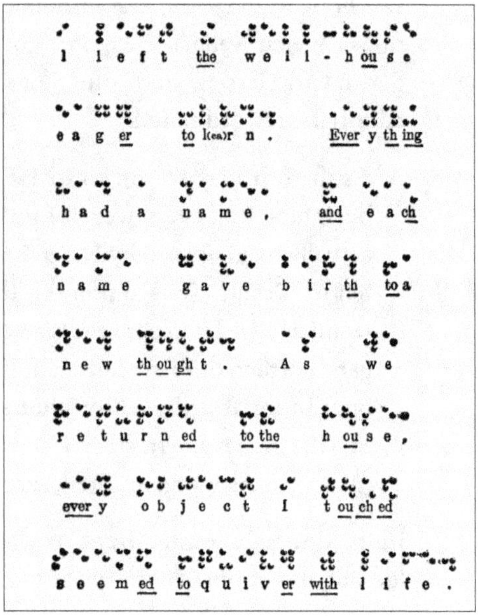

FIG. 5.4 Facsimile of Keller's handwritten letter to Phillips Brooks, in the unnumbered pages between the table of contents and part 1 of *The Story of My Life* (1903).

FIG. 5.5 Facsimile of a passage on page 24 of Keller's braille manuscript. Placed after the facsimile of Keller's letter to Brooks (figure 5.4) in *The Story of My Life* (1903).

page contains the famous water-pump scene, when Keller uses her hands to become a speaking subject. The Braille facsimile is less a "spoiler" than a proleptic disclosure, Keller's self-certification, of the text's authenticity and her autonomy.

Macy's emphasis on the place of the typewriter does the same. The typewriter, first invented as a writing instrument for the blind, appears here as an instrument that helps Keller "overcome" the crisis of disabled authorship, for it produces a text that erases embodied difference. Whereas with blind handwriting, letters and words are clearly guided by grids and a special writing stylus, with the typewriter, standardized type obscures the intimate bodily trace. Marta Werner argues further that the typewriter "made possible autobiography" because it encouraged Keller to abandon the doubled self of tactile language for the distanced, singular self of visual print.[96] Accordingly, then, the linear progression of type across the space of the page redoubles the linear progression of the self over historical time; the typewriter is an autobiography machine. Yet because it standardizes the self in print, hiding the individual imprimatur of handwriting, the facsimiles are necessary for reincorporating the author's body into her story. Further, however, at a linguistic level, these facsimiles ultimately reproduce the unconventional duality of Keller's self. Indeed, there is a notable quirk in her writing, the "tendency in her letters and memoirs to refer to herself in the third person."[97] Werner attributes Keller's penchant for writing in the third person to the "double practice of transmission and reception" inhering in manual languages.[98] The letter to Brooks bears out this tendency: "Helen sends you a loving greeting this bright May-day." Given that the facsimile precedes part 1, Keller's narrative begins not with an *I* but a *Helen*—not with a subject, but an object. In the tension between print and holograph, the third-person self-reference is less a quirky effect of double sensation than a literal texturing of the self.

Writing machines like the typewriter show Keller moving into the conventions of the autobiographical form, while Sullivan—her "co-consciousness"—shows the author moving out of them. In *Midstream*, Keller explained her writing process: "Into the tray of one's consciousness are tumbled thousands of scraps of experience. Your problem is to synthesize yourself and the world you live in into something like a coherent whole. I put together my pieces this way and that; but they will not dovetail properly."[99] A poignant remaking of Locke's tabula rasa, the mind is not a blank sheet but more like a scrapbook. Sullivan's active role in Keller's consciousness, an assemblage of "scraps of experience," is like her editorial-authorial role in the making of Keller's autobiographies. Sullivan sorted through the typed pages that Keller wrote but could not read, then cut the pages and pasted the fragments together into a linear narrative, then spelled that narrative into Keller's hands, and finally Keller spelled back corrections for Sullivan to make. The book was, in body and in spirit, dually authored. For even if a transcript existed of the women's tactile signing, Werner points out, "it would be impossible to tell whose words ended up on the paper."[100] Student and teacher became physically and psychically entangled in the process of the life story's composition. The manual communication that textual production required confused all categories of selfhood. When Sullivan read Keller's manuscript to her, did *my* refer to Sullivan, Keller, or both? And when Keller gave Sullivan her corrections, did not the first person carry a trace of Sullivan? In *The World I Live In* Keller explained, "It is not a complete conception, but a collection of object-impressions which . . . are disconnected and isolated."[101] Keller is describing her consciousness, but the same applies to the production of autobiography. In the process of telling a life story, the singular *I* of autobiography becomes inescapably plural. Autobiography, like consciousness, could only ever be collective. Keller's disability turned autobiography from a genre of self-development into a means of "discovering alternate ways of being in the world."[102]

By describing the ontological otherness at the heart of tactile experience, *The Story of My Life* reveals that consciousness is not independent but interdependent. And by narrating the story of its uniquely material production alongside its author's life story, *The Story of My Life* registers a crucial link between collaboration and contingency: that Keller's self is a story always subject to revision in the hands of others. This is perhaps why the paratextual apparatus of authorization, while fairly successful in slave narratives and mendicant literature, did not entirely succeed for Keller, who never escaped from under the ableist shadow of the "Frost King" plagiarism controversy. *The Story of My Life* was a best seller, but that did not stop more skeptical readers from treating it as evidence that Keller did in fact plagiarize her life story. A reviewer for the *Nation* scoffed:

> In Helen Keller's life and education we have an experiment tried under perfect conditions, showing how little essential are observation and experience to the trade of author. All her knowledge is hearsay knowledge, her very sensations are for the most part vicarious, and yet she writes of things beyond her power of perception with the assurance of one who has verified every word.... In making herself over on the everyday pattern, we lose what she could teach us by showing wherein she varies from the normal. It seems almost as if every fact of real psychological value had been perversely withheld; the few observations of importance that she does record being so mingled with her imaginings in regard to the perceptions of others as to be worthless.[103]

Doubts about the validity of Keller's authorship centered on the presumption that her life story was simply an evidentiary archive, one capable of proving that "she varies from the normal." Because she incorporated other people's experiences into her life story, however, Keller effaced her particularity, thereby reducing the "psychological value" that the text might offer. Keller's friend Mark Twain responded to such critics with the assertion that "all ideas are second-hand, consciously and unconsciously drawn from a million outside sources."[104] Twain's punny language takes aim at those who literalize the trope of firsthand knowledge—there is none, insofar as all experience is mediated through the body. Both thematizing and materializing the tactile contours of her mind, *The Story of My Life* demonstrates the impossibility of mastery over one's own coming-into-being.

Jastrow was far more pleased with *The Story of My Life* as "a psychological autobiography" than was the *Nation*. For him, it constituted a major contribution to "the interpretation of the role of sensation in the building up of intellectual acquisitions; it furnishes pertinent illustrations of the delicate interlacing of the strands of experience in the composite pattern of the mental texture."[105] The "interlacing of the strands of experience" described in Keller's autobiography proved the possibility of a chiastic self—the possibility that physical surface and psychical depth are not binaries but the same entity. Touch emerges in Keller's autobiographical corpus as a double sensation that turns her into subject and object, which is why hers is a story of *our* life: that of a woman who was both self and other, and that of two women who constituted a singular *I*. Formed through others, Keller communicated her doubleness at the level of the text's composition, the autobiographical *I*'s that blend in the very process of touching and typing. "Partly from the conditions of her work," Macy remarked, *The Story of My Life* is something "other than a unified narrative."[106] For Keller, touch was a double sensation and a representational strategy that othered autobiography's ocular-centric self. Disability "places a higher premium on interdependence and cooperation than on individualism and autonomy," hence Keller stretched the first person into the third.[107] Capturing the fruitful crisis of authorship created around disability, *The Story of My Life* offers a theory of embodied consciousness that undoes singular selfhood and original authorship. *I* always precedes and accompanies *her*. Touch makes you an autobiographer of someone else, a biographer of yourself.

THE HAPTICS OF DOUBLE CONSCIOUSNESS

Taken together, the substance, style, production, and reception of *The Story of My Life* reveal that tactile impressions engender a self deformation, or perhaps more precisely a selves transformation. Rotating impressibility's linear trajectory of self-directed formation, Keller's body is too pliant—so responsive to its environment that she becomes it. Inside and outside, self and world, subject and object, now become indistinct. While black feminist activist Frances E. W. Harper endeavored to evolve the racial body by regulating "the pleasurable power of touch" and directing the "flow of tactile pressures" toward the impressible body, as Kyla Schuller argues, W. E. B. Du Bois viewed Keller's excessive impressibility as instructive for the project of racial uplift.[108] The two met through William James, when in 1892 James took his psychology class to the Perkins Institution for the Blind to meet Keller. Du Bois later reflected, "Perhaps just because she was blind to color differences in this world, I became intensely interested in her. This woman who sits in darkness has a spiritual insight clearer than that of many wide-eyed people who stare uncomprehendingly at this prejudice[d] world."[109] Du Bois redirects the long-standing trope of the oracular blind person toward antiracism; touch constitutes a "spiritual insight" hidden by the scopic regime of race. Thus, whereas for James and Jastrow, Keller's tactile sensitivity revealed truths about below-threshold consciousness, for Du Bois, it subverted the visual epistemology of race, the (skin) color line. Keller said as much when in 1916 she sent the NAACP a hundred-dollar donation and a letter that its official publication, *The Crisis*, reprinted, which read, "The U.S. stands shamed before the world whilst ten million of the people remain victims of a most blind, stupid, and inhuman prejudice. . . . I feel with those suffering, toiling millions."[110] For Du Bois, Keller's "sensory anomalies" proved useful for "destabiliz[ing] the ideology of color prejudice."[111] Aslant the self-making properties of touch that activists like Harper directed toward racial uplift, it was the self-undoing properties of touch that Du Bois and Keller used to pressure the optics of the color line.

In 1903, the year *The Story of My Life* was printed as a book, Du Bois published *The Souls of Black Folk*, an experimental text that mixes autobiography and sociology, fables and slave spirituals, to limn the "peculiar sensation" of the color line. Du Bois, like Keller, sought to "find expressive forms to represent the experience of those least able to narrate Enlightenment stories of *Bildung* cultivation and self-sovereignty."[112] Their shared efforts to theorize a delocalized self through autobiography demonstrate that the "politics of disability is not separate from, nor analogous to, but always intersectional with, the politics of race," as Susan Schweik argues.[113] The ontological othering of touch, therefore, reframes the social othering of the black self as a *haptic* sensation, as mediated through the kindred functions of the hand and the eye. The haptic is a turn-of-the-century concept that emerged out of the confluence of psychology and art history, which began with Fechner's efforts to link sensory responses to mental judgments of art in *Vorschule der Aesthetik* (1876). By century's end, a psychophysical approach to art analysis emerged that moved beyond materials and technique to include the perception of form. Adjacent to this development, James claimed in *Principles of Psychology* that "touch-images," the tactile sensations accompanying ideas derived from physical perceptions, can define the imagination. Joining Fechner's "aesthetics from below" to the Jamesean touch-image, art historian Bernard Berenson argued in *The Florentine Painters of the Renaissance* (1894) that classical paintings evince a "tactile imagination" that lends "tactile values to retinal impressions."[114] Touch, then, is a seeing at close range and sight a touching at a distance. In 1901, Austrian art historian Aloïs Riegl added that, whereas modern art deploys a pure optic style of looking (i.e., perspective), classical art deploys *haptic vision*, a feeling for the texture and grain of a visual object. Both Keller's *The Story of My Life* and Du Bois's *The Souls of Black Folk* relocate haptic vision to lived experience, applying it to the perception of the color line rather than to art objects. For Du Bois in particular, haptic vision is the key modality of double consciousness, the psychologically split black self that experiences the scopic regime of skin color through the double sensation of touch.

Haptic vision reveals not only the otherness but also the others involved in Keller's self-recognition. The daughter of a Confederate veteran and a native Alabaman, Keller came of age during the consolidation of Jim Crow segregation in the 1880s and 1890s. Her earliest memory involved a childhood friend who "had as great a love of mischief as I. Two little children were seated on the veranda steps one hot afternoon. One was black as ebony, with bunches of fuzzy hair tied with shoestrings sticking out all over her head like corkscrews. The other was white, with long golden curls. One child was six years old, the other two or three years older. The younger child was blind—that was I—and the other was Martha Washington."[115] Reproducing the ontological reversibility of self and other, the scene begins in the first person, slides into the third, and finally discloses who the "younger child" and the "other" child are: the white *I* and the black *her*. Touch manifests at the level of perspectival instability, the pronomial disruption of the third-person into the first-person narrative. By emphasizing the color (rather than the feel) of skin, however, this scene establishes the disabled white girl as psychically able to move beyond herself and the black child as trapped within her body. The fluid grammar of double sensation absorbs and diffuses embodied difference. Yet crucially, the narrative structure of Keller's life story reproduces the postbellum racial order. By staging Sullivan's entrance into Keller's life immediately afterward, it establishes Keller's "overcoming" of her disability as a shift from identifying with a racial other to identifying with an abler-bodied white woman. The ensuing "marriage plot" between Keller and Sullivan shuts out black children like Martha Washington from autobiography's progress narrative while invoking the reconciliation romance (a postbellum genre that restored racial order through the intersectional union of a white northerner and a white southerner) to sanction their queer marriage.[116] Within this homonationalist frame, the haptic vision of child's play—moving between the materiality and the melanin of skin—establishes that, for all the fluidity of tactile consciousness, there can be no comparison between the two girls.

The scene reveals that Keller was not color-blind, as Du Bois had written. She knew that the color line extended into consciousness. *The Story of My Life* includes a report from Sullivan, dated 1887: "'What color is think?' was one of the restful questions she [Keller] asked, as we swung to and fro in the hammock. I told her that when we are happy our thoughts are bright, and when we are naughty they are sad. Quick as a flash she said, 'My think is white, Viney's think is black.' You see, she had an idea that the color of our thoughts matched that of our skin."[117] The skin is the seat of consciousness, but because skin has color and texture, consciousness is as subject to racialization as the rest of the body. This idea had started developing at century's end with physiological studies of the skin, which revealed that the skin, like the mind, has two layers. According to *Manufacturer and Builder*, the "inner, or deeper portion" of the skin, called the *corium*, or *true skin*, is "composed of firm and elastic connective tissue fibers," while the "outer layer," called the *epidermis*, is composed of "separate roundish elements called cells" that are "piled upon each other in layers to a varying extent in different parts of the body."[118] Further, the racial difference marked by melanin is all surface. "In the negro, the dark hue of the skin is due to the presence of pigment . . . in the epidermis. The corium, or true skin . . . does not share this pigmentation."[119] Scottish thinker Alexander Bain similarly explained that whereas "the blackness of the skin in the negro depends entirely" on the epidermis, "the *true skin* or *corium* is a sentient and vascular fibrous texture."[120] This physiological topography bifurcates race and feeling; the visual layer signifies human difference but is not itself responsive to the world, while the tactile layer is sentient and elastic. It also reverses the racial ontology of flesh and skin—flesh signifying not the visceral depths of being but its visual surface.

Germane to Du Bois's theory of double consciousness was the revelation of a hidden skin, the domain of feeling beneath the epidermal surface. The physiology of skin added another layer, as it were, to psychological theories of a hidden self. In the essay "Psychology and Mysticism" (1899) in the *Atlantic Monthly*, psychologist Hugo Münsterberg discussed the theory of "a deeper self and a double consciousness," specifically affirming the "phenomena which suggest that deeper personality lies hidden under the experience of our surface personality."[121] The skin, split between surface-level melanin and a fleshier feel, materialized double consciousness. The deeper true skin is the tactile component of the hidden self, while the epidermis is the visual component of the conscious self. Phrased otherwise: the conscious self and the epidermis are visual, while the hidden self and the true skin are tactile. Both the skin and the self are double. Around this time, Du Bois began redefining Jamesean double consciousness, no longer a pathological condition in which "a person leads two lives" but now a psychological burden whereby racism alienates the black subject in the process of his own identity formation. Du Bois did so in part by experimenting with the haptic properties of skin.[122] He begins *The Souls of Black Folk*, his autobiography not of a person but of a people, with the declaration, "The negro is a sort of seventh son, born with a veil, and gifted with second-sight in this American world—a world which yields him no true self-consciousness, but only lets him see himself through the revelation of the other world. It is a peculiar sensation, this double-consciousness, this sense of always looking at one's self through the eyes of others. . . . One ever feels his twoness."[123] If for psychologists, touch evidenced a hidden self, coded as primitive and pathological, then for sociological thinkers like Du Bois, it materialized the drama of being the nation's hidden self, coded as racially other.

Double consciousness names the emergence of black personhood through white people's racist perceptions. Writing against the pathologizing discourse of the Negro Problem, Du Bois turned the veil into a protective gift that activates racial consciousness. He transformed "what seems to be a curse of repression and blindness into the transpersonal gift of second sight which has been in one's possession since birth but must be awakened and harnessed in order to effect real change."[124] With its emphasis on seeing the self through the eyes of others, double consciousness appears to be a visually stimulated feeling. In keeping with the Paris Exposition of 1900, where Du Bois had used photographic portraits of black people to challenge racist constructs, *The Souls of Black Folk* frames racial consciousness through visual imagery.[125] Yet "second sight" also gestures toward the "spiritual insight" that Du Bois had found in Keller. It echoes the "strange, new sight" that Keller had attributed to her hands at the water pump, when tactile language made her a speaking subject and an object. Metaphorical and material blindness is, for both thinkers, an engine of mystical sight, with the power to disclose inner realities, the lived experience of bodily difference. This shared preoccupation with the haptic materiality of in/sight helps account for the dominant trope of the veil in both their autobiographies. *The Souls of Black Folk* begins, "I have stepped within the Veil, raising it that you may view faintly its deeper recesses," and describes the event that inaugurates double consciousness: a dismissive glance from a white classmate caused Du Bois to realize that he was "shut out from their world by a vast veil."[126] Keller meanwhile gives readers "a glimpse into the darkness that veils my eyes," describing "the veil that clings about my childhood" before the twinned arrivals of Sullivan and language—a veil that excluded her from civilization.[127] This figural similarity reframes the Du Boisian veil, considered a psychological manifestation of the color line, as the "true skin" that, in a very material way, textures the color line.

Literalizing the question posed to Du Bois, and the question with which *Sensory Experiments* began, "How does it feel to be a problem?" *The Souls of Black Folk* responds with a haptic account of racial double consciousness. This tactile "feeling" is most clearly articulated in the story that culminates *The Souls of Black Folk*, "The Coming of John," a story replete with doubles: consciousness, skin, and Johns. With its protagonist based loosely on Du Bois, "The Coming of John" is a third-person life story that distills the internal drama of segregation. It tracks the intertwined lives of two men named John as they come of age in Georgia. The town's white and black communities accept the black John Jones as a respectful plow hand and as the childhood playmate of the wealthy and white John Henderson. But as the Johns become conscious of the color line, their lives both diverge and converge. Both men attend separate colleges in the North, and one night they cross paths at a New York City performance of Wagner's opera *Lohengrin*. There, close encounters with racism make John Jones "feel almost for the first time the veil that lay between him and the white world" and cause him to "chafe at the color-line that hemmed in him and his."[128] When John Jones returns to Georgia, he dedicates himself to the work of racial uplift, specifically by opening a school for the rural black population. Yet as a figure of the black elite, John Jones's ambition and education alienates him from his community. When he speaks at a church meeting about the pettiness of "religious and denominational bickering," the audience sits in silence. Then an elderly man climbs to the pulpit: "He seized the Bible with his rough, huge hands; twice he raised it inarticulate, and then fairly burst into the words, with rude and awful eloquence.... John never knew clearly what the old man said; he only felt himself held up to scorn and scathing denunciation for trampling on the true Religion, and he realized with amazement that all unknowingly he had put rough, rude hands on something this little world held sacred."[129] An elder's rough hands mobilize a moment of aesthetic transport that pierces the tactile skin and visual surface of the veil. The nameless black elder embodies the "primitive" coarsely textured skin of John's hidden self; he represents the haptic "feel" that John, a representative of the "Talented Tenth" charged with uplifting the race, cannot shake. Indeed, the repetitive figure of the elder's "rough, huge hands" and John's "rough, rude hands" underscores that, however well intentioned, John is in fact turned against the African American religious community—when he should be turned against the "smooth-faced" John Henderson.[130] Quite literally out of touch with his own blackness, John faces skepticism from the black community. Capturing second sight in the process of becoming second skin, the scene routes double consciousness through the twoness of skin—the haptic materiality of consciousness that cuts across the visual color line and that cuts into the tactile black community.

Only through his double, John Henderson, does John Jones's racial consciousness, the below-threshold "hidden self" materialized by the black church elder, fully awaken. Shortly after the Henderson family closes the black school that he had headed, John Jones finds the white John trying to rape his sister Jennie, the Henderson family's house servant, and kills him. While awaiting his death by lynch mob, John Jones "thought of the boys at Johnstown. He wondered how Brown had turned out, and Carey? And Jones—Jones? Why, *he* was Jones, and he wondered what they would all do when they knew."[131] Bearing out the psychical split not simply between the urbane and the rural black self but also between the black and white self, experiencing *I* as *he*, the black John awaits his reunion in death with the white doppelgänger, the white self, that he had killed. In his final moments, John internally hears "the strange melody, away from the dark shadows where lay the noise of horses galloping, galloping on. With an effort he roused himself, bent forward, and looked steadily down the pathway, softly humming the 'Song of the Bridge'" from Wagner's *Lohengrin*.[132] Here, the violent destruction of the black John's body occurs from within his consciousness. As Nancy Bentley compellingly argues, the "composite form of a Wagnerian lynching gives the 'peculiar sensation' of double consciousness a concrete and distressing texture, as if to stage such violence openly as the height of sublimity within a white pleasure economy," thus offering a shocking juxtaposition that allows readers "to experience a literary version of double consciousness."[133] Moving across the sensory registers of touch and sight as well as sound, double consciousness constitutes in "The Coming of John" specifically and in *The Souls of Black Folk* more broadly a haptic medium that structures the alienated feeling of the color line, ultimately showing that the tactile hidden self is not only racially marked but also perpetually unspooling the yarn of self-directed improvement that autobiography spins. Enfleshing double consciousness, Du Bois reveals the perceptual thresholds that support and subvert the color line.

With their autobiographical bodies emerging alongside the psychophysical-aesthetic concept of the haptic, Keller and Du Bois reorganize consciousness around the skin, not the soul. Both, after all, wrote to limn and lift the veils between segregated communities: the color line separating white from black people and the seeing and "hearing line," following Christopher Krentz, separating sighted and hearing from deaf-blind people.[134] Reading *The Story of My Life* against the grain and reading it with *The Souls of Black Folk* reveals a concerted effort by minoritized writers to elasticize subjectivity. Indeed, Keller and Du Bois's haptic formulations of consciousness move between what Petra Kuppers calls the "tactility of disability" on the one hand and the retinal impressions of racial difference on the other—a movement that yields a moment of intimacy without identification, when the disabled *I* slips into *we* or the racial *I* slips into *him*. Insofar as touch is a "way of thinking through different positions and bringing them in contact with one another," as Kuppers observes, it usefully proffers a "rhizomatic model of disability that can hold a wide variety of experiences and structured positions in moments of precarious productive imbalance."[135] A relational as well as synaesthetic modality, haptic vision shows how race becomes a central apparatus through which disability takes shape, and conversely how the trope of blindness as oracular insight inflects the second sight of racial consciousness. Haptic vision names the chiastic traversal of race and disability at the turn of the twentieth century—a moment of contact and of displacement. Illuminating double sensation and double consciousness as distinct yet interrelated experiences of social oppression, Keller and Du Bois mediate the feeling of the self as other(s) by rewiring seeing as tactility, a haptic modality that imagines the relations that might emerge in between the nodes of surface and depth, skin and flesh, conscious and unconscious life.

....

The haptic was not the only sensory layer that the capacious sense of touch acquired at century's end. A "sixth sense" emerged as well called kinesthesia: the unconscious feeling of one's body as it moves through space. The idea of a "muscular sense" had emerged decades prior, with Alexander Bain's psychophysiological theory that touch is "really not a simple sense, but a compound of sense and motion."[136] Around that time, Helmholtz conducted studies of the role of muscle movement in the eyes, and he revealed that the sensation of movement is entirely unconscious. Based partly on Helmholtz's work, British neurologist Henry Charlton Bastian later assembled clinical evidence that the muscular sense was dependent on sensory endings in muscles, tendons, joints, and skin. Spurred by the locomotion studies of Eadweard Muybridge and Étienne-Jules Marey, psychologist George Van Ness Dearborn later asserted that kinesthesia "is about to come into its own as the primary and essential sense. Without it, coordinated and adapted bodily movement and strain, concomitant to every kind of mental process, is inconceivable."[137] That year as well the *Washington Post* declared "Kinesthesia Queen of the Senses," reporting that although the "highest rank among the senses is usually awarded to sight," from the "standpoint of physiology another sense deserves the crown," the "so-called 'muscular sense' through which we are conscious of the motions of our body and its parts."[138] Kinesthesia became central to the twentieth-century notion of the body image, first articulated in S. Weir Mitchell's study of phantom limbs and formally identified by neurologist Henry Head as the mind's visual representation of the body to itself. In Merleau-Ponty's meditation on the phenomenological contours of the body image, he argued that kinesthesia is the synaesthetic background, the intersensory field where body-subjects graft themselves onto each other and the world.

Kinesthesia, a perception "in league with the mind's attempt to experience its embodiment as an animate form," turns touch into a vibrant force.[139] Tactile language—finger spelling, embossed print, sign language—was part of what Hillel Schwartz identifies as the "new kinaesthetic" that insisted on a psychophysical link "between the bodiliness of the inner core and the outer experience of the inner self" in everyday as well as artistic choreographies.[140] Indeed, it is through the "motion of hands" that "my sense of kinship with the rest of the world" grew "more joyous and confident," Keller remarked in *The Story of My Life*.[141] As a child, Keller was made into an aesthesiometer, but by her early twenties, she had remade herself into an instrument of vibration: "Every atom of my body is a vibroscope," she avowed.[142] In describing her body as a vibroscope and her selfhood as relational, Keller offers an important reminder that *kin* refers both to the English word for family and to the Greek prefix for bodily movement. Kinesthesia explodes the very notion of consciousness as singular because it captures the moment when kinship and kinesis, relationality and proprioception, are caught in the act of becoming each other. Keller's life writings amplify the doubleness of kinesthesia; they track the ways in which *kin* as movement and *kin* as affiliation become close without ever converging. When touch becomes understood as "a family of senses" that includes kinesthesia and the haptic—movement and optics—it no longer names a singular category of feeling but instead a process of becoming other and more than oneself.[143]

If touch is the feeling where skin and flesh meet, then kinesthesia might be the sensation that moves the law of tact toward the law of genre. In Jacques Derrida's meditation on touch, he writes that "among the senses, touch is an exception, because it has as its object more than one quality—in truth, it potentially has *all* sensory qualities."[144] When Derrida defines the law of tact as the untouchability of touch, he suggests that touch is a law that forbids too much touching, even though touch is "already too much."[145] Rather than plumb the depths of the body's interiority, touch is an experience of the limit. "It is always the law of *parting and sharing* at the heart of touching and contact," he explains.[146] Keller's life writings demonstrate the impossibility of the act of touching, the law of tact. They also point to the impossibility of the act of classifying, that is, the impossibility of the law of genre that attempts to contain "disruptive anomalies" through the demarcation of types, kinds, and classes.[147] Within every genre exists the implication of its other, the Derridean "counter-law that constitutes this very law."[148] To belong to a genre is always to exceed it. Simultaneously contained by and in excess of autobiography, Keller and Du Bois together theorize touch as a genre that can only ever operate by opening itself up to the limits of the self. The law of tact, they powerfully demonstrate, is the law of genre. With *The Story of My Life* in particular, marked as it is by the strike of the typewriter key and the stroke of the sensitive hand, autobiography comes to disrupt self-presence by touching the limits of genre. The limits of consciousness are always too much (Keller, Sullivan, Macy) and never enough (Keller "as far as she can know" herself). To be touch sensitive, then, is to discern the inescapable gap between self and others, as well as to discern the others in our self. Turning *I* into an intersubjective locution, life writing proved central to the project of psychophysical aesthesis, for it made space to experiment with the textures, the gestures, the skins, and the kins of embodied difference.

Coda

**AFTERLIVES AND ANTELIVES
OF FEELING**

> Our senses are not yet theoreticians because they are bound up by the rule, the map, the inherited fantasy, and the hum of worker bees that fertilize materially the life we're moving through. Then again, maybe we did not really want our senses to be theoreticians: because then we would see ourselves as an effect of an exchange with the world, beholden to it, useful for it, rather than sovereign, at the end of the day.
> —Lauren Berlant, *Cruel Optimism*

> The forming of the five senses is a labor of the entire history of the world down to the present.
> —Karl Marx, *Economic and Philosophic Manuscripts of 1844*

From using acoustics to mobilize social harmony and finger spelling to multiply selfhood, the U.S. project of psychophysical aesthesis reshuffles dominant narratives that conflate sensation and emotion with sentiment in the nineteenth century. *Sensory Experiments* has examined a wide range of postbellum writers, thinkers, and cultural producers who creatively engaged with the experimental science of sense experience to propose an alternate, more phenomenological model of feeling: a set of sense-specific genres that mediate the lived vicissitudes of being and belonging. Unfolding within and against the hierarchical social arrangements increasingly certified by biological concepts of human difference, psychophysical aesthesis served the larger purpose of sketching out the metaphysical but no less material implications of raced, gendered, queer, and disabled embodiment. Exploiting the signification immanent in sense experience, it captures a variegated and historically specific set of sensory experiments that explored how subjective feeling both mediates the relation between self and social world and is itself a world-making activity. What emerges from this wide-ranging aesthetic project is a new story about the past and present of affect as a spectrum of feeling that runs from distinction to dissolution, a spectrum along which body-subjects varyingly oscillate.

The era in which psychophysical aesthesis flourished, from 1860 to 1910, was both socially and epistemologically turbulent. By around 1890, psychophysics was already on the wane. Psychologist Wilhelm Wundt played a major role in this development, for unlike Gustav Fechner or William James, he was "much less eager to combine the personae of the physiologist and the philosopher."[1] This particular chapter in the philosophy and science of mind was all but closed by 1896, when *Littell's Living Age* observed that "no science has undergone within the last thirty years so deep a transformation in all its conceptions, its methods, and its very language, as has been the case with psychology." Today's psychologists "do not consider their science as philosophy, but know very well that they only contribute, in common with all other sciences, the necessary stepping-stones to build up the philosophy of the universe."[2] Although U.S. writers and artists continued to exploit psychophysical concepts for another decade, the direct heirs of psychophysics—experimental psychologists like Joseph Jastrow—no longer pressed physiology into the service of metaphysical hypothesis. Thus, when James died in 1910, so too did the last philosophical remainder of psychology and, in effect, the entire psychophysical enterprise. Under the reigning positivist paradigm, what had been one of the most "modern" sciences of the nineteenth century was now a misguided "proto-science." Or, following Thomas Kuhn: in the competitive epistemic environment of the late nineteenth century, psychophysics was a pre-paradigmatic science that had simply lost out to the positivism that would allow psychology to survive and thrive as a "human science" in the twentieth century.[3]

Around the turn of the twentieth century, the New Psychologists determined that the "wider problem [of the soul] should be studied by philosophers, linguists, and anthropologists," and that is precisely what happened.[4] The decades during which psychophysical concepts circulated in the United States were also a kind of epistemic interval "before cultures," when the definition of *culture*—as a system of shared meaning (e.g., beliefs, gestures, behaviors) that organizes a group of people—was taking shape but had not yet taken hold in cultural anthropology.[5] Hence, psychophysics was coming under pressure not only from its positivist offspring, experimental psychology, but also from the emergent social sciences, which used ethnographic rather than experimental methods to research lived human experience. The very origin story of American anthropology, in fact, is told in near-Oedipal terms as a wholesale rejection of psychophysics. In the 1880s, Franz Boas wrote a dissertation, under Helmholtz no less, on how different intensities of light create different colors when interacting with different kinds of water. But after observing how the Inuit of Baffin Island perceive the color of arctic water, he realized that culture, not physiology, is the variable driving sense experience. The fatal flaw of psychophysics is assuming a universal perceiving subject (predictably, white men were Weber's, Helmholtz's, and Fechner's test subjects). Boas argued that slight variations in perception were not physiologically subjective—that is, not attributable to individual quirks like astigmatism—but, rather, culturally specific. Sensation may be a sign, but the symbolic domain of culture makes that sign what it is. Not light waves but language, not tactile nerves but received traditions, shape consciousness. Once Boas discredited these ontological and ethnocentric assumptions, psychologists studied feeling's quantifiable aspects, while sociologists and cultural anthropologists relocated the study of feeling's qualitative aspects from the artificial setting of the laboratory to the "natural" field of the lived world.

But psychophysics, like the phantom limb it had helped S. Weir Mitchell to identify, did not die so much as animate new bodies of knowledge. This returns us to W. E. B. Du Bois, when at the turn of the twentieth century he described double consciousness as the sense of "measuring one's soul by the tape of a [white supremacist] world."[6] Measuring the immeasurable spirit may seem a strange way to define double consciousness, but we can now recognize this formulation as born of psychophysics, the first science to measure the "soul," or psyche, of individual people. A sociologist himself, Du Bois contends that if the social sciences are to undertake the psychophysical work of measuring a people's soul, then, as per the new concept of cultural relativism, the tape being used must belong to that people—not to white Euro-Americans. His response to "How does it feel to be a problem?" therefore serves as the hinge on which two related philosophical and aesthetic traditions pivot. After all, when looking backward at the nineteenth century, double consciousness is a clear summation of psychophysical aesthesis, which used psychophysics to explore embodied difference as a fact of consciousness. But when looking forward to the twentieth century, it is an inauguration of a more phenomenological practice. Once it was established that consciousness is embodied, writers and thinkers then sought to assess how social oppression shapes embodied consciousness—perhaps most notably anthropologist Zora Neale Hurston, in her essay *How It Feels to Be Colored Me* (1928). It also became possible to describe social spaces as an embodied mode of consciousness or "state of mind," such as when Chicago school sociologist Robert Park called the modern city a kind of "psychophysical mechanism in and through which private and political interests find not merely a collective but a corporate expression."[7]

In the first half of the twentieth century, a range of creative and critical writers in the United States took a cue from Du Bois by using these ethnographic accounts of feeling to contest the state-secured hegemony of biology, evidenced by the implementation of eugenics policies and the institution of the "one drop rule" as a legal principle of racial segregation. And with the rise of psychoanalysis and of Frankfurt school social criticism in this era, the sensorium transformed from a set of distinct perceptual faculties into an apparatus fragmented by the violent incursions of technology and consumer culture. What mattered now was the phenomenological entanglement of the sensory and the symbolic in the *un*making of the feeling body. Thus, rather than limn the five senses as genres that mediate the metaphysical contingencies of human difference, many writers and thinkers instead delineated what Adrienne Brown calls "racial perception," the learned behaviors and techniques that allow subjects "to believe they are having an experience of race."[8] From the peripatetic rhythm of Gertrude Stein's "Melanctha" to the urban sounds of Langston Hughes's jazz poetry, a range of early twentieth-century projects advanced the aesthetics laid out by psychophysical aesthesis—though they did so by treating sense experience not as a stabilizing convention but rather as a fitful style of encounter with the world in which embodied subjects live. In this fashion, literature became an important means of advancing the sensory phenomenologies of race and gender that the social sciences helped to shape.

Disciplinary debates about the place of sense experience in how we study and organize our knowledge of the world—the debates of which psychophysics was born—did not end with this historical moment. In fact, these debates have been renewed. In response to the "sensory deadening" of criticism after the poststructuralist "linguistic turn" of the late twentieth century, the interdisciplinary field of sensory studies was founded.[9] It grew out of cultural anthropology, a field that has made good on Karl Marx's declaration—and this coda's second epigraph—that the senses are a historical development. Within this important field, scholars redefine the senses as cultural modes of experience and historical memory, thereby freeing sense experience from the positivism of neuroscience and the essentialism of phenomenology.[10] Sensory studies describes itself as poised to challenge "the monopoly that the discipline of psychology has long exercised over the study of the senses and sense perception by foregrounding the sociality of sensation."[11] This is something of a redux of anthropology's Boasian origin story, as feeling is wrested from the universalist hands of hard science. But to distance sense experience from psychology is necessarily to distance it from psychophysics. Likely done unwittingly, this move ends up displacing psychophysics from the history of feeling that has animated cultural, aesthetic, and critical practices past and present.

In a moment marked by the violent retrenchment of reactionary politics, psychophysics offers us today a means to consider the perceptual processes that have made it possible to value certain lives over others, across differences of race, gender, as well as species. Focused on the five senses as they connect eye, ear, nose, tongue, and skin to the psyche, psychophysics was a science wholly committed to mapping out the perceptual capacities that make us human, all while advancing the position that sensation is a matter of consciousness irreducible to the human. At its boldest, it outlined the auditory, gustatory, visual, olfactory, and tactile limits of being human in a material universe composed of interlocking souls, including those of plants, planets, and animals. Today it offers up a generative account of the imaginative processes inhering in the physical act of feeling—that is, an account of the *aesthesis* through which humans and nonhumans emerge. If psychophysics helped postbellum Americans make sense of the experience of difference in a biologized social order, then in an era of neoliberal biopower, it can perhaps equip us with the means to rethink the "distribution of the sensible," defined by Jacques Rancière as the aesthetic regimes that position people within a community according to what can be sensed (e.g., what is inaudible and audible).[12] If, as Marx declared, power relations "enable or inhibit particular sensory modalities of human existence," then how do sensory modalities enable or inhibit what counts as human existence, or "life itself"?[13] Keeping close kinship with the impossible forms of embodiment psychophysical aesthesis sketched out—phantom limbs, racially pure souls, collaborative *I*'s—is a distinctly contemporary iteration of impossible embodiment, one born of inaudible sound waves: the prenatal ultrasound. As such, it offers a fitting postscript to the query that organized the postbellum crisis of *not-seeing*: What does life look like on the threshold of perception? The prenatal ultrasound is a "body image" of a spectral figure that resides on the threshold of visibility—and, further, on the threshold of the human. Viewing this image through a psychophysical lens brings into focus how the lived genre of not-seeing powerfully converges with the ultrasonic "genre" of (bare) life in the twenty-first century, in the effort to contain the indeterminacies of being human.

The prenatal ultrasound is something like a twenty-first-century spirit photograph. It is a visual form that first became part of common medical practice in the 1980s to evaluate the viability of a fetus—its capacity to live successfully—though its cultural function is to assign gender. Ultrasound technology involves using an electronic device called a transducer to send and receive inaudible high-frequency sound waves at different speeds. The ritual is such: A medical technician runs the transducer over the surface of the gestating patient's abdomen; the transducer sends sound waves through skin, muscle, bone, and fluids until the sound waves strike and bounce off the organs/organisms inside (placenta, fetus, amniotic sac); the transducer then picks up and converts these echoes into an electronic moving image displayed on a screen. Although different in many obvious ways, Mumler's spirit photographs and prenatal ultrasounds share important commonalities. Photography may be "light writing" and sonography "sound writing," but Mumler emphasized that his camera required the magnetic powers of his wife Hannah to visually capture the spirits of the dead. In this sense, Mumler's spirit photographs served as a kind of medical body imaging—from the X-ray to the MRI—that, like the prenatal ultrasound, circumnavigates optics to make visible or to "diagnose" inner truths. In addition, the two body images both serve a familial function, though in dialectically opposed ways. Spirit photographs of the dead were a means of keeping the past present, and today the prenatal ultrasound—a moving image that is frozen and printed out, to be interpreted and used like a photograph—serves as a celebratory revelation that the life to come is already here. But perhaps above all, these figures on the edges of life, the undead and the unborn, sit on the edge of sight. As with spirit photographs, there is not all that much to see when viewing a prenatal ultrasound. Far from self-evident, the imaged body is akin to the double-exposed photographic figure disappearing into its own appearance. The imaged fetus's visual transparency, its grainy ghostliness, bespeaks an ontological opacity that disrupts medicine's visual epistemology—not unlike the existential dilemma precipitated by George Dedlow's "larval" body. The viewer beholds *something* that is called life, but that something is not a clearly human thing; it requires a medical apparatus and robust cultural industry to produce its claim to the human.

The prenatal ultrasound requires not-seeing, but it is also both more and less than what we think it is. Although the fetus has a biological and, for the gestating person, a phenomenological existence apart from the ultrasound image, as that representation moves in cultural contexts—archived in photo albums, shared on social media, deployed by antiabortion activists—it has come to exist *as* that image. In other words, the impossible embodiment of the fetus at least partly rests with the fact that, like a phantom limb or a photographed spirit, representation is what makes it real. "Fetus" is an icon, not a preexisting agent awaiting medical disclosure. As such, the image leads us no more to the separation of life and nonlife ("unborn"), or, for that matter, of mother and fetus, than it does to the separation of human and nonhuman being. In fact, because race historically has been foundational to notions of species difference, the prenatal ultrasound illuminates the dynamic relay between race and not-seeing in the production of the human. The sound waves that represent the fetus both reflect and refract what Nicholas Mirzoeff identifies as "our desire to see racially."[14] As an electronic image (via the conversion of vibrations into electricity), the prenatal ultrasound offers up a body that is only organs, a body that may be assigned sex but cannot be assigned race. And yet, as a body stripped of skin and flesh it registers as racially white, as the unmarked synonym for universal humanity. The fetus has become a national icon, Lauren Berlant has argued, because it is seemingly afloat in an empty vacuum (the amniotic sac), and so appears as a kind of monad that transcends the human body and history itself.[15] It therefore instantiates the fantasy that human life can precede race, can precede flesh. It is a nonvisual representation of a naked body, a "bare" life, but its unsettled semiotic excess and iconic force demonstrate that the human itself is the flesh that it wears—or rather, what we dress it up as.

Indeed, looking at fetal ultrasounds invokes a peculiar kind of relationality. In its sensual and bodily address to the viewer, the image solicits not-seeing, a perceptual modality that embraces rather than eschews what it cannot behold. And yet this modality, or style of seeing, has been deployed not simply to accord "life" to the fetal body but to manage the lives of raced and gendered subjects. Feminists have long grappled with the liberal ideology of agential personhood that the prenatal ultrasound perpetuates, which has the effect of bifurcating mother and fetus, pitting the one against the other. But further, the

Western fantasy of human autonomy and universality powered by not-seeing is tightly woven into systematic efforts, legislative and otherwise, to extend to the fetus the protections and aura of innocence that, Robin Bernstein shows, historically has been afforded to white children.[16] The innocence more recently extended to the fetus—an ephemeral subject associated with yet entirely distinct from the infant and the child—is constitutive of a biopolitics that manages racial populations on the basis not simply of their vitality (capacity for life) but of their "viability" or potential for life, all while sanctioning governmental and social violence against them. Showing how not-seeing turns a ghostly body—living but unborn, not human but also not nonhuman—into one of the most privileged political subjects of the current moment, the psychophysics of feeling pushes us to reconsider a politics of human ontology that embraces rather than eschews its own indeterminacy.

As the perceptual processes that course through the biopolitics of fetal ultrasounds bear out, psychophysics shows how sensory modalities and technologies continue to be used in ways that push at dominant paradigms of embodiment, from differences of race and gender to the question of the human as such. When looking back at psychophysics from the contemporary moment, it is easy to see a long history of disciplining the feeling body that continues today, as the capacity for fine-grained feeling—the complexity of consciousness—still functions as a metric of human difference. Nonetheless, psychophysics represents a speculative science that opened up space for a surprising number of aesthetic experiments. Late nineteenth- and early twentieth-century writers creatively exploited the aesthetic dimensions of sense experience to produce theories of racial, gendered, and disabled being irreducible to biological configurations. From Pauline Hopkins's radical repurposing of sympathetic vibration to Emily Dickinson's gastronomic archive, psychophysical aesthesis reveals that ongoing efforts to define but also imagine the human through sensory processes and affective capacities has roots in the nineteenth century. Psychophysical aesthesis therefore anticipates the vexed negotiations of the human in the present moment, even as its afterlife has fallen under thresholds of critical perception.

NOTES

INTRODUCTION

1. Du Bois, "Strivings of the Negro People," 194.
2. Crary, *Suspensions of Perception*, 4. See also Kittler, *Gramophone, Film, Typewriter*; Sterne, *Audible Past*.
3. See Canto and Shuttleworth, *Science Serialized*.
4. Helmholtz's texts are the exception; they received English translations within a decade of publication. Weber's and Fechner's major texts, however, were not translated into English until the 1960s and 1970s.
5. Sprague, "What We Feel," 740.
6. See Schuller, *Biopolitics of Feeling*.
7. *Oxford English Dictionary Online*, s.v., "aesthesis (n.)," accessed October 18, 2016, https://www-oed-com.libproxy.albany.edu/view/Entry/3234?redirectedFrom =aesthesis#eid.
8. See Ahmed, *Queer Phenomenology*; Berlant, *Cruel Optimism*; Cvetkovich, *Depression*; Sedgwick, *Touching Feeling*; K. Stewart, *Ordinary Affects*.
9. See in particular Gregg and Seigworth, *Affect Theory Reader*; Massumi, *Politics of Affect*; Schaefer, *Evolution of Affect Theory*.
10. Nyhart, *Biology Takes Form*, 5.
11. Hawkins, "William James, Gustav Fechner," 2.
12. Menand, *Metaphysical Club*, 269.
13. Rusert, *Fugitive Science*, 4, 18.
14. Kazanjian, *Brink of Freedom*, 123.
15. See Hyde, *Civic Longing*; Kazanjian, *Brink of Freedom*.
16. W. James, *Principles of Psychology*, 538, 192.

17. W. James, *Principles of Psychology*, 549.
18. Münsterberg, "Danger of Experimental Psychology," 165.
19. W. James, introduction, ix, x.
20. Emerson, *Nature*, 13.
21. Dames, *Physiology of the Novel*, 181. See also Coriale, "Reading through Deafness."
22. Fechner, *Elements of Psychophysics*, 7.
23. Fechner, *Elements of Psychophysics*, 199.
24. Fechner, *Elements of Psychophysics*, 569.
25. Fechner, *Elements of Psychophysics*, 44.
26. Heidelberger, *Nature from Within*, 73.
27. W. James, "World of Pure Experience," 315.
28. W. James, "Hidden Self," 361.
29. W. D. Smith, *Politics and the Sciences of Culture*, 207.
30. Nichols, "Psychology Laboratory at Harvard," 399.
31. "Notices of New Books," 562.
32. See Berlant's national sentimentality trilogy, which includes *Anatomy of National Fantasy*, *Queen of America Goes to Washington City*, and *Female Complaint*; Schuller, *Biopolitics of Feeling*; Wexler, *Tender Violence*.
33. Alexander Baumgarten, quoted in Cooper, *Companion to Aesthetics*, 40.
34. Heidelberger, *Nature from Within*, 252.
35. Peña, *Body Electric*, 3.
36. Oken, *Elements of Physiophilosophy*, xi.
37. Oken, *Elements of Physiophilosophy*, 651.
38. Fechner, *Elements of Psychophysics*, 42.
39. Hetrick, "Aisthesis in Radical Empiricism," 151.
40. Howell, "In the Realms of Sensibility," 409.
41. Allen, *Physiological Aesthetics*, 48.
42. Allen, *Physiological Aesthetics*, 147.
43. Trower, *Senses of Vibration*, 55.
44. Bain, *Emotions and the Will*, 566.
45. Schuller, *Biopolitics of Feeling*.
46. See Galton, *Life, Letters and Labours of Francis Galton*.
47. Galton, *Inquiries into Human Faculty*, 24.
48. Galton, *Inquiries into Human Faculty*, 28.
49. Galton, *Inquiries into Human Faculty*, 29.
50. Allen, *Physiological Aesthetics*, 50.
51. Gaskill, *Chromographia*.
52. Parisi, *Archaeologies of Touch*, 98.
53. Theodore Dreiser, "The Training of the Senses," c. 1899, unpublished manuscript, Annenberg Rare Book and Manuscript Library, Theodore Dreiser Collection, Folder 12433, 1.
54. Dreiser, "Training," 5.
55. Dreiser, "Training," 2.
56. Freeman, *Beside You in Time*, 12.
57. Alexander, *Kinesthetic Knowing*, 14.

58. Riskin, *Science in the Age of Sensibility*, 27.
59. Müller, *Elements of Physiology*, 712.
60. Otis, *Müller's Lab*, 9.
61. Crary, *Techniques of the Observer*, ch. 3.
62. Reed, *From Soul to Mind*, 181.
63. Hermann von Helmholtz, "The Theory of Vision," in Cahan, *Science and Culture*, 195, 202.
64. Grimstad, *Experience and Experimental Writing*, 1, 14.
65. Connolly, *World of Becoming*, 49.
66. Helmholtz, *Physiological Optics*, 443.
67. Heidelberger, *Nature from Within*, 80.
68. R. Williams, *Marxism and Literature*, 132.
69. Jackson, "Function of Criticism."
70. Berlant, *Female Complaint*, 4.
71. Berlant, *Female Complaint*, 259.
72. Highmore, *Cultural Feelings*, 51.
73. Musser, *Sensational Flesh*, 1.
74. "Recent Experiments with the Senses," 518.
75. See Goldstein, *Sweet Science*; Cecire, *Experimental*; Rusert, *Fugitive Science*; Schuller, *Biopolitics of Feeling*.
76. Latour, "How to Talk about the Body?" 206.
77. Latour, "How to Talk about the Body?" 210.
78. Gaskill, *Chromographia*, 35.
79. Heller-Roazen, *Inner Touch*, 250.
80. Buck-Morss, *Dreamworld and Catastrophe*, 101.
81. E. M. Dillon, "Atlantic Aesthesis."
82. See in particular Murison, *Politics of Anxiety*; Coghlan, *Sensational Internationalism*; Reckson, *Realist Ecstasy*.
83. See Siebers, *Disability Theory*.
84. Puar, *Terrorist Assemblages*, 200.
85. Mitchell and Snyder, *Matter of Disability*, 9.
86. Yergeau, *Authoring Autism*, 4.
87. See M. M. Smith, *How Race Is Made*.
88. See McLuhan, "Inside the Five Sense Sensorium."
89. Cytowic, *Man Who Tasted Shapes*, 253.
90. Nordau, *Degeneration*, 142.
91. Connolly, *World of Becoming*, 50.

CHAPTER 1. SIGHT

1. Sacks, *Man Who Mistook His Wife for a Hat*, 66.
2. Finseth, *Civil War Dead*, 89.
3. "Concerning Things Spiritual," 53.
4. H. James, *Turn of the Screw*, 229.

5. S. M. Smith, *At the Edge of Sight*, 6.
6. Thurschwell, "Refusing to Give Up the Ghost," 234.
7. See Chen, *Animacies*.
8. Luciano, *Arranging Grief*, 1.
9. Hammond, "Physics and Physiology of Spiritualism," 234.
10. Strathausen, *Look of Things*, 54.
11. Connolly, *Neuropolitics*, 20.
12. McGarry, *Ghosts of Futures Past*, 17.
13. Mao, *Fateful Beauty*, 124.
14. "Transcendental Physics," 417.
15. Carus, "Fechner's View of Life After Death," 84.
16. W. James, introduction, x.
17. Helmholtz, *Physiological Optics*, 130.
18. Abbot, "Eye and the Camera," 478.
19. H. W. Williams, *Our Eyes*, 6.
20. "Can We Believe Our Eyes?" 66.
21. Beer, "'Authentic Tidings of Invisible Things,'" 85.
22. Smajić, *Ghost-Seers, Detectives, and Spiritualists*, 7.
23. Hermann von Helmholtz, "On the Conservation of Force," in Cahan, *Science and Culture*, 98.
24. Helmholtz, "On the Conservation of Force," 126.
25. Riskin, *Restless Clock*, 211.
26. Rabinbach, *Eclipse of the Utopias of Labor*, 7.
27. Trower, *Senses of Vibration*, 10.
28. Fechner, *Life after Death*, 53. I use the 1882 English translation, which includes the appendix "On the Principle of Heavenly Vision."
29. Fechner, *Life after Death*, 70.
30. Fechner, *Elements of Psychophysics*, 526.
31. Fechner, *Elements of Psychophysics*, 78.
32. Fechner, *Elements of Psychophysics*, 74.
33. Fechner, *Life after Death*, 92.
34. Fechner, *Life after Death*, 81—82.
35. Draper, "Popular Exposition of Some Scientific Experiments," 892.
36. Kittler, *Gramophone, Film, Typewriter*, 120.
37. Carus, "Fechner's View," 87.
38. Fiske, "Unseen World," 274.
39. Fiske, "Unseen World," 266.
40. Hedge, "Ghost Seeing," 298.
41. "Optical Illusions," 153.
42. Carus, "Fechner's View," 85.
43. S. W. Mitchell, "Phantom Limbs," 565.
44. S. W. Mitchell, "Phantom Limbs," 565.
45. S. W. Mitchell, "Medical Department in the Civil War," 1445.
46. Sacks, *Musicophilia*, 286.

47. S. W. Mitchell, "Case," 1.
48. Satz, "'Conviction of Its Existence,'" 114.
49. S. W. Mitchell, "Phantom Limbs," 563.
50. Nelson, *Ruin Nation*, 179.
51. See Schweik, *Ugly Laws*.
52. S. W. Mitchell, "Case," 5.
53. Streeby, *American Sensations*, 31.
54. S. W. Mitchell, "Case," 8.
55. S. W. Mitchell, "Case of George Dedlow," in *Autobiography of a Quack*, 137.
56. S. W. Mitchell, "Case," 11.
57. Altschuler, *Medical Imagination*, 188.
58. S. W. Mitchell, "Case," 7.
59. Berlant, *Female Complaint*, 110.
60. Nelson, *Ruin Nation*, 169.
61. S. W. Mitchell, "Case," 9.
62. S. W. Mitchell, "Case," 10–11.
63. Ogden, *Credulity*.
64. Murison, "Quacks, Nostrums, and Miraculous Cure," 437.
65. S. W. Mitchell, "Phantom Limbs," 564.
66. W. James, "Consciousness of Lost Limbs," 257.
67. S. W. Mitchell, "Phantom Limbs," 564.
68. S. W. Mitchell, *Injuries of Nerves*, 349.
69. S. W. Mitchell, "Phantom Limbs," 565.
70. S. W. Mitchell, "Phantom Limbs," 565.
71. S. W. Mitchell, *Injuries of Nerves*, 349.
72. Ogden, *Credulity*, 229.
73. McGarry, *Ghosts of Futures Past*, 15.
74. S. W. Mitchell, *Injuries of Nerves*, 364, 348.
75. Cervetti, *S. Weir Mitchell*, 108.
76. S. W. Mitchell, "Phantom Limbs," 568.
77. Ngai, *Ugly Feelings*, 91.
78. Ngai, *Ugly Feelings*, 31.
79. G. S. Hall, "Negro in Africa and America," 355.
80. Schuller, *Biopolitics of Feeling*, 14.
81. Morris, *Culture of Pain*, 152.
82. West, "Camera Fiends," 186.
83. "Spirit Photography Scientifically Considered," *Banner of Light* (November 29, 1862), cited in Kaplan, *Strange Case of William Mumler*, 44.
84. Taylor, *Veil Lifted*, 15–16.
85. "Spirit Photography Scientifically Considered," 44.
86. Weinstein, "Technologies of Vision," 128.
87. M. Warner, *Phantasmagoria*, 218.
88. Register, "Spirit Photograph," 122.
89. Register, "Spirit Photograph," 123.

90. Register, "Spirit Photograph," 124.
91. More specifically, with Ramachandran's mirror box, the sight of what appears to be the missing limb convinces the brain that the lost limb has been recovered, so it no longer needs to send it sensory messages—like a flare gun or distress signal. See Ramachandran, *Phantoms in the Brain*; Ramachandran, *Tell-Tale Brain*.
92. Newman, "Wounds and Wounding," 64.
93. Goler, "Loss and the Persistence of Memory," 164.
94. Newman, "Wounds and Wounding," 75.
95. Seltzer, *Bodies and Machines*, 95.
96. Sheehan, *Doctored*, 21.
97. S. W. Mitchell, "Phantom Limbs," 565.
98. Mumler, "Personal Experiences of William H. Mumler in Spirit Photography," in Kaplan, *Strange Case of William Mumler*, 69–139.
99. Taylor, *Veil Lifted*, 18.
100. Holmes, "Doings of the Sunbeam," 14.
101. Finseth, *Civil War Dead*, 100.
102. S. M. Smith, *Edge of Sight*, 12.
103. Bennett, *Transatlantic Spiritualism*, 149.
104. Luciano, "Touching Seeing," 144.
105. Dyer, *White*, 14.
106. Strick, *American Dolorologies*, 73.
107. McGarry, *Ghosts of Futures Past*, 66.
108. See in particular Romero, *Home Fronts*.
109. Digitized images from William Stainton Moses's spirit photograph album are not presently available, but the album itself—page 18, which I discuss here—is housed in the William Stainton Moses Collection at the College of Psychic Studies, London.
110. Strick, *American Dolorologies*, 121.
111. Dyer, *White*, 122.
112. Woodward, "Army Medical Museum in Washington," 243.
113. Cobb, *Picture Freedom*, 64.
114. Weinstein, "Possessive Matters," 277.
115. S. W. Mitchell, "Medical Department," 1445.
116. A. Gordon, *Ghostly Matters*, 172.
117. Fleetwood, *Troubling Vision*, 18.
118. Howells, *Imperative Duty*, 86.
119. Howells, *Imperative Duty*, 86.
120. Habegger, *Henry James and the "Woman Business,"* 209.
121. See Sharpe, *In the Wake*.
122. H. James, *Notes of a Son and Brother*, 298.
123. Coviello, *Tomorrow's Parties*, 188.
124. H. James, *Bostonians*, 7.
125. H. James, *Bostonians*, 32.
126. H. James, *Bostonians*, 28, 34.
127. H. James, *Bostonians*, 31.

128. Funchion, "Critical Oversights," 283.
129. H. James, *Bostonians*, 32.
130. Hartman, *Scenes of Subjection*, 116.
131. Coviello, *Tomorrow's Parties*, 184.
132. DeLue, "Diagnosing Pictures," 65.
133. Beard, *American Nervousness*, 45.
134. H. James, *Bostonians*, 53.
135. H. James, *Bostonians*, 414.
136. H. James, *Bostonians*, 435.
137. W. James, "Consciousness of Lost Limbs," 249, 258.
138. "Phantom Limbs," 504.
139. Merleau-Ponty, *Phenomenology of Perception*, 181.
140. Merleau-Ponty, *Phenomenology of Perception*, 94.
141. Ahmed, "Phenomenology of Whiteness," 158.
142. Hartman, *Scenes of Subjection*, 73.
143. Hartman, *Scenes of Subjection*, 74.
144. Mackey, *Discrepant Engagement*, 235.
145. Mackey, *Discrepant Engagement*, 236.
146. Mackey, *Discrepant Engagement*, 169.

INTERVAL 1. COLORFUL SOUNDS

1. Cytowic, *Synesthesia*, 8.
2. Galton, *Inquiries into Human Faculty*, 256.
3. Downey, "Literary Synesthesia," 497.
4. See Abrams and Harpham, *Glossary of Literary Terms*. See also Postle, *Essentials of Cognitive Neuroscience*.
5. Rimbaud, "Voyelles," in *Rimbaud*, 140–41.
6. In Baudelaire, *Flowers of Evil*, 27–28.
7. Dann, *False Colors Brightly Seen*, 78.
8. Pourciau, *Writing of Spirit*, 163.
9. Binet, "Problem of Color Audition," 813.
10. W. James, "Theodore Flournoy," 466.
11. Gaskill, *Chromographia*, 19.
12. Millet, *L'Audition colorée* (1892), quoted in Dann, *False Colors Brightly Seen*, 29.
13. Babbitt, *New Laokoon*, 172, 174, 183.
14. Coriat, "Unusual Type of Synesthesia," 111.
15. Dann, *False Colors Brightly Seen*, 95.
16. Ellis and Symonds, *Sexual Inversion*, 186.
17. Rée, *I See a Voice*, 31.
18. Schooling, "Color-Music," 349.
19. Gaskill, "Articulate Eye," 487.
20. Schooling, "Color-Music," 349.
21. Rée, *I See a Voice*, 41.
22. Doyle, "Will Color Music Become an Art?" 401.

23. Gaskill, "Articulate Eye," 489.
24. Doyle, "Will Color Music Become an Art?" 399.
25. Gilman, "Dr. Clair's Place," in *Yellow Wall-Paper*, 301.
26. Gilman, "Dr. Clair's Place," 302.
27. Crary, *Suspensions of Perception*, 94.
28. Marvick, "René Ghil," 291.
29. Helmholtz, *Sensations of Tone*, 157.
30. Eidsheim, *Race of Sound*, 5.
31. Howells, *Imperative Duty*, 171.

CHAPTER 2. SOUND

1. Lane, *Mizora*, 16.
2. Lane, *Mizora*, 82.
3. Lane, *Mizora*, 57.
4. Lane, *Mizora*, 92, 93.
5. Benjamin Steege, "Acoustics," in Novak and Sakakeeny, *Keywords in Sound*, 27.
6. *Oxford English Dictionary Online*, s.v., "aural (*adj.*)," accessed September 5, 2017, https://www-oed-com.libproxy.albany.edu/view/Entry/13160?rskey =NnmYsA&result=3&isAdvanced=false#eid. See also Jonathan Sterne, "Hearing," in Novak and Sakakeeny, *Keywords in Sound*, 65–77.
7. Cahan, *Helmholtz*, 199.
8. Helmholtz, *Sensations of Tone*, 1.
9. Helmholtz, *Sensations of Tone*, 3.
10. Thrailkill, *Affecting Fictions*, 154.
11. Darwin, *Descent of Man*, 572.
12. Gurney, *Power of Sound*, v.
13. Galton, *Inquiries into Human Faculty*, 25, 323.
14. See Pfaelzer, *Utopian Novel in America*.
15. Stadler, "Whiteness and Sound Studies."
16. Stoever, *Sonic Color Line*.
17. Kun, *Audiotopia*.
18. Jameson, *Archaeologies of the Future*, 171.
19. English, *Unnatural Selections*, 29, 18.
20. Lanier, "Orchestra of Today," 897.
21. Gottschalk, "Notes of a Pianist," 177.
22. Helmholtz, *Sensations of Tone*, 4.
23. See Steege, *Helmholtz and the Modern Listener*.
24. Steege, *Helmholtz and the Modern Listener*, 60.
25. Picker, *Victorian Soundscapes*, 87.
26. Helmholtz, *Sensations of Tone*, 129.
27. Helmholtz, *Sensations of Tone*, 129.
28. Stoever, *Sonic Color Line*, 39.
29. Helmholtz, *Sensations of Tone*, 98.
30. Helmholtz, *Sensations of Tone*, 368.

31. W. James, *Principles of Psychology*, 456.
32. Helmholtz, *Sensations of Tone*, 368.
33. Cahan, *Helmholtz*, 198.
34. Helmholtz, *Sensations of Tone*, 56.
35. Helmholtz, *Sensations of Tone*, 51.
36. Helmholtz, *Sensations of Tone*, 369.
37. Hui, *Psychophysical Ear*, 62.
38. Hanslick, *Beautiful in Music*, 128.
39. Hanslick, *Beautiful in Music*, 134, 135.
40. "Recent Literature," 683.
41. Thompson, *Soundscape of Modernity*, 47.
42. Helmholtz, *Sensations of Tone*, 234.
43. Helmholtz, *Sensations of Tone*, 235.
44. Helmholtz, *Sensations of Tone*, 363.
45. Stoever, *Sonic Color Line*, 149.
46. Helmholtz, *Sensations of Tone*, 236.
47. Helmholtz, *Sensations of Tone*, 369.
48. Gurney, *Power of Sound*, 258.
49. David Novak, "Noise," in Novak and Sakakeeny, ed. *Keywords in Sound*, 127.
50. Helmholtz, *Sensations of Tone*, 348.
51. Gryzanowski, "Wagner's Theories of Music," 56.
52. Gryzanowski, "Wagner's Theories of Music," 81.
53. Gryzanowski, "Wagner's Theories of Music," 75.
54. Bramen, *Uses of Variety*, 23, 29.
55. W. James, "One and the Many," 60.
56. Sugden, *Emergent Worlds*, 156.
57. Bellamy, *Religion of Solidarity*, 56.
58. Bellamy, *Religion of Solidarity*, 35.
59. Helmholtz, *Sensations of Tone*, 367.
60. Courtemanche, "Satire and the 'Inevitability Effect,'" 230.
61. Bellamy, *Looking Backward*, 63, 57.
62. Bellamy, *Looking Backward*, 63.
63. Ahmad, *Landscapes of Hope*, 27.
64. Bellamy, *Looking Backward*, 88.
65. Bellamy, *Looking Backward*, 146.
66. Bellamy, *Looking Backward*, 108.
67. Bellamy, *Looking Backward*, 109.
68. Dwight, "Music as a Means of Culture," 328, 329.
69. Samson, "Great Composer," 281.
70. Dwight, "Music as a Means of Culture," 326.
71. Brower, "Is the Musical Idea Masculine?" 328.
72. Yablon, "Echoes of the City," 636.
73. Helmholtz, *Sensations of Tone*, vii.
74. Girdner, "Plague of City Noises," 296.
75. Attali, *Noise*, 62, 26.

76. Helmholtz, *Sensations of Tone*, 8, 7.
77. J. Bernstein, *Five Senses of Man*, 282.
78. Stoever, *Sonic Color Line*, 13.
79. Darwin, *Descent of Man*, 568.
80. Ellis, *Sexual Selection in Man*, vi.
81. Hamlin, *From Eve to Evolution*, 130.
82. Bellamy, *Looking Backward*, 201.
83. Bellamy, *Equality*, 365.
84. Bellamy, *Equality*, 365.
85. Bellamy, *Looking Backward*, 56.
86. Courtemanche, "Satire and the 'Inevitability Effect,'" 230.
87. Bellamy, *Looking Backward*, 221.
88. Bellamy, *Looking Backward*, 223.
89. Michaels, *Our America*, 49.
90. Davenport, "Effects of Race Intermingling," 367.
91. Bellamy, *Looking Backward*, 223.
92. Bellamy, *Looking Backward*, 89.
93. Bellamy, *Religion of Solidarity*, 31.
94. Bellamy, *Looking Backward*, 147, 150.
95. Bellamy, *Looking Backward*, 125–26.
96. Novak, "Noise," 127.
97. Hui, *Psychophysical Ear*, 125.
98. Matt Sakakeeny, "Music," in Novak and Sakakeeny, *Keywords in Sound*, 127.
99. Bentley, *Frantic Panoramas*, 15.
100. Hopkins, "Famous Women of the Negro Race," 46.
101. Dwight, "Intellectual Influence of Music," 621.
102. Helmholtz, *Sensations of Tone*, 36.
103. Peters, "Helmholtz, Edison, and Sound History," 183.
104. Eidsheim, *Race of Sound*, 24.
105. Ahmad, *Landscapes of Hope*, 132.
106. Fabi, *Passing*, 47.
107. Hopkins, *Of One Blood*, 8.
108. Hopkins, *Of One Blood*, 11.
109. Brooks, *Bodies in Dissent*, 309.
110. Brooks, *Bodies in Dissent*, 309.
111. Eidsheim, *Race of Sound*, 76.
112. Cruz, *Culture on the Margins*, 3–4.
113. Stoever, *Sonic Color Line*, 133.
114. "Negroes as Singers," 6.
115. Dana Luciano addresses the chronobiopolitics of the Native American voice in the frontier romance in chapter 2 of *Arranging Grief*.
116. "Negroes as Singers," 6.
117. Eidsheim, *Race of Sound*, 52.
118. Hopkins, *Of One Blood*, 14.
119. Brooks, *Bodies in Dissent*, 301.

120. Brooks, *Bodies in Dissent*, 305.
121. Hopkins, *Of One Blood*, 54.
122. Schrager, "Pauline Hopkins and William James," 199.
123. Hopkins, *Of One Blood*, 67.
124. Brooks, *Bodies in Dissent*, 318.
125. Hopkins, *Of One Blood*, 30.
126. Hopkins, *Of One Blood*, 137, 141, 147.
127. Hopkins, *Of One Blood*, 174, 186.
128. Hopkins, *Of One Blood*, 186.
129. Hopkins, *Of One Blood*, 82, 179.
130. Hopkins, *Of One Blood*, 187.
131. Farooq, *Undisciplined*, 96.
132. "Parlor Singing," 412.
133. Barnard, *Empire of Ruin*, 6.
134. Hopkins, *Of One Blood*, 113.
135. Friedner and Helmreich, "Sound Studies Meets Deaf Studies," 73. On the disability history of sound and communications technology, see Mills, "Deaf Jam." For a rigorous critique of the anthropocentrism of aural experiences of sound, see Roosth, "Nineteen Hertz and Below."
136. Ngai, *Ugly Feelings*, 38.
137. Helmholtz, *Sensations of Tone*, 251.
138. Ngai, *Ugly Feelings*, 31.

INTERVAL 2. NOTES ON SCENT

1. Lane, *Mizora*, 81.
2. Allen, *Physiological Aesthetics*, 83.
3. Allen, *Physiological Aesthetics*, 83.
4. Cranch, "Plea for the Sense of Smell," 317.
5. Cristiani, *Perfumery and Kindred Arts*, 18.
6. G. W. S. Piesse, *Art of Perfumery*, 85.
7. "Taste and Smell," 234.
8. C. H. Piesse, *Olfactics and the Physical Senses*, 98.
9. Higginson, "Maroons of Surinam," 151; Higginson, "April Days," 389.
10. "Sound and Smell," 4.
11. Finck, "Aesthetic Value of the Sense of Smell," 798.
12. Ellman, *Oscar Wilde*, 351.
13. Hartmann, "Perfume Land," 221.
14. Hartmann, "Perfume Land," 217.
15. Hartmann, "Perfume Land," 218.
16. Hartmann, "Perfume Land," 217, 219, 222.
17. Hartmann, "Perfume Land," 223, 224.
18. Bradstreet, "*Trip to Japan in Sixteen Minutes*," 55.
19. Bradstreet, "*Trip to Japan in Sixteen Minutes*," 224.
20. "Newest Public Amusement," 15.

21. "Comparisons Most Odorous," 8.
22. Quoted in Krolz, *Creative Composites*, 15.
23. J. Park, *Apparitions of Asia*.
24. Hartmann, "Perfume Land," 224.
25. The performance *A Trip to Japan in Sixteen Minutes, Revisited* cannot be archived in any material sense, but the institute made a brief video about the performance's production: "A Trip to Japan in Sixteen Minutes, Revisited—BTS," the Institute for Art and Olfaction, August 13, 2016, video, 4:03, https://www.youtube.com/watch?time_continue=43&v=rKPpW3hyNQA.
26. Hartmann, "Perfume Land," 224.
27. Jasper and Wagner, "Notes on Scent."
28. Hartmann, "Perfume Land," 224.
29. Hartmann, "Perfume Land," 226.
30. Hartmann, "Perfume Land," 223.
31. Babbitt, *New Laokoon*, 128.
32. Babbitt, *New Laokoon*, 184–85.
33. Nordau, *Degeneration*, 503.
34. Bradstreet, "*Trip to Japan in Sixteen Minutes*," 52.
35. Hartmann, "Perfume Land," 228.

CHAPTER 3. SMELL

1. Hartmann, "Perfume Land," 221.
2. "Newest Public Amusement," 15.
3. "Olfactory Crusade," 1.
4. "Comparisons Most Odorous," 8.
5. Kant, *Anthropology from a Pragmatic Point of View*, 161.
6. Bell, "Discovery and Invention," 652. Early twentieth-century Dutch physiologist H. Zwaardemaker invented olfactometers to measure subjective responses to olfactory stimuli.
7. Duncan, *Chemistry of Commerce*, 157–58.
8. "Studying the Sense of Smell," 32.
9. Finck, "Aesthetic Value of the Sense of Smell," 794.
10. Jastrow, "Plea for the Sense of Smell," 520.
11. Jasper and Wagner, "Notes on Scent."
12. Dussauce, *Practical Guide*, iii, iv.
13. Leslie, *Synthetic Worlds*, 78.
14. "Fashionable Odors," 182.
15. "Taste and Smell," 234.
16. Dussauce, *Practical Guide*, 27.
17. Alaimo, *Bodily Natures*, 2.
18. Dugan, *Ephemeral History of Perfume*, 15.
19. Brennan, *Transmission of Affect*, 9.
20. Rimmel, *Book of Perfumes*, 2.
21. B. Brown, *Sense of Things*, 90.

22. Hsu, "Naturalist Smellscapes," 791.
23. Maxwell, *Scents and Sensibility*, 3.
24. Frost, *Problem with Pleasure*, 39.
25. Nordau, *Degeneration*, 260.
26. Carlisle, *Common Scents*, 4.
27. Fleissner, *Women, Compulsion, Modernity*, 22.
28. Evans, "Howellsian Chic," 807.
29. Cranch, "Plea for the Sense of Smell," 315.
30. Cranch, "Plea for the Sense of Smell," 316.
31. J. Bernstein, *Five Senses of Man*, 284.
32. E. H. Weber, *E. H. Weber on the Tactile Senses*, 120.
33. Fechner, *Elements of Psychophysics*, 202.
34. E. Dillon, "Neglected Sense," 504.
35. Ogle, *Anosmia*, 276.
36. Finck, "Aesthetic Value of the Sense of Smell," 793.
37. Harrington and Rosario, "Olfaction and the Primitive," 16.
38. Finck, "Aesthetic Value of the Sense of Smell," 794.
39. Finck, "Aesthetic Value of the Sense of Smell," 798.
40. Darwin, *Descent of Man*, 23.
41. Finck, "Aesthetic Value of the Sense of Smell," 794.
42. Rimmel, *Book of Perfumes*, 1.
43. Askinson, *Perfumes and Their Preparation*, 1.
44. Cristiani, *Perfumery and Kindred Arts*, 31.
45. "Ambrosia," 58.
46. "To Collect the Perfume of Flowers," 249.
47. Muhammad, *Condemnation of Blackness*, 22.
48. Jefferson, *Notes on the State of Virginia*, 146.
49. "Do the Various Races of Man Constitute a Single Species?" 138.
50. Hoffer, *Sensory Worlds in Early America*, 5.
51. "Odor of Race," 6.
52. Ellis, *Sexual Selection in Man*, 97, 96.
53. Howes, *Varieties of Sensory Experience*.
54. Hooper, "Perfumes of France," 4.
55. Corbin, *Foul and the Fragrant*, 76, 141.
56. Scarry, *Dreaming by the Book*, 62.
57. Corbin, *Foul and the Fragrant*, 186.
58. Cooley, *Toilet and Cosmetic Arts*, 553.
59. Finck, "Aesthetic Value of the Sense of Smell," 796.
60. Looby, "Flowers of Manhood," 118.
61. Stott, "Floral Femininity," 68.
62. Cranch, "Plea for the Sense of Smell," 317.
63. Classen, Howes, and Synnott, *Aroma*, 162.
64. "Flower Odors," 470.
65. Desmarais, "Perfume Clouds," 64.
66. "Perfumes, Soaps, and Pomades," 18.

67. Whitman, *Democratic Vistas*, 48.
68. Clifford, *Romance of Perfume Lands*, 4.
69. Clifford, *Romance of Perfume Lands*, 13–14.
70. Clifford, *Romance of Perfume Lands*, 62, 120.
71. Keeney, *Botanizers*, 70.
72. Reinarz, *Past Scents*, 136.
73. In describing Clifford's novel as transnational plantation fiction, I am building on the work of scholars who have situated U.S. Reconstruction as part of broader global imperial order. See Greeson, *Our South*; A. Kaplan, *Anarchy of Empire*.
74. Cranch, "Plea for the Sense of Smell," 318.
75. "Chemical Perfumes," 8.
76. Thomas, "Notes from the Wild Garden," 174.
77. Allen, *Physiological Aesthetics*, 87.
78. "Perfumery," 4.
79. Duncan, *Chemistry of Commerce*, 172.
80. "Perfumes, Soaps, and Pomades," 18.
81. Stace, "Plant Odors," 266.
82. Rimmel, *Book of Perfumes*, 238.
83. Howells, *Imperative Duty*, 146.
84. Nyong'o, *Amalgamation Waltz*, 83.
85. Rimmel, *Book of Perfumes*, 3.
86. Snively, "Art of Perfumery," 579.
87. Evans, "*Vogue* and Ephemera."
88. Bentley, *Frantic Panoramas*, 140.
89. Review in *Literature*, June 23, 1899, 570; review of Chopin, *Awakening*, New Orleans *Times-Democrat*, June 18, 1899, 14.
90. Review of Chopin, *Awakening*, *Los Angeles Sunday Times*, June 25, 1899, 12.
91. See "The Awakening," Arabesque Aromas, accessed December 12, 2019, http://www.arabesquearomas.com/product/the-awakening-1-ml-sample-natural-botanic-perfume.
92. Stamelman, *Perfume*, 19.
93. Fleissner, *Women, Compulsion, Modernity*, 25.
94. Chopin, *Awakening*, 50, 51.
95. Chopin, *Awakening*, 67.
96. Chopin, *Awakening*, 51.
97. Chopin, *Awakening*, 68.
98. Chopin, *Awakening*, 55.
99. Chopin, "The Storm," in *Awakening*, 194.
100. Chopin, *Awakening*, 158.
101. Chopin, *Awakening*, 164.
102. Chopin, *Awakening*, 115.
103. Frost, *Problem with Pleasure*, 39.
104. W. James, *Principles of Psychology*, 488.
105. Chopin, *Awakening*, 96.

106. Birnbaum, "'Alien Hands,'" 304.
107. Fleissner, *Women, Compulsion, Modernity*, 244.
108. Cheng, "Ornamentalism," 404.
109. Dussauce, *Practical Guide*, 40.
110. Hartmann, "Perfume Land," 221.
111. Ellis, *Sexual Selection in Man*, 55.
112. Holmes, "Autocrat of the Breakfast Table," 460.
113. Heywood and Vortriede, "Some Experiments," 537, 539.
114. Chopin, "Lilacs," 135–36.
115. Benjamin, "On Some Motifs in Baudelaire," in *Illuminations*, 184.
116. Ellis, *Sexual Selection in Man*, 88.
117. Chopin, "Lilacs," 142–43.
118. Chopin, "Lilacs," 131.
119. I borrow the phrase "lilac time" from Nathaniel Mackey, who meditates on the obtuse temporality of odor memory in his jazz novel *From a Broken Bottle Traces of Perfume Still Emanate*.
120. Chopin, "Lilacs," 144.
121. Bentley, *Frantic Panoramas*, 143. My reading of "Lilacs" is indebted as well to Peter Coviello's wonderful account of queer intimacy and the untimely in nineteenth-century America; see Coviello, *Tomorrow's Parties*.
122. Sadtler, "Chemical Classification of Odoriferous Principles," 221.
123. Johnson, *Autobiography of an Ex-Colored Man*, 13.
124. Goldsby, *Spectacular Secret*, ch. 4.
125. Johnson, *Autobiography of an Ex-Colored Man*, 87.
126. "Senses—Smell," 494.
127. Simmel, "Sociology of the Senses," 118.
128. See Freeman, *Time Binds*, ch. 2.
129. Johnson, *Autobiography of an Ex-Colored Man*, 88.
130. A. L. Wood, *Lynching and Spectacle*, 11.
131. Tucker, *Lockstep and Dance*, 58.
132. Patterson, *Rituals of Blood*, 198.
133. Patterson, *Rituals of Blood*, 201.
134. Hartmann, "Perfume Land," 219.
135. Hartmann, "Perfume Land," 220.
136. Reckson, *Realist Ecstasy*, 160.
137. Johnson, *Autobiography of an Ex-Colored Man*, 26.
138. Johnson, *Autobiography of an Ex-Colored Man*, 33.
139. Higginson, *Army Life in a Black Regiment*, 111.
140. Davis, "How Do You Sniff?" 422; Turin, *Secret of Scent*, 14; Classen, Howes, and Synott, *Aroma*, 3.
141. Le Guérer, *Scent*, 144.
142. Higginson, "Procession of Flowers," 657.
143. Latour, "How to Talk about the Body?" 206.

INTERVAL 3. OLFACTORY GUSTO

1. Finck, *Food and Flavor*, 59–60.
2. Ellis, *Sexual Selection in Man*, 57–58.
3. Ellis, *Sexual Selection*, 72.
4. Gilman, "Yellow Wall-Paper," 648.
5. Gilman, "Yellow Wall-Paper," 654, 656.
6. Ellis, "Psychology of Yellow," 456.
7. Nordau, *Degeneration*, 503.
8. Freud, *Civilization and Its Discontents*, 54.
9. Harrington and Rosario, "Olfaction and the Primitive," 11.
10. See Seitler, *Atavistic Tendencies*.
11. Howells, *Imperative Duty*, 89.
12. Howells, *Imperative Duty*, 91.
13. Taves, *Fits, Trances, and Visions*, 3.
14. Fessenden, *Culture and Redemption*, 114.
15. See Tompkins, *Racial Indigestion*.
16. C. D. Warner, "Modern Fiction," 464.

CHAPTER 4. TASTE

1. Korsmeyer, *Making Sense of Taste*, 96.
2. Sprague, "What We Feel," 742.
3. J. Bernstein, *Five Senses of Man*, 295.
4. "Taste and Smell," 234.
5. Allen, *Physiological Aesthetics*, 76.
6. Bain, *Senses and the Intellect*, 105–6.
7. Finck, *Food and Flavor*, xviii.
8. Burke, *Philosophical Enquiry*, 130.
9. See Tompkins, *Racial Indigestion*.
10. R. Bernstein, *Racial Innocence*, 12.
11. Floyd and Forster, "Recipe in its Cultural Contexts," in *Recipe Reader*, 3.
12. Tompkins, "Consider the Recipe," 440.
13. See Cohen, *Social Lives of Poems*.
14. Jackson, *Dickinson's Misery*, 21. See also Socarides, *Dickinson Unbound*.
15. Finck, *Food and Flavor*, 121.
16. Brillat-Savarin, *Physiology of Taste*, 52.
17. Allen, *Physiological Aesthetics*, 67.
18. Allen, *Physiological Aesthetics*, 85.
19. "Good Cookery," 11.
20. "Impaired Taste," 245.
21. C. H. Piesse, *Olfactics and the Physical Senses*, 48.
22. Fleissner, "Henry James's Art of Eating," 51.
23. Darwin, *Descent of Man*, 12.
24. "Pleasures of the Palate," 6.

25. Blot, "Dinner," 173.
26. "Pleasures of the Palate," 6.
27. Shapiro, *Perfection Salad*, 68.
28. Montanari, *Food Is Culture*, 57.
29. Kellogg, *Science in the Kitchen*, 2.
30. Lane, *Mizora*, 45.
31. Gabaccia, *We Are What We Eat*, 127.
32. For a more contemporary iteration, on molecular gastronomy's devaluation of women's culinary knowledge, see Roosth, "Foams and Formalisms."
33. Haley, "Nation before Taste," 71.
34. Rhodes, "What Shall We Eat?" 671.
35. "Art of Cookery," 91.
36. Tompkins, *Racial Indigestion*, 17.
37. Gigante, *Taste*, 3.
38. Harrison, "Philosophy of Frying," 265.
39. Elias, *Food on the Page*, 33.
40. Witt, *Black Hunger*, 36.
41. Tipton-Martin, *Jemima Code*, 2.
42. Gayarré, "Louisiana Sugar Plantation," 620–21.
43. S. W. Mitchell, introduction, xiii.
44. Christian Women's Exchange, *Creole Cookery Book*, 5.
45. E. W. Smith, *Collected Works*, 129.
46. Finck, *Food and Flavor*, xiv.
47. Allen, *Physiological Aesthetics*, 69.
48. Allen, *Physiological Aesthetics*, 67, 71.
49. Allen, *Physiological Aesthetics*, 77.
50. Allen, *Physiological Aesthetics*, 77.
51. Mintz, *Sweetness and Power*.
52. Morton, *Poetics of Spice*, 173.
53. Weiss, "Horrors of San Domingo [1862]," 734.
54. Weiss, "Horrors of San Domingo [1863]," 303.
55. Gikandi, *Slavery and the Culture of Taste*, 109.
56. Jones, "Simians, Negroes, and the 'Missing Link,'" 194.
57. Dubois, *Avengers of the New World*, 2.
58. "Sugar-Refining," 7.
59. "Obligations of Sugar-Refiners," 78.
60. "Sweets," 2.
61. Thorpe, "Sugar and the Sugar Region of Louisiana," 761.
62. Woloson, *Refined Tastes*, 9.
63. Rhodes, "What Shall We Eat?" 671.
64. Bryan, *Kentucky Housewife*, 280–81.
65. Bryan, *Kentucky Housewife*, viii.
66. Tompkins, *Racial Indigestion*, 23.
67. Russell, *Domestic Cook Book*, 3.
68. Russell, *Domestic Cook Book*, 4.

69. Russell, *Domestic Cook Book*, 5.
70. Russell, *Domestic Cook Book*, 8.
71. Witt, *Black Hunger*, 109.
72. Fisher, *What Mrs. Fisher Knows*, 4.
73. Zafar, "Recipes for Respect," 141.
74. Fisher, *What Mrs. Fisher Knows*, 30.
75. Dickinson to Nellie Sweetser, L835 and L835a, in *Selected Letters*. Further references to Dickinson's letters are to this edition, edited by Thomas H. Johnson, and will be cited by letter number.
76. See Emilie Hardman and Emily Walhout, "Baking Emily Dickinson's Black Cake," Houghton Library Blog, Harvard University, December 11, 2015, https://blogs.harvard.edu/houghton/baking-emily-dickinsons-black-cake/.
77. Randolph, *Virginia Housewife*, 162.
78. Coghlan, "Tasting the Archive," 23.
79. Farmer, *Boston Cooking School Cook Book*, 426.
80. Dickinson, Fr598, in *Complete Poems*. Further references to Dickinson's poems are to this variorum edition and will be cited by editor and poem number.
81. Higginson, "Emily Dickinson's Letters," 443.
82. Lang, "American Sappho," in Buckingham, *Emily Dickinson's Reception*, 201.
83. Lang, "Literary Causierie," in Buckingham, *Emily Dickinson's Reception*, 108.
84. "Emily Dickinson's Poems," in Buckingham, *Emily Dickinson's Reception*, 48.
85. "Third of the Gray Sisters," in Buckingham, *Emily Dickinson's Reception*, 484.
86. Bates, "Books and Authors," in Buckingham, *Emily Dickinson's Reception*, 29.
87. Koopman, "Emily Dickinson," in Buckingham, *Emily Dickinson's Reception*, 509.
88. Wyman, "Emily Dickinson as Cook and Poetess," 14.
89. "Grim Slumber Songs," in Buckingham, *Emily Dickinson's Reception*, 85.
90. Certeau, Giard, and Mayol, *Practice of Everyday Life*, 216.
91. Osborne, "Dickinson's Lyric Materialism," 70.
92. Witt, *Black Hunger*, 11.
93. Cameron, "Dickinson's Fascicles," 155.
94. hooks, "Eating the Other: Desire and Resistance," in *Black Looks*, 39.
95. Dickinson, Fr95.
96. Dickinson, L265.
97. Dickinson, L280.
98. E. Andrews, "This Foreshadowed Food," 211.
99. Richards, "How News Must Feel When Traveling," 174.
100. Dickinson, Fr135.
101. Whitman, *Leaves of Grass* (1867).
102. Cheng, "Sushi, Otters, Mermaids," 73.
103. Higginson, "Open Portfolio," in Buckingham, *Emily Dickinson's Reception*, 8.
104. Higginson, preface to *Poems* by Emily Dickinson, iv.
105. Dickinson, L353.
106. Wardrop, "That Minute Domingo," 76.
107. Martha Dickinson Bianchi, introduction to *Single Hound*, by Emily Dickinson, viii.
108. Dickinson, L907.

109. Bianchi, *Emily Dickinson Face to Face*, 5.
110. Dickinson, L545.
111. Moten, *Black and Blur*, 145.
112. Dickinson, L444a.
113. Jenkins, "Child's Remembrance of Emily Dickinson," in Buckingham, *Emily Dickinson's Reception*, 216.
114. Dickinson, L851.
115. Bianchi, *Emily Dickinson Face to Face*, 13.
116. Dickinson, L840.
117. Fleissner, "Henry James's Art of Eating," 51.
118. Dickinson, Fr135.
119. Ahmed, *Cultural Politics of Emotion*, 85.
120. Ahmed, *Cultural Politics of Emotion*, 85.

INTERVAL 4. MOUTHFEEL

1. Levenstein, *Revolution at the Table*, 32.
2. "Sugar-Refining," 7.
3. See "Creative Time Presents Kara Walker," Creative Time, accessed December 13, 2019, http://creativetime.org/projects/karawalker/.
4. Barnard, *Empire of Ruin*, 173.
5. Burke, *Philosophical Enquiry*, 130.
6. Moten, *Black and Blur*, 29.
7. Korsmeyer, *Making Sense of Taste*, 4.
8. Moten, *Black and Blur*, 145.
9. Chen, *Animacies*, 185, 207.
10. Moten, *Black and Blur*, 145, 138.
11. W. W. Brown, "Narrative of the Life and Escape of William Wells Brown," in *Clotel*, 27.
12. Prince, *History of Mary Prince*, 42.
13. Weheliye, *Habeas Viscus*, 129.
14. *Oxford English Dictionary Online*, s.v., "lick (n.)," accessed September 21, 2014, https://www-oed-com.libproxy.albany.edu/view/Entry/108001?rskey=SDDDNr&result=1&isAdvanced=false#eid.
15. Prince, *History of Mary Prince*, 66.
16. Prince, *History of Mary Prince*, 67.
17. Prince, *History of Mary Prince*, 62.
18. See Gadsby, *Sucking Salt*, ch. 2.
19. Moten, *Black and Blur*, 139.
20. Walker and Sargent, "Interview."
21. Moten, *Black and Blur*, 145.
22. Luciano, *Arranging Grief*, Ch. 4.
23. Moten, *Black and Blur*, 142.
24. Panagia, *Political Life of Sensation*, 126.
25. Keller, *World I Live In*, 33.

CHAPTER 5. TOUCH

1. "Notes," 317.
2. "Second Laura Bridgman," 315.
3. Robertson, "Blind-Deaf-Mute Helen Keller," 309.
4. Le Conte, "Evidence of the Senses," 92.
5. "Senses—Touch," 180.
6. Jastrow, "Bridgman, Laura and Helen Keller," 144.
7. Hitz, "Helen Keller," 308.
8. Keller, *Midstream*, 256.
9. S. Smith, "Identity's Body," 267.
10. S. Stewart, *Poetry and the Fate of the Senses*, 178.
11. Butler, *Senses of the Subject*, 43.
12. Starobinski, "Style of Autobiography," 78.
13. Keller, *World I Live In*, xiii.
14. C. D. Warner, "Editor's Study," 962.
15. Couser, *Altered Egos*, 13.
16. D. T. Mitchell, "Body Solitaire," 313.
17. Nielsen, *Radical Lives of Helen Keller*, 11.
18. D. T. Mitchell, "Body Solitaire," 310.
19. Kleege, "Helen Keller and 'The Empire of the Normal,'" 322.
20. Fuss, *Sense of an Interior*, 118.
21. Merleau-Ponty, *Phenomenology of Perception*, 106.
22. Ahmed, *Queer Phenomenology*, 106.
23. Price and Shildrick, "Bodies Together," 69.
24. Mitchell and Snyder, *Biopolitics of Disability*, 43.
25. Schuller, *Biopolitics of Feeling*, 8.
26. See Spillers, "Mama's Baby, Papa's Maybe."
27. Schuller, *Biopolitics of Feeling*, 3.
28. Cheng, *Second Skin*, 11.
29. Stephens, *Skin Acts*, 2–3.
30. Folkenflik, "Self as Other," 234.
31. Keller, *Midstream*, 13.
32. Halliday, "Helen Keller, Henry James," 185.
33. Le Conte, "Evidence of the Senses," 94.
34. Hitz, "Helen Keller," 312.
35. Jastrow, "Eye-Mindedness and Ear-Mindedness," 600.
36. DeSantis, "Feeling of a Line," 256.
37. Carter, *Object Lessons*, 2, 7.
38. Parisi, *Archaeologies of Touch*, 98.
39. Titchener, *Experimental Psychology*, xx.
40. Weber, *E. H. Weber on the Tactile Senses*, 148.
41. Paterson, "Biopolitics of Sensation," 75.
42. Parisi, "Tactile Modernity," 203.
43. W. James, *Principles of Psychology*, 105.

44. W. James, *Principles of Psychology*, 107.
45. W. James, "Hidden Self," 365.
46. W. James, "Hidden Self," 369.
47. W. James, "Hidden Self," 368–69.
48. Gordon, *Dances with Darwin*, 14.
49. W. James, "Notes on Automatic Writing," 42.
50. W. James, "Notes on Automatic Writing," 40.
51. W. James, "Notes on Automatic Writing," 42.
52. W. James, *Psychology*, 176.
53. G. S. Hall, "Laura Bridgman," 161.
54. Jastrow, "Psychological Notes," 362.
55. Jastrow, "Psychological Notes," 357.
56. Keller, *Midstream*, 256.
57. "Little Helen Keller," 11.
58. Edwards, *Words Made Flesh*, 159.
59. Baynton, *Forbidden Signs*, 55.
60. Bell, *Memoir upon the Formation*, 3.
61. Lash, *Helen and Teacher*, 114.
62. Keller, *World I Live In*, 35.
63. W. James, "Laura Bridgman," 98.
64. Jastrow, "Helen Keller," 81.
65. William James to Helen Keller in appreciation of the book *The World I Live In*, December 9, 1908, Helen Keller Archival Collection, American Foundation for the Blind, Arlington, Virginia.
66. Keller, *World I Live In*, 25.
67. Keller, *Midstream*, 257.
68. Kudlick, "Outlook of The Problem," 200.
69. Siebers, *Disability Theory*, 54.
70. "Helen Keller's Autobiography," 3.
71. "Remarkable Biography," A7.
72. Kleege, *Blind Rage*, 34.
73. Walters, *Rhetorical Touch*, 27.
74. Kleege, "Helen Keller Who Still Matters," 104.
75. Keller, *Story of My Life*, 12.
76. Keller, *Story of My Life*, 26, 27.
77. Swan, "Touching Words," 58.
78. Fuss, *Sense of an Interior*, 112.
79. Keller, *Story of My Life*, 67.
80. See Fretwell, "1832–1933."
81. Keller, *Story of My Life*, 28.
82. Keller, *Story of My Life*, 28.
83. Keller, *Midstream*, 256.
84. Keller, *World I Live In*, 62.
85. Cressman, "Helen Keller and the Mind's Eyewitness," 111.
86. Keller, *World I Live In*, 39.

87. Ahmed, *Queer Phenomenology*, 107.
88. Macy, in Helen Keller, *Story of My Life*, 391.
89. Keller, *Midstream*, 34.
90. Keller, *World I Live In*, 13.
91. Keller, *Teacher*, 51.
92. Manning, *Politics of Touch*, 115.
93. Keller, "Helen Keller's Own Story," 7.
94. Bérubé, "Autobiography as Performative Utterance," 340.
95. Macy, in Helen Keller, *Story of My Life*, 285.
96. Werner, "Helen Keller and Anne Sullivan," 7.
97. Fuss, *Sense of an Interior*, 112.
98. Werner, "Helen Keller and Anne Sullivan," 5.
99. Keller, *Midstream*, 3.
100. Werner, "Helen Keller and Anne Sullivan," 22.
101. Keller, *World I Live In*, 16.
102. Kafer, *Feminist, Queer, Crip*, 83.
103. Review of *The Story of My Life*, 361.
104. Twain, *Mark Twain's Letters*, 731.
105. Jastrow, "Helen Keller," 71.
106. Macy, in Helen Keller, *Story of My Life*, 11.
107. Couser, *Recovering Bodies*, 227.
108. Schuller, *Biopolitics of Feeling*, 70, 77.
109. Du Bois, "Helen Keller," 164.
110. Keller, "From a Friend," 305.
111. S. Andrews, "Toward a Synaesthetics of *Souls*," 176.
112. Bentley, *Frantic Panoramas*, 283.
113. Schweik, "Disability Politics," 222. On the intersections of race and disability on questions of labor, see Todd Carmody, "Work Requirements."
114. Berenson, *Florentine Painters of the Renaissance*, 4.
115. Keller, *Story of My Life*, 19.
116. On Keller's autobiography and the "romance of reunion," see Montgomery, "Radicalizing Reunion."
117. Sullivan, in Helen Keller, *Story of My Life*, 170.
118. "Skin," 163.
119. "Skin," 164.
120. Bain, *Senses and the Intellect*, 174.
121. Münsterberg, "Psychology and Mysticism," 74.
122. H. C. Wood, "Study of Consciousness," 74.
123. Du Bois, *Souls of Black Folk*, 5.
124. Farooq, *Undisciplined*, 92.
125. S. M. Smith, *Photography on the Color Line*.
126. Du Bois, *Souls of Black Folk*, 1, 5.
127. Keller, *Story of My Life*, 51, 12.
128. Du Bois, *Souls of Black Folk*, 191.
129. Du Bois, *Souls of Black Folk*, 196.

130. Du Bois, *Souls of Black Folk*, 155.
131. Du Bois, *Souls of Black Folk*, 166.
132. Du Bois, *Souls of Black Folk*, 166.
133. Bentley, *Frantic Panoramas*, 285.
134. See Krentz, *Writing Deafness*.
135. Kuppers, *Disability Culture and Community Performance*, 92.
136. Bain, *Senses and the Intellect*, 172.
137. Dearborn, "Kinesthesia and the Intelligent Will," 204.
138. "Kinesthesia Queen of the Senses," MS 2.
139. Noland, *Agency and Embodiment*, 10.
140. Schwartz, "Torque," 140.
141. Keller, *Story of My Life*, 28.
142. Keller, *World I Live In*, 33.
143. R. Smith, "Kinesthesia and Touching Reality," 1.
144. Derrida, *Touching*, 47.
145. Derrida, *Touching*, 67.
146. Derrida, *Touching*, 199.
147. Derrida, "Law of Genre," 57.
148. Derrida, "Law of Genre," 58.

CODA

1. Bordogna, *William James at the Boundaries*, 47.
2. Kropotkin, "Recent Science," 729.
3. See Kuhn, *Structure of Scientific Revolutions*.
4. Reed, *From Soul to Mind*, 144.
5. See Evans, *Before Cultures*.
6. Du Bois, "Strivings of the Negro People," 194.
7. R. Park, *City*, 2.
8. A. Brown, *Black Skyscraper*, 23.
9. Luciano, "*How the Earth Feels*."
10. See in particular Taussig, *Mimesis and Alterity*; Seremetakis, *Senses Still*.
11. Howes, "Expanding Field of Sensory Studies."
12. Rancière, *Politics of Aesthetics*.
13. Marx, *Economic and Philosophic Manuscripts*, 87.
14. Mirzoeff, "Shadow and the Substance," 112.
15. See Lauren Berlant, "America, 'Fat,' the Fetus," in *Queen of America Goes to Washington City*.
16. See R. Bernstein, *Racial Innocence*.

BIBLIOGRAPHY

ARCHIVAL COLLECTIONS

Annenberg Rare Book and Manuscript Library, University of Pennsylvania, Philadelphia.
Keller, Helen. Archival Collection. American Foundation for the Blind, Arlington, Virginia.
Moses, William Stainton. Collection. College of Psychic Studies, London.

PUBLISHED SOURCES

Abbot, Austin. "The Eye and the Camera." *Harper's Monthly*, September 1869, 476–82.
Abrams, M. H., and Geoffrey Galt Harpham. *A Glossary of Literary Terms*. Stamford, CT: Cengage, 2015.
Ahmad, Dohra. *Landscapes of Hope: Anti-Colonialism in Utopian America*. Oxford: Oxford University Press, 2009.
Ahmed, Sara. *The Cultural Politics of Emotion*. Edinburgh: Edinburgh University Press, 2004.
Ahmed, Sara. "A Phenomenology of Whiteness." *Feminist Theory* 8, no. 2 (2007): 149–68.
Ahmed, Sara. *Queer Phenomenology: Orientations, Objects, Others*. Durham, NC: Duke University Press, 2006.
Alaimo, Stacy. *Bodily Natures: Science, Environment, and the Material Self*. Bloomington: Indiana University Press, 2010.
Alexander, Zeynep Çelik. *Kinesthetic Knowing: Aesthetics, Epistemology, Modern Design*. Chicago: University of Chicago Press, 2017.

Allen, Grant. *The Colour-Sense: Its Origin and Development*. London: Trübner, 1879.
Allen, Grant. *Physiological Aesthetics*. London: King, 1877.
Altschuler, Sari. *The Medical Imagination: Literature and Health in the Early United States*. Philadelphia: University of Pennsylvania Press, 2018.
"Ambrosia—A Nose Offering." *Harper's New Monthly Magazine*, June 1856, 58–62.
Andrews, Elizabeth. "'This Foreshadowed Food': Representations of Food and Hunger in Emily Dickinson's American Gothic." In *Culinary Aesthetics and Practices in Nineteenth-Century American Culture*, edited by Marie Drew and Monika Ebert, 205–19. New York: Palgrave, 2009.
Andrews, Steve. "Toward a Synaesthetics of *Souls*: W. E. B. Du Bois and the Teleology of Race." In *Re-cognizing W. E. B. Du Bois in the Twenty-First Century: Essays on W. E. B. Du Bois*, edited by Mary Keller and Chester Fontenot Jr., 142–85. Macon, GA: Mercer University Press, 2007.
"The Art of Cookery." *Godey's Lady's Book and Magazine*, January 1876, 91–92.
Askinson, George. *Perfumes and Their Preparation*. New York: Henley, 1892.
Attali, Jacques. *Noise: The Political Economy of Music*. Translated by Brian Massumi. Minneapolis: University of Minnesota Press, 1985.
Babbitt, Irving. *The New Laokoon: An Essay on the Confusion of the Arts*. Boston: Houghton, 1910.
Bain, Alexander. *The Emotions and the Will*. 2nd ed. London: Longmans, 1865.
Bain, Alexander. *The Senses and the Intellect*. 1865. 4th ed. New York: Appleton, 1902.
Barnard, John Levi. *Empire of Ruin: Black Classicism and American Imperial Culture*. Oxford: Oxford University Press, 2017.
Baudelaire, Charles. *Flowers of Evil and Other Works: A Dual-Language Book*. Edited and translated by Wallace Fowlie. New York: Dover, 1963.
Baynton, Douglas. *Forbidden Signs: American Culture and the Campaign against Sign Language*. Chicago: University of Chicago Press, 1996.
Beard, George Miller. *American Nervousness*. New York: Putnam, 1881.
Beecher, Catharine. *A Treatise on Domestic Economy*. New York: Harper, 1841.
Beer, Gillian. "'Authentic Tidings of Invisible Things': Vision and the Invisible in the Later Nineteenth Century." In *Vision in Context: Historical and Contemporary Perspectives on Sight*, edited by Teresa Brennan and Martin Jay, 83–100. New York: Routledge, 1996.
Bell, Alexander Graham. "Discovery and Invention." *National Geographic*, June 1914, 649–55.
Bell, Alexander Graham. *Memoir upon the Formation of a Deaf Variety of the Human Race*. New Haven, CT: National Academy of Sciences, 1884.
Bellamy, Edward. *Equality*. Toronto: Morgan, 1897.
Bellamy, Edward. *Looking Backward, 2000–1887*. Edited by Alex MacDonald. 1888. Peterborough, ON: Broadview, 2003.
Bellamy, Edward. *The Religion of Solidarity*. Yellow Springs, OH: Antioch, 1940.
Benjamin, Walter. *Illuminations: Essays and Reflections*. Edited by Hannah Arendt. Boston: Houghton Mifflin Harcourt, 2019.
Bennett, Bridget. *Transatlantic Spiritualism and Nineteenth-Century American Literature*. New York: Palgrave, 2007.

Bentley, Nancy. *Frantic Panoramas: American Literature and Mass Culture, 1870–1920*. Philadelphia: University of Pennsylvania Press, 2009.
Berenson, Bernard. *The Florentine Painters of the Renaissance*. New York: Putnam, 1894.
Berlant, Lauren. *The Anatomy of National Fantasy: Hawthorne, Utopia, and Everyday Life*. Chicago: University of Chicago Press, 1991.
Berlant, Lauren. *Cruel Optimism*. Durham, NC: Duke University Press, 2012.
Berlant, Lauren. *The Female Complaint: The Unfinished Business of Sentimentality in American Culture*. Durham, NC: Duke University Press, 2008.
Berlant, Lauren. *The Queen of America Goes to Washington City: Essays on Sex and Citizenship*. Durham, NC: Duke University Press, 1997.
Bernstein, Julius. *The Five Senses of Man*. New York: Appleton, 1876.
Bernstein, Robin. *Racial Innocence: Performing American Childhood from Slavery to Civil Rights*. New York: New York University Press, 2011.
Bérubé, Michael. "Autobiography as Performative Utterance." *American Quarterly* 52, no. 2 (2000): 343–93.
Bianchi, Martha Dickinson. *Emily Dickinson Face to Face: Unpublished Letters, with Notes and Reminiscences*. New York: Houghton, 1932.
Binet, Alfred. "The Problem of Color Audition." *Popular Science Monthly*, October 1893, 813–23.
Birnbaum, Michelle. "'Alien Hands': Kate Chopin and the Colonization of Race." *American Literature* 66, no. 2 (June 1994): 301–23.
Blot, Pierre. "A Dinner." *Galaxy* 5, no. 2 (February 1868): 173.
Bordogna, Francesca. *William James at the Boundaries: Philosophy, Science, and the Geography of Knowledge*. Chicago: University of Chicago Press, 2008.
Bradstreet, Christina. "*A Trip to Japan in Sixteen Minutes*: Sadakichi Hartmann's Perfume Concert and the Aesthetics of Scent." In *Art, History, and the Senses, 1830 to the Present*, edited by Patrizia Di Bello and Gabriel Koureas, 51–66. London: Ashgate, 2010.
Bramen, Carrie Tirado. *The Uses of Variety: Modern Americanism and the Quest for National Distinctiveness*. Cambridge, MA: Harvard University Press, 2000.
Brennan, Teresa. *The Transmission of Affect*. Ithaca, NY: Cornell University Press, 2004.
Brillat-Savarin, Jean Anthèlme. *The Physiology of Taste*. Translated by Anne Drayton. 1825. New York: Penguin, 1994.
Brooks, Daphne. *Bodies in Dissent: Spectacular Performances of Race and Freedom, 1850–1910*. Durham, NC: Duke University Press, 2006.
Brower, Edith. "Is the Musical Idea Masculine?" *Atlantic Monthly*, March 1894, 332–39.
Brown, Adrienne. *The Black Skyscraper: Architecture and the Perception of Race*. Baltimore, MD: Johns Hopkins University Press, 2017.
Brown, Bill. *A Sense of Things: The Object Matter of American Literature*. Chicago: University of Chicago Press, 2003.
Brown, William Wells. *Clotel; or, The President's Daughter*. London: Partridge and Oakey, 1853.
Bryan, Lettice. *The Kentucky Housewife*. Cincinnati, OH: Shepard and Stearns, 1839.
Buckingham, Willis, ed. *Emily Dickinson's Reception in the 1890s: A Documentary History*. Pittsburgh, PA: University of Pittsburgh Press, 1989.

Buck-Morss, Susan. *Dreamworld and Catastrophe: The Passing of Mass Utopia in East and West*. Cambridge, MA: MIT Press, 2002.

Burke, Edmund. *A Philosophical Enquiry into the Origin of Our Ideas of the Sublime and the Beautiful*. New York: Cosimo, 2009.

Butler, Judith. *Senses of the Subject*. New York: Fordham University Press, 2015.

Cahan, David. *Helmholtz: A Life in Science*. Chicago: University of Chicago Press, 2018.

Cameron, Sharon. "Dickinson's Fascicles." In *The Emily Dickinson Handbook*, edited by Gudrun Grabher, Roland Hagenbüchle, and Cristanne Miller, 138–60. Amherst: University of Massachusetts Press, 1998.

Canto, Geoffrey, and Sally Shuttleworth, eds. *Science Serialized: Representations of the Sciences in Nineteenth-Century Periodicals*. Cambridge, MA: MIT Press, 2004.

"Can We Believe Our Eyes?" *Manufacturer and Builder*, March 1873, 66.

Carlisle, Janice. *Common Scents: Comparative Encounters in High-Victorian Fiction*. Oxford: Oxford University Press, 2004.

Carmody, Todd. "Work Requirements: Race, Disability, and Reform in Progressive America." Durham, NC: Duke University Press, forthcoming.

Carter, Sarah Anne. *Object Lessons: How Nineteenth-Century Americans Learned to Make Sense of the World*. Oxford: Oxford University Press, 2018.

Carus, Paul. "Fechner's View of Life after Death." *Monist* 16, no. 1 (1906): 84–95.

"A Case for Sympathy." *Harper's Weekly*, September 1, 1900, 812.

Cecire, Natalia. *Experimental: American Literature and the Aesthetics of Knowledge*. Baltimore, MD: Johns Hopkins University Press, 2020.

Certeau, Michel de, Luce Giard, and Pierre Mayol. *The Practice of Everyday Life*. Vol. 2, *Living and Cooking*. Translated by Timothy Tomasik. Minneapolis: University of Minnesota Press, 1998.

Cervetti, Nancy. *S. Weir Mitchell, 1829–1914: Philadelphia's Literary Physician*. University Park: Pennsylvania State University Press, 2012.

"Chemical Perfumes." *New York Times*, October 28, 1906, 8.

Chen, Mel Y. *Animacies: Biopolitics, Racial Mattering, and Queer Affect*. Durham, NC: Duke University Press, 2012.

Cheng, Anne Anlin. "Ornamentalism: A Feminist Theory for the Yellow Woman." *Critical Inquiry* 44 (2018): 415–46.

Cheng, Anne Anlin. *Second Skin: Josephine Baker and the Modern Surface*. Oxford: Oxford University Press, 2010.

Cheng, Anne Anlin. "Sushi, Otters, Mermaids: Race at the Intersection of Food and Animal; or, David Wong Louie's Sushi Principle." *Resilience: A Journal of Environmental Humanities* 2, no. 1 (2014): 66–95.

Child, Lydia Maria. *The Frugal Housewife*. Boston: Marsh and Capen, 1829.

Chopin, Kate. *The Awakening and Other Writings*. Edited by Suzanne Disheroon, Barbara Ewell, Pamela Menke, and Susie Scifres. New York: Broadview, 2011.

Chopin, Kate. "Lilacs." 1896. In *A Vocation and a Voice*, edited by Emily Toth, 131–46. New York: Penguin, 1991.

Christian Women's Exchange, ed. *The Creole Cookery Book*. New Orleans: Thomason, 1885.

Classen, Constance, David Howes, and Anthony Synnott, eds. *Aroma: The Cultural History of Smell*. New York: Routledge, 1994.
Clifford, Frank Sanford. *A Romance of Perfume Lands; or, The Search for Capt. Jacob Cole, with Interesting Facts about Perfumes and Articles Used in the Toilet*. Boston: Clifford, 1875.
Cobb, Jasmine Nichole. *Picture Freedom: Remaking Black Visuality in the Early Nineteenth Century*. New York: New York University Press, 2015.
Coghlan, J. Michelle. *Sensational Internationalism: The Paris Commune and the Remapping of American Memory in the Long Nineteenth Century*. Edinburgh: Edinburgh University Press, 2016.
Coghlan, J. Michelle. "Tasting the Archive: Nineteenth-Century American Literature and the Sensory Turn." *Resilience: A Journal of the Environmental Humanities* 5, no. 3 (Fall 2018): 10–30.
Cohen, Michael. *The Social Lives of Poems in Nineteenth-Century America*. Philadelphia: University of Pennsylvania Press, 2015.
"Comparisons Most Odorous." *New York Times*, October 6, 1902, 8.
"Concerning Things Spiritual." *Nation*, January 17, 1867, 53.
Connolly, William. *Neuropolitics: Thinking, Culture, Speed*. Minneapolis: University of Minnesota Press, 2002.
Connolly, William. *A World of Becoming*. Durham, NC: Duke University Press, 2011.
Cooley, Arnold. *The Toilet and Cosmetic Arts in Ancient and Modern Times*. London: Hardwicke, 1866.
Cooper, David E., ed. *A Companion to Aesthetics*. Malden, MA: Blackwell, 2009.
Corbin, Alain. *The Foul and the Fragrant: Odor and the French Social Imagination*. Cambridge, MA: Harvard University Press, 1986.
Coriale, Danielle. "Reading through Deafness: Francis Galton and the Strange Science of Psychophysics." In *Strange Science: Investigating the Limits of Knowledge in the Victorian Age*, edited by Pauline Karpenko and Rae Claggett, 105–24. Ann Arbor: University of Michigan Press, 2016.
Coriat, Isador H. "An Unusual Type of Synesthesia." *Journal of Abnormal Psychology* 8, no. 2 (June–July 1913): 109–12.
Courtemanche, Eleanor. "Satire and the 'Inevitability Effect': The Structure of Utopian Fiction from *Looking Backward* to *Portlandia*." *Modern Language Quarterly* 76, no. 2 (2015): 225–46.
Couser, G. Thomas. *Altered Egos: Authority in American Autobiography*. Oxford: Oxford University Press, 1989.
Couser, G. Thomas. *Recovering Bodies: Illness, Disability, and Life Writing*. Madison: University of Wisconsin Press, 1997.
Coviello, Peter. *Tomorrow's Parties: Sex and the Untimely in Nineteenth-Century America*. New York: New York University Press, 2013.
Cranch, C. P. "A Plea for the Sense of Smell." *Putnam's Monthly*, March 1869, 315–18.
Crary, Jonathan. *Suspensions of Perception: Attention, Spectacles, and Modern Culture*. Cambridge, MA: MIT Press, 2001.
Crary, Jonathan. *Techniques of the Observer: On Vision and Modernity in the Nineteenth Century*. Cambridge, MA: MIT Press, 1999.

Cressman, Jodi. "Helen Keller and the Mind's Eyewitness." *Western Humanities Review* 44, no. 2 (2000): 108–23.

Cristiani, Richard. *Perfumery and Kindred Arts: A Comprehensive Treatise on Perfumery*. Philadelphia: Baird, 1877.

Cruz, Jon. *Culture on the Margins: The Black Spiritual and the Rise of American Cultural Interpretation*. Princeton, NJ: Princeton University Press, 1999.

Cvetkovich, Ann. *Depression: A Public Feeling*. Durham, NC: Duke University Press, 2012.

Cytowic, Richard. *The Man Who Tasted Shapes*. Cambridge, MA: MIT Press, 2008.

Cytowic, Richard. *Synesthesia: A Union of the Senses*. New York: Springer, 2012.

Dames, Nicholas. *The Physiology of the Novel: Reading, Neural Science, and the Form of the Novel*. Oxford: Oxford University Press, 2007.

Dann, Kevin. *False Colors Brightly Seen: Synaesthesia and the Search for Transcendental Knowledge*. New Haven, CT: Yale University Press, 1998.

Darwin, Charles. *The Descent of Man, and Selection in Relation to Sex*. 1871. New York: Appleton, 1876.

Davenport, Charles. "The Effects of Race Intermingling." *Proceedings of the American Philosophical Society* 56, no. 4 (1917): 364–68.

Davis, Hugh. "'How Do You Sniff?' Havelock Ellis and Olfactory Representation in 'Nausicaa.'" *James Joyce Quarterly* 41, no. 3 (2004): 421–40.

Dearborn, George Van Ness. "Kinesthesia and the Intelligent Will." *American Journal of Psychology* 24, no. 2 (1913): 204–55.

DeLue, Rachael Ziady. "Diagnosing Pictures: Sadakichi Hartmann and the Science of Seeing, circa 1900." *American Art* 21, no. 2 (2007): 42–69.

Derrida, Jacques. "The Law of Genre." *Critical Inquiry* 7, no. 1 (1980): 55–81.

Derrida, Jacques. *On Touching—Jean-Luc Nancy*. Stanford, CA: Stanford University Press, 2005.

DeSantis, Alicia. "The Feeling of a Line: Nineteenth-Century American Literature and the Psychology of Imagination." PhD diss., Columbia University, 2013.

Desmarais, Jane. "Perfume Clouds: Olfaction, Memory, and Desire in Arthur Symons's *London Nights* (1895)." In *Economies of Desire at the Victorian Fin-de-Siècle*, edited by Jane Ford, Kim Edwards Keates, and Patricia Pulham, 62–69. New York: Routledge, 2015.

Dickinson, Emily. *The Complete Poems of Emily Dickinson*. Variorum ed. Edited by R. W. Franklin. Cambridge, MA: Harvard University Press, 1998.

Dickinson, Emily. *Emily Dickinson: Selected Letters*. Edited by Thomas H. Johnson. Cambridge, MA: Harvard University Press, 1958.

Dickinson, Emily. *Poems*. Boston: Robert, 1892.

Dickinson, Emily. *The Single Hound: Poems of a Lifetime*. Boston: Little, Brown, 1914.

Dillon, Edward. "A Neglected Sense." *Littell's Living Age*, May 26, 1894, 502–10.

Dillon, Elizabeth Maddock. "Atlantic Aesthesis: Books and Sensus Communis in the New World." *Early American Literature* 51, no. 2 (2016): 367–95.

"Do the Various Races of Man Constitute a Single Species?" *U.S. Democratic Review*, August 1842, 113–39.

Downey, June. "Literary Synesthesia." *Journal of Philosophy, Psychology and Scientific Methods* 9, no. 18 (August 29, 1912): 490–98.
Doyle, Edward Rice. "Will Color Music Become an Art?" *Bookman: A Review of Books and Life*, June 1915, 399–401.
Draper, John William. "Popular Exposition of Some Scientific Experiments." *Harper's Monthly*, May 1877, 888–906.
Dubois, Laurent. *Avengers of the New World: The Story of the Haitian Revolution*. Cambridge, MA: Harvard University Press, 2005.
Du Bois, W. E. B. "Helen Keller." In *Writings by W. E. B. Du Bois in Non-Periodical Literature Edited by Others*, edited by Herbert Aptheker, 164. New York: Knaus, 1982.
Du Bois, W. E. B. *The Souls of Black Folk*. Edited by Brent Hayes Edwards. 1903. New York: Oxford University Press, 2007.
Du Bois, W. E. B. "Strivings of the Negro People." *Atlantic Monthly*, August 1897, 194–98.
Dugan, Holly. *The Ephemeral History of Perfume*. Baltimore, MD: Johns Hopkins University Press, 2011.
Duncan, Robert Kennedy. *The Chemistry of Commerce: A Single Interpretation of Some New Chemistry in Its Relation to Modern Industry*. New York: Harper, 1907.
Dussauce, Hyppolite. *A Practical Guide for the Perfumer*. Philadelphia: Baird, 1868.
Dwight, John Sullivan. "The Intellectual Influence of Music." *Atlantic Monthly*, November 1870, 614–25.
Dwight, John Sullivan. "Music as a Means of Culture." *Atlantic Monthly*, September 1870, 321–31.
Dyer, Richard. *White*. New York: Routledge, 1997.
Ebbinghaus, Hermann. *Memory: A Contribution to Experimental Psychology*. Translated by Henry A. Ruger and Clara E. Bussenius. 1885. New York: Columbia University Teachers College, 1913.
Edwards, R. A. R. *Words Made Flesh: Nineteenth-Century Deaf Education and the Growth of Deaf Culture*. New York: New York University Press, 2012.
Eidsheim, Nina Sun. *The Race of Sound: Listening, Timbre, and Vocality in African American Music*. Durham, NC: Duke University Press, 2019.
Eidsheim, Nina Sun. *Sensing Sound: Singing and Listening as Vibrational Practice*. Durham, NC: Duke University Press, 2015.
Elias, Megan. *Food on the Page: Cookbooks and American Culture*. Philadelphia: University of Pennsylvania Press, 2017.
Ellis, Havelock. "The Psychology of Yellow." *Popular Science Monthly*, May 1906, 456–63.
Ellis, Havelock. *Sexual Selection in Man: Touch, Smell, Hearing, Vision*. Philadelphia: Davis, 1905.
Ellis, Havelock, and John Addington Symonds. *Sexual Inversion*. 1897. Philadelphia: Davis, 1901.
Ellman, Richard. *Oscar Wilde*. New York: Vintage, 1987.
Emerson, Ralph Waldo. *Nature*. Boston: Munroe, 1836.
English, Daylanne. *Unnatural Selections: Eugenics in American Modernism and the Harlem Renaissance*. Chapel Hill: University of North Carolina Press, 2004.

Evans, Brad. *Before Cultures: The Ethnographic Imagination in American Literature, 1865–1920*. Chicago: University of Chicago Press, 2005.
Evans, Brad. "Howellsian Chic: The Local Color of Cosmopolitanism." ELH 71, no. 3 (2004): 775–812.
Evans, Brad. "*Vogue* and Ephemera: The Little Magazines of the 1890s." *Modernist Journals Project*, n.d. https://modjourn.org/essay/vogue-and-ephemera-the-little-magazines-of-the-1890s/.
Fabi, M. Giulia. *Passing and the Rise of the African American Novel*. Urbana: University of Illinois Press, 2001.
Farmer, Fannie. *The Boston Cooking School Cook Book*. 1896. New York: Dover, 1997.
Farooq, Nihad. *Undisciplined: Science, Ethnography, and Personhood in the Americas, 1830–1940*. New York: New York University Press, 2016.
"Fashionable Odors." *Manufacturer and Builder*, August 1871, 182.
Fechner, Gustav. *Elements of Psychophysics*. Edited by Davis Howes and Edward Boring. Translated by Helmut Adler. 1860. New York: Holt, 1966.
Fechner, Gustav. *The Little Book of Life after Death*. Translated by Mary C. Wadsworth. Boston: Little, Brown, 1904.
Fechner, Gustav. *Nanna; oder, Über das Seelenleben der Pflanzen*. Leipzig: Voss, 1848.
Fechner, Gustav. *On Life after Death*. Translated by Hugo Wernekke. London: Open Court, 1882.
Fechner, Gustav. *Vorschule der Aesthetik*. Leipzig: Breitkopf, 1876.
Fechner, Gustav. *Zend-Avesta; oder, Über die Dinge des Himmels und des Jenseits*. Leipzig: Voss, 1851.
Fessenden, Tracy. *Culture and Redemption: Religion, the Secular, and American Literature*. Princeton, NJ: Princeton University Press, 2007.
Finck, Henry T. "The Aesthetic Value of the Sense of Smell." *Atlantic Monthly*, December 1880, 793–99.
Finck, Henry T. *Food and Flavor: A Gastronomic Guide to Health and Good Living*. New York: Century, 1913.
Finseth, Ian. *The Civil War Dead and American Modernity*. Oxford: Oxford University Press, 2018.
Fisher, Abby. *What Mrs. Fisher Knows about Old Southern Cooking*. 1881. Bedford, MA: Applewood, 1995.
Fiske, John. "The Unseen World." *Atlantic Monthly*, March 1876, 266–78.
Fleetwood, Nicole. *Troubling Vision: Performance, Visuality, and Blackness*. Chicago: University of Chicago Press, 2011.
Fleissner, Jennifer. "Henry James's Art of Eating." ELH 75, no. 1 (2008): 27–62.
Fleissner, Jennifer. *Women, Compulsion, Modernity: The Moment of American Naturalism*. Chicago: University of Chicago Press, 2004.
"Flower Odors." *Continental Monthly*, October 1864, 469–72.
Floyd, Janet, and Laurel Forster, eds. *The Recipe Reader: Narratives, Contexts*. New York: Routledge, 2003.
Folkenflik, Robert. "The Self as Other." In *The Culture of Autobiography*, edited by Robert Folkenflik, 215–34. Stanford: Stanford University Press, 1993.

Freeman, Elizabeth. *Beside You in Time: Sense Methods and Queer Sociability in the American Nineteenth Century*. Durham, NC: Duke University Press, 2019.

Freeman, Elizabeth. *Time Binds: Queer Temporalities, Queer Histories*. Durham, NC: Duke University Press, 2010.

Fretwell, Erica. "1832–1933: American Literature's Other Scripts." In *Timelines of American Literature*, edited by Cody Marrs and Christopher Hager, 21–36. Baltimore, MD: Johns Hopkins University Press, 2019.

Freud, Sigmund. *Civilization and Its Discontents*. New York: Norton, 1989.

Friedner, Michele, and Stefan Helmreich. "Sound Studies Meets Deaf Studies." *Senses and Society* 7, no. 2 (2012): 72–86.

Frost, Laura. *The Problem with Pleasure: Modernism and Its Discontents*. New York: Columbia University Press, 2013.

Funchion, John. "Critical Oversights: The Aesthetics and Politics of Reading." *Henry James Review* 34, no. 3 (2013): 279–84.

Fuss, Diana. *The Sense of an Interior: Four Writers and the Rooms that Shaped Them*. New York: Routledge, 2004.

Gabaccia, Donna. *We Are What We Eat: Ethnic Food and the Making of Americans*. Cambridge, MA: Harvard University Press, 1998.

Gadsby, Meredith. *Sucking Salt: Caribbean Women Writers, Migration, and Survival*. Columbia: University of Missouri Press, 2006.

Galton, Francis. *Inquiries into Human Faculty and Its Development*. London: Macmillan, 1883.

Galton, Francis. *Life, Letters and Labours of Francis Galton*. Vol. 3. Edited by Karl Pearson. Cambridge: Cambridge University Press, 1930.

Gaskill, Nicholas. "The Articulate Eye: Color-Music, the Color Sense, and the Language of Abstraction." *Configurations* 25, no. 4 (2017): 475–505.

Gaskill, Nicholas. *Chromographia: American Literature and the Modernization of Color*. Minneapolis: University of Minnesota Press, 2018.

Gayarré, Charles. "A Louisiana Sugar Plantation of the Old Regime." *Harper's Monthly*, March 1887, 606–22.

Gigante, Denise. *Taste: A Literary History*. New Haven, CT: Yale University Press, 2005.

Gikandi, Simon. *Slavery and the Culture of Taste*. Princeton, NJ: Princeton University Press, 2011.

Gilman, Charlotte Perkins. "The Yellow Wall-Paper." *New England Magazine*, January 1892, 647–56.

Gilman, Charlotte Perkins. *The Yellow Wall-Paper, and Other Stories*. Edited by Robert Shulman. Oxford: Oxford University Press, 2009.

Girdner, John H. "The Plague of City Noises." *North American Review* 163, no. 478 (September 1896): 296–303.

Goldsby, Jacqueline. *A Spectacular Secret: Lynching in American Life and Literature*. Chicago: University of Chicago Press, 2006.

Goldstein, Amanda Jo. *Sweet Science: Romantic Materialism and the New Logics of Life*. Chicago: University of Chicago Press, 2017.

Goler, Robert. "Loss and the Persistence of Memory: 'The Case of George Dedlow' and Disabled Civil War Veterans." *Literature and Medicine* 23, no. 1 (2004): 160–83.
"Good Cookery a Flower of Evolution." *New York Times*, December 14, 1884, 11.
Gordon, Avery. *Ghostly Matters: Haunting and the Sociological Imagination.* Minneapolis: University of Minnesota Press, 1997.
Gordon, Rae Beth. *Dances with Darwin, 1875–1910: Vernacular Modernity in France.* Burlington, VT: Ashgate, 2009.
Gottschalk, Louis. "Notes of a Pianist." *Atlantic Monthly*, February 1865, 177–82.
Greeson, Jennifer Rae. *Our South: Geographic Fantasy and the Rise of National Literature.* Cambridge, MA: Harvard University Press, 2010.
Gregg, Melissa, and Gregory J. Seigworth, eds. *The Affect Theory Reader.* Durham, NC: Duke University Press, 2010.
Grimstad, Paul. *Experience and Experimental Writing: Literary Pragmatism from Emerson to the Jameses.* Oxford: Oxford University Press, 2013.
Gryzanowski, Ernst. "Richard Wagner's Theories of Music." *North American Review* 124, no. 254 (January 1877): 53–81.
Gurney, Edmund. *The Power of Sound.* London: Smith, Elder, 1880.
Habegger, Alfred. *Henry James and the "Woman Business."* Cambridge: Cambridge University Press, 1989.
Haley, Andrew. "The Nation before Taste: The Challenges of American Culinary History." *Public Historian* 34, no. 2 (May 2012): 53–78.
Hall, G. Stanley. "Laura Bridgman." *Mind* 4, no. 14 (1879): 149–72.
Hall, G. Stanley. "The Negro in Africa and America." *Pedagogical Seminary* 12 (March 1905): 350–68.
Hall, Stuart. "Old and New Identities, Old and New Ethnicities." In *Culture, Globalization, and the World System: Contemporary Conditions for the Representation of Identity*, edited by Anthony King, 41–68. Minneapolis: University of Minnesota Press, 1997.
Halliday, Sam. "Helen Keller, Henry James, and the Social Relations of Perception." *Criticism* 48, no. 2 (2006): 175–201.
Hamlin, Kimberly. *From Eve to Evolution: Darwin, Science, and Women's Rights in Gilded Age America.* Chicago: University of Chicago Press, 2014.
Hammond, William. "The Physics and Physiology of Spiritualism." *North American Review* 110, no. 227 (1870): 233–60.
Hanslick, Eduard. *The Beautiful in Music.* Translated by Gustav Cohen. 1854. London: Novello, 1891.
Harney, Stefano, and Fred Moten. *The Undercommons: Fugitive Planning and Black Study.* New York: Minor Compositions, 2013.
Harrington, Anne, and Vernon Rosario. "Olfaction and the Primitive: Nineteenth-Century Medical Thinking on Olfaction." In *Science of Olfaction*, edited by Michael Serby and Karen Chobor, 3–12. New York: Springer, 1992.
Harrison, Randolph. "The Philosophy of Frying." *Southern Planter and Farmer*, April 1876, 264.
Hartman, Saidiya. *Scenes of Subjection: Terror, Slavery, and Self-Making in Nineteenth-Century America.* Oxford: Oxford University Press, 1997.
Hartmann, Sadakichi. "In Perfume Land." *Forum*, July 1913, 217–28.

Hawkins, Stephanie. "William James, Gustav Fechner, and Early Psychophysics." *Frontiers in Physiology* 2, no. 68 (2011): 1–10.
Hedge, Frederic. "Ghost Seeing." *North American Review* 133, no. 298 (September 1881): 286–302.
Heidelberger, Michael. *Nature from Within: Gustav Theodor Fechner and His Psychophysical Worldview*. Translated by Cynthia Klohr. Pittsburgh, PA: University of Pittsburgh Press, 2004.
"Helen Keller's Autobiography." *New York Times*, February 14, 1903, 3.
Heller-Roazen, Daniel. *The Inner Touch: Archaeology of a Sensation*. Cambridge, MA: MIT Press, 2007.
Helmholtz, Hermann von. *On the Sensations of Tone: As a Physiological Basis for the Theory of Music*. 3rd ed. Translated by Alexander Ellis. 1863. London: Longmans, 1895.
Helmholtz, Hermann von. *Science and Culture: Popular and Philosophical Essays*. Edited by David Cahan. Chicago: University of Chicago Press, 1995.
Helmholtz, Hermann von. *Treatise on Physiological Optics*. Edited by James P. C. Southall. 1867. Mineola, NY: Dover, 1962.
Hetrick, Jay. "Aisthesis in Radical Empiricism: Gustav Fechner's Psychophysics and Experimental Aesthetics." *Proceedings of the European Society for Aesthetics* 3 (2011): 139–53.
Heywood, Alice, and Helen Vortriede. "Some Experiments on the Associative Power of Smells." *American Journal of Psychology* 16, no. 4 (October 1905): 537–41.
Higginson, Thomas Wentworth. "April Days." *Atlantic Monthly*, April 1861, 385–94.
Higginson, Thomas Wentworth. *Army Life in a Black Regiment and Other Writings*. Edited by R. D. Madison. New York: Penguin, 1997.
Higginson, Thomas Wentworth. "Emily Dickinson's Letters." *Atlantic Monthly*, October 1891, 441–56.
Higginson, Thomas Wentworth. "The Maroons of Surinam." *Atlantic Monthly*, May 1860, 549–57.
Higginson, Thomas Wentworth. "The Procession of the Flowers." *Atlantic Monthly*, December 1862, 649–57.
Highmore, Ben. *Cultural Feelings: Mood, Mediation, and Cultural Politics*. New York: Routledge, 2017.
Hitz, John. "Helen Keller." *American Anthropologist* 8, no. 2 (April–June 1906): 308–24.
Hoffer, Peter Charles. *Sensory Worlds in Early America*. Baltimore: Johns Hopkins University Press, 2005.
Holmes, Oliver Wendell. "The Autocrat of the Breakfast Table." *Atlantic Monthly*, February 1858, 467–69.
Holmes, Oliver Wendell. "Doings of the Sunbeam." *Atlantic Monthly*, July 1863, 1–16.
hooks, bell. *Black Looks: Race and Representation*. Boston: South End, 1992.
Hooper, Lucy. "The Perfumes of France." *Ladies' Home Journal*, November 1892, 4.
Hopkins, Pauline. "Famous Women of the Negro Race—Phenomenal Vocalists." *Colored American Magazine*, November 1901, 45–53.
Hopkins, Pauline. *Of One Blood; Or, the Hidden Self*. New York: Washington Square, 2004.

Howell, William Huntting. "In the Realms of Sensibility." *American Literary History* 25, no. 2 (2013): 406–17.

Howells, William Dean. *An Imperative Duty*. Edited by Paul Petrie. 1891. New York: Broadview, 2010.

Howes, David. "The Expanding Field of Sensory Studies." *Sensory Studies*, August 2013. https://www.sensorystudies.org/sensorial-investigations/the-expanding-field-of-sensory-studies/.

Howes, David, ed. *Varieties of Sensory Experience: A Sourcebook in the Anthropology of the Senses*. Toronto: University of Toronto Press, 1991.

Hsu, Hsuan L. "Naturalist Smellscapes and Environmental Justice." *American Literature* 88, no. 4 (2016): 787–814.

Hui, Alexandra. *The Psychophysical Ear: Musical Experiments, Experimental Sounds, 1840–1910*. Cambridge, MA: MIT Press, 2012.

Hurston, Zora Neale. *How It Feels to Be Colored Me*. 1928. Bedford, MA: Applewood, 2015.

Huysmans, Joris-Karl. *Against Nature*. 1884. New York: Penguin, 2003.

Hyde, Carrie. *Civic Longing: The Speculative Origins of U.S. Citizenship*. Cambridge, MA: Harvard University Press, 2018.

"Impaired Taste." *Scientific American*, October 16, 1869, 245.

Jackson, Virginia. *Dickinson's Misery: A Theory of Lyric Reading*. Princeton, NJ: Princeton University Press, 2005.

Jackson, Virginia. "The Function of Criticism at the Present Time." *Los Angeles Review of Books*, April 12, 2015. https://lareviewofbooks.org/article/function-criticism-present-time/.

James, Henry. *The Bostonians*. 1885. Oxford: Oxford University Press, 2009.

James, Henry. *Notes of a Son and Brother*. New York: Scribner's, 1914.

James, Henry. *The Turn of the Screw and Other Tales*. Edited by Kimberly C. Reed. New York: Broadview, 2010.

James, William. "The Consciousness of Lost Limbs." *Proceedings of the American Society for Psychical Research* 1 (1887): 249–58.

James, William. "The Hidden Self." *Scribner's Monthly*, March 1890, 361–73.

James, William. Introduction to *The Little Book of Life After Death* by Gustav Fechner, vii–xix. Boston: Little, Brown, 1904.

James, William. "Laura Bridgman." *Atlantic Monthly*, January 1904, 95–98.

James, William. "Notes on Automatic Writing." 1889. In *Essays in Psychical Research*, 37–55. Cambridge, MA: Harvard University Press, 1986.

James, William. "The One and the Many." In *Pragmatism: A New Name for Some Old Ways of Thinking*, 127–64. New York: Longman Green, 1907.

James, William. *The Principles of Psychology*. Vol. 1. New York: Holt, 1890.

James, William. *Psychology: A Briefer Course*. London: Macmillan, 1892.

James, William. "Theodore Flournoy (1894)." In *Essays, Comments, and Reviews*, edited by Frederick Burkhardt and Fredson Bowers, 466–68. Cambridge, MA: Harvard University Press, 1987.

James, William. "A World of Pure Experience." In *Pragmatism and Other Writings*, edited by Giles Gunn, 314–36. New York: Penguin, 2000.

Jameson, Fredric. *Archaeologies of the Future: The Desire Called Utopia and Other Science Fictions*. New York: Verso, 2007.
Jasper, Adam, and Nadia Wagner. "Notes on Scent." *Cabinet* 32 (Winter 2008–9). http://cabinetmagazine.org/issues/32/jasper_wagner.php.
Jastrow, Joseph. "Bridgman, Laura and Helen Keller." In *Dictionary of Philosophy and Psychology*, vol. 1, edited by James Mark Baldwin, 143–46. New York: Macmillan, 1901.
Jastrow, Joseph. "Eye-Mindedness and Ear-Mindedness." *Popular Science Monthly*, September 1888, 597–608.
Jastrow, Joseph. "Helen Keller: A Psychological Autobiography." *Popular Science Monthly*, May 1903, 71–83.
Jastrow, Joseph. "A Plea for the Sense of Smell." *Science* 8, no. 200 (December 3, 1886): 520–21.
Jastrow, Joseph. "Psychological Notes on Helen Kellar [sic]." *Psychological Review* 1, no. 4 (1894): 355–62.
Jefferson, Thomas. *Notes on the State of Virginia*. Edited by Frank Shuffelton. 1785. New York: Penguin, 1998.
Johnson, James Weldon. *Autobiography of an Ex-Colored Man*. 1912. New York: Dover, 1995.
Jones, Jeanette Eileen. "Simians, Negroes, and the 'Missing Link': Evolutionary Discourses in Transatlantic Debates on 'The Negro Question.'" In *Darwin in Atlantic Cultures*, edited by Jeanette Eileen Jones and Patrick B. Sharp, 191–207. New York: Routledge, 2010.
Kafer, Alison. *Feminist, Queer, Crip*. Bloomington: Indiana University Press, 2013.
Kant, Immanuel. *Anthropology from a Pragmatic Point of View*. Translated by Robert B. Louden. Cambridge: Cambridge University Press, 2006.
Kaplan, Amy. *The Anarchy of Empire in the Making of U.S. Culture*. Cambridge, MA: Harvard University Press, 2005.
Kaplan, Louis, ed. *The Strange Case of William Mumler, Spirit Photographer*. Minneapolis: University of Minnesota Press, 2008.
Kazanjian, David. *The Brink of Freedom: Improvising Life in the Nineteenth-Century Atlantic World*. Durham, NC: Duke University Press, 2016.
Keeney, Elizabeth. *The Botanizers*. Chapel Hill: University of North Carolina Press, 2012.
Keller, Helen. "From a Friend." *Crisis* 11, no. 6 (April 1916): 305.
Keller, Helen. "Helen Keller's Own Story of Her Life, Written Entirely by the Wonderful Girl Herself." *Ladies' Home Journal*, April 1902, 7–8.
Keller, Helen. *Midstream: My Later Life*. New York: Doubleday, 1929.
Keller, Helen. *The Story of My Life*. Edited by Roger Shattuck. 1902–3. New York: Norton, 2003.
Keller, Helen. *Teacher: Anne Sullivan Macy*. New York: Doubleday, 1955.
Keller, Helen. *The World I Live In*. Edited by Roger Shattuck. 1908. New York: New York Review Books Classics, 2004.
Kellogg, E. E. *Science in the Kitchen*. Battle Creek, MI: Modern Medicine, 1893.
"Kinesthesia Queen of the Senses." *Washington Post*, December 21, 1913, MS 2.

Kittler, Friedrich. *Gramophone, Film, Typewriter*. Translated by Geoffrey Winthrop-Young and Michael Wutz. Stanford: Stanford University Press, 1999.

Kleege, Georgina. *Blind Rage: Letters to Helen Keller*. Washington, DC: Gallaudet University Press, 2006.

Kleege, Georgina. "Helen Keller and 'The Empire of the Normal.'" *American Quarterly* 52, no. 2 (2000): 322–25.

Kleege, Georgina. "The Helen Keller Who Still Matters." *Raritan* 24, no. 1 (2004): 100–112.

Korsmeyer, Carolyn. *Making Sense of Taste: Food and Philosophy*. Ithaca, NY: Cornell University Press, 1999.

Krentz, Christopher. *Writing Deafness: The Hearing Line in Nineteenth-Century American Literature*. Chapel Hill: University of North Carolina Press, 2007.

Krolz, Lauren. *Creative Composites: Modernism, Race, and the Stieglitz Circle*. Berkeley: University of California Press, 2012.

Kropotkin, Petr Alekseevich. "Recent Science." *Littell's Living Age*, July–September 1896, 717–31.

Kudlick, Catherine. "The Outlook of *The Problem* and the Problem with the *Outlook*: Two Advocacy Journals Reinvent Blind People in Turn-of-the-Century America." In *The New Disability History: American Perspectives*, edited by Paul Longmore and Lauri Umansky, 187–213. New York: New York University Press, 2001.

Kuhn, Thomas. *The Structure of Scientific Revolutions*. Chicago: University of Chicago Press, 2012.

Kun, Josh. *Audiotopia: Music, Race, and America*. Berkeley: University of California Press, 2005.

Kuppers, Petra. *Disability Culture and Community Performance: Find a Strange and Twisted Shape*. New York: Palgrave, 2011.

Lane, Mary E. Bradley. *Mizora: A Prophecy*. Edited by Jean Pfaelzer. 1881. Syracuse, NY: Syracuse University Press, 2001.

Lanier, Sidney. "The Orchestra of Today." *Scribner's Monthly*, April 1880, 897–904.

Lash, Joseph. *Helen and Teacher: The Story of Helen Keller and Anne Sullivan Macy*. New York: Delacorte, 1980.

Latour, Bruno. "How to Talk about the Body? The Normative Dimension of Science Studies." *Body Society* 10, no. 2 (2004): 205–29.

Le Conte, John. "The Evidence of the Senses." *North American Review* 140, no. 338 (January 1885): 85–96.

Le Guérer, Annick. *Scent: The Mysterious and Essential Powers of Smell*. Translated by Richard Miller. New York: Random House, 1992.

Leslie, Esther. *Synthetic Worlds: Nature, Art, and the Chemical Industry*. Baltimore, MD: Johns Hopkins University Press, 2005.

Levenstein, Harvey. *Revolution at the Table: The Transformation of the American Diet*. Berkeley: University of California Press, 2003.

"Little Helen Keller, the Blind Deaf-Mute." *New York Times*, September 8, 1889, 11.

Looby, Christopher. "Flowers of Manhood: Race, Sex and Floriculture from Thomas Wentworth Higginson to Robert Mapplethorpe." *Criticism* 37, no. 1 (Winter 1995): 109–56.

Luciano, Dana. *Arranging Grief: Sacred Time and the Body in Nineteenth-Century America*. New York: New York University Press, 2007.
Luciano, Dana. "*How the Earth Feels*: A Conversation with Dana Luciano." Interview by Cécile Roudeaux. *Transatlantica* 1 (2015). https://journals.openedition.org/transatlantica/7362.
Luciano, Dana. "Touching Seeing." *American Literary History* 28, no. 1 (2016): 140–50.
Mackey, Nathaniel. *Discrepant Engagement: Dissonance, Cross-Culturality, and Experimental Writing*. Cambridge: Cambridge University Press, 1993.
Mackey, Nathaniel. *From a Broken Bottle Traces of Perfume Still Emanate*. New York: New Directions, 2010.
Manning, Erin. *Politics of Touch: Sense, Movement, Sovereignty*. Minneapolis: University of Minnesota Press, 2005.
Mao, Douglas. *Fateful Beauty: Aesthetic Environments, Juvenile Development, and Literature, 1860–1960*. Princeton: Princeton University Press, 2010.
Marvick, Louis. "René Ghil and the Contradictions of Synesthesia." *Comparative Literature* 1, no. 4 (1999): 289–308.
Marx, Karl. *Economic and Philosophic Manuscripts of 1844*. Edited by Martin Milligan. New York: Dover, 2012.
Massumi, Brian. *Politics of Affect*. Cambridge, UK: Polity, 2015.
Maxwell, Catherine. *Scents and Sensibility: Perfume in Victorian Literary Culture*. Oxford: Oxford University Press, 2017.
McGarry, Molly. *Ghosts of Futures Past: Spiritualism and the Cultural Politics of Nineteenth-Century America*. Berkeley: University of California Press, 2008.
McLuhan, Marshall. "Inside the Five Sense Sensorium." *Canadian Architect* 6 (June 1961): 49–54.
Menand, Louis. *The Metaphysical Club: A Story of Ideas in America*. New York: Farrar, Straus and Giroux, 2001.
Merleau-Ponty, Maurice. *Phenomenology of Perception*. Translated by Donald A. Landes. New York: Routledge, 2012.
Michaels, Walter Benn. *Our America: Nativism, Modernism, Pluralism*. Durham, NC: Duke University Press, 1995.
Mills, Mara. "Deaf Jam: From Inscription to Reproduction to Information." *Social Text* 28, no. 1 (2010): 35–58.
Mintz, Sidney. *Sweetness and Power: The Place of Sugar in Modern History*. New York: Penguin, 1986.
Mirzoeff, Nicholas. "The Shadow and the Substance: Race, Photography, and the Index." In *Only Skin Deep: Changing Visions of the American Self*, edited by Coco Fusco and Brian Wallis, 110–27. New York: International Center of Photography, 2003.
Mitchell, David T. "Body Solitaire: The Singular Subject of Disability Autobiography." *American Quarterly* 52, no. 2 (2000): 311–15.
Mitchell, David T., and Sharon L. Snyder, *The Biopolitics of Disability: Neoliberalism, Ablenationalism, and Peripheral Embodiment*. Ann Arbor: University of Michigan Press, 2015.
Mitchell, David T., and Sharon L. Snyder. *The Matter of Disability*. Ann Arbor: University of Michigan Press, 2019.

Mitchell, S. Weir. *The Autobiography of a Quack and Other Stories*. New York: Century, 1915.
Mitchell, S. Weir. "The Case of George Dedlow." *Atlantic Monthly*, July 1866, 1–11.
Mitchell, S. Weir. *Injuries of Nerves and Their Consequences*. Philadelphia: Lippincott, 1872.
Mitchell, S. Weir. Introduction to *Cooking in Old Creole Days*, by Célestine Eustis, xiii–xiv. New York: Russell, 1903.
Mitchell, S. Weir. "The Medical Department in the Civil War." *Journal of the American Medical Association* 62, no. 19 (May 1914): 1445–50.
Mitchell, S. Weir. "Phantom Limbs." *Lippincott's Monthly Magazine*, December 1871, 563–69.
Montanari, Massimo. *Food Is Culture*. Translated by Albert Sonnenfeld. New York: Columbia University Press, 2006.
Montgomery, Travis. "Radicalizing Reunion: Helen Keller's *The Story of My Life* and Reconciliation Romance." *Southern Literary Journal* 42, no. 2 (2010): 34–51.
Morris, David B. *The Culture of Pain*. Berkeley: University of California Press, 1991.
Morton, Timothy. *The Poetics of Spice: Romantic Consumerism and the Exotic*. Cambridge: Cambridge University Press, 2000.
Moten, Fred. *Black and Blur*. Durham, NC: Duke University Press, 2017.
Muhammad, Khalil Gibran. *The Condemnation of Blackness: Race, Crime, and the Making of Modern Urban America*. Cambridge, MA: Harvard University Press, 2011.
Müller, Johannes. *Elements of Physiology*. Translated by W. M. Baly. Philadelphia: Lea and Blanchard, 1843.
Münsterberg, Hugo. "The Danger of Experimental Psychology." *Atlantic Monthly*, February 1898, 159–66.
Münsterberg, Hugo. "Psychology and Mysticism." *Atlantic Monthly*, January 1899, 67–85.
Murison, Justine. *The Politics of Anxiety in Nineteenth-Century American Literature*. Cambridge: Cambridge University Press, 2011.
Murison, Justine. "Quacks, Nostrums, and Miraculous Cures: Narratives of Medical Modernity in the Nineteenth-Century United States." *Literature and Medicine* 32, no. 2 (2014): 419–40.
Musser, Amber. *Sensational Flesh: Race, Power, and Masochism*. New York: New York University Press, 2014.
"Negroes as Singers." *Washington Post*, April 25, 1903, 6.
Nelson, Megan Kate. *Ruin Nation: Destruction and the American Civil War*. Athens: University of Georgia Press, 2012.
"Newest Public Amusement." *New York Times*, September 14, 1902, 15.
Newman, Kathy. "Wounds and Wounding in the American Civil War: A (Visual) History." *Yale Journal of Criticism* 6, no. 2 (1993): 63–86.
Ngai, Sianne. *Ugly Feelings*. Cambridge, MA: Harvard University Press, 2007.
Nichols, Herbert. "The Psychology Laboratory at Harvard." *McClure's* 1, no. 5 (1893): 399–409.
Nielsen, Kim. *The Radical Lives of Helen Keller*. New York: New York University Press, 2004.
Noland, Carrie. *Agency and Embodiment: Performing Gestures/Producing Culture*. Cambridge, MA: Harvard University Press, 2009.

Nordau, Max. *Degeneration*. 1892. New York: Appleton, 1895.
"Notes." *Mind* 13, no. 50 (April 1888): 317.
"Notices of New Books." *New Englander and Yale Review* 45 (June 1886): 560–66.
Novak, David, and Matt Sakakeeny, eds. *Keywords in Sound*. Durham, NC: Duke University Press, 2015.
Nyhart, Lynn. *Biology Takes Form: Animal Morphology and the German Universities, 1800–1900*. Chicago: University of Chicago Press, 1995.
Nyong'o, Tavia. *The Amalgamation Waltz: Race, Performance, and the Ruses of Memory*. Minneapolis: University of Minnesota Press, 2009.
"The Obligations of Sugar-Refiners and Consumers to Physics and Chemistry." *Manufacturer and Builder*, April 1871, 78.
"The Odor of Race." *New York Times*, May 22, 1904, 6.
Ogden, Emily. *Credulity: A Cultural History*. Chicago: University of Chicago Press, 2018.
Ogle, William. *Anosmia, or Cases Illustrating the Physiology and Pathology of the Sense of Smell*. London: Adlard, 1870.
Oken, Lorenz. *Elements of Physiophilosophy*. Translated by Alfred Tulk. London: Ray, 1847.
"An Olfactory Crusade." *New York Times*, May 14, 1903, 1.
"Optical Illusions." *Scientific American*, September 2, 1868, 145–60.
Osborne, Gillian. "Dickinson's Lyric Materialism." *Emily Dickinson Journal* 21, no. 1 (2012): 57–78.
Otis, Laura. *Müller's Lab*. Oxford: Oxford University Press, 2007.
Panagia, Davide. *The Political Life of Sensation*. Durham, NC: Duke University Press, 2009.
Parisi, David. *Archaeologies of Touch: Interfacing with Haptics from Electricity to Computing*. Minneapolis: University of Minnesota Press, 2018.
Parisi, David. "Tactile Modernity: On the Rationalization of Touch in the Nineteenth Century." In *Media, Technology, and Literature in the Nineteenth Century: Image, Sound, Touch*, edited by Colette Colligan and Margaret Linley, 189–213. New York: Ashgate, 2011.
Park, Josephine. *Apparitions of Asia: Modernist Form and Asian American Poetics*. Oxford: Oxford University Press, 2014.
Park, Robert. *The City*. Chicago: University of Chicago Press, 1925.
"Parlor Singing." *Atlantic Monthly*, October 1869, 410–20.
Paterson, Mark D. "The Biopolitics of Sensation, Techniques of Quantification, and the Production of a 'New' Sensorium." *Resilience: A Journal of the Environmental Humanities* 5, no. 3 (Fall 2018): 67–95.
Patterson, Orlando. *Rituals of Blood: Consequences of Slavery in Two American Centuries*. New York: Perseus, 1998.
Peña, Carolyn Thomas de la. *The Body Electric: How Strange Machines Built the Modern American*. New York: New York University Press, 2003.
"Perfumery." *New York Times*, December 17, 1894, 4.
"Perfumes, Soaps, and Pomades." *New York Times*, August 12, 1894, 18.
Peters, John Durham. "Helmholtz, Edison, and Sound History." In *Memory Bytes: History, Technology, and Digital Culture*, edited by Lauren Rabinowitz and Abraham Geil, 177–98. Durham, NC: Duke University Press, 2004.

Pfaelzer, Jean. *The Utopian Novel in America, 1886–1896: The Politics of Form*. Pittsburgh, PA: University of Pittsburgh Press, 1984.
"Phantom Limbs," *Scientific American*, May 17, 1919, 504.
Picker, John. *Victorian Soundscapes*. Oxford: Oxford University Press, 2003.
Piesse, Charles Henry. *Olfactics and the Physical Senses*. London: Piesse and Lubin, 1887.
Piesse, G. W. Septimus. *The Art of Perfumery*. Philadelphia: Lindsay and Blakiston, 1857.
"Pleasures of the Palate." *New York Times*, June 15, 1879, 6.
Postle, Bradley. *Essentials of Cognitive Neuroscience*. West Sussex, UK: Wiley, 2015.
Pourciau, Sarah. *The Writing of Spirit: Soul, System, and the Roots of Language Science* New York: Fordham University Press, 2017.
Price, Janet, and Margrit Shildrick. "Bodies Together: Touch, Ethics and Disability." In *Disability/Postmodernity: Embodying Disability Theory*, edited by Mairian Corker and Tom Shakespeare, 62–75. London: Bloomsbury, 2002.
Prince, Mary. *The History of Mary Prince, a West Indian Slave*. Edited by Moira Ferguson. 1831. Ann Arbor: University of Michigan Press, 1993.
Puar, Jasbir. *Terrorist Assemblages: Homonationalism in Queer Times*. Durham, NC: Duke University Press, 2007.
Rabinbach, Anson. *The Eclipse of the Utopias of Labor*. New York: Fordham University Press, 2018.
Ramachandran, V. S. *Phantoms in the Brain: Probing the Mysteries of the Human Mind*. New York: Harper Collins, 1999.
Ramachandran, V. S. *The Tell-Tale Brain: A Neuroscientist's Quest for What Makes Us Human*. New York: Norton, 2012.
Rancière, Jacques. *The Politics of Aesthetics: The Distribution of the Sensible*. Edited and translated by Gabriel Rockhill. London: Bloomsbury, 2013.
Randolph, Mary. *The Virginia Housewife: or, Methodical Cook*. Columbia: University of South Carolina Press, 1984.
"Recent Experiments with the Senses." *Littell's Living Age*, July 1872, 515–33.
"Recent Literature." *Atlantic Monthly*, November 1879, 675–86.
Reckson, Lindsay V. *Realist Ecstasy: Religion, Race, and Performance in American Literature*. New York: New York University Press, 2019.
Rée, Jonathan. *I See a Voice: Deafness, Language and the Senses—A Philosophical History*. New York: Holt, 2000.
Reed, Edward S. *From Soul to Mind: The Emergence of Psychology, from Erasmus Darwin to William James*. New Haven, CT: Yale University Press, 1998.
Register, Seely. "The Spirit Photograph." *Harper's Monthly*, June 1863, 122–24.
Reinarz, Jonathan. *Past Scents: Historical Perspectives on Smell*. Urbana: University of Illinois Press, 2014.
"A Remarkable Biography." *Los Angeles Times*, April 4, 1903, A7.
Review of *The Story of My Life*. *Nation*, April 30, 1903, 361.
Rhodes, Albert. "What Shall We Eat?" *Galaxy* 22 (November 1876): 665–774.
Richards, Eliza. "'How News Must Feel When Traveling': Dickinson and Civil War Media." In *A Companion to Emily Dickinson*, edited by Martha Nell Smith and Mary Loeffelholz, 157–79. Malden, MA: Blackwell, 2008.

Rimbaud, Arthur. *Rimbaud: Complete Works, Selected Letters.* Translated by Wallace Fowlie. Chicago: University of Chicago Press, 2005.
Rimington, Alfred Wallace. *Colour-Music: The Art of Mobile Colour.* London: Hutchinson, 1912.
Rimmel, Eugène. *The Book of Perfumes.* London: Chapman and Hall, 1867.
Riskin, Jessica. *The Restless Clock: A History of the Centuries-Long Argument over What Makes Living Things Tick.* Chicago: University of Chicago Press, 2016.
Riskin, Jessica. *Science in the Age of Sensibility: The Sentimental Empiricists of the French Enlightenment.* Chicago: University of Chicago Press, 2002.
Robertson, George Croom. "The Blind-Deaf-Mute Helen Keller." *Mind* 14, no. 54 (April 1889): 305–9.
Rodaway, Paul. *Sensuous Geographies: Body, Sense and Place.* London: Routledge, 1994.
Romero, Lora. *Home Fronts: Domesticity and Its Critics in the Antebellum United States.* Durham, NC: Duke University Press, 1997.
Roosth, Sophia. "Nineteen Hertz and Below: An Infrasonic History of the Twentieth Century." *Resilience: A Journal of the Environmental Humanities* 5, no. 3 (2018): 109–24.
Roosth, Sophia. "Of Foams and Formalisms: Scientific Expertise and Craft Practice in Molecular Gastronomy." *American Anthropologist* 115, no. 1 (2013): 4–16.
Rusert, Britt. *Fugitive Science: Freedom and Empiricism in Early African American Culture.* New York: New York University Press, 2017.
Russell, Malinda. *A Domestic Cook Book: Containing a Careful Selection of Useful Receipts for the Kitchen.* 1866. Ann Arbor: William Clements Library, 2007.
Sacks, Oliver. *The Man Who Mistook His Wife for a Hat.* New York: Simon and Schuster, 1998.
Sacks, Oliver. *Musicophilia: Tales of Music and the Brain.* Toronto: Knopf, 2007.
Sadtler, Samuel. "A Chemical Classification of Odoriferous Principles." *American Journal of Pharmacy* 72 (May 1900): 220–26.
Samson, Jim. "The Great Composer." In *The Cambridge History of Nineteenth-Century Music*, edited by Jim Samson, 259–85. Cambridge: Cambridge University Press, 2008.
Satz, Aura. "'The Conviction of Its Existence': Silas Weir Mitchell, Phantom Limbs and Phantom Bodies in Neurology and Spiritualism." In *Neurology and Modernity: A Cultural History of Nervous Systems, 1800–1950*, edited by Laura Salisbury and Andrew Shail, 113–29. London: Palgrave, 2010.
Scarry, Elaine. *Dreaming by the Book.* Princeton, NJ: Princeton University Press, 2001.
Schaefer, Donovan O. *The Evolution of Affect Theory.* Cambridge: Cambridge University Press, 2019.
Schooling, William. "Color-Music: A Suggestion of a New Art." *Littell's Living Age*, August 10, 1895, 349.
Schrager, Cynthia. "Pauline Hopkins and William James: The New Psychology and the Politics of Race." In *The Unruly Voice: Rediscovering Pauline Elizabeth Hopkins*, edited by John Cullen Gruesser, 182–210. Urbana: University of Illinois Press, 1996.
Schuller, Kyla. *The Biopolitics of Feeling: Race, Sex, and Science in Nineteenth-Century America.* Durham, NC: Duke University Press, 2018.

Schwartz, Hillel. "Torque: The New Kinaesthetic of the Twentieth Century." In *Incorporations*, edited by Jonathan Crary and Sanford Kwinter, 70–127. New York: Zone, 1992.
Schweik, Susan. "Disability Politics and American Literary History: Some Suggestions." *American Literary History* 20 (2008): 217–37.
Schweik, Susan. *The Ugly Laws: Disability in Public*. New York: New York University Press, 2009.
"A Second Laura Bridgman." *Mind* 13, no. 50 (April 1888): 315.
Sedgwick, Eve Kosofsky. *Touching Feeling: Affect, Pedagogy, Performativity*. Durham, NC: Duke University Press, 2002.
Seitler, Dana. *Atavistic Tendencies: The Culture of Science in American Modernity*. Minneapolis: University of Minnesota Press, 2008.
Seltzer, Mark. *Bodies and Machines*. London: Routledge, 1992.
"The Senses—Smell." *Harper's Monthly*, March 1856, 495–96.
"The Senses—Touch." *Harper's Monthly*, January 1856, 179–85.
Seremetakis, C. Nadia. *The Senses Still: Perception and Memory as Material Culture in Modernity*. Chicago: University of Chicago Press, 1994.
Serres, Michel. *The Five Senses: A Philosophy of Mingled Bodies*. Translated by Margaret Sankey and Peter Cowley. London: Bloomsbury, 2016.
Shapiro, Laura. *Perfection Salad: Women and Cooking at the Turn of the Century*. Berkeley: University of California Press, 1986.
Sharpe, Christina. *In the Wake: On Blackness and Being*. Durham, NC: Duke University Press, 2016.
Sheehan, Tanya. *Doctored: The Medicine of Photography in Nineteenth-Century America*. University Park: Pennsylvania State Press, 2011.
Siebers, Tobin. *Disability Theory*. Ann Arbor: University of Michigan Press, 2008.
Sigourney, Lydia. *Lucy Howard's Journal*. New York: Harper, 1858.
Simmel, Georg. "Sociology of the Senses." 1907. In *Simmel on Culture: Selected Writings*, edited by David Frisby and Mike Featherstone, 109–19. London: Sage, 1997.
"The Skin." *Manufacturer and Builder*, July 1883, 163.
Smajić, Srdjan. *Ghost-Seers, Detectives, and Spiritualists: Theories of Vision in Victorian Literature and Science*. Cambridge: Cambridge University Press, 2010.
Smith, Effie Waller. *The Collected Works of Effie Waller Smith*. Oxford: Oxford University Press, 1991.
Smith, Mark M. *How Race Is Made: Slavery, Segregation, and the Senses*. Chapel Hill: University of North Carolina Press, 2006.
Smith, Roger. "Kinesthesia and Touching Reality." *19: Interdisciplinary Studies in the Long Nineteenth Century* 19 (2014): 1–27.
Smith, Shawn Michelle. *At the Edge of Sight: Photography and the Unseen*. Durham, NC: Duke University Press, 2013.
Smith, Shawn Michelle. *Photography on the Color Line: W. E. B. Du Bois, Race, and Visual Culture*. Durham, NC: Duke University Press, 2004.
Smith, Sidonie. "Identity's Body." In *Autobiography and Postmodernism*, edited by Kathleen Ashley, Leigh Gilmore, and Gerald Peters, 266–92. Amherst: University of Massachusetts Press, 1994.

Smith, Woodruff D. *Politics and the Sciences of Culture in Germany, 1840–1920*. Oxford: Oxford University Press, 1991.
Snively, John. "The Art of Perfumery." *Harper's Monthly*, September 1874, 570–79.
Socarides, Alexandra. *Dickinson Unbound: Paper, Process, Poetics*. Oxford: Oxford University Press, 2012.
"Sound and Smell." *New York Times*, November 24, 1882, 4.
Spillers, Hortense. "Mama's Baby, Papa's Maybe: An American Grammar Book." *Diacritics* 17, no. 2 (Summer 1987): 64–81.
Sprague, C. J. "What We Feel." *Atlantic Monthly*, December 1867, 740–44.
Stace, Arthur. "Plant Odors." *Botanical Gazette*, November 1887, 265–68.
Stadler, Gustavus. "On Whiteness and Sound Studies." *Sounding Out!* July 6, 2015. https://soundstudiesblog.com/2015/07/06/on-whiteness-and-sound-studies/.
Stamelman, Richard. *Perfume: A Cultural History of Fragrance from 1750 to the Present*. New York: Rizzoli, 2006.
Starobinski, Jean. "The Style of Autobiography." In *Autobiography: Essays Theoretical and Critical*, edited by James Olney, 73–83. Princeton, NJ: Princeton University Press, 1980.
Steege, Benjamin. *Helmholtz and the Modern Listener*. Cambridge: Cambridge University Press, 2012.
Stephens, Michelle. *Skin Acts: Race, Psychoanalysis, and the Black Male Performer*. Durham, NC: Duke University Press, 2014.
Sterne, Jonathan. *The Audible Past: Cultural Origins of Sound Reproduction*. Durham, NC: Duke University Press, 2003.
Stewart, Kathleen. *Ordinary Affects*. Durham, NC: Duke University Press, 2007.
Stewart, Susan. *Poetry and the Fate of the Senses*. Chicago: University of Chicago Press, 2002.
Stoever, Jennifer Lynn. *The Sonic Color Line: Race and the Cultural Politics of Listening*. New York: New York University Press, 2016.
Stott, Annette. "Floral Femininity: A Pictorial Definition." *American Art* 6, no. 2 (Spring 1992): 60–77.
Strathausen, Carsten. *The Look of Things: Poetry and Vision around 1900*. Chapel Hill: University of North Carolina Press, 2003.
Streeby, Shelley. *American Sensations: Class, Empire, and the Production of Popular Culture*. Berkeley: University of California Press, 2002.
Strick, Simon. *American Dolorologies: Pain, Sentimentalism, Biopolitics*. Albany: SUNY Press, 2014.
"Studying the Sense of Smell." *Harper's Weekly*, December 30, 1905, 32.
"Sugar-Refining." *Chicago Daily Tribune*, May 18, 1873, 7.
Sugden, Edward. *Emergent Worlds: Alternative States in Nineteenth-Century American Culture*. New York: New York University Press, 2018.
Swan, Jim. "Touching Words: Helen Keller, Plagiarism, Authorship." In *The Construction of Authorship: Textual Appropriation in Law and Literature*, edited by Martha Woodmansee and Peter Jaszi, 57–100. Durham, NC: Duke University Press, 1994.
"Sweets." *Chicago Daily Tribune*, April 4, 1874, 2.
"Taste and Smell—A New Theory." *Scientific American*, April 10, 1869, 234.
Taussig, Michael. *Mimesis and Alterity: A Particular History of the Senses*. London: Routledge, 1993.

Taves, Ann. *Fits, Trances, and Visions: Experiencing Religion and Explaining Experience from Wesley to James.* Princeton, NJ: Princeton University Press, 1999.

Taylor, J. Traill. *The Veil Lifted: Modern Developments of Spirit Photography.* London: Whitaker, 1894.

Thomas, Edith. "Notes from the Wild Garden." *Atlantic Monthly,* August 1891, 172–78.

Thompson, Emily. *The Soundscape of Modernity: Architectural Acoustics and the Culture of Listening in America, 1900–1933.* Cambridge: MIT Press, 2002.

Thorpe, T. B. "Sugar and the Sugar Region of Louisiana." *Harper's Monthly,* November 1853, 746–67.

Thrailkill, Jane. *Affecting Fictions: Mind, Body, and Emotion in American Literary Realism.* Cambridge, MA: Harvard University Press, 2007.

Thurschwell, Pamela. "Refusing to Give Up the Ghost: Thoughts on the Afterlife from Spirit Photography to Phantom Films." In *The Sixth Sense Reader,* edited by David Howes, 223–46. London: Berg, 2009.

Tipton-Martin, Toni. *The Jemima Code: Two Centuries of African American Cookbooks.* Austin: University of Texas Press, 2015.

Titchener, E. B. *Experimental Psychology: A Manual of Laboratory Practices.* Vol. 2. London: Macmillan, 1910.

"To Collect the Perfume of Flowers." *Scientific American,* April 21, 1855, 249.

Tompkins, Kyla Wazana. "Consider the Recipe." *J19: The Journal of Nineteenth-Century Americanists* 1, no. 2 (2013): 439–45.

Tompkins, Kyla Wazana. *Racial Indigestion: Eating Bodies in the 19th Century.* New York: New York University Press, 2012.

"Transcendental Physics." *Atlantic Monthly,* July 1881, 417–20.

Trower, Shelley. *Senses of Vibration: A History of the Pleasure and Pain of Sound.* New York: Continuum, 2012.

Tucker, Linda. *Lockstep and Dance: Images of Black Men in Popular Culture.* Jackson: University of Mississippi Press, 2007.

Turin, Luca. *The Secret of Scent: Adventures in Perfume and the Science of Smell.* New York: Harper Collins, 2006.

Twain, Mark. *Mark Twain's Letters.* Vol. 2. Edited by Albert Paine. New York: Harper, 1917.

Walker, Kara, and Antwaun Sargent. "Interview: Kara Walker Decodes Her New World Sphinx at Domino Sugar Factory." *Complex,* May 13, 2014. https://www.complex.com/style/2014/05/kara-walker-interview.

Walters, Shannon. *Rhetorical Touch: Disability, Identification, Haptics.* Columbia: University of South Carolina Press, 2014.

Wardrop, Daneen. "'That Minute Domingo': Dickinson's Cooption of Abolitionist Diction and Franklin's *Variorum Edition*." *Emily Dickinson Journal* 8, no. 2 (1991): 72–86.

Warner, Charles Dudley. "Editor's Study." *Harper's Monthly,* May 1896, 962–64.

Warner, Charles Dudley. "Modern Fiction." *Atlantic Monthly,* April 1883, 464–74.

Warner, Marina. *Phantasmagoria: Spirit Visions, Metaphors, and Media into the Twenty-First Century.* Oxford: Oxford University Press, 2006.

Weber, E. H. *E. H. Weber on the Tactile Senses.* Edited and translated by Helen E. Ross and David J. Murray. East Sussex, UK: Taylor and Francis, 1996.

Weber, E. H. *Der Tastsinn und das Gemeingefühl*. N.p., 1846.
Weheliye, Alexander. *Habeas Viscus: Racializing Assemblages, Biopolitics, and Black Feminist Theories of the Human*. Durham, NC: Duke University Press, 2014.
Weinstein, Sheri. "Possessive Matters in 'The Ghostly Rental.'" *Henry James Review* 21, no. 3 (2000): 270–78.
Weinstein, Sheri. "Technologies of Vision: Spiritualism and Science in Nineteenth-Century America." In *Spectral America: Phantoms and the National Imagination*, edited by Jeffrey Weinstock, 124–40. Madison: University of Wisconsin Press, 2004.
Weiss, John. "The Horrors of San Domingo." *Atlantic Monthly*, June 1862, 732–54.
Weiss, John. "The Horrors of San Domingo." *Atlantic Monthly*, March 1863, 289–306.
Werner, Marta. "Helen Keller and Anne Sullivan: Writing Otherwise." *Textual Cultures* 5, no. 1 (2010): 1–45.
West, Nancy. "Camera Fiends: Early Photography, Death, and the Supernatural." *Centennial Review* 40, no. 1 (1996): 170–206.
Wexler, Laura. *Tender Violence: Domestic Visions in the Age of U.S. Imperialism*. Chapel Hill: University of North Carolina Press, 2000.
Whitman, Walt. *Democratic Vistas: The Original Edition in Facsimile*. Edited by Ed Folsom. 1870. Iowa City: University of Iowa Press, 2010.
Whitman, Walt. *Leaves of Grass* (1855). Edited by Ed Folsom and Kenneth Price. Walt Whitman Archive. Accessed January 30, 2018. https://whitmanarchive.org/published/LG/1855/whole.html.
Whitman, Walt. *Leaves of Grass* (1867). Edited by Ed Folsom and Kenneth Price. Walt Whitman Archive. Accessed September 5, 2015. https://whitmanarchive.org/published/LG/1867/index.html.
Williams, Henry Willard. *Our Eyes, and How to Take Care of Them*. London: Tegg, 1871.
Williams, Raymond. *Marxism and Literature*. Oxford: Oxford University Press, 1977.
Witt, Doris. *Black Hunger: Food and the Politics of U.S. Identity*. Oxford: Oxford University Press, 1999.
Woloson, Wendy. *Refined Tastes: Sugar, Confectionery, and Consumers in Nineteenth-Century America*. Baltimore, MD: Johns Hopkins University Press, 2002.
Wood, Amy Louise. *Lynching and Spectacle: Witnessing Racial Violence in America, 1890–1940*. Chapel Hill: University of North Carolina Press, 2009.
Wood, H. C. "A Study of Consciousness." *Century Magazine* 40, no. 1 (1890): 72–77.
Woodward, J. J. "The Army Medical Museum in Washington." *Lippincott's Monthly Magazine*, March 1871, 233–42.
Wyman, Helen Knight. "Emily Dickinson as Cook and Poetess." *Boston Cooking School Magazine of Culinary Science and Domestic Economics*, June 1906, 14–15.
Yablon, Nick. "Echoes of the City: Spacing Sound, Sounding Space, 1888–1916." *American Literary History* 19, no. 3 (2007): 629–60.
Yergeau, Melanie. *Authoring Autism: On Rhetorical and Neurological Queerness*. Durham, NC: Duke University Press, 2018.
Zafar, Rafia. "Recipes for Respect: Black Hospitality Entrepreneurs before World War I." In *African American Foodways: Explorations of History and Culture*, edited by Anne Bower, 139–52. Urbana: University of Illinois Press, 2007.

INDEX

Page numbers in italics refer to illustrations.

abolitionism, 13, 75
abstraction, 45, 142, 166; of aesthetics, 15; color music and, 84; embodiment and, 49; mathematical, 92; perfumes and, 148, 161; smell sense and, 159; spirit photographs and, 63
acoustics, 31, 85, 88, 257; physical, 88, 89, 122; psychophysical, 89, 90, 97, 118, 126; of social harmony, 90
Adams, Henry, 27
aesthesiometer, 229–32, *230*, 235, 255
aesthesis, psychophysical, 20, 25–31, 122, 199, 211, 257–58, 264; body images and, 39; defined, 4; five senses and, 22; life writing (autobiography) and, 256; ontology and, 5, 6; perfumery and, 135, 142, 163; sense experience as, 25; synaesthesia and, 34; taste sense and, 175, 177, 178; of touch, 227; utopian fiction and, 91
aesthetics, 2, 6, 13; atmospheric, 145–53; from below, 20, 25; biopower and, 29; dissolute, 212; floral perfumes and, 142; Japanese, 128; Kantian "aesthetics from above," 16; musical, 89, 92, 96, 97, 122; Orientalist, 34; sensual corporeality and, 214; smell sense and, 124, 130; taste sense and, 175, 176, 187
"The Aesthetic Value of the Sense of Smell" (Finck), 132, 138, 168

African Americans, 17, 30, 135, 136; black Protestant church, 172–73; as Civil War soldiers, 60, 68, 69, 164, 203; culinary reform and racist stereotypes, 183–87; and "fugitive science," 7; and music, 109–19, New Negro, 115; perfume and racial terror (lynching), 157–63; post-Reconstruction political visibility of, 71–76; smell sense and, 136–37, 138, 141, 143; and sweetness, 187–98; "Talented Tenth," 253; and three-fifths personhood, 49, 50; in utopian fiction, 71, 72, 110, 146, 172. *See also* blackness; double consciousness
afterimages, 43, 45, 80
agency, 5, 123, 177, 226, 235; fetal personhood and, 263–64; of the hidden self, 232; of matter, 38, 45; of nature, 42; perceptual sensitivity and, 15; of the soul, 9
Ahmad, Dohra, 110
Ahmed, Sara, 77, 212, 225, 241
Alexander, Zeynep Çelik, 20
Allen, Grant, 16, 18, 27, 33, 130, 193; on color sense as measure of civilization, 84; on gastronomy, 180, 187; smell sense, 124; on synthetic perfumes, 145; on taste and aesthetics, 176
Altschuler, Sari, 49
American Anthropologist, 223
American Nervousness (Beard), 75

American Society for Psychical Research, 39
American Sugar Refining Company (ASRC), 213
Anagnos, Michael, 237
animacy, 38, 48, 54, 55
Anosmia, or Cases Illustrating the Physiology and Pathology of the Sense of Smell (Ogle), 138
anthropology, cultural, 259, 260–61
"Apple Sauce and Chicken Fried" (Smith), 186
À Rebours [Against Nature] (Huysmans), 126, 134–35
Aristotle, 14, 21, 22, 33, 222
Army Life in a Black Regiment (Higginson), 164–65
Army Medical Museum (AMM), U.S., 38, 51, 59, 70
The Art of Perfumery (Piesse), 125
Asians and Asian Americans, 128, 130, 170
Askinson, George, 140
astronomy, 15
Atlantic aesthesis, 29
Atlantic Monthly, 39, 45, 47, 52, 92, 102, 202
Attali, Jacques, 104
L'Audition colorée (Millet), 81
Aunt Jemima pancake mix, 184
Autobiography of an Ex-Colored Man (Johnson), 136, 157–58, 163
The Awakening (Chopin), 136, 148–53, 154, 163

Babbitt, Irving, 82, 129, 130
Bacon, Francis, 7
Bain, Alexander, 16–17, 176, 250, 254–55
Banner of Light, 56
Barnard, John Levi, 214
Barnum., P. T., 56
Bastian, Henry Charlton, 255
Bates, Arlo, 199–200
Baudelaire, Charles, 80, 169
Baynton, Douglas, 233
Beard, George Miller, 75, 168
Beardsley, Aubrey, 148
The Beautiful in Music (Hanslick), 96
beauty, 16, 89, 96, 130, 142, 176
becoming/unbecoming, 6, 8, 23, 26, 256, 138, 140, 218
Beecher, Catharine, 182
Beer, Gillian, 41
being, 4, 257; gendered, raced, and disabled, 5; "pure being," 28, 31, 100, 104, 107; subjectivity and, 220
Bell, Alexander Graham, 102, 122, 132, 223, 233
Bellamy, Edward, 31, 91, 99–100, 118
belonging, 4, 91, 184, 257
Benjamin, Walter, 156, 160
Bentley, Nancy, 109, 157, 253
Berenson, Bernard, 249

Berkeley, George, 84
Berlant, Lauren, 13, 24, 49, 257, 263
Bernstein, Julius, 27, 104, 137, 175
Bernstein, Robin, 177, 264
Bianchi, Martha Dickinson, 206, 208, 209–10
Binet, Alfred, 81, 230
biology, 3, 15, 26, 122, 135, 260
bioluminescence, 34
biopolitics, 20, 25, 134, 161, 162, 264
biopower, 2, 17, 19, 30, 261
Bishop, Bainbridge, 82, 83
blackness, 2, 30, 72, 115, 149, 253; ambivalence about, 163, 173; in cake recipes, 194, 207, 208; as occult consciousness, 116; owning of, 172; as skin pigmentation, 250
black women, 119–20, 152; body as site of white consumption, 216–17, 218; culinary abilities of, 184, 193–96; and rape, 119; sweetness and racial embodiment, 192, 198, 216, 218, 220. *See also* African Americans
Blake, William, 80
blindness, 37, 43, 75, 138. *See also* Keller, Helen
Blot, Pierre, 181
Boas, Franz, 259
body image, 31, 35–38, 54, 91, 176, 179; kinesthesia and, 255; phenomenology and, 76, 78; prenatal ultrasound and, 262; Reconstruction and, 71; spirit photographs and, 55
body-soul relation, 10, 26
body-subjects, 2, 25, 26, 49, 255, 258. *See also* interiority (selfhood); subjectivity
Bontecou, Reed, 59, 63, 68, 70
The Book of Perfumes (Rimmel), 134, 139
Booth, John Wilkes, 75
Boston Cooking School Cook Book (Farmer), 183, 197
Boston Cooking School Magazine of Culinary Science and Domestic Economics, 200, 210
The Bostonians (James), 39, 72–76
botany, 144
Brace, Julia, 138
Brady, Mathew, 56, 61, 70
Braille, 239, 243, 244
Brennan, Teresa, 134
Bridgman, Laura, 221, 223, 232, 235
Brillat-Savarin, Jean Anthèlme, 180
Brook Farm, 102
Brooks, Daphne, 111, 113
Brooks, Phillips, 243, 245
Brower, Edith, 103
Brown, Adrienne, 260
Brown, William Wells, 217
Bryan, Lettice, 192, 196, 198, 211

Bryant, William Cullen, 52
Buck-Morss, Susan, 29
Burke, Edmund, 177, 187, 214
Burrage, Henry, 52
Butler, Judith, 223

Cahan, David, 88, 94
Canby, Margaret, 237
capitalism, 63, 77, 106, 198, 214
carceral state, 19
Carus, Paul, 39, 45, 46
"A Case for Sympathy" (*Harper's Weekly*), 1
"The Case of George Dedlow" (Mitchell), 47–53, 100, 262
Castel, Louis-Bertrand, 82
Cecire, Natalia, 26
Certeau, Michel de, 174
Cervetti, Nancy, 53
Charcot, Jean-Marie, 232
chemistry, 15, 133, 134, 135; cooking and, 179, 183; and metaphysics, 141
The Chemistry of Commerce (Duncan), 132
Chen, Mel Y., 38, 216
Cheng, Anne Anlin, 153, 205
Child, Lydia Maria, 182, 201
children, 17, 36; black, 249; culinary science and, 183; mixed-race, 119; and sweetness, 187; thought process of, 82, 170; white, 264
Chopin, Kate, 29, 32, 135, 148–52, 163
Christianity, 42
chromola, 84, 86
citizenship, 49, 136
civilization, 20, 84; African, 111, 117, 120, 121; biblical and classical (Greco-Roman) sources, 120–21; decline and decadence of, 170; as ethnological designation, 90; gastronomy and, 179, 181, 182; music and, 88; perfumes and, 139, 140; skin and, 229; smell sense and, 124, 144; Western, 118; whiteness, 143, 169
Civil War, 4, 39, 59, 73, 202, 203; amputee veterans, 35, 47, 48, 52–53, 55, 221; odors in, 163–64; photographs and, 56, 61, 70; visual epistemology of modernity and, 36; wounded black soldiers, 60, 68, 69
class differences/divisions, 13, 53, 65, 84, 132, 133; culinary practices and, 168, 179–80, 184, 193, 198, 201, 213; disability and, 30; free white manhood, 99; New Woman and, 148; and odor, 141–42
Clifford, Frank Sanford, 144, 278n73
Clotel (Brown), 217
Cobb, Jasmine Nichole, 70
Coghlan, J. Michelle, 197

Cole, Brad, 144
Colored American Magazine, 91, 109; "Harp of David" advertisement, 119–20, *120*
color hearing/music, 81–86, 129, 130, 168
color organ (musical instrument), 82–83, *83*, *84*, *86*
color sense, 18
The Colour-Sense (Allen), 84
Connolly, William, 23, 34, 39
consciousness, 8, 11, 22, 25, 43, 151; awakened, 149; below-threshold, 248; black music and, 109; body and, 4, 28, 37; as chemical compound, 140; collaborative, 241, 242, 261; corporeal excess and, 211; embodied, 26, 133, 174, 177, 260; eugenics and, 18; "hand consciousness" of hysterics, 231, 233; as "heavenly vision," 39; human difference and, 2; integrated totality of, 14; interdependence and, 245; kinesthesia and, 255; as light wave, 44; limits of, 256; music and utopian change in, 120; as set of sense-specific capacities, 33; skin and, 250; threshold of, 100, 107, 151, 154, 229, 232; touch sense and, 221, 222, 235; transpersonal, 31, 91, 104, 109, 115, 116, 121, 135; as universal ordering principle, 9; utopian ideals and, 102. *See also* double consciousness
conservation of energy, law of, 41
consumer culture, 13, 260
Cooking in Old Creole Days (Eustis), 185
Cooley, Arnold, 142
Corbin, Alain, 142
"Correspondences" (Baudelaire), 80
Corti, Alfonso, 93
Couser, G. Thomas, 224
Coviello, Peter, 73
Cranch, C. P., 125, 136, 143, 145, 152, 157
Crary, Jonathan, 2, 21–22, 85
The Creole Cookery Book, 185
Cressman, Jodi, 241
crime, 19
Cristiani, Richard, 140
Cruel Optimism (Berlant), 257
Cruz, Jon, 111–12
culinary science, 179, 182–85, 187, 188, 199, 211. *See also* gastronomy
cultural relativism, 108, 259
cultural studies, 33
Cytowic, Richard, 33, 78

Darwin, Charles, 13–14, 17, 89, 140, 233; on music/noise binary, 104–5; on smell sense, 139; on taste sense, 181. *See also* sexual selection
Davenport, Charles, 106
day view, 9, 10–12, 40, 43, 55, 91

Index · 315

deafness, 122, 138
De Anima [On the Soul] (Aristotle), 14
Dearborn, George Van Ness, 255
"The Death of Slavery" (Bryant), 52
decadence, 34, 134, 147, 170, 216. *See also* perfumes, decadent
Degeneration (Nordau), 34, 170
Deleuze, Gilles, 5
Deliverance (film), 240
democracy, 99
Democratic Vistas (Whitman), 143
Derrida, Jacques, 256
The Descent of Man (Darwin), 13, 89, 104–5, 139, 181
De Tactu [Concerning Touch] (Weber), 228
Dickinson, Emily, 29, 32, 40, 178, 196–211, 218
Dictionary of Philosophy and Psychology, 223
dietetics, 175, 181
difference, human, 1, 3, 6, 25, 32, 225; psychophysical configurations of, 4, 15, 26, 28, 97, 139, 166, 171–72, 174, 233, 257
difference, racial, 2, 20, 29, 31, 189, 202
Dillon, Edward, 138
Dillon, Elizabeth Maddock, 29
disability, 26, 30, 48, 225, 232, 238, 247, 254; literature and communication regarding, 31, 225, 233–34, 243; and race and gender, 53, 226, 248
"Dr. Clair's Place" (Gilman), 85, 100
"Doings of the Sunbeam" (Holmes), 61
A Domestic Cook Book (Russell), 193–94
Domingo (San Domingo, Saint-Domingue), 32, 188, 189, 192, 196, 198–211, 218. *See also* sugar
double consciousness, 1–2, 110, 227, 232, 234, 235, 247–54, 259
Downey, June, 80, 171
Doyle, Edward Rice, 84
Draper, John, 45
dreams, 45
Dreiser, Theodore, 18–19
dualism, 9
Dubois, Laurent, 188
Dubois, Raphäel, 34
Du Bois, W. E. B., 1–2, 30, 247–54, 259
Dugan, Holly, 134
Duncan, Robert, 132, 145
Dussauce, Hyppolite, 133, 134, 153
Dvořák, Antonin, 109
Dwight, John Sullivan, 102, 109
Dyer, Richard, 65, 68

ear, human, 87–88, 92–95, 97, 104. *See also* hearing
Ebbinghaus, Hermann, 154
Economic and Philosophic Manuscripts of 1844 (Marx), 257

Eidsheim, Nina Sun, 86, 110, 111, 122
electricity, 22, 42, 102, 263
Elements of Physiophilosophy (Oken), 9, 14
Elements of Psychophysics (Fechner), 1, 10, 15, 17, 43, 44, 154
Ellis, Alexander, 108
Ellis, Havelock, 27, 82, 105, 141, 154, 168, 169
Emerson, Ralph Waldo, 9, 74, 136
"Emily Dickinson as Cook and Poetess" (Wyman), 200
"Emily Dickinson's Letters" (Higginson), 199
emotions (affect), 9, 24, 123, 257; affect theory, 5; five senses and, 174, 176; management of, 6; music as stimulus of, 84, 89, 97, 109; perfumes/odors and, 133, 134, 164; sentimental literature and, 13; smell sense and, 124, 126, 127; taste sense and, 177
empiricism, 2, 6, 11; and enlightenment, 40; music theory and, 92; night view of reality, 15; philosophies of existence and, 7; radical, 11, 12, 22, 29, 235; scientific materialism and, 9; visual, 59
Enlightenment, 11, 21, 22, 40, 42, 129, 214, 248
epistemology, 5, 13, 20, 88, 227, 238. *See also* knowledge
Equality (Bellamy), 105
Essentials of Cognitive Neuroscience (Postle), 80
ethnocentrism, 259
ethnology, 15, 139
ethnosympathy, 111–12, 114
eugenics, 6, 18, 106, 260; acoustics and, 31, 91; "eugenic Atlantic," 30; synaesthesia and, 33; as "utopian" project, 89
Eustis, Célestine, 185
evolution, 13–14, 83
exogamy, 108
eye, human, 36, 40, 43, 45, 56, 70. *See also* vision/sight

Farmer, Fannie, 178, 183, 197–98, 211
Fechner, Gustav, 1, 2, 11, 20, 127, 133, 258, 265n4; aesthetics and, 12–13, 15–16, 25, 175; 249; afterlife theory of, 31, 39, 40, 44–45, 47; day view of, 8, 9, 10, 14, 26, 40; materialism of, 7, 9, 22; mysticism and spiritualism and, 39, 91; and synaesthesia, 33, 79. *See also Elements of Psychophysics* (Fechner); *The Little Book of Life after Death* (Fechner); *Vorschule der Aesthetik [Introduction to Aesthetics]* (Fechner)
"feeble-mindedness," 19
feeling, theory of, 5, 8, 19
feminism, 73, 182; black feminists, 247; eugenic, 105; feminist phenomenology, 5; prenatal

ultrasound technology and, 263–64; and racism and classism, 224–25; socialist feminist utopia, 87–88
Finck, Henry T., 27, 132, 138; on cooking, 176, 186; on plant-based perfumes, 142; on the psychology of eating, 167, 179; on smell sense, 139
finger spelling, 236, 238, 239–40, 239, 243, 255, 257
Fisher, Abby, 178, 195, 196, 211
Fiske, John, 45
Fisk Jubilee Singers, 111, 112, 113–14
The Five Senses (Serres), 131
The Five Senses of Man (Bernstein), 104
flavor, 175, 176–77, 185
Fleissner, Jennifer, 135, 149, 181, 211
Fletcherism, 181
The Florentine Painters of the Renaissance (Berenson), 249
Flournoy, Theodore, 81
Food and Flavor: A Gastronomic Guide to Good Living (Finck), 167, 168, 176
form/matter distinction, 22
Fortune, Harper S., 120
Foucault, Michel, 46
Fougère Royale (perfume), 147, 150
Fourier, Charles, 99
Frankfurt school, 260
Franklin, Benjamin, 65, *68*
Freeman, Elizabeth, 19, 160
Freud, Sigmund, 2, 170
From a Broken Bottle Traces of Perfume Still Emanate (Mackey), 279n119
Frost, Laura, 151
"Frost Fairies" (Canby), 237
The Frugal Housewife (Child), 182, 201
Fuller, Sarah, 233
Funchion, John, 74
Fuss, Diana, 225, 238

Gabaccia, Donna, 183
Gallaudet, Edward, 233
Galton, Francis, 17–18, 19, 33, 78, 81, 89
Gardner, Andrew, 56
Gaskill, Nicholas, 18, 28, 81
gastronomy, 32, 176, 180, 181, 182, 187, 211. *See also* culinary science
Gates, Elmer, 18
Gayarré, Charles, 184–85
gender, 13, 26, 30, 261
genres of feeling, 4–5, 20, 21, 25, 26
"Ghost Seeing" (*North American Review* article), 45
Giard, Luce, 174, 201
Gilman, Charlotte Perkins, 85, 86, 100, 105, 169, 172

Glossary of Literary Terms (Abrams and Harpham), 80
Godey's Lady's Book and Magazine, 183
Goldsby, Jacqueline, 158
Goldstein, Amanda Jo, 26
"Good Cookery a Flower of Evolution" (*New York Times* article), 180
Good Housekeeping magazine, 225
Gottschalk, Louis, 92
Greenfield, Elizabeth Taylor, 109
Griggs, Sutton, 110
Gryzanowski, Ernst, 27, 99
Gurney, Edmund, 89, 98

Haitian Revolution, 188, 199, 203
Hall, G. Stanley, 8, 54, 232
Hall, Stuart, 174
hallucinations, 45, 47, 80
Hammond, William, 38, 59
Hanslick, Eduard, 96
haptic sense, 18, 248–54, 256
Harewood Hospital (Washington, DC), 59, *60*
Harmony Society, 99
Harper, Frances, 72, 172, 247
Harper's Monthly, 1, 27, 58, 140, 185, 224
Harper's Weekly, 57, 132
"Harp of David" advertisement, 119–20, *120*
Harrington, Anne, 171
Harris, Charles, *60*, 68
Harrison, Randolph, 184
Hartman, Saidiya, 74, 77
Hartmann, Sadakichi, 29, 126–30, 131, 154, 161
Hawthorne, Nathaniel, 99
Haymarket riot (1886), 90
Head, Henry, 35, 255
hearing, 92–93, 126, 130; evolutionary primacy of, 129–30; physiology of, 97; sexually selective, 105, 106, 108, 122. *See also* ear, human
Hedge, Frederick, 45
Hegel, G. W. F., 84
Heidelberger, Michael, 11
Heller-Roazen, Daniel, 29
Helmholtz, Hermann von, 2, 21, 27, 35, 90, 127, 167; on conservation of energy and thermodynamics, 41, 46; on Darwinian evolution and early anthropology, 13, 259; on materiality of sense experience, 7, 22–23, 93; optics studied by, 40, 41, 46, 75, 88, 132, 255; and psychophysical acoustics, 88, 89, 92, 93, 95–96, 100; and sign theory perception, 20, 22–24, 25, 81; and synaesthesia, 80, 85. *See also On the Sensations of Tone* (Helmholtz)
heredity, 3, 18

Index · 317

hermeneutics, 80
Heywood, Alice, 154–55
"The Hidden Self" (James), 229–31
hidden self, theory of, 110, 116, 253
Higginson, Thomas Wentworth, 126, 163–64, 199, 202, 203, 205
History of Mary Prince (Prince), 217–18
Hitz, John, 223
Hoffer, Peter, 141
Holmes, Oliver Wendell, 61, 154
homeopathy, 85
homosexuality, 19, 82, 156
hooks, bell, 202
Hooper, Lucy, 142
Hopkins, Pauline, 27, 29, 31, 91, 109, 123
Horace Mann School for the Deaf, 233
"The Horrors of San Domingo" (Weiss), 188, 202
Howe, Samuel Gridley, 221, 237
Howells, William Dean, 29, 71, 86, 146, 172
How It Feels to Be Colored Me (Hurston), 260
"How to Talk about the Body?" (Latour), 28
Hsu, Hsuan, 134
Hughes, Langston, 260
Hui, Alexandra, 96, 108–9
humanities ("human sciences"), 7
Hume, David, 11
Hurston, Zora Neale, 260
Huysmans, Joris-Karl, 126, 134, 148, 169, 171
Hyers sisters (Anna Madah and Emma Louise), 109
hygiene codes, 141
hysteria, 36, 53, 171, 229–31, 233, 235

idealism, 9
immigrants, 30, 90, 170
An Imperative Duty (Howells), 71–72, 86, 146, 172–73
imperialism, 13
Imperium in Imperio (Griggs), 110
impressibility, 17
incest, 106, 107, 108, 119
indigenous people, 17
individualism, 103, 247
induction, aesthetic, 20, 21, 25
industrialization, 154
inference, unconscious, 22, 23
Injuries of Nerves and Their Consequences (Mitchell), 47, 52, 53, 76
Inquiries into Human Faculty and Its Development (Galton), 17–18, 33, 78–79
Institute for Art and Olfaction, 128–29
interiority (selfhood), 72, 226; African American, 112, 114; and autobiography, 223; and corporeality, 65; formed from outside, 236, 241; phantom limb and, 54, 72; recursive, 163; taste sense and, 175; touch sense and, 222, 224. *See also* body-subjects; subjectivity
intersubjectivity, 5, 226, 256
Iola Leroy (Harper), 72, 172
I See a Voice (Rée), 87

Jackson, Helen Hunt, 209
Jackson, Virginia, 178
James, Henry, 36, 37, 39, 72
James, William, 3, 8, 12, 27, 152, 226, 258; and American Society for Psychical Research, 39; on color hearing, 81; on double consciousness, 110, 232, 235; on Fechner's day view, 40; "The Hidden Self," 229–31; on Keller, 235, 248; music theory and, 99; "Notes on Automatic Writing," 231; on partial tones, 94; on phantom limbs, 52, 76; radical empiricism and, 11; on touch and mental states, 229; on "touch-images," 248–49
Jameson, Fredric, 91
Janet, Jules, 230
Janet, Pierre, 230
japonisme, 128, 153
Jastrow, Joseph, 27, 132–33, 136, 223, 226–29, 232–33, 248
Jefferson, Thomas, 141
Jenkins, Macgregor, 209
Jicky (perfume), 147
Jim Crow, 1, 132, 159, 249
Johnson, Edward A., 110
Johnson, James Weldon, 136, 157, 162, 163
Journal (Keller), 224
just-noticeable difference (JND), 10, 27

Kant, Immanuel, 21, 22, 132
Kazanjian, David, 7
Keller, Helen, 31, 32, 220; color of thought and, 249–50; Du Bois and, 247–48, 251–52, 256; as feminist, 224–25; finger spelling and, 238–39, 239; Jastrow's aesthesiometer experiment and, 232; life and autobiographies of, 221–25, 227, 241–43, 249–50; as "motor-minded" type, 228; oralism (lip reading) of, 233–34, 234; support for African Americans, 248; touch as epistemological narcissism, 227; writing process, 245. *See also The Story of My Life* (Keller)
Kellogg, Ella, 182
The Kentucky Housewife (Bryan), 192
kinesthesia, 254–56
Kittler, Friedrich, 2
Kleege, Georgina, 225, 237

knowledge, 20, 21, 76, 259; aesthetic ways of knowing, 28; culinary science and, 183, 186; firsthand, 246; occult, 33. *See also* epistemology; science
Koopman, Harry Lyman, 200
Korsmeyer, Carolyn, 174–75, 216
Krentz, Christopher, 254
Kudlick, Catherine, 235–36
Kuhn, Thomas, 258
Kuppers, Petra, 254

Ladies' Home Journal, 142, 242, 243
Lamarck, Jean-Baptiste, 14
Lane, Mary Bradley, 87, 124, 182
Lang, Andrew, 199
language, 28, 29, 158, 159; and consciousness, 259; finger spelling, 238; manual language, 236, 240; sign language, 233, 236; smell sense and, 165, 166; tactile, 241, 244, 251, 255
Lanier, Sidney, 92
Lash, Joseph, 234
Latour, Bruno, 28, 165–66
Leaves of Grass (Whitman), 35
Le Conte, John, 222
Le Guérer, Annick, 131, 165
"Letter to a Young Contributor" (Higginson), 202
liberalism, 99
life/death binary, 38, 43, 54, 151
life science, 13
light, 10, 40–42, 80, 92, 168; color music and, 83, 84, 86; and consciousness, 44, 45, 259; photography and, 56, 59, 68, 70, 262; physics of, 175; and psychophysical parallelism, 11; and sound, 156
Light Ahead for the Negro (Johnson), 110
"Lilacs" (Chopin), 136, 155–58
Lincoln, Abraham, 63, 64, 68, 70, 71, 75–76
Lincoln, Mary Todd, 63, 64
Lincoln, Tad, 63, 64
Linnaeus, Carl, 14, 125
Lippincott's magazine, 27, 52
lip reading, 233–34, 234, 236
literature, 28, 29, 260; domestic novel, 173; mendicant, 243, 246; as mode of scientific inquiry, 26; sensory embodiment and, 27; sentimental, 13; synaesthesia and, 170
Littel's Living Age (magazine), 138, 258
The Little Book of Life after Death (Fechner), 35, 40, 42, 43, 46, 221
lived experience, 3, 22, 24, 172, 174, 228, 240
Locke, John, 11, 21, 22, 245
Lombroso, Cesare, 19

Looking Backward, 2000–1887 (Bellamy), 31, 91, 99–108, 118, 119, 121, 122
"A Louisiana Sugar Plantation of the Old Regime" (Gayarré), 184–85
Lubin Perfumes advertisement, *162*
Luciano, Dana, 63, 112, 220
Lucy Howard's Journal (Sigourney), 201
Lundborg Perfumes, 146, 147, *147*

Mackey, Nathaniel, 77, 279n119
Macy, John, 236, 241, 242, 243, 244, 256
magnetism, 42
Maher, Margaret, 207
Manning, Erin, 242
Manufacturer and Builder, 40, 56, 133, 189, 250
Marey, Étienne-Jules, 255
Martin, Lewis, 68, 69
Marx, Karl, 257, 261
Mary Todd Lincoln with the Spirit of Her Husband President Abraham Lincoln and Son Thaddeus (Mumler spirit photograph), 63, *64*, 68
masculinity, white, 49, 70
Massumi, Brian, 5
Master Herrod with Spirits of Europe, Africa, and America (Mumler spirit photograph), 65, *66*, 68
The Master's House (Thorpe), 189
materialism, transcendental, 42, 51, 74
mathematics, 11
matter, 9, 12, 22, 38, 42, 88, 175
matter-mind relation, 9, 10, 11, 21, 210; body image and, 37; as correlation, 2–3, 28; flavor and, 179; Keller and, 240; as psychophysical correspondence, 38; psychophysics of feeling and, 5, 25; sense experience and, 23
Mayol, Pierre, 174
McGarry, Molly, 39
McLuhan, Marshall, 33
medical case studies, 4, 39, 47–53, 70, 80, 81
medical gaze, 46, 58
medicine, 9, 51, 59, 68, 82, 169, 186, 231
"Melanctha" (Stein), 260
memoirs, 4, 243, 245
memory, 45, 84, 129, 261; hysteria and, 229, 231; odor memory, 156, 161, 279n119; perfumery and, 133, 135, 148, 151, 153–64; psychology of, 154; taste sense and, 211
Menand, Louis, 7
mental illness, 19
Merleau-Ponty, Maurice, 76–77, 225, 236, 255
mesmerism, 51, 102, 115
metaphysics, 2, 6–7, 122, 141
Michaelis, Theodor, 108

Index · 319

Michaels, Walter Benn, 106
Middle Passage, 77
Midstream: My Later Life (Keller), 224, 240, 245
Miller, Preston, 84
Millet, Jules, 81
mimesis, 145, 146
Mind (journal), 221
mind, science of, 10
mind-body parallelism, 43, 46
Mintz, Sidney, 188
Mirzoeff, Nicholas, 263
Mrs. French (Mumler photograph), 62
Mitchell, David T., 30
Mitchell, S. Weir, 27, 31, 35–36, 46, 76, 255; on black cooks, 185; Lincoln and, 71; medical case studies, 39, 55; on phantom limb phenomenon, 59, 222, 259; treatments by, 85, 169
Mizora: A Prophecy (Lane), 87–88, 124, 182
Molyneux problem, 222
monism, 9
The Monist, 39
monogenesis, 110, 119
Montanari, Massimo, 182
Montessori, Maria, 18, 228, 229
More, Thomas, 89
Moses, William Stainton, 65
Moten, Fred, 209, 214, 216, 220, 221
mouthfeel, 216, 217, 220
Muhammad, Khalil Gibran, 141
Müller, Johannes, 21, 22, 24
Mumler, Hannah, 37, 55
Mumler, William, 31, 37, 38, 39, 55, 59, 73, 76. *See also* spirit photographs
Münsterberg, Hugo, 8, 250–51
Murison, Justine, 51
music, 88; African American, 109–19; color music, 82, 83–85; European tonal music, 98–99, 109; harmonic, 98, 99, 101, 107, 117; jazz, 216, 260, 279n119; in *Looking Backward*, 101–2, 104, 107; noise and, 104–5, 107, 108; non-Western, 98, 107; pitch, 93, 95, 97; as psychophysical phenomenon, 92; scent correspondence to musical notes, 125–30, *125*; sexual selection and, 89, 105; smell sense and, 125–30, *125*; timbre, 85, 86, 109–10, 111, 112, 114; tonality, 98, 99, 110, 176, 179; unconscious effects of, 100
Musser, Amber, 25
Muybridge, Eadweard, 255
My Religion (Keller), 224

Nanna; or, On the Soul Life of Plants (Fechner), 9
Native Americans, 30, 65, 68, 112, 233
natural history, 2, 14, 15
naturalism, 134
natural science, 2, 12, 15, 42, 228, 258
"Negroes as Singers" (*Washington Post* article), 112
Negro Problem, 1, 251
nervous system, 17, 21, 72, 168, 226
neurasthenia, 53–54, 104, 168, 169, 171, 173
neuroscience, 261
New Harmony, 99
New Psychology, 8, 12, 221, 222, 258
Newton, Isaac, 41, 82
New Woman, 32, 135, 148–49, 152–54, 157
Ngai, Sianne, 54, 122–23
Nichols, Herbert, 12
night view, 15, 80
Nordau, Max, 34, 81–82, 83, 84, 129, 130, 135
North American Review, 99
"Notes on Automatic Writing" (James), 231
Notes on the State of Virginia (Jefferson), 141
not-seeing, 31, 37, 72, 262, 263; as bodily cognition, 40; body images and, 38; cultural ascendance of, 41; fetal ultrasound technology and, 264; phantom limb and, 46–55; spirit photographs and, 55–71, 57, 60, 62, 64, 66–67, 69; spiritualist, 39; transcendental materialism and, 74
Novak, David, 98
Nyhart, Lynn, 7
Nyong'o, Tavia, 146

odophone, 125–26, 127, 168
Of One Blood (Hopkins), 31, 91, 109–19, 121, 122
Ogden, Emily, 51
Ogle, William, 138
Oken, Lorenz, 9, 14–15, 30, 33
"Old and New Identities, Old and New Ethnicities" (Hall), 174
Olney, Edward, 146
On the Sensations of Tone (Helmholtz), 85, 88, 91, 97, 122–23; Bell's "harmonic telegraph" and, 102; on harmonic music, 98; English translation (Ellis), 108; on music/noise binary, 104; on timbre, 109–10
ontogenesis, 82, 151, 233
ontology, 6, 20, 36, 264; materialist ontology of the soul, 38, 45, 70; matter and mind as two sides of, 9; psychophysics of smell and, 135; relational, 5; smell sense and race, 153
ophthalmoscope, 40, 132
optics, 40, 41, 46, 70, 75, 88
Optimism (Keller), 224
Orientalism, 34, 108, 128, 130, 153
O'Sullivan, Timothy, 56
Out of the Dark (Keller), 224
Owen, Robert Dale, 99

Panagia, Davide, 220
Papier à cigarettes JOB (Atché), 163
Paris Commune, 29
Park, Josephine, 128
Park, Robert, 260
"Parlor Singing" (*Atlantic* essay), 120
Paterson, Mark D., 228
patriarchy, 72, 75, 76, 118–19, 152, 169
Patterson, Orlando, 160
Peirce, C. S., 2, 132–33, 233
Peña, Carolyn Thomas de la, 13
people of color, 19, 54, 177
perceptual sensitivity, 6, 12–20, 22, 26, 30, 33, 34, 168
perceptual threshold, 10, 43
Perfumery and Kindred Arts (Cristiani), 140
perfumes, 4, 6, 26, 176, 179; in Chopin's *The Awakening*, 148–53; decadent, 147, 148, 150, 153, 154, 162, 168; distillation and, 140–41, 143, 145; global imperial order and, 144, 278n73; and inner life, 133–34; lynching and, 157–63; "olfactory training" and, 28; Orientalist aesthetics of, 34, 153; perceptual sensitivity and, 15; perfume concerts, 127, 129, 130, 168; professionalization of science and, 133; psychophysics of, 136–53; racial discourses and, 139–40, 141, 142, 146; recollection and, 153–64; and sound/music, 125–30, 168; synthetic, 145–53. *See also* smell sense
Perkins Institution for the Blind, 237, 248
phantom limb, 5, 27, 38, 46, 71, 174, 255; and bodily presence, 63; and disability, 35–36, 231; named, 35; not-seeing and, 37; ontology of, 47; and race, 30, 77–78; representation and, 263; and war, 31, 53–54, 76
"Phantom Limbs" (Mitchell), 47, 48, 52
phenomenology, 76–78, 225, 261
photography, 26, 36, 58–59, 60. *See also* spirit photographs
phrenology, 15
phylogenesis, 82, 151, 233
physics, 7, 15, 89, 97, 179, 183
Physiological Aesthetics (Allen), 16, 18, 84, 124, 176
physiology, 7, 12, 22, 89, 97, 259
The Physiology of Taste (Brillat-Savarin), 180
Piesse, Charles Henry, 125–26, 181
Piesse, G. W. Septimus, 125, 140, 168
Pindell, Anne Pauline, 109
plantation fiction, 144, 278n73
"A Plea for the Sense of Smell" (Cranch), 136, 143, 157
"A Plea for the Sense of Smell" (Jastrow), 132
pleasure, 16, 89, 127; gustatory, 176, 186, 199, 202, 204; racialized experiences of, 178; tonal music and, 99

Poe, Edgar Allan, 80
Popular Science Monthly, 27, 81, 170, 225, 227
positivism, 47, 92, 222, 258
poststructuralism, 260
Pourciau, Sarah, 80
The Power of Sound (Gurney), 89
A Practical Guide for the Perfumer (Dussauce), 133
The Practice of Everyday Life (Certeau, Giard, and Mayol), 174
pragmatism, 2, 7, 23
Price, Janet, 226
"primitive" peoples, 82, 138, 141, 170, 233
Prince, Mary, 217–18
Principles of Psychology (James), 8, 94, 229, 248–49
Pvt. Lewis Martin (Bontecou photo), 68, 69
"The Procession of Flowers" (Higginson), 165
progress, 89
Prometheus: Poem of Fire (Scriabin), 84
psychoanalysis, 2, 260
Psychological Review, 232
psychology, experimental, 2, 228, 258, 259
"Psychology and Mysticism" (Münsterberg), 250–51
"The Psychology of Yellow" (Ellis), 170
psychophysical parallelism, law of, 11, 12, 23
psychophysics, 2–3, 6, 122; biopolitics and, 20; cultural life of, 4; evolutionary racial science and, 13; as precursor to experimental psychology, 2; smell sense and, 133, 135, 136–53; of sound, 88; as speculative science, 6–12, 25, 264; spiritualism and, 38–39; synaesthesia and, 78, 80–81; taste sense and, 133, 175; of touch, 225, 228; waning of, 258, 259
Puar, Jasbir, 30
public sphere, 49, 90, 102, 184

queerness/queer theory, 5, 6, 32, 225

Rabinbach, Anson, 42
race, 3, 13, 260, 261; consciousness and, 26; cross-racial desire, 32; and difference, 2, 20, 29, 31, 189, 202; disability and, 30, 31; gender politics and, 75; musical aesthetics and, 98; and odor, 137, 141–44, 146, 151–52, 159, 173; perfumery and, 135–36; photography and, 68, 70; and psychophysical acoustics, 118; and purity, 28, 31, 90, 104–8, 261; and science, 3, 13, 17, 19, 32; and sensory taxonomy, 14–15, 30, 33; smell sense and, 138–39; sounds and, 86; species difference and, 263; spirit photographs and, 6. *See also* blackness; whiteness

racialization, 4, 5; of consciousness, 250; of disabled male body, 54; impressibility and, 17; not-seeing and, 39; sound and, 90
Ramachandran, V. S., 58
Rancière, Jacques, 261
Randolph, Mary, 194, 197
Rapp, George, 99
recipes, 4, 28, 32, 178, 192–98, 211
Reckson, Lindsay, 161
Reconstruction, 1, 39, 71–76, 89, 136, 278n73
Rée, Jonathan, 83, 87
The Religion of Solidarity (Bellamy), 99–100
resonance, 90, 93, 116; affective, 111; ethnosympathy and, 114; gender and, 119; social harmony and, 6; theory, 92, 96, 97, 122
"Retreat from Lenoir and the Siege of Knoxville" (Burrage), 52
Rhodes, Albert, 183, 189–90
Rice, Edward E., 129
Riegl, Aloïs, 249
Rimbaud, Arthur, 80, 81, 84, 85–86
Rimington, Alexander Wallace, 82–83
Rimmel, Eugène, 134, 139, 146
Riskin, Jessica, 41
Robertson, George Croom, 221
Rodaway, Rod, 87
A Romance of Perfume Lands (Clifford), 144, 278n73
Romanticism, 12, 26, 41, 47, 65, 158
Roosevelt, Theodore, 49
Rosario, Vernon, 171
Rusert, Britt, 26
Russell, Malinda, 178, 193–95, 196, 197, 211

Sacks, Oliver, 47
Sadtler, Samuel, 157
Salomé (Wilde), 126
San Domingo/Saint-Domingue. *See* Domingo (San Domingo, Saint-Domingue)
"savages" (primitive or indigenous peoples), 38, 75, 144; developmental belatedness of, 138; smell sense and, 139, 140; taste sense and, 181–82, 199, 204, 205, 206; yellow color and, 170
Scent (Le Guérer), 131
Schooling, William, 83, 84
Schuller, Kyla, 13, 17, 26, 226, 247
Schwartz, Hillel, 255
Schweik, Susan, 248
science, 26, 45, 126; arrogance of, 9; feeling and, 261; as philosophy, 7, Romantic, 12, 41, 47. *See also* knowledge
Science (journal), 136
Science in the Kitchen (Kellogg), 182

science studies, 5
Scientific American, 45–46, 76, 126, 140, 175, 180
Scriabin, Alexander, 84–85
Scribner's Monthly, 92
sensation, 99, 257; double, 225, 227, 240–41, 245, 247, 249, 254; theories of, 21–24; sociality of, 261
sensationalism, 48, 50
sense ability, 124
"sense discrimination," 18
sense experience, 2, 5, 17, 133, 264; as aesthesis, 12, 25, 27; as bodily cognition, 6–7, 23; materiality of, 3, 21, 22, 226
senses, five, 6, 132, 220; and aesthetics, 4, 20, 22, 24, 176; lived experience of, 33, 147; sensory hierarchy, 14, 16, 32, 33, 124, 126
The Senses and the Intellect (Bain), 176
sensibility, 13
sensitive threshold, 10
sensitivity, 15, 124, 139, 204; aural/auditory, 17, 31; gustatory, 180, 182; hierarchy of, 16, 17; nervous, 168, 173; olfactory, 28, 127; perceptual, 6, 12–20, 22, 26, 30, 33, 34, 168; training and, 14, 19, 34, 84, 140, 229; tactile, 18, 31, 238, 248
sensory studies, 32, 260–61
Sensuous Geographies (Rodaway), 87
sensus communis, 29, 178
sentimentalism/sentimentality, 13
Serres, Michel, 131
settler colonialism, 14
sexuality, 105, 135, 141, 148, 152, 170, 233
sexual selection, 13, 89, 105, 106, 108, 119, 121
Sexual Selection in Man: Touch, Smell, Hearing, Vision (Ellis), 105
Sharpe, Christina, 72
Shelley, Percy, 80
Shildrick, Margrit, 226
sight. *See* eye, human; vision/sight
sign language, 233, 236, 255
sign theory of perception, 6, 20, 21, 23, 25, 81, 92
Sigourney, Lydia, 201
Simmel, Georg, 159
slavery, 14, 70, 78, 188, 214, 226; black music and, 111; historical amnesia and, 220; sexual selection and, 118–19; slave insurrections, 198; slave narratives, 217–18, 243
smell sense, 33, 124–30; industrial odors, 131–32, 134–35, 162; language and, 158, 159; odor memory, 156, 161, 279n119; olfactory essences, 161, 174; scientific neglect of, 168. *See also* perfumes; race, and odor
Smith, Effie Waller, 186
Smith, Mark M., 32

Smith, Shawn Michelle, 37
Smith, Sidonie, 223
Smith, Woodruff D., 12
Snively, John, 146–47
Snyder, Sharon, 30
Socarides, Alexandra, 178
social Darwinism, 90, 148
social harmony, 90, 91, 99, 100, 109, 121, 257
socialism, 99, 100, 106, 108
social sciences, 16, 259, 260
Society for Psychical Research (Great Britain), 39
"Sociology of the Senses" (Simmel), 159
solidarity, 99–100, 101, 106, 107, 108, 174
soul food, 187
The Souls of Black Folk (Du Bois), 32, 227, 248–49, 251–54
sound, 90–91, 94, 122
South, Global, 144
Spillers, Hortense, 226
Spinoza, Baruch, 5
"The Spirit Photograph" (Victor), 58
spirit photographs, 6, 31, 38, 62, 64, 66; double exposure in, 63; not-seeing and, 37; prenatal ultrasound technology and, 262; purposes of, 55–56, 59; Reconstruction and, 71. *See also* Mumler, William; photographs
spiritualism, 36, 38–40, 51; James's *The Bostonians* and, 72–73, 75, 76
Sprague, C. J., 3, 175
Stace, Arthur, 146
Stadler, Gustavus, 90
Stamelman, Richard, 149
Steege, Benjamin, 88, 92
Stein, Gertrude, 260
Stephens, Michelle, 226
Stewart, Susan, 223
Stoever, Jennifer, 90, 94
"The Storm" (Chopin), 150
The Story of My Life (Keller), 31, 32, 224, 227, 233, 235–38, 240–46, 250, 254–55
Stott, Annette, 143
subjectivity, 220, 254; black, 111; inflection and, 123; liberal, 218; ontological reversibility of, 225, 249; racial, 118; touch sense and, 223, 236. *See also* body-subjects; interiority (selfhood)
A Subtlety, or the Marvelous Sugar Baby (Walker), 213–14, 215, 216, 218, 219, 220
sugar, 177, 188, 202, 217; brown, 189, 190, 192, 193, 197–98, 200, 212, 213; Caribbean black cake and, 190, 207; white, 189, 192, 212, 213, 214, 220. *See also* sweetness
"Sugar and the Sugar Region of Louisiana" (Thorpe), 189, *191*

Sullivan, Anne, 227, 234, 236–38, 239, 241, 252, 256
Swan, Jim, 238
Swedenborg, Emanuel, 80, 222
sweetness, 32, 175, 183, 211–12; African Americans and, 189, 190; aesthetics and, 177, 214; Afro-Caribbean black cake recipes, 32, 178, 190, 192–98; colonial sugar plantations and, 188–89, 213; freedom and, 217; state of nature and, 187; white women and, 5, 32, 177, 183, 187, 189–90. *See also* sugar
Sweetser, Nellie, 196, 207
symbolists, 33, 134
Symonds, John Addington, 82
sympathetic vibration, 90, 93, 101–4, 109–10, 115–16
sympathy, 13, 17
synaesthesia, 33–34, 129, 131, 173; color hearing/music, 81–82, 83–85; color smell, 169–72; Fechner's psychophysics and, 78; mouthfeel and, 216, 220; odophone and, 126; psychophysics and, 80–81

taste sense, 32, 33, 168, 174–87, 204, 216. *See also* culinary science; gastronomy; sweetness
Der Tastsinn und das Gemeingefühl [*The Sense of Touch and the Common Sensibility*] (Weber), 228
Taylor, J. Traill, 56, 61
Teacher: Anne Sullivan Macy (Keller), 224, 242
thermodynamics, 45, 50
Thomas, Edith, 145
Thorpe, T. B., 189
time, 154, 156
Titchener, E. B., 8, 228
Todd, Mabel Loomis, 199
The Toilet and Cosmetic Arts in Ancient and Modern Times (Cooley), 142
Tomkins, Silvan, 122
Tompkins, Kyla Wazana, 173, 177–78, 183–84
touch sense, 6–7, 32, 33, 168, 221–25, 227–28, 230–31, 235, 256
transcendentalism, 9
"Transcendental Physics" (*Atlantic Monthly* article), 39
trauma, 53, 58
A Treatise on Domestic Economy (Beecher), 182
Treatise on Physiological Optics (Müller), 22, 40
A Trip to Japan in Sixteen Minutes (Hartmann), 128, 130, 131
A Trip to Japan in Sixteen Minutes, Revisited (Institute for Art and Olfaction tribute performance), 128–29, 276n25
Tucker, Linda, 160

"Turkish Reveille" (Michaelis), 107, 108
The Turn of the Screw (James), 36
Twain, Mark, 246
typewriter, 244

ultrasound, prenatal, 261–64
unbecoming/becoming, 6, 8, 23, 26, 256, 138, 140, 218
The Undercommons (Harney and Moten), 221
U.S. Army Medical Museum (AMM), 38, 51, 59, 70
Utopia (More), 89
utopian fiction, 31, 87, 89, 122, 124. See also *Looking Backward, 2000–1887* (Bellamy); *Mizora: A Prophecy* (Lane); *Of One Blood* (Hopkins)
utopianism, 86, 91, 99, 101, 110

The Veil Lifted: Modern Developments of Spirit Photography (Taylor), 61
vibration, tonal, 96
Victor, Metta Victoria Fuller, 58
The Virginia Housewife (Randolph), 194
vision/sight, 33, 40, 41, 70, 88, 129–30, 231. See also eye, human
visual studies, 32
vitalism/vital force, 9, 12
Vogue magazine, 148
Volta Bureau, 223
Vorschule der Aesthetik [Introduction to Aesthetics] (Fechner), 16, 33, 78
Vortriede, Helen, 154–55
"Voyelles" (Rimbaud), 80, 81

Wagner, Richard, 80, 126
Walker, Kara, 213, 214, 220
Warner, Charles Dudley, 173, 224
Warner, Marina, 56
Washington, Martha, 249
wave theory, 41
Weber, E. H., 2, 11, 20, 26–27, 265n4; as "father of psychophysics," 9–10; on materiality of sense experience, 22; psychophysical studies of tactile sensitivity, 226–28; on smell sense, 137
Weheliye, Alexander, 217
Weiss, John, 188, 202
Werner, Marta, 244, 245
West, Julian, 100

Westphal, Carl, 232
Wexler, Laura, 13
What Mrs. Fisher Knows about Old Southern Cooking (Fisher), 195
"What We Feel" (Sprague), 3, 175
White, George, 111
whiteness, 30, 50, 54, 65, 152; loss of, 172; New Woman and, 153; perfumed floral femininity and, 142–44; phenomenology of, 77; representation of, 68; sexually selective hearing and, 105, 106
white supremacy, 14, 30, 104, 106, 121, 214, 220, 259
white women, 115, 143, 189–90; ambiguously "white," 173; culinary science and, 184; deviant, 163; and music, 120–21; suffragists, 75, 90; and sweetness, 5, 32, 177, 183, 187, 189–90. See also New Woman
Whitman, Walt, 35, 126, 143, 205
Wilde, Oscar, 126
Williams, Henry Willard, 40
Williams, Raymond, 24
Winsor, Anna, 231
Witt, Doris, 184, 194, 201
Wöhler, Friedrich, 133
women, 19, 54; and cooking, 175–83, 211; innate character of, 145; and neurasthenia, 171; perfumery and, 28, 135–36, 142–44, 147, 151, 152, 160, 161; and spiritualism, 36, 53; and sweetness, 5, 32, 177, 183, 187, 189–90; "yellow woman," 153. See also black women; New Woman; white women
Woodward, J. J., 70
The World I Live In (Keller), 221, 224, 235, 245
world soul, 43, 44, 91, 100, 106, 121
World War I, 85
Wundt, Wilhelm, 8, 12, 229, 258
Wyman, Helen Knight, 200, 210

Yablon, Nick, 103
"yellow peril," 170
"The Yellow Wall-Paper" (Gilman), 169–72, 170
Yergeau, Melanie, 30
Young, Thomas, 41

Zafar, Rafia, 195
Zend-Avesta (Fechner), 9

www.ingramcontent.com/pod-product-compliance
Lightning Source LLC
Chambersburg PA
CBHW070335240426
43665CB00045B/2031